Praise for Patricia Bell-Scott's

THE FIREBRAND
AND THE
FIRST LADY

"Bold, fast-paced, and vividly written, Patricia Bell-Scott's dual portrait of Pauli Murray and Eleanor Roosevelt significantly enhances the story of two luminous activists who learned much from each other across the color line." —Blanche Wiesen Cook, author of *Eleanor Roosevelt*, vols. 1, 2, and 3

"Extraordinary and inspiring." —*Shelf Awareness*

"A fresh look at a fascinating friendship between two vivid individuals from very different worlds—as well as a chronicle of the age-old conflict between the highest ideals and the art of the possible." —Geoffrey C. Ward, author of *The Roosevelts: An Intimate History*

"A groundbreaking portrait. . . . Essential and edifying." —*Booklist* (starred review)

"Should inspire all readers. Rarely has a friendship been dissected and analyzed with such verve and open-eyed compassion." —Wil Haygood, author of *Showdown: Thurgood Marshall and the Supreme Court Nomination That Changed America*

"Deftly reveals two women's crucial involvement in the struggle for civil rights. . . . An absorbing historical page-turner." —*Publishers Weekly* (starred review)

"The extraordinary life of Pauli Murray, activist, poet, teacher, priest and 'firebrand' for all seasons, is beautifully detailed in Patricia Bell-Scott's book. . . . [Murray and Roosevelt's] history together reverberates today as the fight for equality continues, making this book important reading for all of us." —Jane Alexander, award-winning actress

"Bell-Scott shines a bright light on this significant relationship. A fresh look at Eleanor Roosevelt and a fascinating exploration of a cherished, mutually beneficial friendship." —*Kirkus Reviews* (starred review)

"What an exquisite book! Patricia Bell-Scott has done the painstaking research on two women who in many respects couldn't have been more different, but in at least one respect—their unique friendship—shared a passion for truth. . . . Patricia Bell-Scott has given us a book that will inspire and give hope to all who read it."
—The Rt. Rev. Mary D. Glasspool,
Bishop Suffragan, Diocese of Los Angeles

"Biography at its best: intimate while revealing of society in its time. Patricia Bell-Scott sees all, and her view is both engrossing and encouraging."
—Nell Irvin Painter,
author of *Sojourner Truth: A Life, A Symbol*

PATRICIA BELL-SCOTT

THE FIREBRAND AND THE FIRST LADY

Patricia Bell-Scott is professor emerita of women's studies and human development and family science at the University of Georgia. Her previous books include *Life Notes: Personal Writings by Contemporary Black Women*, *Flat-Footed Truths: Telling Black Women's Lives*, and *Double Stitch: Black Women Write About Mothers and Daughters*, which won the Letitia Woods Brown Memorial Book Prize. She lives in Athens, Georgia, with her husband, Charles V. Underwood Jr.

www.patriciabellscott.com

THE FIREBRAND
AND THE
FIRST LADY

Pauli Murray, 1946   Eleanor Roosevelt, 1934

THE FIREBRAND
AND THE
FIRST LADY

PORTRAIT OF A FRIENDSHIP

Pauli Murray, Eleanor Roosevelt,
and the Struggle for Social Justice

PATRICIA BELL-SCOTT

VINTAGE BOOKS
A Division of Penguin Random House LLC
New York

FIRST VINTAGE EDITION, JANUARY 2017

Grateful acknowledgment is made to The Estate of Pauli Murray for
permission to reprint excerpts of letters, notes, previously published poems,
and photographs by Pauli Murray. Other materials are reprinted by courtesy of
The Franklin D. Roosevelt Presidential Library, The Literary Estate of Eleanor
Roosevelt, and The Walter P. Reuther Library at Wayne State University.

The Library of Congress has cataloged the Alfred A. Knopf edition as follows:
Name: Bell-Scott, Patricia
Title: The firebrand and the first lady : portrait of a friendship : Pauli Murray,
Eleanor Roosevelt, and the struggle for social justice / Patricia Bell-Scott.
Other titles: Portrait of a friendship, Pauli Murray, Eleanor
Roosevelt, and the struggle for social justice
Subjects: LCSH: Roosevelt, Eleanor, 1884–1962—Friends and associates. | Murray, Pauli,
1910–1985—Friends and associates. | Women social reformers—United States—Biography.
| Presidents' spouses—United States—Biography. | African American women civil rights
workers—Biography. | African American feminists—Biography. | Episcopal Church—
Clergy—Biography. | African American intellectuals—Biography. | Female friendship—
United States. Classification: LCC E807.1.R48 B45 2016 | DDC 973.917092—dc23
LC record available at http://lccn.loc.gov/2015033959

Vintage Books Trade Paperback ISBN: 978-0-679-76729-9
eBook ISBN: 978-1-101-94692-3

Author photograph © Anne Yarbourgh
Book design by Iris Weinstein

www.vintagebooks.com

Printed in the United States of America
10 9 8 7 6 5 4 3 2 1

In memory of Louis Wilbanks Jr., Patrick C. McKenry, and Hilda A. Davis

and for

Charles Vernon Underwood Jr.

For me, becoming friends with Mrs. Roosevelt was a slow, painful process, marked by sharp exchanges of correspondence, often anger on my side and exasperation on her side, and a gradual development of mutual admiration and respect.

—PAULI MURRAY, "Challenging Mrs. R.,"
The Hunter Magazine, September 1983

One of my finest young friends is a charming woman lawyer—Pauli Murray, who has been quite a firebrand at times but of whom I am very fond.

—ELEANOR ROOSEVELT, "Some of My Best
Friends Are Negro," *Ebony,* February 1953

The measure of her greatness was her capacity for growth, her ruthless honesty with herself, and the generosity with which she responded to criticisms.

—PAULI MURRAY, *Song in a Weary Throat,* 1987

I have known Miss Murray for a long time
and she is a very brilliant girl.

—ELEANOR ROOSEVELT to David Morse of the International
Labour Organization in Geneva, concerning Pauli Murray's
application for a staff position, June 14, 1951

She asked me of my future plans and seemed to approve. You would have thought I was talking to either you or Aunt Sallie, the way she talked to me.

—PAULI MURRAY to Mother [Pauline Fitzgerald Dame], regarding
her first White House visit with Eleanor Roosevelt, June 4, 1943

When more whites and Negroes become friends and lose whatever self-consciousness they started out with, we shall have a much happier world.

—ELEANOR ROOSEVELT, "Some of My Best
Friends Are Negro," *Ebony,* February 1953

CONTENTS

PART VI

DRAWING CLOSER AS FRIENDS, 1952–55

PART VII

FIGHTING FOR A JUST WORLD, 1956–59

INTRODUCTION: THE HAND OF FRIENDSHIP

*You need to know some of the veterans of the
battle whose shoulders you now stand on.*

—PAULI MURRAY TO PATRICIA BELL-SCOTT, DECEMBER 12, 1983

The letter that carried these words launched a twenty-year odyssey that gave birth to *The Firebrand and the First Lady*. It was Pauli Murray's second response to my invitation to serve as a consulting editor to *SAGE: A Scholarly Journal on Black Women,* of which I was co–founding editor. She sprinkled her missive with encouragement and what I self-consciously took as an overstatement, hailing the journal as "a formidable undertaking" with the potential to transform "the mainstream of American scholarship." That this groundbreaking activist, lawyer, writer, and priest had high expectations for my work filled me with excitement and apprehension—lest I fall short.

Prior commitments prevented Murray from contributing to the inaugural issue of *SAGE,* but she would share reminiscences of people and events that became guideposts along my way. She mentioned the President's Commission on the Status of Women, for which she served as a subcommittee member and to which John F. Kennedy appointed Eleanor Roosevelt as commission chair. Murray praised the women activists who had taken the lessons learned in the labor and civil rights movements and applied them to the women's movement. She also boasted that she was "finally . . . free to do the creative writing" she had longed to do "since 1939." Her top priority, she quipped, was a "dratted autobiography."

Although I dashed off an appreciative reply, I never got the chance to ask Murray about the veterans on whose shoulders I stood. Her death, eighteen months later at age seventy-four from pancreatic cancer, caught me off guard. Having no knowledge of her illness, I had respected her wish to write undisturbed "until late in 1984." I kept a list of topics I hoped to discuss when she had a breathing spell. That moment never came.

Pauli Murray had been dead for nine years when I decided to write about her friendship with Eleanor Roosevelt. My interest, piqued by a reference to ER in what proved to be Murray's last letter to me, intensified when I read her autobiography, *Song in a Weary Throat,* published two years after her death. Upon examining the letters in the Pauli Murray Papers Collection at the Schlesinger Library at Harvard University and in the Eleanor Roosevelt Papers Collection at the Franklin D. Roosevelt Presidential Library, I immediately recognized that their relationship deserved attention beyond its mention by previous biographers and historians.

Unlike Eleanor Roosevelt's friendships with the black civil rights leaders Mary McCleod Bethune and Walter White, which have been duly noted, ER's friendship with Pauli Murray has not been fully examined. Bethune and White were powerful political figures; a relationship with the first lady was beneficial to them, the organizations they represented, and the Roosevelt administration. Bethune and White were also "veterans who knew when to advance and when to retreat, how to swallow a humiliation with a smile and how to bide their time," observed ER's friend and biographer Joseph P. Lash.

Murray, on the other hand, was of a younger generation, determined to challenge authority and inequality head-on. She filed her first discrimination complaint with her adoptive mother when she was barely six years old. "How come you give Grandfather *three* pancakes," Murray asked, "and me only one?" A self-described individualist, she was most comfortable working alone and setting her own course outside bureaucratic institutions. Because she did not speak for an established group, Murray could not deliver votes—nor did she want to. What she offered instead was the honest and often brash opinion of an independent thinker who could not be still in the face of injustice.

Murray's politics, temperament, and resolve to be herself frequently frustrated her family, her friends, and people in organizations to which she was devoted, such as the National Association for the Advancement of Colored People and the Episcopal Church. Her personal writings suggest that she believed that these difficulties set her apart from her better-known male and conventional female peers. And I believe that these difficulties also contributed to her marginalization, until recently, in the historical record.

· · ·

I WAS FOUR YEARS INTO the research for this book and writing the foreword to a new edition of Murray's family memoir *Proud Shoes* when I came across the August 19, 1971, letter to her friend Caroline F. Ware, a historian. In it, Murray spoke of the notes she was making for a future biographer whose work would probably not be published in her lifetime. I felt a haunting presence, as if Murray were hovering near my writing desk, when I read that she had envisioned a biography that began with her battle to enroll at the University of North Carolina and the "friendship with Mrs. R." That I had responded to a wish Murray made long before I imagined this book confirmed my instinct that her letter to me was more than coincidence. I would sense Murray's presence again during conversations with her friends and on pilgrimages to Bear Mountain, Howard University, Val-Kill, and other sites that were the backdrop of important moments in her relationship with ER.

In the beginning, I concentrated on the period between December 6, 1938—when Pauli Murray introduced herself in a protest letter to Franklin and Eleanor Roosevelt—and November 7, 1962, the day ER died. Further research led me to expand the scope from Murray's first glimpse of ER in 1934 to Murray's death on July 1, 1985. Because I wanted these women to speak for themselves, I initially constructed this book as a collection of letters linked together by explanatory text. But the story felt fragmented and incomplete. It lacked the complexity and depth of their friendship, which had bridged generational, racial, class, and political differences.

I put the manuscript aside and determined to write a narrative with two views. One would be a close-up that followed the evolving friendship of two human rights activists. The other would use a wider-angle lens to place their relationship in context on the historical stage during the Great Depression, World War II, McCarthyism and the Cold War, and the civil and women's rights movements of the twentieth century. Such a narrative required that I consider not only the letters they wrote to each other but what they said about the friendship, and how it influenced their thinking and actions.

Having settled on the parameters and architecture of my work, I began anew with these questions: What drew Pauli Murray, the granddaughter of a mulatto slave, and Eleanor Roosevelt, whose ancestry entitled her to membership in the Daughters of the American Revolution, together in friendship? What was the nature of their friendship, and how did they sustain it over time? What needs did they satisfy in each other, and how were they changed by the relationship? And what significance did their friendship have for the cause of social justice?

Despite the difference in family origin and the fact that Pauli Murray was twenty-six years junior to Eleanor Roosevelt, they had several things in common. They shared the given name Anna, which neither preferred or used. Both lost their parents as children and were raised by elderly kin. Highly sensitive, they had an abiding compassion for the helpless that stemmed in part from their childhoods as orphans, their experience with chronically ill relatives, and their need for acceptance, which was compounded in Murray's case by discrimination on multiple fronts. They were both baptized as Episcopalians and—except for a brief period when Murray left the church—remained lifelong congregants.

They had inquiring minds. They were voracious readers. They loved poetry, and they loved to write. They were unpretentious, and they conveyed a seriousness of purpose that made them seem humorless, which was not the case. Both endured ridicule—Murray for her boyish physique, ER for her protruding teeth. They had presence and phenomenal energy. They rarely slept more than five or six hours a night. ER's daily schedule left those around her breathless, and Murray's intensity exhausted even her most patient friends.

Yet they were not immune to low spirits or anxiety. Pauli Murray experienced sporadic mood swings until diagnosed, at age forty-three, with a thyroid disorder. Eleanor Roosevelt manifested depression-like symptoms when she felt unappreciated by those whose opinions she valued and when she thought she had failed. Both fought a tendency toward shyness and learned to be resolute and outspoken in the face of opposition. Their well-being required meaningful work, physical activity, and the company of cherished friends, including their dogs. ER favored Scottish terriers. Murray had a soft spot for large breeds and strays.

· · ·

THE TWENTY-THREE-YEAR-OLD Murray, whose 1933 Hunter College yearbook photograph appears on the jacket of this book, was not a "fan" of the recently installed first lady, also pictured. Their relationship started as a confrontation in words, fueled by Murray's desire for dramatic social change and the first lady's obligation to the measured approach FDR's administration took on the question of civil rights.

They respectfully addressed their early letters to "Mrs. Roosevelt" and "Miss Murray." By 1944, ER had adopted the use of "Pauli." But Murray, who came to regard the first lady as a maternal figure, could not bring herself to use "Eleanor" as invited. Because ER belonged to the same generation as Murray's mother, the first lady would always be "Mrs. Roosevelt," "Mrs. R.," or occasionally "Mrs. Rovel," a nickname Murray created by shortening the name Roosevelt. Their closings, like their salutations, evolved from the formal "Sincerely" and "Truly yours" to the personal "Affectionately" and "Fondly."

They supplemented more than three hundred letters, notes, and birthday, get-well, sympathy, and holiday greeting cards with clippings, reports, manuscripts, photographs, flowers, and candy. ER's missives were concise and—except for an occasional postscript—typed, for which Murray must have been grateful, given the first lady's hard-to-read handwriting. Murray, who was at her best hashing out her thoughts and feelings on paper, invariably wrote longer letters. Sometimes she typed several drafts before mailing the final document, to which she periodically attached a gracious cover note to ER's confidential secretary, Malvina Thompson. When time was of the essence or a typewriter inconvenient, Murray wrote with a fountain pen in her favorite blue-green ink.

There were instances when the letters flowed with a sense of urgency, as was the case during the 1940–42 campaign to overturn the death sentence of the young black sharecropper Odell Waller. There were also infrequent periods when they were out of touch for more than six months, such as 1960–61, when Murray taught at the law school in Ghana.

Their first face-to-face discussions focused on labor and civil rights and took place over tea at the first lady's New York City apartment and the White House. After FDR's death, their conversations expanded to include an array of issues, including personal concerns. They met at ER's New York City residences and her Hyde Park retreat Val-Kill. While ER did visit Bethune and White in their homes and would have surely welcomed an invitation to Murray's place, I have found no evidence that this happened. This is, perhaps, understandable, given Murray's limited resources. In contrast to Bethune and White, Murray moved frequently and was periodically unemployed or underemployed. She did not own a home in ER's lifetime, and she often shared her living space with friends and relatives. Out of respect for ER's time and commitment to others, Murray deferred to ER on when and where they would meet.

When one considers the disparate demands in the daily lives of Pauli Murray and Eleanor Roosevelt, it is remarkable that neither drifted away from the relationship. On the contrary, they drew closer, grounded by the needs they satisfied in each other. Murray had a need to speak out and feel heard. ER had a need to respond and make a difference. Murray's friend Maida Springer-Kemp, a labor leader, who saw them together more than anyone other than Malvina Thompson, told me that Murray could be embarrassingly direct, which must have bothered ER; and it was "a credit to Mrs. Roosevelt's courage and awareness that this young woman . . . not be left crying in the wilderness." In due course, ER came to rely upon the woman she dubbed "a firebrand," who dared say what she thought.

As I followed their heated exchange on such issues as the Roosevelt administration's response, or lack thereof, to lynching or ER's defense of Adlai Stevenson's tepid support of the *Brown* decision during the 1956 presidential campaign, I found myself reflecting on the combatants in Murray's poem "The Quarrel," posted on the wall near my desk:

> *Two ants at bay*
> *on curved stem of an apple*
> *are insufficient cause*
> *to fell the tree*

Pauli Murray and ER reminded me of the ants in this poem tenaciously fixed to the apple stem. No disagreement weighed enough to upend the sturdy tree that was their friendship. Disagreement over politics and strategy sometimes left them disturbed and disappointed. But in time, their perspectives converged.

They helped each other see possibilities beyond their immediate vision, and this broadened view reverberated in the causes they served. Murray, who had never voted for FDR or trusted the two-party system, became a registered voting Democrat. She would always find compromise, incremental change, and hierarchal institutions trying. Nonetheless, she would lean away from the radical left.

Eleanor Roosevelt, who once cautioned Murray against flouting segregation statutes, moved "further along the road in the civil-rights struggle than she might otherwise have traveled" without Murray's influence, biographer Blanche Wiesen Cook has written. ER indeed progressed from sharing Murray's sentiments with her "My Day" readers, FDR, and other opinion makers to defying threats against her own life when she publicly aligned herself with civil rights activists.

Pauli Murray and Eleanor Roosevelt were more than political allies.

They developed an enduring friendship that came to be characterized by honesty, trust, affection, empathy, support, mutual respect, loyalty, acceptance, a commitment to hearing the other's point of view, pleasure in each other's company, and the ability to pick up where they'd left off, irrespective of the miles that had separated them or the time lapsed. ER did not live to see Murray complete her work with the President's Commission on the Status of Women, earn a doctorate of juridical science, become a distinguished professor, cofound the National Organization for Women, help lead the fight to preserve Title VII of the 1964 Civil Rights Act, or become an Episcopal priest. However, Pauli Murray carried her memory of ER into each endeavor.

· · ·

SEVERAL YEARS AGO, I discovered an unexpected gem tucked inside an autographed first edition of *Proud Shoes* I purchased online. That gem, Murray's five-page, single-spaced newsletter to friends, was dated July 5, 1970, and printed on what was once white paper in the fading purple ink of a ditto machine. In it, she recounts her delight in church work, teaching at Brandeis University, the formation of a "women's caucus at the ACLU biennial conference," and the publication of her poetry collection, *Dark Testament and Other Poems.* As she did in the letter that planted the seed for *The Firebrand and the First Lady,* Pauli Murray closed with a tribute and a challenge: "Eleanor Roosevelt lighted the candle in the darkness, and left behind a noble tradition for women of my generation whose lives she personally touched. I can do no less than to try to follow in her massive footsteps and to ask my contemporaries to do the same."

I believe that biography, as the British biographer Richard Holmes has said, "is a handshake across time" and "an act of friendship." My hope is that this book honors Pauli Murray's wish to share the story of her friendship with Eleanor Roosevelt, the path they lit for future generations, and the hand of friendship Pauli extended to me. This story and the challenge of telling it have changed my life, as I suspect Pauli knew it would.

PRELUDE

CAMP TERA,
1933–35

First Lady Eleanor Roosevelt, age forty-eight, and Jessie I. Mills, the Camp Tera business manager, exit a cabin eight days after the facility opened. "I like this place very much," ER said to the staff and the press, "but I think the requirements too strict." Bear Mountain, New York, June 18, 1933. *(Bettmann/CORBIS)*

I sing of Youth, imperious, inglorious
Dissatisfied, unslaked, untaught, unkempt Youth.

—PAULI MURRAY, "Youth, 1933"

We can not pass over the fact that the world is a hard
world for youth and that so far we have not really given
their problems as much attention as we should.

—ELEANOR ROOSEVELT, "Facing the Problems of Youth," 1935

Pauli Murray was sitting in the hallway outside the social hall at Camp Tera when Eleanor Roosevelt drove up in a convertible coupe in late fall 1934. On the passenger side sat the first lady's private secretary, Malvina "Tommy" Thompson. In back was a man Murray took to be a Secret Service agent. Gasps and cheers erupted as the first lady walked briskly around the premises. The ting of forks dropping echoed from the dining area as residents rushed to tidy their quarters. While some scurried to put their craftwork on display, others trailed their honored guest like chicks behind a mother hen. Such commotion on a quiet Sunday startled Murray, a newcomer and one of the few African American residents. Having no handiwork to lay out, she sneaked back to her cabin to wash up, brush her hair, and put on a fresh blouse.

Camp Tera, so named for the Temporary Emergency Relief Administration, was the first government-sponsored residential facility for unemployed women. It had been in operation for a year when Murray stepped off the boat that brought recruits up the Hudson River from New York City. Suffering from poor nutrition, respiratory problems, and exhaustion, she had quit her job as a representative for the National Urban League magazine *Opportunity* and enrolled in the camp on the advice of her physician, Dr. May Chinn. Although Pauli was twenty-four, her "slight figure and bobbed hair" gave her the appearance of "a small teen-age boy." She typified the needy women Eleanor had in mind when she'd proposed a camp to rehabilitate their physical and emotional health.

. . .

WHEN CAMP TERA OPENED, on June 10, 1933, on a two-hundred-acre site in the Bear Mountain area of upstate New York, one in four Americans was unemployed. In New York City alone, over 250,000 were on relief. The economic depression and Franklin Delano Roosevelt's campaign pledge "to put people to work and restore the American economy" persuaded voters to send him, instead of the Republican Herbert Hoover, to the White House in the 1932 election.

True to his word, Roosevelt launched a series of economic initiatives hailed as the New Deal. One of the earliest and most popular programs was the Civilian Conservation Corps. The goal of the CCC was to rebuild the health and morale of unemployed men between the ages of seventeen and twenty-eight with work, food, and shelter. CCC enrollees, trained by military personnel to work on roads, flood control, forestry, and beautification projects, wore uniforms, lived in camps, and got three meals a day. The pay was thirty dollars a month, twenty-five of which went directly to their families. It was the first time Harley Jolley, a white enrollee from North Carolina, got a toothbrush, a vaccination, and a daily bath.

By August 1935, there would be over 500,000 enrollees, 50,000 of whom were black. The majority of the blacks lived in segregated camps, were limited to subordinate positions, and were supervised by white officers, even though the legislation that authorized the CCC forbade discrimination on the basis of race, color, or creed. "They never believed that we could work," recalled Houston Pritchett, a black enrollee from Detroit, "but once we'd get the chance, that's what did it."

The segregated and militaristic character of the CCC bothered the first lady. Yet she was encouraged by the reports of young men whose strength and optimism were renewed by the camp experience. She also believed that women would benefit from a comparable program that gave them a breather from the heartache of unemployment.

The idea of women living in camps away from family, doing any kind of manual labor, made some government officials uncomfortable. Even those who ran the CCC generally viewed camps for women, who could presumably turn to family for support, as an extravagance that would undercut relief for men. Some program directors maintained that women, especially if unrelated, were too temperamental to live together. Others, influenced by Sigmund Freud's theories of the role of unconscious drives in human development, the belief that idleness encouraged immorality, and the fear that radicals were endangering the American way of life saw women's camps as a breeding ground for unacceptable behavior, such as homosexuality, and subversive ideas, such as communism.

Undaunted by these objections, ER pushed the Roosevelt administration to create a pilot camp for women. Fueling her determination were firsthand observations of the difficulties poor women and their families faced. As a nineteen-year-old volunteer, ER had investigated sweatshops in New York City for the National Consumers League and taught calisthenics and dance at the College Settlement on Rivington Street for the Junior League. These experiences exposed her to a world where immigrant families lived in unspeakable poverty and where children, who labored alongside their parents, sometimes collapsed.

What ER saw and learned from working with women in the labor movement and FDR's administration influenced her decision to host three White House conferences on the needs of women. These meetings were vital, she told conferees at the first gathering, for "women had been neglected in comparison with others, and throughout this depression have had the hardest time of all." Among the proposals put forth at the second conference was a program of camps for unemployed women.

Eleanor Roosevelt's desire to establish these camps was, to be sure, an expression of her compassion, her fierce desire to see the New Deal help women, and her commitment to progressive politics. Her tenacity, coupled with the support of Secretary of Labor Frances Perkins, the first woman to serve in a presidential cabinet; Harry Hopkins, the director of the Federal Emergency Relief Administration; Ellen Woodward, the director of the FERA women's division; and Hilda Worthington Smith, the director of the FERA Workers' Education Project, gave birth to Camp Tera. Skeptics sarcastically dubbed Camp Tera and subsequent facilities set up for women as "She-She-She Camps," playing on the abbreviation CCC for the men's camps.

Eight days after the first residents arrived at Camp Tera, the first lady made the scenic drive, approximately forty-five miles south of her Hyde Park residence, to check things out for herself. She was disappointed to find just thirty women. She had hoped to see close to the three hundred called for in the plans. She stayed for three hours, talking with the residents and staff. And what she discovered made her angry.

To be eligible, women had to be single, divorced, or widowed residents of New York State between eighteen and thirty-five years of age. They could have no resources, and none of their close relatives could be employed. More than one thousand had applied. Delays and a stringent screening process had turned most away. That Camp Tera offered no pay and the rumor that residents did hard labor and wore uniforms in return for little to eat further discouraged prospective enrollees.

Stirred by estimates of 250,000 jobless women who reportedly scavenged for food, rode all night on subways, and slept in jails, boxcars, and abandoned buildings, ER vowed to cut through the red tape. "There must be two hundred girls in New York City who need to get back their health and spirits in a place like this," she told the press. "You can't make me believe there aren't."

Within a month of her visit, the registration bureau streamlined the screening process, raised the age limit to forty, and admitted women whose fathers worked part-time. Native and immigrant, they soon numbered one hundred. They varied from those with little formal education to those with college degrees, like Murray. Among their ranks were former maids, entertainers, factory workers, secretaries, store clerks, and women who had never worked outside the home.

The first lady was not content with the reports from agency officials. She returned periodically to the camp with her secretary and her Scottish terrier Meggie. They usually stayed all day, inspecting the facility, conferring with residents and staff, joining them at meals. In addition to Tommy and Meggie, ER often brought along friends, such as Elinor F. Morgenthau, wife of Secretary of the Treasury Henry Morgenthau Jr.; Democratic Party activists, such as Nancy Cook, Marion Dickerman, and Caroline O'Day; and newspaperwomen, such as Genevieve Forbes Herrick of the *Chicago Tribune*.

Camp Tera had twenty-six log cabins plus a dining and recreation hall. Whatever residents and staff needed—winterized facilities, blankets, sports equipment, art supplies, books, holiday treats, or funds for field trips—ER lobbied officials for or donated money she earned from her radio broadcasts and publications to provide it. Her commitment to the camp inspired others to give money, supplies, and their time. Kate Smith, the popular singer known as the "Songbird of the South," donated a shiny floor-console radio.

Making sure the camp was adequately staffed and equipped was no less important to the first lady than that it be open to women irrespective of racial background. This sensitivity to discrimination, a consciousness she did not have in her youth, was due in part to her close friendships with Mary McLeod Bethune and Walter Francis White. Bethune, whom the first lady met in 1927 at a conference of women club leaders, was one of seventeen children born in Mayesville, South Carolina, to Samuel and Patsy McLeod, both former slaves. Bethune was educated at Scotia Seminary in North Carolina and the Institute for Home and Foreign Missions in Chicago. Her childhood dream was to do missionary work in Africa.

Charismatic and very dark-skinned, Bethune rose from abject poverty to found Bethune-Cookman College for blacks. From her post as an influential educator, she expanded her reach and became president of the National Association of Colored Women, founding president of the National Council of Negro Women, and special adviser to FDR. In 1936, with the first lady's backing, she was named head of the National Youth Administration Office of Minority Affairs, which aided unemployed youths through grants, work-study, and job training. Bethune was also the only female member of the Federal Council of Negro Affairs, an informal group of black advisers to the president that came to be known as the Negro Cabinet.

Eleanor Roosevelt regarded Bethune as one of her closest friends in her age group. Whenever Bethune came to the White House, the first lady "always went running down the driveway to meet her, and they would walk arm in arm into the mansion" to talk for hours about the needs of African Americans. "Few heads of State received such a welcome," observed White House usher J. B. West.

Unlike Bethune, who fought her way past deprivation, discrimination, and disparaging remarks about her complexion, the blue-eyed, fair-skinned White grew up in a middle-class family in Atlanta, Georgia. He was one of seven children born to George W. White, a postal worker, and Madeline Harrison, a teacher. In 1918, two years after graduating from Atlanta University, Walter White joined the NAACP headquarters staff. He became national executive secretary in 1931.

Using his ability to pass for white, he gathered data about racial violence in the South that he hoped would convince Franklin Roosevelt to back a federal anti-lynching bill. But the president, eager to avoid a fight with southern legislators whose support he needed in Congress, would not grant White an audience. White found an ally in Eleanor Roosevelt. Not only did she meet with him privately in the White House, she ultimately secured an hour-long meeting for him with her husband. Their efforts to convince FDR to speak out in support of anti-lynching legislation failed, yet White and ER refused to give up, forging a friendship in the process.

What ER learned about racial discrimination from Bethune, White, and African Americans she met or who wrote to her encouraged her to examine her own behavior and be ever watchful for problems at Camp Tera. She promptly contacted William H. Matthews, director of the Emergency Work Bureau, which handled registration for the camp, after she heard a complaint in August 1933. "One of the colored girls told me that when she registered for Camp Tera she was told that they did not want colored girls," the first lady wrote. "However, there are several there, and I thought you would like to know that this question has been brought up."

Matthews read ER's letter as a directive. The first lady wanted black residents admitted to the camp, and she wanted them to feel welcomed. He promised to investigate. By the end of the month, Matthews reported, the situation had "changed." There were now "ten colored girls in the camp."

· · ·

BEING A RESIDENT at Camp Tera was not what Murray had envisioned when she'd migrated to New York City to escape the social and legal system of racial segregation in the South known as Jim Crow. Born on November 20, 1910, in Baltimore, Maryland, she was christened Anna Pauline Murray after her paternal grandmother, Annie Price Murray, and her maternal aunt Mary Pauline Fitzgerald Dame. Pauli was the fourth of six children born to William Henry Murray, a teacher educated in the College Preparatory Department of Howard University, and Agnes Georgiana Fitzgerald Murray, a nurse trained at Hampton Institute. Pauli's siblings were Grace, born in 1905, Mildred in 1907, William in 1909, Rosetta in 1912, and Robert, later known as Raymond, in 1913.

Two tragedies marked Pauli's childhood. The first was the death of her thirty-five-year-old, seven months pregnant mother, Agnes, from a cerebral hemorrhage. Three-year-old Pauli went to Durham, North Carolina, to live in the household of her elderly maternal grandparents, Robert George Fitzgerald and Cornelia Smith Fitzgerald, and two middle-aged aunts. Sarah "Sallie" Fitzgerald, to whom Pauli bore a striking resemblance, and Pauline Dame, who would become Pauli's adoptive mother, were teachers as Grandfather Robert had been. Grandmother Cornelia was the acknowledged daughter of Sidney Smith, a white lawyer from a prominent North Carolina family, and a part-Cherokee slave named Harriet, owned by the Smiths.

The second tragedy struck when Murray's father, William, nearly died from typhoid fever and what relatives believed to be encephalitis. From then on, he suffered "unpredictable attacks of depression and violent moods." Job stress and his wife's death intensified his instability. Relatives took custody of Murray's siblings, who had remained in Baltimore, and committed William to the Hospital for the Negro Insane of Maryland in Crownsville. There, he would live in filthy quarters and receive no meaningful treatment.

Murray saw her father once after his institutionalization. Instead of the "dapper gentleman" in family photographs from whom it was said she'd inherited her keen intellect, she was introduced to an inmate in tattered overalls with sad, lifeless eyes. His shoes were falling apart, his hair uncombed. She saw no likeness to the teacher who had inspired his students to excel or the artist who had labored through the night over his writing and musical compositions. William's appearance, the fact that he had had no previous visitors, and the revelation that the authorities were willing to release him to the custody of an adult relative—but no one had agreed to take him—broke Murray's heart. She vowed to rescue him when she reached majority age. Unfortunately, a burly white hospital attendant with a habit of using racial epithets clubbed William to death. He was fifty-one. Pauli was thirteen.

At the time of William's murder, there were 275 patients and only four attendants at the hospital. That all the attendants and professional staff were white exacerbated tensions in the crowded facility. "It was a common occurrence," reported the *Baltimore Afro-American*, "for attendants to beat the inmates with clubs and broomsticks."

William's mood swings and his violent death left Pauli apprehensive about her own health. She developed "an irrational fear of being hemmed in or struck from behind," as William had reportedly been. She also worried that his illness might be hereditary and that someday "she might go berserk."

The loss of her mother, the racially motivated murder of her father in a mental institution, and the embrace of proud elder kin instilled in Murray a compassion for the helpless, a commitment to social justice, and a lifelong hunger for knowledge. The caption next to her picture in Durham's Hillside High yearbook—"The best I can do to help others is to be the best I can myself"—aptly characterized the life of individual achievement and social uplift to which she aspired. In her senior year, she was voted "most studious girl," and she served as editor in chief of *Ski-Hi*, the student newspaper. She graduated with honors in 1926, but Hillside did not go beyond the eleventh grade.

Murray's pursuit of excellence meant leaving the South, where the law required her to attend an all-black college. Legally defenseless, she fought segregation with her conscience; it was the only weapon she had. Rather than ride a segregated bus, she walked or bicycled wherever she went. She refused to go to theaters that seated blacks in the "peanut gallery."

In 1925, Murray fell in love with New York City during a summer visit to see cousins who lived in Queens. Its ethnic and artistic enclaves were a hotbed of cultural and social ferment. In Harlem, where three-fourths of the black population lived, a new cultural movement was in full bloom. Everything about the Big Apple awed Murray—Lady Liberty's welcoming majesty, buildings that soared into the sky, theater marquees on Broadway, and the freedom to sit and ride wherever she pleased. She decided on the spot: here is where she would live.

Murray was also attracted to New York City for another reason. She had no money for college, and qualified graduates of a New York City high school could attend a city college tuition-free. It might have been more practical for Murray to attend the North Carolina College for Negroes in Durham and live at home, but she ruled that out. She also turned down a tuition scholarship to Wilberforce, a highly regarded black school in Ohio.

Murray's first choice, Columbia University, was a private school that did not admit women. Her best and only option proved to be Hunter College. Founded in 1870 as a city school for women, Hunter had tough admissions standards, a first-class curriculum, and a practice of admitting bright students without regard to race, religion, ethnicity, or class. To satisfy the residency requirement and complete a fourth year of high school at Richmond Hill High, Murray moved in with her Queens relatives. The household included Murray's cousin Maude Womack; Maude's husband, James; and their three young sons.

Because Murray needed more credits than the maximum allowable load in order to graduate in a year, she was permitted to audit the extra courses. The hours required to pass the courses for which she was enrolled and prepare for the state exams for the courses she audited left her no time for chores at home. Her inability to pitch in compounded the tensions with her relatives over another matter. That matter was the suspicion Murray's "yellow-brown skin, kinky-curly hair, and Southern accent" created in the minds of neighbors, who did not know that her fair-skinned cousins were black. The neighbors, assuming Murray's relatives were immigrants from Europe, had not asked about their racial identity, and they had been silent on the issue.

Despite the difficulties at home and her heavy courseload, Murray graduated in 1927 with honors and her second high school diploma. She entered Hunter College in the fall of 1928, intent on becoming a writer and a member of the Phi Beta Kappa honor society. But the confidence of having earned two diplomas with honors was replaced with insecurity and trepidation. Murray was a southerner in a student population of five thousand New Yorkers, where only a few hundred were black. Most of her classmates and teachers welcomed her; still, she felt self-conscious and nervous about competing with whites. She concentrated in English and history. She embraced Phi Beta Kappa's motto, "Love of learning is the guide of life," though her grades put membership out of reach. She joined the Journalism Club and the International Student Club. She adopted Pauli as her official name.

The recognition that her presence upset "the delicate balance in neighborhood relationships," a pride in race instilled by Aunt Pauline, and an inability to help with housework led Murray to move out of her relatives' home the summer before the stock market crashed. She lived for a while at the Emma Ransom House of the Harlem YWCA, commuted to school, and worked a series of jobs as a dishwasher, waitress, night-shift elevator operator, maid, and switchboard operator. The pay was meager, the hours long. She survived on coffee and rummaged through refuse for food and cigarettes. She rarely slept more than two hours at a stretch.

Murray's efforts to keep her eyes open in class amused her classmates. She sat near the windows, wiggled in her seat, wrung her hands, and ran to the restroom to douse her face in cold water. Nothing helped. Her academic performance declined, as did her health. By the year's end, she was anemic and underweight.

The strain of working round the clock, the lack of time to study, the disappointment over her grades, and the shame of not having soap, toothpaste, medicine, or school supplies precipitated a "nervous breakdown." She left Hunter at the close of her sophomore year. She was entirely self-supporting, so she worked full-time while she tried to recover.

On November 28, 1930, Murray married William "Billy" Roy Wynn, another struggling student. "It was a dreadful mistake," she would write years later. Attracted by "mutual loneliness and rootlessness," they married secretly, fearing that Murray would be evicted from the YWCA if the marriage became public. "Sexually inexperienced," penniless, and without a place of their own, the couple soon separated. They would remain legally married for the next eighteen years but would lead separate lives.

Desperate for a change, in the spring of 1931 Murray jumped at the chance to drive to California with a friend. During this trip, her first to the West Coast, she penned the poem "The Song of the Highway." The opening lines—"I am the Highway, / Long, white winding Highway"—celebrated her "wanderlust."

Murray's exuberance was soon squelched by a letter from Aunt Pauline that had been forwarded from New York to Vallejo, California. Her aunt was ill, and she wanted Murray to come home immediately. Since Murray had no money and hitchhiking by car might take too long, she risked hopping an eastbound freight train at the Southern Pacific Railroad yard. Hundreds of thousands of youths, males and females from all ethnic groups, rode freight trains in search of work and a better life.

Riding the rails, in contrast to the pleasant drive west, terrified Murray. She was in danger of being apprehended, shot, crushed on the tracks or inside a boxcar, or assaulted should male riders discover she was female. Everyone assumed, to her relief and as she intended, that she was a boy. She was wearing "scout pants," high-top shoes, a leather jacket, and a newsboy cap. Murray's adolescent build, her cropped hair, and her clothing—like that of other young women alone on the road, for whom comfort and security were constant concerns—reinforced a male persona. After ten days as a stowaway, she reached the Jersey City trainyard "so cinder-blackened" that it took three baths to cleanse the stains from her body.

Aunt Pauline's health took a turn for the better, and Murray resumed her life in New York City. Her thirst for travel was satisfied for now, but her desire to write grew more intense. She transformed her diary entries about her train adventure into the short story "Three Thousand Miles on a Dime in Ten Days." In it, she recounted the "jail-birds, veteran hoboes, suckers, gamblers, murderers" she had met as she jumped freight cars carrying cattle, food, and lumber products. This story, which would be published in 1934 along with "Song of the Highway" in Nancy Cunard's *Negro* anthology, placed Murray in the company of such Harlem Renaissance icons as Zora Neale Hurston, Langston Hughes, and Countee Cullen and that of influential white writers such as Theodore Dreiser, Ezra Pound, and William Carlos Williams. Murray was perhaps the youngest of the 150 contributors, and she had the distinction of being "the only one in the book not represented by a purely *racial* piece of writing," Cunard boasted.

Cunard, a British writer-activist who had rejected her upper-class family background, loved Murray's writing and the accompanying photograph of Pete, a baby-faced male character featured in her story. Pete was actually Murray, and she asked Cunard to publish this image with no mention of the author's sex in the contributors' notes. Cunard thought the snapshot of Murray's "boy-self" adorable, she wrote back, adding that "we will use that" and list the author as "Pauli Murray, a name for boy or girl."

Murray reenrolled at Hunter in the fall of 1931. She managed to stay in school, working odd jobs, for the next two years. She lived and shared expenses with Louise E. Jefferson, an art student at Hunter. Crippled by polio in childhood, Jefferson would nonetheless become an accomplished swimmer, photographer, illustrator, publishing house art director, and cofounder of the Harlem Artists Guild. Jefferson's self-discipline and purposive approach to her studies had a positive impact on Murray, who was sometimes scattered and impetuous. Murray's writing improved, and she went from barely passing to make making Bs and As in her courses. The academic fraternity for English majors, Sigma Tau Delta, tapped her for membership in her senior year. Her essay "A Working Student" appeared in the 1932 Christmas issue of the *Hunter College Echo* magazine.

Murray graduated with a bachelor of arts in January 1933. She was one of four blacks in a class of 247 women. It was the peak of the Depression and a few months before Franklin and Eleanor Roosevelt moved into the White House. Unemployment, which was above the national average in New York City, was estimated to be as high as 50 percent for blacks, regardless of educational background. It took Murray most of the year to find a job, and after ten months with *Opportunity* magazine, her health failed. She resigned and signed up for Camp Tera on her doctor's orders.

. . .

CAMP TERA WAS AN OASIS for Murray. Frail and shy, she was happy to discover among the residents an old friend of hers from the YWCA, who was now escorting newcomers around the site. Margaret "Pee Wee" Inniss was an immigrant from Trinidad and one of the earliest recruits. Though she had only a married half brother in the United States and no college training, she dreamt of running her own interracial camp for children. An indomitable spirit, she availed herself of every free course and training opportunity she could find. Pee Wee, who was a prankster, was well liked; she directed plays, organized sports teams, and served as circulation manager for the camp's biweekly bulletin, *Tera Topics*. She also made a practice of writing frank letters about her concerns to public officials, including Eleanor Roosevelt. Murray was impressed by both Pee Wee's audacity and the fact that the first lady wrote back. Murray would one day wage her own "confrontation by typewriter," she called it, with ER and the president.

Murray and Pee Wee might have been assigned to the same room in an old wooden cabin because they were among a handful of black enrollees. The "narrow cubicle" they shared held their cots, footlockers, and a dresser. Ordinarily, any hint of racial segregation raised Murray's ire. However, she was ill and lonely, and it pleased her to have the company of a friend.

Surrounded by the smooth, red-brown cliffs of Bear Mountain, stands of mountain laurel and hemlock, the glistening waters of Lake Tiorati, and a congregation of birds, chipmunks, deer, and rabbits, Murray felt a serenity she had never before known. There were no work requirements other than keeping her personal space and the common areas clean. Even as a child, she had not had this kind of leisure.

Life at Camp Tera reflected Eleanor Roosevelt's belief that exercise in the open air enhanced one's overall well-being. Here, Murray could choose activities from hiking, swimming, canoeing, and relay racing to ice-skating, tobogganing, and horseback riding. She could participate in dramatic skits, discussion groups, and songfests. She could play an assortment of ball, board, or card games and take art, crafts, and dance classes.

Murray's favorite pastimes were hiking and curling up in a corner to read and write. She had no aptitude for or interest in the domestic arts. She had not learned to cook, and she never would. More comfortable "with a pen than a needle," she hated sewing. Athletic and tomboyish, she preferred outdoor work, like chopping wood, to housekeeping.

The food at Camp Tera was wholesome and plentiful, and Murray's appetite was insatiable. For breakfast, there was fruit, cereal, eggs, toast, and coffee; for lunch and dinner, ham or frankfurters, sauerkraut, scalloped potatoes, cabbage, bread and butter, cocoa, and tea. Thanks to the first lady, the residents enjoyed turkey, dressing, and holiday sweets at Thanksgiving and Christmas.

Food, shelter, exercise, and rest brought Murray nearly to full strength in a month. Her sense of well-being got an additional boost from a new friend, Margaret "Peg" Holmes. Peg was a round-faced, golden-haired camp counselor from an upper-class family in Putnam County, New York. She was athletic, fun-loving, and popular. Residents affectionately nicknamed her "the second Babe Ruth." Peg taught English and dance. She also supervised outdoor sports and *Tera Topics*. She and Murray were close in age. They liked to hike and read poetry together.

The friendship with Peg and the verdant landscape stirred Murray's creative juices. Her poem "Poet's Memo," which appeared in the 1934 Christmas issue of *Tera Topics,* was replete with romantic phrases like "Your face, beloved," sensual imagery such as "wavelets sighing," and allusions to the Greek myth of Pan, the half-human, half-goat god said to watch over all wildlife. That Pan was also known for his seductive powers and that Murray referred to Peg privately as Pan suggests that this poem was perhaps an homage to Peg as well.

. . .

ON THE SUNDAY ELEANOR ROOSEVELT ENTERED the social hall with Jessie Mills, the camp's officious director, Pauli Murray was overtaken by "the tremor of excitement" that engulfed the residents and the staff. She averted her eyes and "pretended to read a newspaper." She had never imagined being so close to the first lady, whose unassuming manner belied her background.

Born in New York City on October 11, 1884, Anna Eleanor Roosevelt was the first of three children and the only daughter of Anna Hall Roosevelt, a beautiful socialite, and Elliott Roosevelt, the dashing younger brother of President Theodore Roosevelt. ER's brothers, Elliott and Gracie Hall, were born in 1889 and 1891, respectively.

Eleanor grew up privileged, yet she was no stranger to personal tragedy. When she was eight, her mother died at twenty-nine of diphtheria, and ER and her brothers went to live with their maternal grandmother, Mary Ludlow Hall. ER's brother Elliott died of diphtheria in 1893, and her father died a year later at thirty-four of alcoholism and a seizure suffered after jumping out of a window in an apparent suicide attempt. Eleanor was ten.

In 1899, ER's grandmother sent her to Allenswood Academy, a private school near London, England, which offered an academic course of study to girls from wealthy families. At Allenswood, Eleanor grew in self-confidence and worldview under the tutelage of headmistress Marie Souvestre. ER wanted to stay at the school for four years. But she came home after three, at her grandmother's insistence, to make her New York society debut.

In 1905, ER married Franklin Roosevelt, her distant cousin—fifth, once removed. She would give birth to seven children in ten years. Her only daughter, Anna, was born in 1906, sons James in 1907, Franklin in 1909 (he died before his first birthday, from influenza), Elliott in 1910, Franklin Delano in 1914, and John in 1916.

John was only two when ER discovered her husband's affair with her former social secretary Lucy Page Mercer. Eleanor offered Franklin a divorce. His mother, Sara Delano Roosevelt, threatened to disinherit him if he left his family. Franklin promised not to see Lucy again and reconciled with his wife.

In 1921, doctors diagnosed FDR with poliomyelitis, which left him permanently paralyzed from the waist down. A rising star in the Democratic Party before paralysis struck, he had been elected to the New York State Senate in 1910, served as assistant secretary of the navy from 1913 to 1920, and run for vice president on the national ticket with James M. Cox in 1920. After a period of rigorous rehabilitation, Franklin resumed his political career with the support of his wife. He was elected governor of New York in 1928 and president in 1932.

ER was glad for the nation, the Democrats, and her husband, but she had "never wanted to be a President's wife. And I don't want it now," she told Associated Press reporter Lorena Hickok, who had covered her during the campaign. Franklin's election to the presidency meant relinquishing several activities that gave ER personal meaning and self-satisfaction. One such commitment was her post as teacher and administrator at the Todhunter School for girls in New York City. ER had commuted between Albany and Manhattan and kept teaching when her husband was governor. This would not be possible for the president's wife. The prospect of what her life might become depressed ER.

Murray, who knew nothing of ER's sorrows, studied her surreptitiously. The first lady was fifty years old and nearly six feet tall. She wore no makeup. She tied her light brown hair back with a ribbon. Her dress had simple lines. Her shoes were low-heeled and practical.

Murray's observations corroborated news stories, such as those written by Hickok, detailing the first lady's resolve to be "plain, ordinary Mrs. Roosevelt," despite her new role. She, and not a chauffeur or Secret Service agent, had driven her party to the camp. She had raised eyebrows in Washington's high society when she positioned herself alongside the waitstaff to serve ham sandwiches at an inaugural luncheon, thereby demonstrating a desire to serve others and a preference for informality. She gave a garden party on the grounds of the White House for residents of the National Training School for Girls, which, in contrast to its name, resembled a prison. It had no teachers or counselors, and the living quarters were "dark" and "unsanitary." When ER was told that politicians would be upset if she hosted black and white girls together, she said, "It may be bad politics, but it's a thing I would like to do as an individual, so I'm going to do it."

This was not the first time Eleanor Roosevelt had acted on her convictions. Six years before she became first lady, she was arrested and charged with disorderly conduct after she joined three hundred picketers in support of a paper box makers' strike in New York City. Now that she was first lady, she would avoid arrest, but she continued to work with union leaders, such as Rose Schneiderman, and to lobby for fair wages, for better working conditions, and against child labor.

ER changed the complexion of the White House by hiring only black maids, much to the chagrin of her mother-in-law. The first lady's dinner guests, a mix of friends, artists, young people, and, sometimes, "destitute" men she had met in the park, reflected her wish to get to know people from all age groups and walks of life. She was said by one journalist to favor unconventional thinkers and "people who do things" over "stuffed shirts, fat-heads and very proper people." Had her husband not been a candidate for president, she confided to a friend, she would have voted for the socialist Norman Thomas.

At the suggestion of Hickok, who would become a lifelong friend, Eleanor Roosevelt set a precedent by holding weekly press conferences with women reporters. She invited the public to write to her about their problems, and more than three hundred thousand did just that in her first year as first lady. While she could not help everyone who asked, she responded to each letter or passed it on to someone—a division chief, cabinet secretary, or the president—who could.

ER's passion for examining issues up close fascinated the public. Indeed, the distances she traveled and the inconveniences she tolerated were unparalleled for a first lady. She braved the squalor and soot of a West Virginia mining town to discuss living conditions with black miners. Mud coated her shoes as she tramped through an army bonus camp to talk with World War I veterans about their unpaid pensions. "An able-bodied man at the pink of condition would have difficulty in keeping up with her when she walks," noted a reporter for the *Washington Post*. The Secret Service appropriately code-named her Rover.

ER was determined that the first camp for women succeed. Given her insistence that Camp Tera be racially inclusive and her practice of counting the number of black residents, ER must have noticed the small brown girl with cropped hair in pants sitting near the social hall. Perhaps because Murray seemed to be reading or because her shyness was so obvious, ER, who normally greeted everyone, simply passed by.

· · ·

AS SOON AS ELEANOR ROOSEVELT LEFT, Jessie Mills summoned Murray to the main office and accused her of disrespecting the first lady by not "standing at attention." Mills, who'd been an ambulance driver in World War I, had the demeanor of a drill sergeant. Her thick eyeglasses and the dark suit she accented with a narrow tie magnified her overbearing personality. She woke residents at six in the morning with a bugle call and signaled changes in the schedule of activities with a shrill bell. Lights went out at ten with taps. She forbade the staff from fraternizing with residents beyond their official duties.

Mills's authoritarianism and her accusation offended Murray, for she had made herself as presentable as possible and stayed out of ER's way. Furthermore, the first lady's unpretentiousness, Murray insisted, showed that she neither wanted nor needed "obsequious behavior" from anyone. Mills resented Murray's assertiveness and soon found an excuse to oust her. During a routine search, Mills came across a copy of Karl Marx's *Das Kapital* in Murray's belongings. This time, Mills accused Murray of being a Communist.

Das Kapital was a required text in a political philosophy course Murray had taken at Hunter. She had brought it along with a stack of novels and books of poetry. Intellectually curious and accustomed to reading widely, Murray vehemently denied that she was a Communist. Mills took her possession of Marx's book as proof otherwise.

Mills often allowed residents to stay until they secured a job or other means of support. Murray's friend Pee Wee, for example, had been at the camp for nearly eighteen months and would remain there until the facility closed, two years later. But Mills expelled Murray immediately, partly out of frustration with her rebelliousness and partly out of fear that groups closely watching the camp, such as the American Legion, would accuse the staff of harboring Communists. It is also possible that Mills, who would shortly lose her job due to alleged improprieties, was motivated by her disapproval of Murray's friendship with Peg. That their relationship was close, interracial, and between a camp staffer and resident made it unacceptable to Mills on several counts.

Pauli Murray's residency at Camp Tera lasted just over three months. After a five-week hitchhiking trip to Nebraska with Peg, Murray returned to New York City, homeless and without a job. She never expected to cross paths with Eleanor Roosevelt again.

PART I

TAKING AIM AT
THE WHITE HOUSE,
1938–40

Pauli Murray, here a twenty-seven-year-old WPA teacher, composes a poem on Election Day, November 8, 1938, on Riverside Drive, New York City. She often marked historical and personally meaningful events by writing poetry and prose. (*The Schlesinger Library, Radcliffe Institute, Harvard University and the Estate of Pauli Murray*)

I

"It Is the Problem of My People"

The clatter of Pauli Murray's old typewriter bounced off the walls of her one-room Harlem apartment on December 6, 1938. Working at breakneck speed, she stopped only to look over a line in her letter or take a drag from her ever-present cigarette. Although she was only five-foot-two and weighed 105 pounds, she hammered the keys with the focus of a prizefighter. She had been forced to move three times because neighbors found the noise intolerable.

The catalyst for Murray's current agitation was Franklin Roosevelt's speech at the University of North Carolina the day before. It was his first address since the 1938 midterm elections and the fourth visit to the university by an incumbent president. The reports of his isolation at his vacation home in Warm Springs, Georgia, and the arrangements for radio broadcasts to Europe and Latin America had sparked international interest in his speech.

Thousands lined the motorcade path to UNC in the drenching rain, holding handmade signs and flags, hoping to catch a glimpse of the fifty-six-year-old president in his open car. When it became apparent that there would be no break in the downpour, organizers moved the festivities from Kenan Stadium to the brand-new Woollen Gymnasium. There, in an over-capacity crowd of ten thousand, a man fainted from the swelter. Many people went to other campus buildings to listen to the broadcast. Countless numbers stood outside the gym in the rain. Before FDR spoke, the university band played "Hail to the Chief," school officials awarded him an honorary doctor of laws degree, and an African American choir sang spirituals.

Under the glare of klieg lights, the warmth of his academic regalia, and the weight of his steel leg braces, the president made his way to the flag-draped platform. He paused often during his twenty-five-minute address for roaring applause, wiping his face with the handkerchief he slipped in and out of his pocket, gripping the lectern to maintain his balance. He praised the university for its "liberal teaching" and commitment to social progress. He declared his faith in youth and democracy. He urged Americans to embrace "the kind of change" necessary "to meet new social and economic needs."

Having listened to the broadcast the day before, Murray underlined passages in the speech from the *New York Times* front-page story "Roosevelt Urges Nation to Continue Liberalism." The "contradiction" between the president's rhetoric and her experience of the South made her boil. She would never forget the day a bus driver told her to "relieve" herself in "an open field" because the public toilets were for whites only. Insulted, she rode in agony for two hours, not knowing if there would be toilet facilities for blacks at the next stop.

Murray wondered if it mattered to the president that the "liberal institution" that had just granted him an honorary doctorate, and of which he claimed to be a "proud and happy" alumnus, barred black students from its hallowed halls and confined those blacks who came to hear him to a segregated section. Did he understand the psychological wounds or the economic costs of segregation? And how could he rationally or morally associate a whites-only admissions policy with liberalism or social progress? Having applied to UNC's graduate program in sociology a month before FDR's visit, Murray aimed to see just how liberal the school was.

. . .

EXACERBATING MURRAY'S FRUSTRATION with the president was his previous condemnation of lynching as "a vile form of collective murder" and his recent silence during a thirty-day Senate filibuster of the Wagner–Van Nuys bill that would have made lynching a federal offense. After the bill died, FDR proposed that a standing committee of Congress or the attorney general investigate "lynchings and incidents of mob violence."

The black press lashed out against his political maneuvering. The *New York Amsterdam News* condemned him for keeping "his tongue in his cheek!" The *Chicago Defender* called him "an artful dodger." The *Louisiana Weekly,* predicting that blacks would abandon the Democratic Party, declared, "You're too late, Mr. President, and what you say is NOTHING."

Murray understood that FDR's reticence on anti-lynching legislation was an attempt to placate conservative politicians from the South, where whites lynched blacks with impunity. Her introduction to politics had begun as a preschooler, reading newspaper headlines to her grandfather Robert Fitzgerald, a Union army veteran whose injury in the Civil War cost him his vision in his old age. Robert, originally from Pennsylvania, settled in North Carolina after the war to teach ex-slaves. He had also nurtured his granddaughter's intellect and her love of African American literature and history. That this year marked the seventy-fifth anniversary of the Emancipation Proclamation made the president's inaction even more objectionable to Murray. Since 1863, more than three thousand blacks had been lynched, and at least seventy of these murders had taken place during FDR's presidency.

Murray's indignation was rooted in bone-chilling stories she had heard as a child of racial brutality and the Klansmen who circled her grandfather's property nightly on horseback, threatening to shut down his school for blacks. Ever brave, Robert had kept "his musket loaded" and the school door open. Murray had her own stories, too.

When she was six years old and on her way to fetch water from a community well, she and a neighbor came upon a group of blacks gathered around the body of young John Henry Corniggins, sprawled near a patch of thorny shrubs. Murray saw "his feet first, the white soles sticking out of the grass and caked with mud, then his scratched brown legs." His eyes were open. Blood seeped through a bullet hole in his shirt near his heart.

John Henry lay motionless as large green flies wandered over his face and into his mouth. Nearby, a solitary "buzzard circled." Murray raced home, trembling in a cold sweat. The word among blacks was that a white man had assumed John Henry was stealing watermelons and shot him. No evidence of theft was found near the boy's body. No one was arrested for his murder.

Six years later, violence touched Murray's family when a white guard at Maryland's Hospital for the Negro Insane murdered her father. At the funeral, she could hardly believe that the "purple" bloated body in the gray casket was her once proud father. She was horrified by the sight of his mangled head, which had been "split open like a melon" during an autopsy "and sewed together loosely with jagged stitches crisscrossing the blood-clotted line of severance."

· · ·

THE FIGHT OVER ANTI-LYNCHING LEGISLATION was but one of Franklin Roosevelt's worries. His attempt to purge Congress of his enemies had failed, and a coalition of anti–New Deal Republicans and Democrats had emerged. Despite the continuing economic depression, important legislation remained deadlocked. Frightening developments loomed on the world stage, as well. Under Adolf Hitler, Germany's aggression in Europe escalated with the annexation of Austria and the Sudetenland of Czechoslovakia. During Kristallnacht, hundreds of synagogues were destroyed. Thousands of Jews were stripped of their citizenship, property, and business rights and sent to concentration camps.

As Murray pounded out her letter to the president, she recalled Eleanor Roosevelt's visit to Camp Tera. Murray had been following reports about the first lady, listening to her radio broadcast, and reading her syndicated newspaper column, "My Day," since it had begun publication, on December 30, 1935. In it, ER chronicled get-togethers with family and friends, meetings with public figures, impressions of what she saw during her travels, and her opinions on a range of cultural and political matters. Writing the column six days a week and meeting her duties as first lady, which frequently went past midnight, required her to compose on the go. After one day-long visit to Camp Jane Addams (as Camp Tera had been renamed, in 1936, in honor of the first American woman to win the Nobel Peace Prize), Tommy sat her typewriter on a rock near the Bear Mountain Bridge so that ER could dictate her copy and meet her deadline.

Southern segregation made ER uncomfortable, and she did not enjoy going to FDR's Warm Springs cottage, despite the delight he took in the place. She did not accompany the president to UNC, but two weeks earlier, she had attended the Southern Conference for Human Welfare in Birmingham, Alabama, on her own. SCHW was an interracial gathering of liberals who met to discuss health, economics, housing, labor, race relations, voting rights, opportunities for young people, and agricultural issues affecting the region. The conferees included a mix of labor, religious, youth, and civil rights activists, politicians, government administrators, journalists, educators, and representatives from organizations affiliated with the socialist and Communist movements.

ER was the most celebrated attendee, and her presence drew the national press. Of her whirlwind schedule, a *New York Times* reporter noted, "Mrs. Roosevelt arrived at 5 o'clock this morning . . . and rested until 8 o'clock and thereafter in rapid succession held a press conference, visited several institutions, spoke informally to an afternoon session meeting on youth problems and tonight gave an address on 'Democracy in Education.'" Seven thousand people, nearly half of them black, jammed into the city auditorium to hear her speak about the importance of "universal education" and the contribution each citizen makes to the nation, "regardless of nationality or race." She fielded questions for the better part of an hour.

The first lady's participation at the SCHW was historic. However, her skillful circumvention of a local ordinance requiring segregated seating was what interested Murray most. When city officials learned that conferees were mingling freely during sessions, without regard to race, the police came and directed everyone to obey local law. Having walked into a session late, ER sat down in the black section near her friend Mary McLeod Bethune, who was now director of the Negro Affairs Division in the National Youth Administration. When the police ordered ER to move, she had her chair placed between the white and black delegations. And it was there she sat, symbolically outside of racial strictures, for the remainder of the conference.

The first lady's deft reaction warmed the hearts of conferees, angered segregationists, and thrilled the black press. The influential *Afro-American* newspaper, of which Murray was a devoted reader, underscored the significance of ER's aisle-straddling tactic by proclaiming, "Sometimes actions speak louder than words."

• • •

AFTER CAMP TERA, Murray got a job with the Works Progress Administration, initially as a remedial reading teacher, then with the Workers'

Education Project. Now that the WPA was in jeopardy, she planned to return to North Carolina, where she could do graduate work at UNC and look after her adoptive mother, Aunt Pauline. The thought of living in the South again filled Murray with dread. On the other hand, it seemed worth the sacrifice to further her education and be with family.

In no mood for armchair liberalism, Murray counted herself among a group of young radicals incensed by FDR's "coziness with white supremacy in the South." She reasoned that if UNC were half the institution the president said it was, its administration would find a way to accommodate her. Murray knew of only one way to challenge his roundly praised address. She typed a bold missive, spelling out what the South was like for blacks, daring him to take a stand as a fellow Christian for democracy and the liberal principles he espoused.

December 6, 1938

Dear President Roosevelt:

I pray that this letter will get past your secretaries and reach your personal consideration.

Have you time to listen to the problem of one of your millions of fellow-citizens, which will illustrate most clearly one of the problems of democracy in America. I speak not only for myself but for 12,000,000 other citizens.

Briefly, the facts are these:

I am a Negro, the most oppressed, most misunderstood and most neglected section of your population.

I am also a WPA worker, another insecure and often misrepresented group of citizens. I teach on the Workers' Education Project of New York City, a field which has received the constant and devoted support of your wife, Mrs. Eleanor Roosevelt.

My main interest, the tradition of my family for three generations, is education, which, I believe, is the basic requirement for the maintenance and extension of democracy.

At present, in order to do a competent teaching job, a job comparable to the work of established educational institutions, like all other professional WPA workers, I feel the need of more training. To understand the knotty economic and social problems of our country and to interpret these problems clearly and simply to workers makes it imperative that we continue our studies. Our wage standards are such that we are unable to further our education. Those of us who do not have degrees are unable to get them because of the general WPA arrangements. Those of us who have degrees, and yet feel an inadequacy of information and formal training, find it impossible to go further and obtain our Master's Degree.

Sometime ago I applied to the University of North Carolina for admission to their graduate school. They sent me an application blank, on the bottom of which was asked, "Race and Religion." (For your information, I am a confirmed Protestant Episcopalian.) As you know, no Negro has ever been admitted to the University of North Carolina. You may wonder then, why I, a Negro knowing this fact, did make application.

My grandfather, a Union Army soldier, gave his eye for the liberation of his race. As soon as the war was over, he went to North Carolina under the Freedmen's Bureau to establish schools and educate the newly freed Negroes. From that time on my entire family has been engaged in educational work in that state. My own father was a principal of one of the Baltimore City schools and my sisters and brothers are also teachers. You passed through Durham, where my family lived and worked, and where my aunt now a woman of sixty-eight years, still plods back and forth to her school training future citizens of America. This aunt has been teaching since she was fifteen years old, and for more than thirty years in the Durham Public Schools, and yet if she were to become disabled tomorrow, there is no school pension system which would take care of her, neither does she qualify for the Old Age Pension system which excludes teachers.

12,000,000 of your citizens have to endure insults, injustices, and such degradation of spirit that you would believe impossible as a human being and a Christian. We are forced to ride in prescribed places in the busses and street cars of those very cities you passed through in our beloved Southland. When your party reached the station at Durham yesterday, you must have noticed a sign which said "White," and then a fence, then another sign which said "Colored." Can you, for one moment, put yourself in our place and imagine the feelings of resentment, the protest, the indignation, the outrage that would rise within you to realize that you, a human being, with the keen sensitivities of other human beings were being set off in a corner, marked apart from your fellow human beings?

We, as Americans and Negroes, actually have few rights as Americans. Laws are passed designed to prevent us from using the ballot, an elementary and fundamental principle of democracy. We have to live in "ghettoes" everywhere, not only in Warm Springs, Ga., but also in the city of Washington, the very heart of our democracy.

It is the task of enlightened individuals to bring the torch of education to those who are not enlightened. There is a crying need for education among my own people. No one realizes this more than

I do. But the un-Christian, un-American conditions in the South make it impossible for me and other young Negroes to live there and continue our faith in the ideals of democracy and Christianity. We are as much political refugees from the South as any of the Jews in Germany. We cannot endure these conditions. Our whole being cries out against inequality and injustice. And so, we come to Northern cities to escape the mental and physical cruelties of the land in which we were born and the land we love.

You said yesterday that you associated yourself with young people, and you emphasized their importance in the current affairs of our nation. Can you ask your young Negroes to return to the South? Do you feel, as we do, that the ultimate test of democracy in the United States will be the way in which it solves its Negro problem? No, President Roosevelt, our problems are not just those of other people. They are far deeper, far more trying, and far more hopeless. Have you raised your voice loud enough against the burning of our people? Why has our government refused to pass antilynching legislation? And why is it that the group of congressmen so opposed to that passing of this legislation are part and parcel of the Democratic Party of which you are leader?

Yesterday, you placed your approval on the University of North Carolina as an institution of liberal thought. You spoke of the necessity of change in a body of law to meet the problems of an accelerated era of civilization. You called on Americans to support a liberal philosophy based on democracy. What does this mean for Negro Americans? Does it mean that we, at last, may participate freely, and on the basis of equality, with our fellow-citizens in working out the problems of this democracy? Does it mean that Negro students in the South will be allowed to sit down with white students and study a problem which is fundamental and mutual to both groups? Does it mean that the University of North Carolina is ready to open its doors to Negro students seeking enlightenment on the social and economic problems which the South faces? Does it mean, that as an alumnus of the University of North Carolina, you are ready to use your prestige and influence to see to it that this step is taken toward greater opportunity for mutual understanding of race relations in the South?

Or does it mean, that everything you said has no meaning for us as Negroes, that again we are to be set aside and passed over for more important problems? I appeal for an answer because I, and my people are perplexed.

Sincerely yours,
Pauli Murray

Hoping to ensure that the president would get her correspondence, Murray sent a copy of it with a cover letter to the first lady.

> December 6, 1938
>
> Dear Mrs. Roosevelt:
>
> You do not remember me, but I was the girl who did not stand up when you passed through the Social Hall of Camp Tera during one of your visits in the winter of 1934–35. Miss Mills criticized me afterward, but I thought and still feel that you are the sort of person who prefers to be accepted as a human being and not a human paragon.
>
> One of my closest friends and pals is "Pee Wee," whom you know as Margaret Inness [*sic*]. I have watched with appreciation your interest in her struggle to improve herself and to secure employment. Often I have wanted to write you, but felt that you had more important problems to consider.
>
> Now I make an appeal to you in my own behalf. I am sending you a copy of a letter which I wrote to your husband, President Roosevelt, in the hope that you will try to understand the spirit and deep perplexity in which it is written, if he is too busy.
>
> I know he has the problems of our nation on his hand, and I would not bother to write him, except that my problem isn't mine alone, it is the problem of my people, and in these trying days, it will not let me or any other thinking Negro rest. Need I say any more?
>
> Sincerely yours,
> Pauli Murray

Given how fired up Murray was when she composed these letters, the clamor coming from her tiny, smoke-filled apartment must have disturbed her fellow tenants. It is not known if her typing led to another eviction. What we do know is that her missives opened a conversation with Eleanor Roosevelt that would continue until ER's death in 1962.

• • •

THE PRESIDENT'S STAFF FORWARDED Murray's correspondence to Ambrose Caliver, senior specialist in Negro education at the federal Office of Education. Caliver would pass it on to Hilda Worthington Smith, specialist in workers' education in the WPA, from whom Murray would hear a month later. ER, on the other hand, responded in two weeks.

December 19, 1938

My dear Miss Murray:

    I have read the copy of the letter you sent me and I understand perfectly, but great changes come slowly. I think they are coming, however, and sometimes it is better to fight hard with conciliatory methods. The South is changing, but don't push too fast. There is a great change in youth, for instance, and that is a hopeful sign.

Very sincerely yours,
Eleanor Roosevelt

While the first lady's plea for patience was not an answer Murray could accept, she was grateful that ER "answered under her personal signature." The contrasting tone in their exchange—Murray the impatient youth and ER the cautious elder—symbolized the tension at the beginning of their friendship.

Even though ER advised Murray against pushing "too fast," the young woman's argument reverberated two days later in "My Day." "I could not help thinking of some of the letters which pass through my hands," the first lady told readers. Paraphrasing Murray's appeal to the president, ER wrote, "Are you free if you cannot vote, if you cannot be sure that the same justice will be meted out to you as to your neighbor; if you are expected to live on a lower level than your neighbor and to work for lower wages; if you are barred from certain places and opportunities?"

Left to right: University of North Carolina president Frank Porter Graham, Eleanor Roosevelt, and *Daily Tar Heel* reporter Louis Harris en route to a luncheon at the Campus Inn, Chapel Hill, North Carolina, 1942. Harris, who would become an influential pollster, covered campus reaction to Pauli Murray's application for admission. *(Southern Historical Collection, Wilson Library, University of North Carolina at Chapel Hill)*

2

"Members of Your Race Are Not Admitted"

On December 12, 1938, shortly after Pauli Murray wrote to the Roosevelts, the U.S. Supreme Court issued a six-to-two decision in the case of *Missouri ex rel. Gaines v. Canada.* The plaintiff, Lloyd Lionel Gaines, was an honors graduate of Lincoln University. Lincoln, an all-black college located in Jefferson City, Missouri, had no law school, and Gaines, a duly qualified state resident, had applied to the University of Missouri School of Law. Because he was African American, the university refused to admit him. Gaines and NAACP counsel Charles Hamilton Houston appealed first to the county and state courts, which upheld the university's decision. From there, they took the case to the U.S. Supreme Court.

To the delight of the NAACP and the dismay of southern segregationists, the high court held that the state of Missouri could not deny Gaines admission to the University of Missouri School of Law on racial grounds and at the same time provide legal education to whites within the state. The court directed Missouri to provide legal education to blacks "substantially equal" to that offered whites, and it forbade the state from using a "limited demand" for legal education by blacks as an excuse for discrimination in favor of whites.

The court also ruled that Missouri could not satisfy the requirements of the equal protection clause of the Fourteenth Amendment by making legal education available to its black residents outside the state, as it had previously done. In short, the *Gaines* decision torpedoed the strategies southern authorities used to maintain segregated schools. Funding Gaines so he could attend law school in another state was no longer an option. Only the possibility of separate and "substantially equal" facilities remained viable.

Thrilled by the court's opinion, Murray sent a letter of congratulations and encouragement to Gaines. This victory marked a milestone for the NAACP legal brain trust. She thought it improved the prospects for her application to the University of North Carolina, as well. By the time Hilda Smith acknowledged Murray's letter to President Roosevelt and offered to help identify a school that would admit her, Murray was determined to see how far she could push UNC.

The *Gaines* decision was barely forty-eight hours old when UNC dean William W. Pierson drafted a letter to Murray that ignored the implications of what the federal court had done. "I am not authorized to grant you admission to our Graduate School," Pierson wrote. "Under the laws of North Carolina, and under the resolutions of the Board of Trustees of the University of North Carolina, members of your race are not admitted to the university. It has long been the social policy of the State to maintain separate schools for the whites and Negroes." Acknowledging that no black college in North Carolina offered graduate degrees, the dean continued, "It is expected that the Legislature of the State will make provision for graduate instruction for Negroes." But the nature of that provision was yet to be announced.

Murray was undeterred. Unlike Thomas R. Hocutt, a graduate of the North Carolina College for Negroes, whose earlier attempt to enroll at UNC was thwarted by the refusal of NCCN president James E. Shepard to release his transcript, Murray had proffered a bachelor of arts from Hunter College and a fully completed application.

Convinced that the scales of justice were tilting in her direction, Murray dispatched a letter of introduction to UNC president Frank Porter Graham on December 17, 1938, opening a three-month exchange with campus leaders. In addition to proposing that she and Graham meet, Murray indicated that she had been reared in North Carolina and that she was a graduate of the state's public schools. She underscored the significance of the *Gaines* decision, and she reminded Graham of the responsibility for liberal leadership Franklin Roosevelt had entrusted to the university.

If Murray's legal argument did not move Graham, her characterization of the moral problem should have made him cringe. "How much longer," she asked, "is the South going to withhold elementary human rights from its black citizens. How can Negroes, the economic backbone of the South for centuries, defend our institutions against threats of fascism and barbarism if we too are treated the same as the Jews of Germany?" To make sure Graham understood her intentions, Murray threatened to follow Gaines's example. "It would be a victory for liberal thought in the South," she wrote, "if you were favorably disposed toward my application instead of forcing me to carry the issue to the courts."

· · ·

FRANK GRAHAM, a native North Carolinian and a UNC alumnus, was a friend of the Roosevelts'. The president had twice tapped Graham, a southern liberal and a supporter of the New Deal, to chair the study committee on unemployment insurance and social security in 1934, and again to head the advisory committee on the economic problems of the South in 1938. FDR's effusive speech at Chapel Hill was in part a reflection of his regard for Graham, whom some believed Roosevelt eyed as a potential running mate.

Eleanor Roosevelt's friendship with Graham began in 1935, when he invited her to speak at graduation. She was the first woman to give a commencement address, and the first first lady to visit the campus. Like Graham, she valued open dialogue. Their mutual concern for the poor and minorities drew them to organizations such as the Southern Conference for Human Welfare, where they became natural allies and their friendship blossomed.

"Dr. Frank," as he was affectionately called around campus, had a record that made liberals proud. He had permitted the black poet Langston Hughes to speak at the university, even though 285 citizens had signed a petition sent to North Carolina governor Oliver Max Gardner opposing Hughes's appearance. On learning that the medical school had a quota system for Jewish applicants, Graham abolished it, over the dean's objection. His leadership of the SCHW, whose racially diverse membership included Republicans and Democrats, along with Communists and socialists, made him a target for conservative critics.

In his keynote address at the founding meeting of the SCHW, Graham, whose short, 125-pound frame bore no relationship to his personal power, brought the audience to its feet when he declared, "The black man is the primary test of American democracy and Christianity." This statement would have pleased Murray had she been present, for she had scribbled a similar thought in one of her notebooks: "It seems to me that the testing ground of democracy and Christianity in the United States is in the South." She had repeated essentially the same argument in her letter to Franklin Roosevelt.

Not one to use words carelessly, Murray meant what she wrote. She viewed her application as a test for UNC, American democracy, and Christianity. And she dared professed liberals, such as Graham and the Roosevelts, to do more than say the right thing.

Graham found himself cornered by political realities antithetical to his personal ideals. He believed in educational opportunity for blacks, and he was "aware of the inequities" Murray pointed out. Yet as a state employee, he felt bound not to admit blacks until state laws were changed. His only recourse, he wrote to Murray, was to advocate for the development and strengthening of programs at black colleges, as he'd done. He was under intense criticism for what he had "tried to do in behalf of Negro people," and he implored Murray not to disrupt the progress made thus far. In the end, the races "go up or down together," he warned.

While Murray could not agree with Graham's obedience to a law she believed unjust, she had to admit that he wrote a "very fine letter." It had the familiar ring of Eleanor Roosevelt's earlier message: to be patient and avoid provoking the opposition. It was advice Murray would not heed.

3

"We Have to Be Very Careful About the People We Select"

In January 1939, Murray sent copies of her correspondence with UNC officials to NAACP executive secretary Walter White. White passed her materials on to Thurgood Marshall, assistant special counsel for the association. While Murray awaited word from Marshall, the local media and then the national press picked up the story of her application.

When Murray saw the January 6, 1939, headline of the *Durham Morning Herald*, "Negress Applies to Enter Carolina," she felt as if she had been slapped in the face. That her name had been withheld did not numb the sting of the offensive noun or the opinion reflected. "Rational members of both races understand that the policy of segregation of races with respect to schools is a fixed one in this part of the country," reported the newspaper. "No one in his right mind favors trying to abandon or materially amend that policy at this juncture."

North Carolina governor Clyde R. Hoey's response to Murray's application lacked Frank Graham's diplomacy and Eleanor Roosevelt's hopefulness. "North Carolina does not believe in social equality between the races and will not tolerate" integrated schools, said Hoey. He favored "equality of opportunity" for blacks "in their respective fields of service." What the governor meant was that he would upgrade black schools, if necessary, to keep UNC all white.

Eager to share her position, Murray launched her own publicity campaign, sending open letters to Hoey and copies of her correspondence with UNC officials to the press. African American newspapers gave prominent coverage to her case. The *Carolina Times,* the black weekly in Murray's hometown edited by her friend Louis E. Austin, reprinted her letter to UNC's President Graham and ran an editorial with a photograph and a warning: "North Carolina will do well to regard the application of the young Negro woman from New York as having the support of a majority of thinking Negroes in the state. There will be many more to follow from points much closer." The *Afro-American,* which reached a national audience, excerpted Murray's letter to Franklin Roosevelt under the title "Did F.D.R. Mean It?" and highlighted the paradox of the president's remarks at UNC and the school's rejection of Murray's application.

According to the *Daily Tar Heel,* sentiment at UNC was mixed. Howard K. Beale, a professor of history, and Paul Green, the Pulitzer Prize–winning playwright and English professor who had invited Langston Hughes to campus, wanted to admit Murray outright. UNC was either a liberal institution or not, argued Beale. If it was the former, then the only option was to welcome qualified blacks. By contrast, Professor Howard W. Odum, who headed the School of Public Welfare and the Sociology Department, to which Murray had applied, said the time was not right. Odum, a native southerner and an influential scholar of race relations, insisted that integration had to be gradual and carefully planned. It was "asking too much" of the South, he said, to admit Murray immediately.

Campus polls and debate revealed bitter opposition and strong support for Murray's application. There were rumors of a lynching posse that promised to "tar and feather any 'nigger' who tried to" enroll. Then again, students like John Alan Creedy were disturbed by the threats of violence, as well as the laurels President Roosevelt had conferred upon UNC. Creedy, editor of the campus-based *Carolina Magazine,* wrote in an editorial entitled "We, the Hypocrites . . .": "We are a conservative University with a little surface froth of liberal foam to keep everyone fooled—even ourselves." Then, to demonstrate "what sort of student" UNC was "missing by excluding Negroes," he published Murray's "Song of the Highway" poem in a special issue on black graduate education in the South. Fifty-seven years later, Creedy would still insist that UNC students missed out because the state denied Murray's admission.

The controversy over Murray's application horrified her aunt Pauline. "Please be careful what you do about this," she wrote. Still teaching in a black segregated school in Durham without benefit of a pension or tenure, she feared that school authorities would dismiss her or that angry whites would lynch her and set her home afire. Dame pleaded with daughter Pauli, "You can make it very uncomfortable for me."

North Carolina College for Negroes president James E. Shepard, who was a "deeply respected friend" of Murray's family, had a different take on the situation. A black conservative, he saw this as a chance to expand the programs and physical plant at his school, and he told the press exactly what legislators wanted to hear: "Negroes could do their best work only in their own schools."

Shepard's political opportunism and Aunt Pauline's vulnerability troubled Murray, but it was impossible to challenge "deep-seated injustice" and accepted customs without "making people uncomfortable," she reasoned. By the time the North Carolina legislature passed a bill enabling the creation of graduate and professional courses at black colleges, and then declined to appropriate funds for them, Murray was ready to go to court.

. . .

WHEN MURRAY MET with Thurgood Marshall in the winter of 1939 and he told her that the NAACP would not handle her appeal, she was flabbergasted. The association had a policy of taking only "airtight" cases, where the legal foundation for the grievance and the background of the plaintiff were flawless, he explained. Murray's New York State residency, notwithstanding her North Carolina roots, weakened her case. Furthermore, the loss of an expensive appeal was a risk the association could not afford. Murray countered with the argument that UNC had violated her Fourteenth Amendment right to equal protection, as it did admit whites from out of state. Nevertheless, Marshall had made up his mind. If Murray wanted to go to court, she would have to proceed without NAACP backing.

Murray left the meeting feeling as if she had been blindsided. Not only had Marshall turned down her case, his comment about the importance of a plaintiff's background—"We have to be very careful about the people we select"—made her wonder if he found *her* undesirable. And, if so, why?

Was it her politics? Murray was certainly to the left of NAACP leadership. Radicalized by her experiences with the Workers' Education Project and a brief residency at Brookwood Labor College—both of which immersed her in a community of labor and leftist activists—she had already been arrested for picketing the *New York Amsterdam News* in support of unionization. Booted from Camp Tera on the charge that she was a Communist, she set out "to educate" herself on the subject and, in the process, joined a group of "intellectual radicals" known as the Communist Party (Opposition) in 1936. From the group's leader, Jay Lovestone, a former Communist Party USA official who had been expelled for criticizing party dogma and strategy, Murray received an extensive "critique" of Soviet communism. What she learned was vital for counteracting Communists who participated in liberal groups with which she worked.

Repulsed by the Communist appeal "Self-Determination for the Black Belt," which had the uncomfortable sound of "another form of segregation," Murray disavowed the CPO in 1938. While she never flirted with communism again, she was still closer ideologically to the democratic socialist Norman Thomas, for whom she voted in the 1932 presidential election, than to NAACP officials who backed FDR and New Dealers in the Democratic Party.

Was the issue her temperament? A self-described individualist with a first-class intellect, Murray found that bureaucracies tried her patience. Her assertive letters to UNC officials bothered black veteran leaders, such as NAACP assistant executive secretary Roy Wilkins. Even friends, such as National Urban League executive Lester B. Granger, who praised Murray's courage, and *New York Post* reporter Ted Poston, who admired her "literary brilliance," saw her audacity and proclivity for working to the point of exhaustion as signs of emotional instability.

Was the problem her family history? If Marshall, a native Baltimorean only two years older than Murray, had not heard about her father's institutionalization and murder at the Hospital for the Negro Insane or the false rumor that her mother had committed suicide, he certainly knew Murray's older brother, William H. Murray Jr. They had been classmates at Howard University School of Law before William, whom Marshall remembered as a talented student, dropped out with financial and emotional difficulties.

Or was the problem Murray's personal life? Because the association was leery of taking on female plaintiffs, especially unmarried women, for fear that something untoward might surface and damage their reputation and the case, the fact that Murray presented herself as single and kept her marriage to Billy Wynn secret was problematic. Even the marriage, given their eight-year estrangement without divorce, would have been cause for concern. Or perhaps NAACP leaders had seen Murray's essay and her photo as the boy Pete in Nancy Cunard's *Negro* anthology. Walter White, for example, was an award-winning author well connected to the New York literary elite. It is also possible, considering the questionable privacy of medical records in the 1930s, that Marshall got wind of Murray's 1937 hospitalization in Amityville, New York, probably at the

Long Island Home for Nervous Invalids. Although she was admitted with symptoms of anxiety and exhaustion, her conversations with the medical staff marked the beginning of a decade-long "inner conflict," during which she acknowledged her attraction to women but rebuffed the medical diagnosis of homosexuality. Murray's notes reveal that she was a patient for eight to ten days between the third and fourth weeks of December. Her care and treatment included a thorough physical examination, wholesome meals, psychotherapy, rest, and relaxation.

As a practice, the NAACP regarded the most desirable plaintiffs as those with no arrest record, no prior association with radical groups, particularly Communists, and no confirmed or alleged family or personal history of mental illness, which by definition included homosexuality. (The American Psychiatric Association would not declassify homosexuality as a mental disorder until 1973.) Even if Marshall knew nothing of Murray's hospitalization or sexuality, he and NAACP officials would have likely looked upon her manner, close relationships with women, and male-sounding first name with suspicion.

Murray would never know the extent to which any of these issues might have influenced Marshall and his colleagues. What she did believe for the rest of her life was that there was more behind the decision not to take her case than he actually disclosed. In his eyes, she felt less than "Simon-pure."

As desperately as Murray wanted to appeal her case in court, she thought it unwise to go forward without the NAACP. She respected Marshall, in spite of their differences. Besides, she could not pay for a court battle on her own.

Having to give up this fight was a "personal defeat" made all the more insufferable by the "irony" of Murray's ancestry. Not only had she been raised in North Carolina, where many of her black relatives still lived and paid taxes that supported UNC, but her white, slave-owning ancestors, the Smiths, had close ties to the school. Murray's great-great-grandfather, Dr. James Strudwick Smith, had been a trustee. His sons, James Sidney Smith, who was Grandmother Cornelia's father, and Francis Jones Smith, her uncle, were alumni. Their sister, Mary Ruffin Smith, who reared Cornelia, left a portion of her estate to a trust fund for student scholarships. That Mary, a devoted member of the Chapel of the Cross, had had Cornelia baptized at the old stone Episcopal church adjacent to the campus gave Pauli, a practicing Episcopalian herself, another connection to the university.

Murray's inability to appeal UNC's decision, and the news that Lloyd

Gaines had vanished mysteriously before classes started at the University of Missouri Law School, fueled the writing of her fiery essay "Who Is to Blame for Disappearance of Gaines?" Published first in the *Carolina Times* and again in the *Black Dispatch* of Oklahoma City, this piece, like Murray's letters to Franklin and Eleanor Roosevelt, was the product of frustration. However, this time, Murray aimed her pen at young blacks who were wasting "precious creative energies," rather than organizing for the greater good. Every sentence was a mouthful, spewing the full range of her emotions.

> We Negroes can throng the streets 300,000 strong, break bottles over resisting heads, stop traffic, commandeer busses and other public vehicles, and show unprecedented aggressiveness, joy and hilarity when a Joe Louis knocks out a single white opponent by appointment, but when a Lloyd Gaines, single-handedly comes up against a whole region of the country, with its hidebound folkways of "white supremacy," with its lynching parties, and with the great majority of its population disfranchised and disinherited; when he battles his way to the Supreme Court and back again, facing the insults, the butts of criticism, the uncertainties, the threats, the great inner struggle between idealism and personal safety; when he does all this alone, with scarcely more than his own conscience and a few loyal friends to reassure him, not a single mass demonstration is held anywhere in the country!

In spite of Murray's biting call to "find Lloyd Gaines if he can be found; if not, finish the job he left uncompleted," Gaines would not be heard from again. Some blacks believed he had been murdered. Some said he accepted a payoff and fled to New York or Mexico City. Neither local authorities nor the Federal Bureau of Investigation looked into his disappearance. Fifty-five years later, the University of Missouri School of Law would grant Gaines an honorary law degree, as a symbolic apology for the injustices of the time.

Eleanor Roosevelt presents the NAACP's Spingarn Medal to contralto Marian Anderson (right) in recognition of "the highest or noblest achievement by an American Negro," Richmond, Virginia, July 3, 1939. "The DAR may not think Marian Anderson is good enough to sing in their Hall," chuckled the black White House servants, "but the First Lady thinks she is good enough to sing for a king and queen." *(Bettmann/CORBIS)*

4

"I Am Resigning"

In January 1939, Eleanor Roosevelt took a public stand against lynching and discrimination. She had been working for five years with Walter White and the NAACP to persuade Congress and Franklin Roosevelt to pass anti-lynching legislation. Disturbed by the Senate filibuster that had blocked a recent bill, she decided to say how she felt about the issue at the Second National Conference on the Problems of the Negro and Negro Youth.

Prefacing her statement with "On the clear understanding that I am speaking for myself, as an individual, and in no other sense," she told a thousand black youths gathered in Washington, D.C., under the auspices of the National Youth Administration that she wanted an anti-lynching bill "as soon as possible." Though she doubted that such a "law would do away with lynching," she believed this kind of legislation was important "because it would put us on record against something we all should be against."

A month later, the first lady spoke out again. The impetus was the Daughters of the American Revolution's refusal to allow Marian Anderson, the celebrated African American contralto, to sing in Constitution Hall. The DAR, an organization whose members claimed bloodline descent from the founders of the American republic, restricted its spacious hall to white artists and patrons only. ER, who'd joined the DAR by invitation when she came to Washington as first lady, had already hosted a concert by Anderson in the White House. The singer had one of the most "moving" voices ER had heard.

Unwilling to sanction DAR policy by keeping quiet, on February 26, the first lady wrote to President General Mrs. Henry M. Robert Jr., "I am in complete disagreement with the attitude taken in refusing Constitution Hall to a great artist. You have set an example which seems to me unfortunate, and I feel obliged to send in to you my resignation. You had an opportunity to lead in an enlightened way and it seems to me that your organization has failed."

In her column the next day, ER discussed the deliberations that led her to resign. While she did not name the organization, press accounts of the Anderson concert controversy left no doubt about the target of the first lady's disapproval.

> I have been debating in my mind for some time, a question which I have had to debate with myself once or twice before in my life. . . . The question is, if you belong to an organization and disapprove of an action which is typical policy, should you resign or is it better to work for a changed point of view within the organization? In the past, when I was able to work actively in any organization to which I belonged, I have usually stayed until I had at least made a fight and had been defeated.
>   . . . But in this case, I belong to an organization in which I can

do no active work. They have taken an action which has been widely talked about in the press. To remain as a member implies approval of that action, and therefore I am resigning.

The first lady's advocacy for Anderson did not end with her resignation or the remarks in her column. After a group known as the Marian Anderson Citizens Committee, cochaired by former Howard University School of Law dean Charles Hamilton Houston and Secretary of the Interior Harold Ickes, arranged for Anderson to give a free concert on the steps of the Lincoln Memorial, ER agreed to serve as honorary cosponsor. Over a hundred politicians, religious and civil rights leaders, and artists joined her. In that distinguished group were Secretary of the Navy Claude A. Swanson, Secretary of the Treasury Henry Morgenthau Jr., Attorney General Frank Murphy, Supreme Court Justices Charles Hughes and Hugo Black, orchestra conductor Leopold Stokowski, and actor Katharine Hepburn.

The Easter Sunday concert was a critical and political success. Its interracial audience, some seventy-five thousand strong, was the largest for a performance of this kind hosted at the Capitol. There were no incidents and no segregation among the platform guests or in the audience. Millions listened to the radio broadcast.

As Anderson, a caramel-skinned woman clad in a full-length fur coat, took her place behind a bank of microphones and sang, "My Country, 'Tis of Thee," a wave of emotion washed over the crowd. Many wept silently, moved by her rich deep voice, the patriotic song, and her prayerful bearing against the backdrop of the Lincoln Memorial. That this magnificent artist could sing in the best venues around the world but not in certain sections of her own country was a message about injustice the nation could not ignore. While Eleanor Roosevelt did not attend the concert, her support assured Anderson the national audience she deserved.

Within weeks of the first lady's resignation, a survey conducted by the American Institute of Public Opinion indicated that 67 percent of the public approved of her decision. Although the survey results were good news, ER had decided to follow her own mind no matter what. "I have by now learned to care little or nothing for what other people may think," she wrote in the May 23 issue of *Look* magazine. "I have a belief that one must hold to personal standards rather than wait for the judgment of others."

ER's personal standards allowed her to wear a comfortable gingham dress and serve Nathan's hot dogs with ham and smoked turkey to the queen and king of England and their entourage at a picnic on the Roosevelt estate. The first lady's attire and the menu embarrassed many social elites, including her mother-in-law, Sara, and some White House staffers. The royals, on the other hand, had "great fun." King George liked his very first hot dog so much he asked for seconds.

Pauli Murray took note of ER's comments and actions. Still roiled by the UNC decision and her inability to challenge it in court, she aimed to see just how far the first lady was willing to go on the question of social justice.

5

"We . . . Are the Disinherited"

In August 1939, shortly before the government eliminated the Workers' Education Project, for which Pauli Murray worked, she took the position of acting executive secretary for the Negro People's Committee for Spanish Refugees. The NPC, an auxiliary of the North American Committee to Aid Spanish Democracy, was established to raise financial and moral support from African Americans for refugees who fled Spain after the dictator Francisco Franco defeated the democratically elected government. Murray's assignment was to raise an operating budget that included her own salary—a tall order for someone not yet thirty with no executive experience. Compounding this challenge was internecine conflict among the organization's leaders.

The NPC board and its sponsors were a contentious group of political figures. Among the most influential were Democrats Mary McLeod Bethune and Lester Granger, Republican Hubert T. Delaney, Communists Paul Robeson and William L. Patterson, and socialist A. Philip Randolph. Murray was personally closest to Granger, her former supervisor at the National Urban League. But she did not share his allegiance to the Democratic Party. After voting for the Socialist Party ticket in the 1932 presidential election and her brief association with the Communist Party (Opposition), she was politically independent.

Notwithstanding the gamesmanship, workload, and uncertain salary, Murray's work put a face on the victims of war. Photographs of grief-stricken refugees, many of whom were children, marched across her desk. These images, plus the updates she received from Brookwood Labor College classmates who had joined the Abraham Lincoln Brigade, the military units of American volunteers fighting in support of the Spanish Republic against Franco, kept her going.

Murray's job gave her reason to contact Eleanor Roosevelt, who was already engaged in refugee relief. The first lady had sponsored Lorenzo Murias, a twelve-year-old who had lost his family in the Spanish Civil War, and she denounced the "propaganda of fear" and discrimination against émigrés. In "My Day," she praised the noted black artist Richmond Barthé for donating "his sculptured figures of two Spanish refugee children" to the NPC.

Looking to capitalize on ER's special interest in refugee children, Murray forwarded an information packet, a thank-you letter for the "mention" of Barthé's gift, and a news clipping featuring photos of four-year-old Aguileo Sardo Alejo and ten-year-old Rosa Marin Gonzalez, whom the NPC had adopted with the proceeds from the sale of the sculpture. Murray was also concerned about the growing number of Ethiopian refugees displaced by Italy's invasion of their homeland. Since the NPC had no resources to help them, she asked ER to bring the "Ethiopian question" to the attention of the American public and the Intergovernmental Commission on Refugees.

Although the first lady acknowledged receipt of Murray's material, she did not explicitly refer to the NPC again in "My Day." She did call, to Murray's satisfaction, for greater coordination in war relief.

· · ·

DURING THE FIRST WEEK of December, Murray wrote to the White House twice. Her first communiqué, dated December 2, went to Franklin Roosevelt, who was considering a replacement for the recently deceased Associate Supreme Court Justice Pierce Butler. Murray's goal was to persuade FDR to name "a qualified Negro" jurist to the high court. Having watched the president's proposal to expand the number of justices go down in defeat, Murray sought to assuage the loss with a missive that bore no resemblance to her testy statement about his UNC speech. She waxed eloquent about the president's charisma and the country's affection for "the second Roosevelt." She suggested, somewhat tactlessly, that there was an upside to Butler's death: "It might be a miracle of history that what you could not gain through personal influence and intelligent persuasion has been achieved for you through what some would be prone to call 'acts of God.'"

White House press secretary Stephen T. Early promptly acknowledged

Murray's letter, but her wish for a black Supreme Court justice was not to be. FDR nominated Attorney General Frank Murphy, and the Senate would confirm him in January.

Murray's second letter, dated December 6, went to Eleanor Roosevelt, and it addressed a personal concern. Murray had left the NPC after only three months. She found it nearly impossible to raise funds from blacks, and the effort was exhausting. And her disagreements with the Communists associated with the NPC reached a breaking point when the Soviet Union signed a nonaggression pact with Nazi Germany and then Hitler invaded Poland, as did the Soviet Union. Not only did Murray "disapprove of the Soviet Union action," she told a board member, she did not "believe in any form of totalitarian government be it nazi or communist," and she had "absolutely no respect for the Communist Party and its tactics."

The stress Murray felt over having to quit her job was exacerbated by the unexpected arrival of her aunt Sallie's seventeen- and twenty-year-old sons, Joshua and James. Their father, the Reverend John Ethophilus Gratten Small, had died of a stroke, leaving the family with no support. The boys were heartbroken, and their mother, awash in her own grief, sent them to Murray. Being unemployed again and unable to provide for her nephews and herself was devastating.

Murray described her situation in an opinion that she sent to several newspapers. Attributing its authorship to a friend, she asked ER to read it "with the hope that you can find some space in your column, 'My Day,' to comment upon the reaction such a letter inspires."

December 6, 1939

To the Editor:

. . . Our family of three has just been subjected to the degrading experience of re-application for relief after four years of WPA, odd jobs and whatever we could turn our hands to. The fact that we prefer to make our way on a combined income of $13.00 weekly from employment at lower wage standards than WPA, is irrelevant.

We say degrading experience, not because the techniques of administering relief have not improved in the last four years. The interviewers are more patient and more courteous, they make an all-too-obvious effort to take the sting out of the situation, there is more dignity in the interview and the effort to interpret a harsh welfare law is commendable.

The fact remains that while there are no longer mass demonstrations of unemployed organizations against the unfairness and inadequacy of the relief system, the position of the applicant is none the less unbearable.

It is the sense of isolation, of being literally driven into these places by the whip of necessity, it is the inevitable loss of dignity, of self-assurance and personal identity when one has mustered the moral courage necessary to cross the threshold of a district office.

It is the surrender of personal pride and self-esteem sacred to the individual when he becomes a mere number on a yellow slip of paper. It is the waste of time and emotional energy that comes with waiting in a bare reception room, on ridiculous stiff-backed benches in an atmosphere of grimness and desolation which makes the applicant feel like a prisoner awaiting trial. The moral and economic responsibility for oneself and loved ones makes the imprisonment all the more real just because the bars are invisible and unfelt.

It is the undeniable fact that no preoccupation with newspapers, knitting, interesting books or a personal philosophy can offset the period of waiting in the relief office. . . .

Because they sit there mutely, inarticulate and helpless, like flies in a huge web of circumstances over which they have no control, they are no less members of the great human family and representatives of the highest creation of nature on this planet.

Looking at all these miserable, frustrated, unused people, we cannot help thinking that the difference between our plight and that of the European refugees is only one of degree.

We, who are the disinherited, who are forced to become public charges in spite of every effort on our parts, conclude that the long-time tragedies of peace may be more devastating, if allowed to continue, than those of war.

Whatever the cause for this state of being, until democratic society can find a dignified use for all the individuals who comprise it, there can be no peace.

Yours very truly,
[unsigned]

The emotional impact of unemployment Murray described, and her reference to the futility of knitting, one of ER's favorite hobbies, got the first lady's attention. "The other day I was sent an extremely interesting letter from a woman who, after four years on WPA, with odd jobs of various kinds to fill in, finds that her family today is forced back on relief," she wrote in "My Day." While ER may not have seen through Murray's subterfuge, the last three paragraphs stayed with her. After quoting them, the first lady told readers, "I don't think there is any way in which we can save people from relief registration, but I do think that letters of this kind should remind us of the necessity of continuing to solve our own economic problems."

Elated, Murray wrote to Malvina Thompson. "Will you kindly extend my appreciation to Mrs. Roosevelt for her use of my enclosure in her column on December 14? Her comment was quite timely." Now that Murray had the first lady's attention, it was time to set up a file for correspondence with the White House.

Eleanor Roosevelt (center) inspects a migrant farmworkers' camp in Visalia, California, April 3, 1940. While she found adequate conditions at this government-run facility, what she saw at other camps disturbed her. *(Bettmann/CORBIS)*

6

"It Was the Highest Honor . . .
to Meet and Talk with You"

In December 1939, Pauli Murray went to work for National Share-croppers Week. NSW was an annual event cosponsored by the Southern Tenant Farmers' Union, an organization founded to combat the exploitation of farmworkers, and the Workers Defense League, an advocacy group formed to protect workers' civil rights. Both the STFU and the WDL had ties to the Socialist Party, and Murray, whose political sentiments leaned in that direction, was more comfortable at NSW headquarters than she had been at the Negro People's Committee. Her assignment as executive secretary brought her to a confluence of the labor and civil rights movements. The letterhead that bore her name and title, along with a logo by artist Rockwell Kent, carried an impressive list of liberal sponsors that included noted educators John Dewey and W. E. B. Du Bois, women's rights and antiwar activist Carrie Chapman Catt, and Murray's previous opponent Frank Porter Graham.

Poor farmers were in desperate straits, and Murray poured herself into her new job. Nearly half a million sharecroppers and tenant farmers were reportedly homeless and unemployed. In January, thousands of black and a few white sharecroppers set up camps with their families along 150 miles of two Missouri interstate highways. They did so to protest eviction notices from their landowner-employers. Because sharecroppers and tenant farmers worked land and lived in shacks owned by their employers, to whom they paid crops or cash in lieu of rent, an eviction notice meant they had no job and no place to live. The sight of displaced farm families huddling in the snow and freezing rain on makeshift beds and in ramshackle cars along some of the nation's most trafficked highways attracted national attention.

Ironically, the Agricultural Adjustment Administration, a New Deal agency created to stabilize falling crop prices, encouraged the evictions by paying landowners to take land out of production. Sharecroppers and tenant farmers were already losing jobs to drought, increased mechanization, and crop rotation. Although the AAA contract provided that workers get a portion of the landowner's payment, landowners subverted this stipulation through their alliance with AAA officials.

Within weeks of joining the staff, Murray sought the first lady's support for National Sharecroppers Week. This year's plan called for a week of consciousness-raising activities in more than twenty cities. The "objectives," as Murray outlined in her letter, were "to raise funds for organization, education and amelioration of conditions among sharecroppers, but particularly to focus public attention on the farm tenancy problem." To accomplish this, the campaign needed ER's "active interest." Murray requested a meeting to explain how the first lady could help.

Murray's timing was perfect. ER was following reports of farmworkers' problems, and she worried about the Missouri roadside encampments, especially the children who were without shelter, adequate food, clothing, or "a chance for education." She and the president had met with Reverend Owen Whitfield, the black sharecropper who organized the Missouri protest, and representatives of the STFU. ER had visited scores of rural communities, and she had seen how hard life was for families, like the Tennessee farm mother of eleven who "broke off one of her chrysanthemums" as a gift for her esteemed guest. Reading *The Grapes of Wrath,* John Steinbeck's novel about the migration of the Joads, a poor Oklahoma farm family, to California, had filled the first lady with "dread." Yet she could not "lay the book down or even skip a page." After she finished, she visited migrant farmworkers' camps in the San Joaquin Valley and confirmed to the press that Steinbeck had told the truth.

ER sent word to Murray through Tommy that she would forward information about NSW "to any of the government groups you might think could help you." The first lady also agreed to meet with Murray and two of her colleagues on January 15, 1940, at the apartment she kept in Manhattan. Once news of the scheduled meeting with ER spread through NSW headquarters, the three-person delegation doubled in size. When they arrived, an understandably "flustered" ER said, "Oh, dear, I thought only three were coming." She "had prepared tea and cakes for three," not six.

At twenty-nine, Murray was the youngest of the group. Still, they all "stammered like schoolgirls." When they stood to introduce themselves, one almost lost her balance. Another tried to curtsy. Murray, who probably wore a dress or skirt because this was a special occasion, "got up and bowed so awkwardly that Mrs. Roosevelt had to suppress a smile." No one touched the refreshments.

It had been nearly six years since Murray first saw ER at Camp Tera. This time, Murray did not shrink behind a newspaper, avoiding eye contact, afraid to speak. Instead she perched on a stool directly facing the first lady's chair. As ER listened, her blue eyes alert with interest, Murray had the sense that she was "talking with an affectionate older relative." Only from Aunts Pauline and Sallie did Murray expect and receive the acceptance she now felt. She also noticed that ER, who was said to be plain, "radiated an inner beauty" that was not obvious in news photographs.

ER was apparently impressed by this diminutive woman with a penchant for penning spirited letters about injustice. The first lady agreed to present the NSW's prizes for the best high school essays on "the conditions of sharecroppers in America." And she signed on to speak at the NSW banquet.

Murray left the gathering "giddy with success." The next day, she apologized for the size of the delegation in a thank-you note, adding, "It was the highest honor of my career to meet and talk with you." Of the issues raised in the meeting with the NSW committee, ER said in "My Day,"

"We should surely make every effort to have people in the cities understand the problems of their country neighbors."

. . .

LESS THAN TWO WEEKS AFTER the meeting at Eleanor Roosevelt's apartment, Pauli Murray cocked her pen again. The trigger was a column the first lady had written after she'd crossed a picket line to attend the premiere of *Abe Lincoln in Illinois* at the Keith Theatre, on January 22, 1940. This premiere, a film adaptation of the Pulitzer Prize–winning play by Robert Sherwood, was a benefit sponsored by the Newspaper Women's Club. A line of protesters, which the first lady and everyone else had to pass to enter the theater, marred the event for Washington society.

ER loved the film as much as she had loved the original play. Raymond Massey's portrayal of Lincoln, on the screen and the stage, as a person who stood up for his beliefs when there was little evidence that his "beliefs would be accepted" never failed to move her. Having to walk by the protesters made the first lady uneasy, and she discussed her feelings with readers the next day.

"I reached the theater last night to find it picketed by the colored people, who are barred from all District of Columbia theaters except their own," she wrote. "It may not have been quite fair or wise to picket this particular show, because the house had been taken over by an organization for a charity and the organization had a right to sell its tickets to whomever it wished." Yet she hated the idea of crossing a picket line. "Though this was not a strike where any question of unfair labor conditions was involved," the first lady had a sense that this was "unjust discrimination," and it made her "unhappy."

ER may not have known that the prohibition on black patrons was not the only insult that angered protesters. The other snub had to do with a Lincoln look-alike contest launched to boost attendance. When theater management learned that the judges had inadvertently selected the photograph of Thomas P. Bomar, a "tall, lanky" fair-skinned African American postal worker, they refused to acknowledge him at the premiere as planned.

For Murray, the first lady's attendance at an event that honored Lincoln and, at the same time, discriminated against blacks was a contradiction made worse by the prospect that ER did not understand how humiliating the situation was. Murray "stewed over it for a week" and then shot off a response.

I was disappointed when I read . . . that you crossed a picket line against your deeper feelings. . . .

The continual day-to-day embarrassment of a group is a greater hardship than the momentary embarrassment of the individuals who attended the Keith Theatre performance of *Abe Lincoln in Illinois*. . . .

Your article, even though it reflected some indecision, was a most effective result of that demonstration. Sympathetic editorial writers have done yeoman service in building public sentiment for the rights of labor. The rights of minority groups are equally important.

There can be no compromise on the principle of equality.

7

"When People Overwork Themselves, . . . They Must Pay for It"

Pauli Murray launched National Sharecroppers Week at the close of February 1940. In Washington, D.C., plans called for a mass meeting, a number of teas, and a dinner at the National Press Club. In New York City, the week opened with more than a hundred events at labor halls, churches, and civic organizations, as well as a theater benefit with performances by fifty celebrities and a dinner forum at the Hotel Commodore. More than 550 supporters came to the March 4 banquet, and $4,052 was raised. By all accounts, NSW was on the road to success. Unfortunately, the young dynamo responsible for the project was unable to witness the fruits of her labor.

The week before the dinner forum, Murray had been admitted to the psychiatric unit at Bellevue Hospital, where she remained for a few days before transferring to a private facility and the care of Dr. Helen Rogers. From there, Murray read with interest the *New York Times* story about the banquet. She was gratified by Franklin Roosevelt's telegram to the organizers and John Steinbeck's tribute to the "migrant Okies and Arkies in California" that was recited by actor Ruth Gordon.

Murray was especially delighted with the first lady, who told the audience that she "had talked at first hand with many sharecroppers and discussed their problems with Dr. Will Alexander, head of the Farm Security Administration." The "problem," as she had come to understand it, was not regional. It was linked to the economic and social woes of the entire nation. Sharing the podium with ER were Southern Tenant Farmers' Union president J. R. Butler, Raleigh *News & Observer* editor

Jonathan W. Daniels, Socialist Party spokesman Norman Thomas, and NAACP assistant executive secretary Roy Wilkins.

Although Murray felt a "quiet joy" about the job she had done, she was worried about her health. Unable to sleep for long stretches, she propped up in bed with her typewriter and notepad. Hoping to make sense of her condition the best way she knew how, she began writing down her troubles and sorting through her thoughts. She had several concerns. One had to do with the pressures of her job and her uncertain employment status. At NSW headquarters, Murray ran a national project without adequate staff, money, or time. She would finish the job in a week or so and then be unemployed again.

Another concern had to do with "family matters." Her closest kin were in distress. Aunt Pauline was on leave from her teaching post because she had broken her leg. Aunt Sallie was unemployed and caring for Aunt Pauline. Aunt Sallie's sons, now in Murray's custody, were jobless, grieving the death of their father, and finding life in New York difficult. As an unmarried daughter, Murray was expected to help financially and, if necessary, return to Durham to care for her maternal aunts. As much as she wanted to be a good daughter, Murray loathed the idea of giving up life in New York for the restrictions of the segregated South.

Work demands and caring for her cousins made it hard for her to take care of herself. Irregular eating and sleeping habits weakened her immune system. She was plagued by viral infections. She suffered from anxiety and mood swings. The lack of time and resources to nurture her fertile creativity made her unhappy. She yearned to write, to try "experimental theatre," and to pursue photography.

Another issue had surfaced on a regular basis since Murray had turned nineteen. That issue, she typed in bold honesty on the page, involved "either falling in love with a member of my sex, or finding no opportunity to express such an attraction in normal ways—sex life, marriage, dating, identification with the person and her environment." In fact, a week before the NSW banquet, a Rhode Island police officer had found Murray walking along the highway in Providence. She was distraught over the "disappearance" of a female friend, possibly Peg Holmes, after what may have been a breakup. Murray was not arrested. However, the officer who took her back to New York reported, according to the FBI, that she "was dressed in men's clothing" and had said "she was a homosexual and was taking treatments at Bellevue Hospital."

Since Murray's hospitalization at the Long Island Home three years earlier, she had been consulting with doctors and scouring the scientific literature in search of an "answer to true homosexuality." That Murray asked one psychiatrist if she had "a mother fixation" demonstrated her familiarity with psychoanalysis. Having rebuffed psychiatric treatment and the theory that her attraction to women was a manifestation of homosexuality, Murray constructed an alternative explanation. She convinced herself that she was a pseudohermaphrodite with secreted testes (and she would hold this belief until X-rays of her uterus, fallopian tubes, and the surrounding area proved her wrong). Such a condition pointed to biology—specifically, the presence of male gonads and hormones—rather than mental illness as the source of her attraction to women, her tomboyishness, and her lack of interest in feminine pursuits, such as housekeeping.

While this idea gave Murray a way to reject a homosexual identity, it did not protect her from the perception of others, including the doctors who refused to prescribe the hormones she hoped would help her, that she was lesbian. Nor did it spare her the prejudice and discrimination against homosexuals. Just a few years earlier, Murray had proudly asked Nancy Cunard to publish a photograph of Pete, her "boy-self." Now the suspicion of people she admired, such as Thurgood Marshall, and possibly the rejection of someone she loved overwhelmed her with shame and despair.

· · ·

TWO DAYS AFTER the NSW banquet, Murray, much improved, wrote an upbeat letter thanking Eleanor Roosevelt for her contribution. Murray admitted that she was physically exhausted, but she said nothing of her emotional difficulties. "When people overwork themselves, even for the best of causes, they must pay for it," she wrote. "And so I was in the Hospital on the night of the Annual Dinner-Forum for National Sharecroppers Week, and my punishment was that I was unable to hear you speak, or to participate in the activities of our campaign, even by listening over the radio. I am still in the Hospital, but hope to be out by the first of next week."

Murray concealed that she was in a psychiatric unit by writing on NSW letterhead and using her home address for the return. The only hint of her anguish was her reaction to a comment ER made about a character in Elizabeth Goudge's book *The Sister of the Angels.* That character, ER had said in her column, "accepts people as they are and does not try to turn them into the kind of people they should be." Murray made no mention of her own longing for acceptance, but she did tell ER that her column had "helped people along in their personal problems."

Murray also apologized for lashing out at ER's remarks about the Keith Theatre protest. The version of "My Day" Murray read in the *New York World-Telegram* had omitted the most important paragraph—the last one. "Here you developed your attitude on the basic rights of minority groups, but it was only after I had written you a critical comment that I discovered this paragraph in one of the Negro news weeklies," Murray explained. That deleted paragraph left no doubt where ER stood on the theater's policy. She had written, "There are basic rights, it seems to me, which belong to every citizen of the United States and my conception of them is not a rule in the nation's capital which bars people freed from slavery from seeing in a public place one of the greatest dramatic presentations of that story."

It pleased Murray that ER had spoken out about the theater's policy. It must have thrilled Murray to learn that Thomas Bomar and his daughter were "sitting in row 5" the night of the premiere. According to the *Philadelphia Afro-American,* the management had given Bomar complimentary tickets before they realized he was black, and he "had slipped unceremoniously past the ticket takers who were unable to distinguish him as colored, as were the judges who had selected him from among hundreds of photographs as the perfect Lincoln double."

ER had no knowledge of the stressors in Murray's life. Yet ER may have sensed the young woman's vulnerability, for she reached out with a bouquet of flowers and a get-well note. She congratulated Murray on an "excellent" banquet and made a one-hundred-dollar donation. She also opened the door to tea "here [in the White House] or in New York later."

Rest and the first lady's "tentative invitation" revitalized Murray. She drafted a list of things she intended to do. Writing was priority number one. Dancing more often and improving her "swimming technique to the point of going into deep water" made the list as well. In good spirits by the next week, Murray wrote to the first lady again: "Your lovely letter and flowers brought happiness to many people—patients, doctors, nurses, neighbors and friends. They lived in almost as many homes as there were flowers for more than a week. My greatest joy was in sharing them and in the realization that those who received them felt as happy and honored as I. And so a great personality touches the lives and hearts of many people unknowingly."

PART II

BUMPING UP AGAINST
THE LAW,
1940–42

A vermin-infested jail in Petersburg, Virginia, where Pauli
Murray and Adelene McBean spent Easter weekend, March 1940.
After this encounter with "southern justice," Murray would no
longer "regard it with the same terror." (*Library of Congress Prints and
Photographs Division*)

8

"Miss Murray Was Unwise Not to Comply with the Law"

By late March 1940, Pauli Murray's recovery and the approaching
Easter holiday made her hungry for family. She decided to go
home to Durham, and Adelene McBean, a former WPA worker
who was one of several women with whom Murray shared a big apartment at 35 Mount Morris Park West, said she wanted to go, too. Mac, as
Murray called her, was a young "peppery, self-assertive woman of West
Indian parentage" and a close friend. Mac had arranged Murray's transfer
from the psychiatric unit at Bellevue to a private hospital under the care
of Dr. Helen Rodgers and had looked after Murray's cousins while she
was away. Mac had not been to the South, and Murray was uneasy about

how she would deal with segregation and how white southerners would respond to such an outspoken black woman.

Their trip began without incident. Murray and Mac took a new, well-appointed Greyhound from New York City to Washington, D.C. The "trouble" started on Saturday, March 23, after they transferred to a small, dilapidated bus in Richmond, Virginia. Unlike the previous coach, where the seating was on a first-come basis, white passengers spread out in the front of the old bus. Blacks sat in the rear.

Murray and Mac took the only vacant seats in the black section, which happened to be atop a wheel well that "protruded into the floor space." The rickety bus nearly hurled them into the aisle when the driver, Frank W. Morris, made sharp turns. The jostling caused "a stabbing pain" in Mac's side, and she suggested to Murray that they move into the white section, where there were several open seats. They were traveling alone, and Murray was apprehensive about defying segregation laws. Nevertheless, she asked Morris if he would move the white passengers forward, so that she and her ill friend could shift to a better seat in the rear. Elbowing Murray away, Morris told her to "get out of his face" and return to her seat. She tried to reason with him again, but he insisted they stay where they were until the bus reached Petersburg, Virginia.

In Petersburg, while Morris was boarding new passengers, Murray and Mac moved up two rows. Although they were "still behind all the white passengers," moving up changed the racial dividing line. When Morris saw what they had done, he ordered them to return to their original seats. They told him their old seat was broken and refused to move back. He went to get the police.

As Murray and Mac sat waiting for the authorities, the anxiety inside the bus became palpable. All the passengers kept their distance. A band of menacing-looking white men gathered outside. Preparing for the worst, Murray wrote her name and Aunt Pauline's address on a note she handed to a black passenger, and she asked him to tell her aunt to contact the NAACP.

Morris returned forty-five minutes later with two white policemen. Officer Andrews was a slim man dressed in a crisp uniform set off by a Sam Browne belt and shiny boots. Officer McGhee, a man of ample girth, touched each seat as he walked down the aisle toward the women. Both men carried weapons. When Andrews asked the pair to move, a young white male passenger heard Mac snap, "You can't scare us. We're not animals. We're not dirt. Just because we're colored, you think you can push us around like sacks of meal! I'm not afraid of you, do you hear me?

You don't frighten me one bit, not one tiny bit, with your gold-plated badge and your shiny bullets." Mac maintained that she had rights, she was in pain, and she would not sit in a broken seat. She had paid the same fare as other passengers; therefore, she deserved the same quality of service.

Mac's argument and her demeanor befuddled the officers. Recognizing the volatility of the situation and that they were dealing with blacks who were not locals, the officers retreated with the driver to reconsider their strategy. Minutes later, McGhee returned and tried to coax the women into compliance. Segregated seating was the law in Virginia, the portly officer said, his voice just above a whisper, his head bowed in their direction. Neither he nor they could change it, and he was obliged to arrest them if they did not move.

Mac glared at McGhee in silence before she let loose again: "I'm a free American citizen. I can travel when and where I please." She did not care about the law in Virginia because she knew the United States Constitution. She was ill, the seat behind her was broken, and she had not paid "good money" to ride in a broken seat. She and Murray stayed put.

At Officer Andrews's request, Morris examined the seat and readjusted the cushion. Murray tested it, judged it satisfactory, and she and Mac moved back. The impasse seemed to be over, until the driver began distributing incident-report cards to the white passengers. When he skipped over the black passengers, Murray asked, "Why he did not hand out some of the cards to the people in the rear?" This question, coming after Mac's insistence that he apologize, was more than Morris could bear. He bolted from the bus and returned with the police. They charged the women with creating a public disturbance and disorderly conduct and took them into custody.

Murray stood up and took her books, briefcase, coat, typewriter, and Mac's hatbox from the overhead rack. As she made her way toward the door, there was a commotion in the rear. Mac, spent from vacillating between anger and tears, had fainted. The officers "half-carried, half-dragged" her off the bus.

The sight of Mac lying on a stretcher, the congregation of white men watching, and the nippy evening wind caused Murray to tremble. That she was apparently dressed in male clothing and had told officers, according to one passenger, that her name was Oliver Fleming must have added to her fears. Then, out of nowhere, a professional-looking black man stepped close and asked for Murray's name "under his breath." That man, E. C. Davis of the local NAACP, would wire Murray's sister Mildred

Murray Fearing and report the incident to the chapter president, who would in turn contact NAACP headquarters.

The officers took Murray and Mac first to Petersburg Hospital, where Mac was "treated for hysteria and minor bruises." As soon as she was conscious and ambulatory, the officers transported them to Petersburg City Prison, whereupon Murray gave her name and clarified her sex status as they were booked. They had little money and refused bail. The authorities confiscated their belongings, except for Murray's coat, in which she had hidden pencils, paper, and a flashlight.

A deputy placed Murray and Mac in a small, cold cell with three women inmates and a fetid "open toilet." Unable to sleep, Murray and Mac sat on the end of their bedbug-infested mattresses and watched their cellmates shoo away large cockroaches with a small fire. Black male prisoners, who were crammed into the corridor outside the women's cell door, tried to watch the women use the toilet. The men also peppered the women with obscenity-laced chatter about "sex and sexual gratification." This banter, coupled with the negative reaction of the women prisoners to Mac's accent and Murray's appearance, kept them on edge.

Murray and Mac thought of testing a Gandhian principle they had read about in Krishnalal Shridharani's *War Without Violence. Satyagraha,* or nonviolence resistance, was a response to oppression that appealed to Murray's philosophical and political instincts. Stirred by this concept, the women drafted three documents. The first was a firm but polite memo to the prison authorities demanding humane treatment for themselves and the other black prisoners. The second was a note to fellow inmates describing the reason for their arrest, "stressing the injustice of racial segregation." The third was a "detailed Statement of Facts on [their] arrest and imprisonment."

News of the arrest spread over the weekend. Their outlook brightened when local NAACP attorneys Raymond J. Valentine and Robert H. Cooley came to see them on Sunday evening. On Tuesday morning, 250 blacks and whites packed the courtroom. The prosecution charged Murray and Mac with disorderly conduct, creating a public disturbance, and violating a state statute that mandated racially segregated seating on public buses. The judge fined them five dollars plus court costs. Their attorneys gave notice that they would appeal. The retrial was set for April.

. . .

THE NAACP INVITED MURRAY and Mac to Washington, D.C., to prepare for the appeal with an elite circle of civil rights attorneys at Howard

University School of Law. Known as the "Capstone of Negro Education," Howard was chartered in 1867. Named in honor of General Oliver O. Howard, the first commissioner of the Freedmen's Bureau, the school was the training ground for the association's legal brain trust. Valentine and Cooley participated in the discussion, as did NAACP counsel Thurgood Marshall, with whom Murray had previously consulted on her UNC application. William H. Hastie, the first black federal judge, now dean of Howard's law school; Leon A. Ransom, a professor of criminal law, also from Howard; and attorneys Oliver W. Hill of Richmond and Henry Lincoln Johnson Jr. of Washington, D.C., also joined the group.

Ransom played the "devil's advocate," arguing the case for the Commonwealth of Virginia. Hastie kept quiet much of the time; yet when he spoke, he went to "the core of an issue." Both men held doctor of juridical science degrees from Harvard. Their brilliance and the debate mesmerized Murray.

Notwithstanding this formidable legal team, they lost the appeal when the prosecution dropped the violation of segregation charge to avert a constitutional challenge. Murray wanted desperately to appeal the disorderly conduct and creating a disturbance charges, but the NAACP declined again to take the case forward. She suspected that a story published in the May 18, 1940, issue of *Opportunity* had influenced the association's decision. That story, "Color Trouble," was an account of a bus incident in Petersburg involving two black passengers who told the police they were from New York City. The author was Harold Garfinkel, a white UNC graduate student who had been a passenger. The basic facts of his story resembled Mac's and Murray's case as they had presented it in their statement. However, Garfinkel's main characters were a feisty young woman named Alice and her companion, a "slight," light-skinned "young man" who said his name was Oliver Fleming.

Garfinkel's story was well received, and it must have heightened misgivings about Murray's desirability as a plaintiff among NAACP officials, who, like Murray, regularly read *Opportunity*. Given the similarities between the story and Murray's case, NAACP leaders probably assumed that Alice was Adelene and Oliver was Pauli.

Murray dismissed the story as pure fiction, but she feared that it raised speculations about her sexuality. That it had the same title and theme as one of her poems was a coincidence that added another layer to her aggravation. Written two years earlier, Murray's "Color Trouble" spoke of acting defiant in the face of prejudice, as she and Mac had done in Petersburg.

Murray and Mac were so frustrated that they refused to pay their fine and went back to jail. This time prison authorities gave them clean bedding, disinfected the cell, and allowed them to keep most of their personal items. Their stay was short-lived. In a few days, officials at the Workers Defense League paid their fines, and they were released.

· · ·

WHEN ELEANOR ROOSEVELT RECEIVED the telegram from Mildred about the arrest, she immediately contacted Virginia's governor, James H. Price. The first lady's message went straight to the point: "Pauli Murray and traveling companion became ill on bus at Petersburg, moved up one seat—now in jail—no funds." After ER heard from the governor, she had Tommy contact Mildred. "Mrs. Roosevelt asks me to write you and say that she had an investigation made after receiving your telegram about your sister," Tommy wrote. "She asked the Governor of Virginia about it, which was all she could do, and he says that Miss Murray was unwise not to comply with the law. As long as these laws exist, it does no one much good to violate them."

Murray certainly appreciated the first lady's concern, but Governor Price's response offended her. Murray doubted if he or ER had any idea about "what it meant to be a Negro." That one should obey segregation because it was the law was an argument Murray could not accept.

Twenty-three-year-old death-row inmate Odell Waller was close in age to Pauli Murray's brothers and cousins, circa 1941. "They are very dear to my heart," she told Odell, and "I know how I would feel if they were in your shoes." *(Department of Corrections, Commonwealth of Virginia)*

9

"Where Were We to Turn for Help?"

In August 1940, Pauli Murray attended a meeting of the Workers Defense League that would draw her into another battle with the Commonwealth of Virginia. She consented to serve on the administration committee out of appreciation for the moral and financial assistance the WDL had given her and Mac during the Petersburg bus ordeal. One of the cases brought to the committee was that of Odell Waller, a twenty-three-year-old African American sharecropper from Gretna, Virginia.

Waller had shot his landlord and employer, Oscar Davis, a forty-six-year-old white tenant farmer, on July 15, 1940, during an argument over the wheat crop they'd raised and owned together. Davis had reduced the tobacco crop he and Waller planted by 95 percent, in accordance with the federal crop allotment program authorized by the Agricultural Adjustment Act, but Davis did not pay Waller his share of the subsidy, as government regulations stipulated. Waller and his family depended on the crops they grew on Davis's land. To help out, Waller took a construction job in Maryland, leaving his foster mother, Annie; his wife, Mollie; and his cousin, Robert, to harvest the crops they shared with Davis. While Waller was away, Davis evicted Annie and Mollie from the shanty they occupied on his property and seized the entire wheat crop. When Waller returned, he went to demand his share of the wheat from Davis. They argued. There was a shooting. Two days later, Davis died in Lynchburg Memorial Hospital. Waller, who had fled to Ohio, awaited extradition.

Because there was no money for legal fees and the details of the case were sketchy, the committee set the matter aside until more information was available. Murray, a newcomer, listened to the discussion but said nothing. Three months later, word came that Waller had been sent back to Virginia, convicted of first-degree murder by an all-white jury, and sentenced to die in the electric chair on December 27. With barely a month and a half to raise $350 and file an appeal, the WDL decided to handle Waller's case. The committee's next decision was to send an emissary to Richmond to raise funds, conduct a field investigation, and generate local support. This strategy seemed sound to Murray—until someone recommended that she go.

The Petersburg bus incident was still fresh in Murray's mind, and the notion of returning to Virginia horrified her. Furthermore, she felt ill-prepared for the job. She begged the group to send a veteran with more knowledge and experience—someone like A. Philip Randolph, president of the Brotherhood of Sleeping Car Porters, the first predominantly black labor union. But all the senior members of the committee, including Randolph, had prior commitments. Murray, the only one free to go, could not refuse. If she did not do whatever she could and the Virginia authorities executed Waller, she would never forgive herself.

On November 6, the morning after Franklin Roosevelt was reelected for an unprecedented third term, Murray set out for Richmond, taking her seat at the helm of a two-year campaign to save Waller's life. That journey officially launched her career as a civil rights activist. To avoid the difficulties of her last trip to the commonwealth, Murray borrowed a friend's car. Gene Phillips, a white woman and former relief worker sympathetic to the case, volunteered to go with her. Together, they had a total of thirty-five dollars. Their car, a "ramshackle 1931 convertible coupe," had a temperamental motor, a tattered canvas top, and broken windshield wipers. The absence of a heater and the bone-chilling weather foretold the hostile reception they would face as an interracial team from the North.

Murray began her investigation in the office of Thomas Hartley Stone, Waller's counsel. Stone's account and court records told a story of two men—one black, the other white—who lost their land and were forced into subsistence farming. Oscar Davis, a tenant farmer, was by virtue of his race marginally better off than Odell Waller. Davis eked out a living with the support of the crop subsidy program. Waller, a black sharecropper, had no control over the conditions of his employment.

Murray quickly found that the prosecution and the defense clashed on every fact in the case except that Odell Waller had shot Oscar Davis. First, there was conflicting testimony on the circumstances of the shooting. Witnesses for the prosecution testified that Waller threatened to kill Davis, that Waller shot Davis without provocation, and that Davis was unarmed. Waller, on the other hand, denied that he had threatened or meant to kill Davis. Waller said that when he went to claim his portion of the wheat, Davis cursed him, and they argued. When Davis reached toward his pocket as if he had a weapon, Waller fired his gun in self-defense—not in cold blood, as prosecution witnesses claimed.

Second, Davis and Waller had been at odds before the shooting. Davis had refused to pay Waller's mother, Annie, for caring for his sick wife, and Annie had stopped working the tobacco crop. Davis retaliated, seizing all the wheat, evicting Annie and Mollie, and castrating the Wallers' dog while Odell was out of the state. Davis's actions were consistent with his reputation in the black community, where he was known as a man who regularly carried a gun, habitually mistreated blacks, and at times fought violently with his own sons. Local whites described Davis as a kind and honorable man.

Third, there was the questionable credibility of the prosecution's only eyewitness, Henry Davis. Henry, a seventeen-year-old black employee of Oscar Davis's, said he saw Waller shoot Davis for no apparent reason. Henry would not talk to the defense until the trial. Yet he spoke to the prosecution several times, raising speculation that he had been coached.

Fourth, there was the inflammatory testimony of Oscar Davis's sons, Frank and Edgar. At the trial, they reported that their father's last words were "Odell shot me without any cause." Neither son had recounted

Oscar's dying statement when questioned at the preliminary hearing. Neither had seen the shooting. Nevertheless, the prosecution used their testimony to bolster the claim that Waller was a cold-blooded killer.

The fifth issue was Waller's constitutional right to a jury of his peers. An all-white jury of men, all of whom had paid the state's $1.50 poll tax for the last three years, had convicted Waller. In Virginia and seven other southern states, payment of this tax was a prerequisite for voting and eligibility for jury service. The poll tax effectively excluded approximately 90 percent of the adult blacks and whites from the pool of potential jurors in Pittsylvania County, where Davis and Waller lived. Although Stone filed a motion to quash the indictment on the grounds that the jury excluded people who had not paid the poll tax, he did not have the time or the resources to gather tangible proof of each juror's or Waller's poll-tax status before the trial. It was a critical flaw in the defense case.

Finally, there was the question of judicial temperament. The sixty-six-year-old white presiding judge, James Turner Clement, denied a change-of-venue request, even though there was testimony that lynch mobs were forming in the vicinity. His dismissive attitude toward the defense, and his remark that "a man charged with a criminal offense has no right to await the action of the Grand Jury," made in the presence of jurors, seemed to suspend the presumption of innocence.

Murray's interviews uncovered other issues that exacerbated Waller's case. His counsel's background was an impediment. Thomas Stone had been hired to handle the preliminary hearing and trial by the Revolutionary Workers League, a Chicago-based group formerly affiliated with the Communist Party USA. The RWL saw Waller's case as an opportunity to earn favorable press by highlighting the injustice of the American judicial system, as the CPUSA had done with its support of the Scottsboro case, in which nine black boys were falsely accused of gang-raping two white women. Stone's ties to the RWL and his confrontational style caused blacks, liberals, socialists, and labor unionists to shy away from the campaign.

Locals, to Murray's frustration, confused the Workers Defense League with the RWL. The organizational names had a similar ring; however, the WDL, unlike the RWL, was an independent body supported by a broad base of progressives. Murray immediately made bringing Waller's appeal under WDL control a priority.

Many white southerners saw the campaign as an affront by outsiders because the case called attention to unjust labor, judicial, and voting practices in Virginia. Only a handful of whites and a small Unitarian

Church group indicated a willingness to help. Murray faced resistance from blacks as well. Administrators at Virginia Union University, a local black school, denied her appeal to address a student assembly. Being turned away by a group from whom she'd expected at least a modicum of consideration left her despondent.

Murray was so afraid of another rejection that she "had to fight off the urge to vomit" before meeting with a conference of black Baptist ministers. As she waited to speak, a number of people came before the group, requesting help with equally compelling cases. Leon Ransom, one of the Howard University School of Law professors she had met during preparations for the Petersburg case appeal, made an impassioned plea for four black men accused of raping a white woman. As Murray listened, she lost her nerve and tried to leave through a side door. Before she escaped, Reverend Joseph T. Hill, the minister who had invited her, called her up front and asked the group to "hear what she has to say."

Stressed and exhausted, Murray blurted out, "Gentlemen, I haven't the strength to give you my message." She then burst into tears. Handing her prepared statement to Reverend Hill, she took a seat and gathered herself as he read. When he finished, Murray stood up and spoke without notes about a poor African American sharecropper on death row, wrongfully convicted of first-degree murder. Having met not one black person or organization in Richmond willing to join the campaign, she pleaded, "If men of God could not take Waller's plight into their hearts, where were we to turn for help?"

At the end of Murray's presentation, Reverend E. H. Bouey, Waller's death-row spiritual counselor, rose and said that Waller was a "fine young feller who needs a chance." Bouey asked his brethren to help in any way they could. Each minister, many of them teary-eyed, stepped forward and put his contribution on the table. They were men of modest means, and their combined offering was barely twenty-five dollars. Nonetheless, Murray believed that their "prayers and blessings" prepared her for the trying months to come.

Pauli Murray, age thirty, WDL field secretary in charge of the Odell Waller campaign. The faint inscription at the bottom right of photograph reads, "To Mother with Love, 1941, Pauli." *(The Schlesinger Library, Radcliffe Institute, Harvard University and the Estate of Pauli Murray)*

I O

"Will You Do What You Can to Help Us?"

Back in New York, Pauli Murray summarized her notes from the Richmond trip. She had raised $37.50 in cash, of which $5.50 had come from relatives. This was merely a drop in the bucket, given the thousands Odell Waller's appeal would surely cost. Since she was not a member of Waller's family or his counsel, the authorities would not let her visit him in jail. From where she sat, the problems with the case seemed insurmountable.

Undaunted by Murray's report, the Workers Defense League hired her full-time as the field secretary for the Waller case. Emboldened by their vote of confidence, she rolled up her sleeves and began to map out a campaign. The first person she reached out to was Odell Waller.

The memory of conditions in the Petersburg prison made Murray concerned about Waller's welfare. On November 15, 1940, she tucked two dollars in an envelope with a note introducing herself and the WDL. "We want you to feel encouraged and to know that you have thousands of friends all over the country. . . . Try to keep well and strong because you have a tough job ahead of you. Many people are praying for you. . . . I am sorry that I could not come . . . to see you in prison," she explained. "The rules would not permit me to do so. . . . Just have courage and believe that life is before you."

Waller was grateful to get Murray's letter and the money. A high school dropout for whom reading and writing were a challenge, he scribbled a reply: "I know I have some friends same time I think every one have gone against me."

That same day, on her thirtieth birthday, Murray sent a packet via special delivery to Eleanor Roosevelt with a cover note to Malvina Thompson. "Will you bring this letter to Mrs. Roosevelt's attention as soon as she has a free moment?" she asked.

November 20, 1940

Dear Mrs. Roosevelt:

At the risk of intruding upon your Thanksgiving, I must write you about an urgent matter. It is the case of a young Negro sharecropper, Odell Waller, condemned to die on December 27th. . . .

The Workers Defense League, defense agency for the Southern Tenant Farmers Union has entered the case and is handling the appeal in cooperation with the NAACP.

Young Waller's plight symbolizes the deep-rooted injustice of the sharecropper-landlord system. It also reveals the essential undemocratic features of the poll-tax law. Since jury lists in Virginia are drawn from lists of those who have paid their poll-tax, Waller was not tried by his peers, but by a jury ten of whom were planters.

This young man deserves a fair trial. We must have $350.00 to file the appeal on Monday, November 26th. To carry this case to the United States Supreme Court, $2,000 is needed.

With intelligent handling, we may be able to get the Supreme Court to review the poll-tax law. John F. Finerty, lawyer for Tom Mooney has entered the case as our special legal counsel. If we are not successful in our appeal, we will find it necessary to apply to Governor Price of Virginia for pardon or commutation.

I have just returned from Richmond where the young man awaits execution in the death cell. I have talked with a number of interested citizens, both Negro and white, including Mr. Virginius Dabney,

Editor of the *Times-Dispatch,* and Reverend Henry Lee Robinson, Director of Religious Work in the State Penal Institutions, 101 N. Jefferson Street. Both gentlemen seem interested in Waller's case. They will be glad to give you further information, if you desire it.

Waller's spiritual adviser in the death cell told me he seems to be a young man of good character and feels he has been condemned unjustly. While we must take our stand against the social evils which have brought about his tragic situation, we do not want to antagonize the good people of Virginia.

Will you do what you can to help us?

Waller's mother, Mrs. Annie Waller, is arriving in New York on Saturday of this week. She will appeal to interested people in her son's behalf. Since she was present at the time of the shooting of Waller's landlord, I am sure she would be glad to answer any questions you care to ask.

May I wish you and your family a happy Thanksgiving, and offer my earnest hope for continued success in the coming four years. We need your intelligent leadership.

> Sincerely yours,
> Pauli Murray,
> Field Secretary in
> Charge Waller Case

Encouraging developments were on the horizon. "We have raised nearly $1,000 within two weeks," Murray wrote to Odell Waller. "Worn dollar bills come in from very poor people who want to see you have another chance." Thanks to her influence, Waller would soon give the WDL complete authority over his case, disavowing the Revolutionary Workers League's support, thus distancing himself from the Communist Party USA.

John Finerty, who represented Tom Mooney, the labor activist unfairly charged and convicted in 1916 for the bombing deaths of ten people, agreed to serve pro bono as special legal counsel, along with WDL counsel Morris Shapiro. The addition of Finerty and Shapiro diminished the role of Thomas Stone, Waller's original counsel, and he would eventually withdraw. Even though Virginius Dabney, the influential editor of the *Richmond Times-Dispatch,* did not see grounds for appeal, he continued to discuss the case with Murray. She took their dialogue as a hopeful sign.

· · ·

MURRAY'S MENTION of the Mooney case and the poll tax in the letter to ER linked Waller's case to two issues that had already stirred the first lady's conscience. ER had followed Mooney's trial and conviction, and she said his release after twenty-two years in prison brought "a great sense of vindication" to his supporters. She was working for anti–poll-tax legislation as well with the white southern activist Virginia Durr and the National Committee to Abolish the Poll Tax.

Given ER's interest in poor workers and minority rights, her natural inclination was to sympathize with Waller. Yet a meeting between the first lady and Waller's mother would further complicate FDR's relations with southern conservatives, whose election to Congress depended on the disenfranchisement of African Americans and poor whites in their home states. For ER to publicly back or lend her name in any way to the appeal of a black sharecropper convicted of first-degree murder by a legally sanctioned all-white jury in Virginia would put the president in a predicament he could ill afford. Not only did he face resistance to his domestic policy, but isolationists opposed his efforts to address Great Britain's desperate need for aid. Germany had invaded France in June, and U.S. preparedness had become FDR's overriding concern.

In deference to political considerations, Eleanor Roosevelt did not meet with Annie Waller. However, she forwarded Murray's material to the governor of Virginia with a cover note that made her feelings clear: "My dear Governor Price— The enclosed correspondence has been sent to me and I hope very much that you will look into the case and see that the young man has a fair trial."

· · ·

MOTHER WALLER, as Annie came to be known among supporters, arrived in New York City late in November 1940. She was a "wraithlike, tiny, brown-skinned woman whose harsh life was etched indelibly in her face." Her "hands were scarred purple," her back "stooped from constant bending in the fields." She had never been away from home. Still, she braved this frighteningly unfamiliar world to speak to religious, labor, and civil rights groups on behalf of her son. Her husband was dead and "there was no one else to do it."

In a "quavering voice that was almost like a sob," she spoke in broken English of a loving son who "worked like a slave." Mother Waller brought audiences to tears with her narrative of the sharecropper's lot. "When it was cold and raining, and so raw no woman ought to been outdoors, there I was working up to my ankles in that red mud in the rain till it was so dark I couldn't even see the rows before me," Annie said. "I worked and I worked, but it was all for Mr. Davis. I didn't see nothing in the ground for Annie."

Murray, with whom Mother Waller stayed during her month-long visit, wrote to ER again. "Mrs. Waller is 65 years old and has come all the way to New York alone to appeal to interested persons to help in the defense of her son. Her story is so heartbreaking. I am convinced you would be glad to hear it. She cannot write and I am writing for her," Murray explained. "Do please give her fifteen minutes of your time if you are anywhere in the vicinity of New York or Washington. I will see to it that she will be present at whatever time and place you suggest."

When Murray's appeal arrived, ER was preparing to testify before the Select Committee to Investigate the Interstate Migration of Destitute Citizens. She had already broken ground as the only first lady to testify before Congress; this would be her second appearance. She dazzled the committee with her observations of the migrant camps in California and the findings in reports she'd received from Murray and other activists on cases, such as that of the Chirillos, a family of seven from Ohio accused of being relief floaters because they'd moved to New York and applied for assistance. Contrary to popular opinion, migrants were often industrious, ER told the legislators. She called for better housing, sanitation, nutrition, and education, as well as an end to discrimination against migrant workers.

Murray was thrilled by the first lady's testimony—and even more excited about a note she received from Tommy. "Mrs. Roosevelt asks me to tell you that she has a letter from the Governor of Virginia, in which he states that the attorneys for the Waller boy have requested an opportunity to present the matter to the Supreme Court of Appeals," the message read. "Additional time is being granted the young man and his attorneys to prepare the case for consideration before the court."

Murray may have had the favorable press sparked by ER's resignation from the DAR in mind when she asked permission to release word of the first lady's letter to Governor Price. Obliged to keep her advocacy out of the spotlight, ER directed Tommy to reply via telegram, "Regret cannot give you permission to release Mrs. Roosevelt's letter."

· · ·

ON MURRAY'S SECOND TRIP to Richmond, in December, the superintendent of the prison allowed her to visit Odell with Mother Waller. As they made their way through the corridor to his death-row cell, Murray's heart sank. The hostility and filth she and Mac had faced in the Petersburg jail paled in comparison to "the oppressiveness of his somber surroundings, the unrelieved gloom of barren walls and darkened cells, the desolate hours spent in waiting, and the terrifying nearness of the electric chair a few yards away." Murray yearned to send Waller her German shepherd, Petie, to ease the isolation, although she knew this was out of the question.

It had been a year since Murray had first written to Waller. She found him to be a "short, stocky young man" with penetrating eyes, eager to see his mother and the young woman who spent every waking minute on his appeal. In the moment they had together, Murray questioned Waller about the shooting. He told her what he had always said about the incident: "I am as sorry as I can be it all happened. I wasn't trying to kill Mr. Davis. I was aiming to keep him from killing me."

Waller's "straightforwardness," his understandable fear of Davis, and the information Murray gleaned from field interviews persuaded her that he was guilty of manslaughter—not premeditated murder. She would never see him again, but she would fight for a defendant's right to a fair trial and against the death penalty for the rest of her life.

· · ·

ENERGIZED BY THE VISIT with Odell and the news that Governor Price had granted a stay of execution until March 14, 1941, Murray generated a steady flow of letters to Waller. She spoke in her missives of faith and her sense of the historical moment. "There is a greater power than our puny efforts at work here," she wrote on January 23, 1941. "Let each day count for something. Read, study, think, write down your thoughts; keep a diary and write a little something in it every day. Remember the great apostle Paul who wrote such beautiful letters while he was in prison. . . . You have no time to get blue and down. You have a stake in democracy also, and you must try to find the part you are playing in all this."

To the first lady, Murray sent a document that combined her summary of the case, with profiles of Waller and Davis by Murray Kempton, a young labor organizer turned journalist. This pamphlet, which they coauthored, took its main title from Annie Waller's testimony, *"All for Mr. Davis": The Story of Sharecropper Odell Waller,* and it became the campaign's primary publicity tool. After ER's friend UNC president Frank Graham endorsed the pamphlet by writing the preface, Murray came to regard him as an ally.

N. A. A. C. P.

Presents the Story of

"Those Who ARE ABOUT TO DIE"

Mother Waller and Pauli Murray

Gripping Saga of the South
Today

ZION CHURCH
WEDNESDAY, MAY, 7th
8:00 P.M.

This flyer announces an appearance by Annie Waller
(top) and Pauli Murray (bottom) at a fund-raiser for the
Odell Waller campaign in Denver, Colorado, on May 7,
1941. During the tour, they gulped vitamins to build up
"resistance against the flu." *(Workers Defense League Collection,
Walter P. Reuther Library, Wayne State University)*

11

"Might as Well Become a Lawyer"

In January 1941, Eleanor Roosevelt began her third term as first lady,
and the nation prepared to enter World War II. The Waller campaign
moved into high gear with Pauli Murray functioning as advance
woman, press secretary, fund-raiser, and liaison between the Workers
Defense League and the Waller family. Although several WDL staffers
helped, only Murray was involved in every aspect of the appeal. She was
encouraged—and for good reason. Waller had an outstanding legal team,
plus the backing of the liberal establishment.

During the first week of the new year, Murray and Mother Waller set out on the first leg of a national tour to raise funds and public awareness. They spoke to more than seven thousand people in twenty cities, including Boston, Chicago, Cleveland, Denver, Detroit, Milwaukee, Minneapolis, Pittsburgh, and Washington, D.C. During the second leg, they went to Los Angeles, Portland, San Francisco, and Seattle, making stops on the way home in Cincinnati, Dayton, Indianapolis, Kansas City, Louisville, Oklahoma City, and St. Louis. They always arrived weary, having sat up all night on a train. Invariably short on money, they carried their own food and boarded with supporters.

On a typical day, Murray and Mother Waller met with members of the local media, YMCAs, YWCAs, unions, and NAACP chapters; students and faculty members in high schools and colleges; religious leaders and their congregations; and liberal groups unaffiliated with the Communist Party USA. Each presentation opened with Mother Waller's gut-wrenching account of her son and the shooting. Murray followed with a discussion of the facts in the case and the impact of the poll tax on the justice system in Virginia. Thirty years old and now under one hundred pounds, Murray was not much bigger than Mother Waller or much older than Odell. But she spoke with the conviction of a veteran, often standing atop a desk or chair in practical sailor pants, drawing people of conscience to the cause.

Whenever she had a quiet moment, Murray reported back on the contacts they made, the funds raised and pledged, and the practical issues they faced. She churned out press releases and columns for the *Workers Defense Bulletin* and other outlets. She kept Odell informed about the campaign and his mother's well-being. She repeatedly urged him to put his story on paper in his own words.

While the tour raised $755 and the profile of the campaign, Murray returned home in an irritated state. The relentless pace had left her little time or energy for creative writing. She had been out of college for eight years, and every job since had brought endless workdays, overwhelming responsibility, low pay, and no opportunity for advancement. Her post as field secretary for the Waller case was more of the same, except that the stakes—a young man's life—were greater than ever before.

An irrepressible desire to write, bone-aching fatigue, and continuing worry over financial and family obligations put Murray in a somber mood. News of the Nazi invasion of Greece and Yugoslavia, and the massive air raids against London, deepened her melancholy.

Eleanor Roosevelt takes flight with Charles "Chief" Anderson
(right) at Moton Airfield, Tuskegee, Alabama, on March 31,
1941. "These boys are good pilots," she wrote in "My Day."
(National Archives)

· · ·

AS MURRAY CRISSCROSSED THE COUNTRY with Mother Waller, Eleanor Roosevelt worked on refugee relief and war preparedness. For five
months, she would serve as assistant director of the Office of Civilian
Defense as a volunteer without pay. She would also do a series of radio
broadcasts that focused on how women could help with the war effort.
With these new duties added to her extensive writing and speaking commitments and her obligations as first lady, she rarely logged less than
fifteen hours of work each day.

In March, ER went to Tuskegee Institute, in Alabama, to meet with the
Julius Rosenwald Fund's board of trustees. On the agenda was a request
for a loan from institute president Frederick D. Patterson to expand the
facilities for the all-black flight-training program at the school. Mary
McLeod Bethune had been lobbying FDR to end the military's "flagrant
discrimination against Negroes" and to allow them to be trained as pilots.

The first lady, a Rosenwald Fund trustee, visited the flight-training
program. The staff and trainees impressed her. Hoping to convince the
administration and the public that blacks could fly, she decided to be
photographed in a Waco biplane piloted by Charles Anderson, the first
African American to earn a pilot's license and the program's chief flight
instructor. When ER announced her intention to fly with Anderson,
"the Secret Service men almost had a conniption, but what can you tell

the First Lady when she says, 'I'm going to do this'?" observed Quentin Smith, a pilot in training.

ER had always loved flying. "It was like being on top of the world," she had said of her 1933 round-trip flight from Washington to Baltimore in a plane piloted by Amelia Earhart, the first woman to fly solo across the Atlantic Ocean. On this day, ER savored the breathtaking view of the Alabama "countryside" for forty minutes from the passenger seat of the small plane. With pride, she presented a snapshot of herself and her confident pilot to FDR. That snapshot appeared in newspapers across the country.

ER encouraged the fund trustees to support the project, and she kept a watchful eye on the squadron that came to be known as the Tuskegee Airmen—or the Red Tails, in deference to the paint on the tail section of their planes. They would distinguish themselves under the command of the black West Point graduate Lieutenant Colonel Benjamin O. Davis Jr. The Tuskegee Airmen would "bless . . . the name of Eleanor Roosevelt" for the rest of their lives.

. . .

IN DIRE NEED OF RESPITE, Murray accepted an offer from the Young People's Socialist League to do a series of talks on sharecropping during the summer in exchange for free housing in a secluded cabin atop Mount Airy, in the Catskills. In this tranquil place, she set her troubles aside and established, for the first time, a daily writing practice. Getting to put her writer self at the forefront of her consciousness was a wondrous experience. She "avoided causes and politics," she wrote in her journal, like "poison ivy."

Murray wrote in the nude, except for a pair of shorts, on a small screened porch attached to her two-room cabin. Sometimes it took her all day, typing and retyping, to eke out a page. Whenever she hit writer's block, she took off for the woods with her dog, Petie. Walking away from the writing when frustrated seemed to refuel Murray's creativity. She often raced back to the typewriter to catch sentences that had sprung into her mind.

The combination of uninterrupted time, release from the strain of the campaign, and reassuring feedback from the Pulitzer Prize–winning poet Stephen Vincent Benét improved Murray's outlook. *John Brown's Body,* Benét's epic poem about the Civil War, was one of her favorites. Reading it always drew her close emotionally to Grandfather Robert, a Civil War veteran who'd left a diary of his experience. Murray had written to

Benét two years earlier, introduced herself, and asked him to read her work. He'd responded with an invitation to meet at his New York City residence. Their periodic meetings and Benét's written critiques nurtured her epic poem "Dark Testament" and a series of sketches that would mature into the family memoir *Proud Shoes.*

The Waller campaign, on the other hand, pulled Murray toward a law career. Indeed, each encounter she had with Leon Ransom or Thurgood Marshall seemed to quicken the path away from creative writing. Ransom, who'd witnessed Murray's presentation to the black ministers in Richmond, had complimented her on her appeal. To deflect the conversation from what she felt was a shamefaced performance, Murray quipped that she "might as well become a lawyer" since she kept "bumping into the law." Ransom took her words literally. He told her she "had what it takes to become a good lawyer," and he urged her to come to Howard University School of Law. Skeptical of his offer and her ability, Murray said that she might, if she got a scholarship. Ransom pledged that she would get one, if she applied.

Murray remained ambivalent about pursing a law degree despite Ransom's encouragement and a letter of recommendation from Marshall. The day notice of her acceptance and a tuition scholarship arrived, she faced a dilemma: Should she become a writer or a lawyer? "I'm really a submerged writer," Murray told writers Lillian E. Smith and Paula Snelling, "but the exigencies of the period have driven me into social action." Murray capulsized her situation in the opening lines of the poem "Conflict":

> *Some day the poet and warrior*
> *Who grapple in my brain*
> *Shall lock in final contest*
> *And I will be ground under.*

As much as Murray wanted to write full-time, it seemed impractical for a black woman without independent means. Only a handful of blacks sustained themselves by writing, and she doubted she could write as well as the acclaimed poet Countee Cullen, who—even with a master's degree in English and French from Harvard—earned his living teaching high school. "Without a trade or profession," Murray believed she was destined for "a grubby existence in rented rooms on the fringes of society." She simply "didn't have the courage" to pursue writing.

Law, Murray reasoned, would equip her with the tools to live a middle-class life *and* fight for civil rights. It also appealed to her love of intellectual inquiry and debate. Convinced that a law degree was her ticket to meaningful work and a better life, Murray left the WDL to enter Howard in the fall of 1941.

The delegation that went to see Franklin Roosevelt about the Odell Waller case at the entrance to the Office of the U.S. Attorney General, July 1, 1942. *Front row, left to right:* Reverend William Lloyd Imes, Mary McLeod Bethune, A. Philip Randolph, Frank R. Crosswaith. *Second row, left to right:* Anna Arnold Hedgeman, Pauli Murray, Ralph Matthews, Layle Lane, Albert Hamilton, Frank D. Reeves, and Channing H. Tobias. When Murray organized this group, she did not know that FDR was in Hyde Park or that he had written to Virginia governor Colgate W. Darden Jr. *(New Pittsburgh Courier Archives)*

I2

"I Have Done Everything I Can Possibly Do"

On December 7, 1941, before Pauli Murray finished her first semester in law school, Japanese bombers attacked the U.S. naval base at Pearl Harbor, destroying eighteen ships. More than two thousand military personnel and civilians died. The next day at a special joint session of Congress, Franklin Roosevelt called for and got a declaration of war. Three days later, Germany and Italy declared war on the United States. Congress responded in kind.

The war tested Murray's philosophical beliefs. She hated violence, yet every fiber of her body was opposed to Hitler and Nazism. A religious pacifist, she had already joined the Fellowship of Reconciliation and spent eight months at the Harlem Ashram, a multiracial commune of Christian pacifists that included James Farmer, the future founder of the Congress of Racial Equality. She would not sign up for military service, as many Howard University students did, but she advocated fiercely for their right to serve according to their ability and without segregation.

Despite her concerns about the war and the demands of her studies, Murray continued to monitor developments in the Odell Waller case. Between March 1941 and June 1942, John Finerty and the WDL defense team argued before the Virginia Supreme Court of Appeals, the U.S. Supreme Court, the U.S. District Court, and the U.S. Fourth Circuit Court of Appeals. They also submitted separate petitions to U.S. Supreme Court Justices Harlan F. Stone, Hugo Black, Robert H. Jackson, and Felix Frankfurter.

Even though Waller's attorneys worked pro bono, there was never enough money to cover the expenses of preparing and filing briefs, travel, telephone bills, printing, and office supplies. For this reason, Annie Waller went on another national tour in the spring of 1942, soliciting assistance from labor unions, churches, and humanitarian groups.

As the case made its way through the judicial system, a coalition of ministers led by Waller's pastor, Reverend Robert L. Gilbert, designated May 31 as a day of prayer. Murray asked Eleanor Roosevelt "to do whatever you can." Odell wrote to the first lady as well. "I have heard lots of people speak of what a nice lady you are and . . . that you believe in helping the poor," he said. "I always worked hard but I couldn't get anything out of it. I raised some wheat with a man named Oscar Davis and he took all of the wheat and I tried to get my share of it. He wouldn't let me have the wheat. We got in a quarrel. And I shot him to keep him from hurting me not meaning to kill him. He carried a gun. . . . I was afraid of him. . . . Please write to the Governor and get him to have mercy on me and allow me a chance. You will never regret it."

· · ·

EVERYTHING ER HAD LEARNED about Waller—from the circumstances surrounding the shooting to the problems with the original trial—spoke to his disadvantaged status as a black sharecropper. She believed, as did Murray and the WDL, that Waller's powerlessness personified the plight of countless poor farmers. Pained by the prospect of his execution, the first lady sent the newly elected governor of Virginia, Colgate Darden, a copy of an opinion letter by Professor John Dewey that had been published in the *New York Times*. In his piece, Dewey discussed how poverty, the poll tax, and the composition of the jury thwarted Waller's ability to get a fair trial. Dewey called on the Supreme Court, which had declined to hear the case without comment, to rehear the case and for Darden to grant clemency should the appeal to the high court fail.

To Dewey's letter, ER attached her own appeal. "My dear Governor Darden," she wrote,

> I have had a great many letters about Odell Waller's case and the thing which impresses me is that one of the women who made the original investigation, writes me that she feels very strongly Odell Waller should not be executed. She begs me to ask you for clemency.
>
> I am, of course, not familiar enough with the case, but the letter from Dr. John Dewey about this case, makes me feel it is important enough to take into consideration. . . .
>
> If the facts as stated by Dr. Dewey are true, I hope very much that you will be able to go over the case very carefully, as it has created a great deal of feeling among both white and colored people and it may have not only national but international implications.

It is hard to imagine that the first lady had as little knowledge of the Waller case as her letter suggested. Murray had been sending ER material since November 1940. By implying that she had not chosen sides, perhaps ER hoped to avoid making Governor Darden defensive.

· · ·

BY THE SUMMER OF 1942, the Waller case was the subject of front-page news stories and editorials around the country. Word of ER's advocacy for the convicted sharecropper leaked and aroused "bitterness" among whites who saw Waller's trial and conviction as a matter of "states' rights"; blacks and their supporters took this catchphrase as a euphemism for white supremacy.

Franklin Roosevelt found himself in a tough spot. He was grieving for his mother, Sara, who had died in September. He was worried about the war and the economy. He knew that his wife wanted him to convince Governor Darden to grant clemency. He also knew that any effort on his part to stop Waller's execution would be politically costly. But the first lady would not relent. She bombarded her husband with "notes and messages," which she dropped into a "small basket" near his bed.

On June 15, a week after the U.S. Navy faced down the Japanese fleet in the Battle of Midway, FDR drafted a "personal and unofficial note" to Governor Darden, describing a case in New York in which a man was convicted of first-degree murder for shooting his neighbor. The man and his neighbor had argued. The neighbor made a threat, and the man shot him. Roosevelt, who happened to be governor at the time, commuted the man's sentence to life in prison. The president had no regrets about his decision, he told Darden. In fact, he was thankful he had shown mercy. FDR closed his letter with the plea that Darden "think of this note as merely a suggestion from an old friend who has let the death sentence take its course in very many cases, but who really hopes that you will recognize that perhaps the killer element in human nature may not have been present in the case of this unfortunate man who might have been just 'scared' for his own life."

· · ·

THE PRESIDENT'S LETTER FORETOLD the onslaught of appeals that would descend on the governor in the countdown to Waller's execution. Among the expanding network of people who would take up Waller's cause were former first lady Grace Anna Goodhue Coolidge, American Federation of Labor president William Green, and Congress of Industrial Organizations president Philip Murray. The *New York Times* published a letter to the editor by the Nobel Prize–winning novelist Pearl S. Buck in which she addressed the unconstitutional aspects of the Waller trial and the problem it posed for the world's leading democracy. Murray saw a commission of inquiry appointed by the president as a practical solution. On June 15, the Waller campaign released to the press a petition to FDR for such an inquiry.

On June 16, Harlem residents and business owners voluntarily shut off their lights to protest Waller's sentence and discrimination in employment. That evening, twenty thousand blacks gathered at a Madison Square Garden rally, where "Save Odell Waller" banners swayed from the ceiling. A. Philip Randolph, whose voice had the resonance of a classically trained actor's, hailed the gathering as the "beginning of a nationwide drive to kill Jim-Crow." Mother Waller, who shared the platform with Randolph, Bethune, and Reverend Adam Clayton Powell Jr., begged the "vast crowd to help save her boy."

Twenty-four hours before Waller's scheduled execution, Governor Darden granted a reprieve—it was Waller's fifth—and announced that he would hold a commutation hearing on June 29. Murray, now on her summer break, traveled to Waller's hometown, the neighboring counties, and Richmond to gather information in preparation for the hearing. She learned that the governor, a Democrat married to the daughter of one of the richest men in the United States, had aspirations of becoming "a national figure noted for his humanitarian attitude." However, the "political repercussions" of commuting Waller's sentence coupled with national criticism of the commonwealth troubled him. Darden needed "a convenient way out" of this dilemma.

On June 28, the day before the hearing, the first lady took the train to Richmond to fulfill two commitments. The first was to give the opening address at the annual meeting of the Virginia Veterans of Foreign Wars. The second was to make a personal appeal for clemency to the governor, whom she planned to see privately. To the veterans, ER spoke of winning the war and the battle for democracy. With Darden, she discussed "a number of questions . . . very important to his state and to all Southern states today," she wrote in her column. While ER did not mention Odell Waller by name, African Americans took her comments as evidence of her support. Waller's opponents accused her of "preaching racial unrest" and "fishing for the Negro vote."

Tens of thousands of people, some from as far away as Europe, sent letters and telegrams urging the governor to spare Waller's life. The pressure came closer to home when Virginius Dabney and a group of prominent Virginians called on Darden to grant clemency. In a commutation-day editorial that bore the imprint of Murray's conversations with him and for which the *Danville Register* would brand him a "pussyfooting" coward, Dabney asserted that "pertinent facts" had not been presented at the original trial, that the climate "was not conducive to an objective hearing of the evidence," and that the testimony of the only eyewitness, Henry Davis, "was unbelievable." Waller's execution would affect the "morale of colored peoples" around the world, Dabney warned. Indeed, the nation's enemies would use the execution as proof that the United States was not the democracy it claimed to be.

. . .

THE HEARING BEGAN at nine-thirty on the morning of June 29 in the Senate chamber at the capitol in Richmond. For the next eleven hours, twelve witnesses testified, including Henry Davis for the prosecution and Mother Waller for the defense. Finerty, Waller's lead counsel, and Edmund M. Preston—a highly regarded local attorney who joined the defense after Thomas Stone, the original counsel, withdrew—argued that circumstantial evidence supported Waller's belief that he was acting in self-defense. Davis was known to carry a gun and have a temper, and tensions between him and Waller had escalated in the weeks leading up to the shooting.

As far as the original trial, the presiding judge had made little effort to appear objective. Stone had erred in not documenting the jurors' and Waller's poll-tax status, and this evidence, had it been presented, was proof Waller had not been tried by a jury of his peers. Because Stone's error was foundational to Waller's first-degree murder conviction, he stood to be executed on the basis of a flawed trial.

The defense seized upon the fact that the story told at the hearing by Henry Davis, the black farmworker who lived in the house with Oscar Davis's family, bore little resemblance to the testimony he gave at the original trial. What Henry now claimed was that Oscar Davis had agreed without argument to give Waller his wheat sometime later, and that when Oscar turned his back to go into his house for breakfast, Odell shot him. After the first two shots, Henry said, he ran to the back of the house, entered the kitchen, and walked through the front door just as Odell stepped over Oscar and shot him twice more in the back. That hospital records indicated that Oscar had been shot in the right arm and near the right side of the head, instead of the left arm and the left side of the head as Henry testified, made his story even more incredible.

Late the next day, Darden released a statement to the press. His conclusion was that Oscar Davis had been unarmed and that Odell Waller shot him without cause or provocation. Dismissing the charge that the poll tax and the background of the jury created a bias against the defense, the governor declared that Waller had "a fair and impartial trial, by an impartial jury" and his conviction rested on "evidence adduced by members of his own race, which upon its face bears the impress of truth."

Although Darden insisted that the volume of mail and media attention had no impact on his decision, he contended that the Waller campaign had distorted the facts and hoodwinked the public. Murray would always believe that pressure from powerful constituents, angered by the unflattering spotlight on the state, made it difficult for the governor to hear Waller's appeal without prejudice.

• • •

AFTER DARDEN'S DECISION, Randolph asked Murray to organize a delegation to go to the White House to persuade President Roosevelt to establish a commission of inquiry. In addition to Randolph, Bethune, and Murray, the group and the organizations they represented included Frank Crosswaith, Harlem Labor Center, New York City Housing Authority; Albert Hamilton, Workers Defense League; Anna Arnold Hedgeman, New York Area Office of Civil Defense; Reverend William Lloyd Imes, St. James Presbyterian Church; Layle Lane, American Federation of Teachers; Ralph Matthews, the *Afro-American;* Ted Poston, Negro News Desk, Office of War Information; Leon Ransom, Howard University School of Law; Frank D. Reeves, NAACP Washington Bureau; and Channing Tobias, National Council, YMCA. Murray, the youngest member of the delegation, represented the NAACP Student Conference, for which she served as chair.

Unable to see the president, whose whereabouts were privileged information during wartime, the group went first to the Justice Department, then to the office of the vice president. No cabinet-level official would grant them a respectable audience. Murray was particularly offended by an aide in the office of one influential senator who "displayed contempt for the delegation by picking up Mrs. Bethune's cane (she suffered from arthritis) and twirling it like a drum major's baton as he talked." Once the rumor spread that the group was planning to picket the White House, Elmer Davis, the director of the War Information Office, met with them and warned that picketing the Executive Mansion would undermine the war effort.

After hours of futile pursuit, the delegation turned to ER. She, too, had been trying to reach the president by telephone, and her requests to speak with him became more insistent as the hour of Waller's execution drew close. FDR's personal adviser Harry Hopkins had the unenviable task of informing the first lady that the president was unavailable. Caught in the crossfire between FDR and ER, Hopkins observed that her persistence so provoked her husband that he finally took the phone.

The president, having avoided his wife's calls all day, told her he would not "interfere again," and he "urged very strongly that she say nothing about it." As a matter of fact, he "thought the Governor was acting entirely within his constitutional rights and, in addition to that, doubted very much if the merits of the case warranted the Governor's reaching any other decision."

At ten that night, ER called Randolph, who was waiting with the delegation at NAACP headquarters. Murray was among those listening on one of "the five telephone extensions in the office" when the first lady said, her voice trembling, "Mr. Randolph, I have done everything I can possibly do. I have interrupted the President twice. He is in an important conference with Mr. Hopkins and will be displeased with me if I interrupt him again. He has said that this is a matter of law and not of the heart. It is in Governor Darden's jurisdiction and the President has no legal power to intervene. I am sorry, Mr. Randolph, I can't do any more."

The finality of Franklin Roosevelt's decision stung the delegation. Some delegates burst into tears. Albert Hamilton, the only white member, "went to the washroom and vomited." Murray and a few members kept trying to reach Darden, but to no avail.

Layle Lane, vice president of the American Federation of Teachers (left, holding hat), and Morris Milgram, national secretary, Workers Defense League (right, holding document) at Odell Waller's funeral, Gretna, Virginia, July 5, 1942. The Waller case would inspire Milgram to pioneer the development of private, integrated housing with support from Pauli Murray, Eleanor Roosevelt, Jackie Robinson, and other liberal activists. *(Workers Defense League Collection, Walter P. Reuther Library, Wayne State University)*

13

"The President Has Let the Negro Down"

Odell Waller had been on death row for 630 days by the time the *Chicago Defender* reported that he was "alternating between periods of violent rage and moody glaring at black, impersonal walls." Prison authorities erected a "screen wire" to contain the objects he threw from his cell. By the time Governor Darden's commutation hearing was over and Annie Waller came to see her son for the last time, Odell had spent himself and was at peace. He told her "he didn't mind going." When she burst into tears, he said, "Mama, don't cry. . . . I know you have done everything you could for me."

Odell thanked, hugged, and kissed his mother twice, before he "said goodbye." Then he sat down with pencil and paper to write his story, as Pauli Murray had suggested.

> . . . This is Odell Waller speaking. I accidentally fell and some good people tried to help me. Others did everything they could against me so the Governor and the courts don't know the true facts. First I will say don't work for a man too poor to pay you. He will steal and take from you. In my case I worked hard from sun up until sun down trying to make a living for my family and it ended up to mean death for me. . . . I wasn't thinking of shooting Mr. Davis. . . . Davis flew hot and began to curse about the wheat. Naturally I got angry. . . . Davis thrust his hand in his pocket . . . to draw a gun. If he didn't have one he was bluffing, he frightened me. I pulled a gun and begin shooting not intending to kill him. I was frightened. . . .

When Waller finished his ten-page narrative, he gave it to his attorney and asked him to release it to the press. At 8:35 a.m. on July 2, 1942, nearly twenty-one months after his conviction, Odell Waller calmly walked to the electric chair without assistance. He was the 156th black man put to death in Virginia. Only twenty-three white men had been electrocuted.

· · ·

MURRAY WAS HAUNTED by visions of Waller's death-row cell and the execution chamber. She did not sleep the night before or for several days after his death. She vented her anguish in the extended essay "He Has Not Died in Vain" and a stanza of "Dark Testament," her most ambitious poem:

> *Put it all down in a time capsule,*
> *Bury it deep in the soil of Virginia,*
> *Bury slave-song with the Constitution,*
> *Bury it in that vineyard of planters*
> *And poll-taxes, sharecroppers and presidents.*
> *For the same red earth is fed*
> *By the white bones of Tom Jefferson*
> *And the white bones of Odell Waller.*
> *In coffin and outhouse all men are equal.*

Murray also sent a missive to the person who had been a beacon throughout the campaign. "With all the heartache of those who were convinced from the start Odell Waller was no murderer, I send you his dying statement," she wrote to Eleanor Roosevelt. "Your compassion during those two trying hours on Wednesday night and the magnificent effort you put forth in behalf of our delegation made us know you were bearing our burden with us and softened the steel which entered our souls. All the members of the delegation feel the same way. You are a splendid American."

On Sunday, July 5, twenty-five hundred mourners came "by foot, car, mule cart and truck" to Fairview Baptist Church, where Odell was a member. Two hundred crammed inside the old white building. The remainder stood outside in the blistering heat. "Simple flowers from the gardens of friends decorated" the open casket. "Thank God for Odell Waller," said Reverend J. R. Redd of Danville. "He died for the thing we're supposed to be fighting for . . . democracy." Odell's minister, Reverend Robert Gilbert, said it was fitting that the campaign to save Waller's life had drawn people together. The discrimination he suffered meant "we're all in the death row."

The only white person Waller's family allowed to participate in the service was Morris Milgram. Milgram was a socialist and the son of Russian Jewish immigrants. He had grown up in New York City, fighting for labor and minority rights. No WDL staffer, except Murray, was closer to the Waller family than Milgram, who'd ridden to Virginia on a train in the dirty, un-air-conditioned Jim Crow section with the African American activist Layle Lane. When it was Milgram's turn to speak, no words came. He wept silently for several minutes before he finally spoke of how the campaign had "awakened" the nation to the problems of poor sharecroppers. He also "stressed the importance" of Mahatma Gandhi's philosophy of nonviolent resistance.

After the service, Waller's casket was taken outside, so those standing in the churchyard could view his body. He was laid to rest in the "red earth of the little cemetery" near his church and the graves of other family members.

. . .

OVERWHELMED WITH GRIEF, Murray did not attend the funeral in Virginia. She, Randolph, and Finerty went to a memorial service at St. James Presbyterian Church in Harlem. Murray welled up as she read sections of Waller's statement. His observations, despite the poor grammar, rang true: "You take big people as the president, governors, judges, their children will never have to suffer. They has plenty money. Born in a mansion nothing to never worry about, I am glad some people are that lucky. The penitentiary all over the United States are full of people who was poor tried to work and have something."

Two weeks after Waller's execution, white mobs lynched two twenty-five-year-old black men: Jessie Smith, an army private, in Flagstaff, Arizona, and Willie Vinson, a dishwasher, in Texarkana, Texas. In Rome, Georgia, the police beat and jailed the internationally renowned black concert singer Roland Hayes and his wife, Helen. Randolph, convinced there was a connection between these racially motivated assaults and the Waller case, asked Murray to draft an open letter to President Roosevelt. That letter, Waller's final testament, and stories about the case appeared in African American newspapers across the country.

Although several members of the delegation that went to Washington, D.C., signed the July 16 letter, its sentiment and argument were quintessentially Murray's. "Waller's death," she wrote, "is a 'stab in the back' to a group of people who are asked to defend their country, but which the leaders of the country apparently do not intend to defend. By his failure to put the White House on record publicly in this case, the President has let the Negro down. In failing us the cause of Hitlerism at home has been aided."

Murray was inconsolable. Her anger at FDR ran deep. "You know as well as we do that Waller was doomed from the start," she asserted. "You know that he was the victim of a vicious economic and political system perpetuated by the poll tax and racial oppression. . . . You know that an impoverished and underprivileged Negro in Southern courts is handicapped in the matter of obtaining competent counsel who will raise and prove the complex technical questions in a manner required by our astute Supreme Court." Of the president's refusal to call for a commission of inquiry, she said, "We view your silence as a tacit political alliance with Southern reactionaries which may maintain the Democratic Party, but does not help democracy."

Murray closed her six-page letter with a warning: "The time will come when a Negro life will not be sacrificed on the altar of reactionary and behind-the-scene politics. As all Americans remember Pearl Harbor, Negro Americans will remember Odell Waller, and we solemnly pledge that he shall not have died in vain."

· · ·

A WEEK LATER, Randolph called on Murray again. This time he wanted her to organize a demonstration to protest Waller's execution and the poll tax. Murray recruited five hundred marchers with the help of local

March on Washington Movement activists and Maida Springer, a young Panamanian immigrant who was a rising star in the International Ladies' Garment Workers' Union. On the afternoon of July 25, 1942, they walked to New York City's Union Square, dressed in white with black armbands, placards in hand, in somber silence to the "throb of muffled drums." Murray and Springer held a "banner that went almost across the street," which read, "We solemnly pledge that our dead shall not have died in vain."

This protest gave Murray a desperately needed outlet for her emotions. She sent a clipping about the parade with a note to the first lady that said, "The significance of this demonstration lies in the fact that it was Negro-inspired, led and executed; non-communist and non-political. It marks an era of independent action on the part of American Negro citizens to see to it our country fulfills the obligations of a democracy at home."

· · ·

POLITICAL CONSIDERATIONS PRECLUDED ER from expressing her frustration in open letters or demonstrations. Still, she spoke out where she could. She told twenty-three hundred students at Columbia University that the nation had to do more than simply talk about the problems of minorities to eliminate discrimination. In an obvious reference to Waller, she added, "There should be no such thing as a sharecropping system in this country." To a correspondent who took issue with her sympathy for Waller, ER replied, "Times without number Negro men have been lynched or gone to their death without due process of law. No one questions Waller's guilt, but they question the system which led to it."

Behind closed doors at the White House, ER was grieving. Her pain, like Murray's, gave way to anger. "If this were a white man," she told Tommy, who knew how much the first lady cared, "he would have gotten a small sentence or life at most. It's one more case of racial injustice."

· · ·

THE WDL HAD RAISED $32,399 for Waller's appeal, and it was $2,844 in debt after his funeral. While the campaign had failed to save Waller's life, it was an important marker in the battle against the poll tax, which the U.S. Supreme Court would rule unconstitutional in 1966. It also fostered an alliance between Pauli Murray and Eleanor Roosevelt that was a turning point in their budding friendship.

PART III

MAKING FRIENDS
WITH THE FIRST LADY,
1942–44

Pauli Murray, now a second-year law school student (third from left, with short hair), and fellow African American delegates at the International Student Assembly in Washington, D.C., September 1942, were photographed by future filmmaker Gordon Parks, who worked for the Farm Security Administration and Office of War Information. Murray was one of eighty-two representatives from the United States, which had the largest delegation. *(Library of Congress Prints and Photograph Division)*

14

"The Race Problem Is a War Issue"

Still smarting over Odell Waller's execution and the failure of Congress to pass anti-lynching legislation, Pauli Murray wrote a brash letter to Franklin Roosevelt on July 23, 1942. In it, she mocked the "rationalization" government officials offered as explanation for Executive Order 9066, granting the military authority to remove American citizens and residents of Japanese ancestry from the West Coast and intern them in detention centers. "As President of a nation at war," Murray asserted, "you have almost unlimited emergency powers. . . . If Japanese Americans can be evacuated to prevent violence being perpetrated upon them by our less disciplined American citizens, then certainly you have the power to evacuate Negro citizens from 'lynching' areas in the South, and particularly in the poll tax states."

Murray accused the president of using "vague and general" language to maintain friendly relations "with the Southern bloc." In contrast, his Republican rival Wendell Willkie boldly compared "race prejudice to imperialism." "You are very much the subject of discussion among Negroes, Mr. President," Murray wrote, and "they feel their votes were among that large balance of power which swung you into office for two successive terms."

Murray was not sure that her letter would reach the president's desk or if it would move him. So she sent it to Eleanor Roosevelt with a cover note: "Will you read this letter and pass it on to the President? I only made one copy and did not want this one to get lost in a maize [*sic*] of secretariats. If there ever were a Woman's Revolution, I'm afraid you'd have to run for President." As justification for the tone of her missive to FDR, Murray added, "If some of our statements are bitter these days, you must remember that truth is our only sword."

Although Murray's intent was to rouse the president, her proposal—that the government evacuate African Americans from the South as it had done on the West Coast with Japanese Americans—angered ER. The first lady's indignation was rooted in her opposition to internment and her inability to persuade the administration that the policy was unjust. "If we can not meet the challenge of fairness to our citizens of every nationality . . . regardless of race, creed or color; if we can not keep in check anti-semitism, anti-racial feelings as well as anti-religious feelings," she had argued, "we shall have removed from the world, the one real hope for the future on which all humanity must now rely." As FDR and his advisers moved forward with the evacuation program, ER implored, "These people are good Americans and have the right to live as anyone else." Despite her entreaty, the president issued his directive on February 19, 1942.

While the first lady did not publicly criticize the internment program after the executive order was issued, knowing that there were "children behind barbed wire looking out at a free world" pained her. She worked diligently to prevent ill treatment in the camps, separation of families, discrimination, and disenfranchisement. In no mood for Murray's sarcastic "outburst," ER penned her sharpest letter to date.

August 3, 1942

Dear Miss Murray:

    I am giving your letter to the President, but on my own I want to answer some of the things which you say and which you imply.

How many of our colored people in the South would like to be evacuated and treated as though they were not as rightfully here as any other people? I am deeply concerned that we have had to do that to the Japanese who are American citizens, but we are at war with Japan and they have only been citizens for a very short time. We would feel a resentment if we had to do this for citizens who have been here as long as most of the white people have.

And now, as to what you say about the President's not having been forthright and the interest with which you are watching Mr. Willkie:

I wonder if it ever occurred to you that Mr. Willkie has no responsibility whatsoever? He can say whatever he likes and do whatever he likes, and nothing very serious will happen. If he were elected President, on that day, he would have to begin not to just plan a program to meet the conditions in the country which he would like to see changed, but he would have to take into consideration the people who are heads of important committees in Congress, none of whom he has chosen but with whom he must work, and who are the people on whom he must depend to pass vital legislation for the nation as a whole. People elect the members of Congress, and they are there and have equal power. The only thing he could do would be to initiate legislation and of course they could refuse to pass it.

For one who must really have a knowledge of the workings of our kind of government, your letter seems to me one of the most thoughtless I have ever read. Of course I can say just how I feel, but I could not say it with as much sense of security unless the President were willing for me to do so. I have no responsibility; I am not elected and not running for office; I am responsible only to myself for what I do; I do not owe the same responsibility to the people as a whole. It is very easy for us as individuals to think of what we would do if we were in office, but we forget that with the election to the office of President go at the same time infinite restrictions and the kind of responsibility which is never ours as private citizens.

The appointment of the Fair Practices Committee in itself indicates where the President stands. That group may not achieve everything we would like to have them achieve, but that only means that we have to face realities and that we cannot move faster than the people wish us to move.

Very sincerely yours,
Eleanor Roosevelt

The first lady's heated reply prompted a fiery epistle from Murray on race, war, and democracy.

August 9, 1942

Dear Mrs. Roosevelt:

Since a letter which I assumed would be handled in routine fash-
ion has evoked a personal response from you, would you bear with
me while I attempt to express my point of view on the great problem of race? . . .

You have been utterly frank with me, and I should like to be
equally frank with you. . . .

I do not deny that my letter to President Roosevelt seems
thoughtless, even reckless. Certainly, it was not intended to offer
any fundamental solution to a major problem. It was written from
a depth of desperation and disgust, such as every thinking Negro
often experiences. Desperation—in that there must be some way
of bringing home to the American people our utterly untenable
position of fighting in democracy's name for supremacy over the
Axis powers, while 13,000,000 of our own citizens are victims of a
racial theory as vicious as Hitler's. Disgust—because our President
has the power and the prestige to set in motion the wheels of public
opinion for the support of legislation and other measures which are
necessary to eliminate some of the very evils of which you and Mrs.
[Pearl] Buck speak, and some of us cannot understand why he does
not use this power more vigorously. Somehow, somebody has got
to find a way to dramatize the fascist-like nature of lynching, segregation, discrimination, disenfranchisement, and the comparable
stupidities of racial supremacy. Somebody has got to make clear to
the entire country that to pursue these policies further is suicidal.

At this moment no person can do this more effectively than Mr.
Roosevelt. . . .

On the point of Mr. Willkie, surely you could not have thought
me so politically immature as to be taken in by any statement or
promise from the Republican Party. Neither the Republican Party
nor the Democratic Party holds any promise for Negro Americans
as I see it. Mr. Roosevelt's party has in it a southern bloc which
is perpetuated by the southern poll tax and the Northern Democrats and which is pledged to the Hitler theory of racial supremacy,
whether we like to admit it or not. But many Negroes do not share
my lack of faith in the possibilities of the Republican Party, and it
was because of this that I raised the question.

The appointment of the Fair Employment Practices Committee
was a step in the right direction but the President issued Executive
Order No. 8802 out of which it grew mainly because the Government was faced with a march on Washington by Negroes throughout the country. If anything, it seems to indicate that the President

will remain aloof from the Negro question until there is an organized resentment and pressure as to make it a national embarrassment if he does not act.

All that I am pleading for is that he take the initiative in these
matters, and point out we cannot come into the world struggle for
democracy with dirty hands. He must search out scathingly the
denials of democracy to Negroes, Asiatics, Jews and other minorities at home, and abroad, as a war measure, that these be corrected
immediately. He must, in some way, make Great Britain realize that
her policy of arresting Indian Nationalist leaders is disastrous to the
cause of democracy. If we really mean what we say, when we speak
of the Four Freedoms, then give India her freedom and release the
creative energies of Gandhi, Nehru and the Indian masses to work
in our behalf. American Negroes cannot separate their struggle for
equality from the Indian's struggle for independence, and the silence
of our government on this crucial question, will be construed to
mean that we too can hope for no real stakes in the peace to follow
this war. . . .

There is no question about your soundness on this problem,
Mrs. Roosevelt, but officially we seem to lack the imagination and
the courage to take the hard road but the straight road. Some of us
cannot compromise with this "race supremacy" any longer, for to
do that would be to give up the last shred of integrity we have left.
We must speak out, appealingly, caustically, bitterly, as long as we
are able that Americans may not forget for one moment this race
problem is a war issue, and that fundamental approaches must be
made to eliminate it, now, not after the war is over.

I do not speak from the generation of Negro leaders whom you
know and respect. I do not even speak from the point of view of
Pauline Redmond whom you know as a splendid representative of
trained Negro youth. I speak out of the hearts of the declassed and
degraded young Negroes who had never had much chance and yet
must bear the responsibilities which fall from the present generation. Trained as an American, my loyalties are divided between race
and country. I look at the American south, I look at our failure to
understand the legitimate demands of the Indian people, I look at
our Oriental exclusion acts, I listen to white Americans speak of the
Japanese as "yellow niggers," thus carrying over their contempt for
the American Negro into their estimate of the people of whom we
are at war. Above all, I have been exposed to the agony of spirit of
my fellow law students as they face Selective Service and are drafted
to fight for a country which even in the face of death, maintains the
official stamp of segregation and inequality in the Armed Forces.

Viewing these stupidities, I wonder whether the white man has the courage or the imagination to save himself and civilization from utter ruin. Three hundred years of oppression have given us patience to bear hardship, but I doubt whether it has given us patience to bear with the instruments of hardship. Though the issue may be freedom and not race, as you say, nevertheless Hitler is taking advantage of our inability to handle our minority question intelligently and still counts up victories while we "muddle along."

With deep appreciation for your patience, and the hope I may someday meet you and discuss these matters more in detail, I am

Very sincerely yours,
Pauli Murray

Murray's letter so disturbed ER that she proposed they meet on August 27 in her New York City apartment. She thought it might be "easier to talk these things over than it is to discuss them through correspondence." The idea of a candid conversation appealed to Murray. However, she was reluctant to go alone, "for fear" of being "mesmerized" by ER's personality. For this reason, she took Anna Arnold Hedgeman, an older activist accustomed to dealing with political figures, as backup.

Pauli Murray and Eleanor Roosevelt had not seen each other since the first lady hosted the National Sharecroppers Week Committee in January 1940. When Murray and Hedgeman arrived, ER opened the door, startling Murray with "an affectionate hug" and the lament "Oh, that was a terrible night, wasn't it?" ER's embrace, as well as her reference to the vigil before Odell Waller's execution, signaled that Waller's death and the "wounds of interracial conflict" weighed heavily on her conscience.

ER's compassion disarmed Murray. She had come to spar over civil rights and found her "militant" armor "replaced by unreserved affection." She left the meeting with permission to address ER as "Mrs. R.," the nickname the first lady encouraged her young friends to use. "I cannot tell you how much personal reassurance I found in the interview yesterday," Murray said in her next letter. "There is no need for any apology to our generation. I only hope we can keep alive the flame of human compassion and freedom as you are doing."

• • •

TWO WEEKS LATER, in September 1942, Murray and ER found themselves on opposing sides at the International Student Assembly. The ISA was a four-day conference of three hundred youth leaders from nearly fifty nations. Conference activities took place in the auditorium at the U.S. Department of Labor, on the campus of American University, and at the White House. In her dual role as an ISA board member and first lady, ER served as host.

The presence of uniformed delegates from the allied nations of Great Britain, Canada, the Netherlands, and the Soviet Union gave the discussions practical urgency. Soviet delegate Lieutenant Lyudmila Pavlichenko, a twenty-six-year-old woman sniper who had killed 309 Germans in battle, quickly became a media darling. Several medals, including the Order of Lenin, embellished the dark green uniform she wore with her tall black boots.

President Roosevelt topped the list of speakers who addressed the assembly. In a speech broadcast to the nation and the troops, he called upon youths everywhere to help win the war and lay the framework for peace. His pledge to provide for those whose lives were interrupted by military service turned Murray's thoughts to the sixty-five men from Howard who had just marched off campus en masse to active duty.

ER, hoping to preserve an atmosphere of goodwill and unity, watched the deliberations closely. She showered the delegates from the Allied nations with attention, taking them to historical sites, such as the Lincoln Memorial, and inviting them to dine and stay overnight at the White House. She soon discovered, to her dismay, that Murray was "a ringleader" in a group of activists backing three controversial resolutions. These resolutions called for the British colonial government to free India, Gandhi, and the imprisoned Indian nationalist leaders; the end to Russian occupation of Lithuania; and the elimination of minority oppression in the United States. Concerned that the debate over these issues would fracture the conference, ER cornered Murray at a picnic for the delegates on the White House lawn and said, "Pauli, I want to talk to you later."

Murray sensed what ER wanted to discuss from the look in her "searching blue eyes." Unable to avoid this tête-à-tête, Murray listened to the first lady argue that the resolutions would undermine the assembly by creating conflict between the United States and her allies. Murray wrestled with the dilemma of going against her beliefs or acceding to ER and U.S. policy. In the end, Murray backed the resolutions.

The delegates passed a compromise that called for renewed negotiations between the British government and the Indian people. They rejected the resolution condemning the Russian occupation, and they unanimously affirmed the principle of human rights and condemned racial discrimination. Though Murray had lobbied fiercely for the original resolutions, she was relieved that the assembly remained intact.

At the close of the conference, ER wrote in her column, "The declaration . . . drafted by the young people and their determination to keep a committee together to work in peace as well as in war, with all the various countries represented, shows a faith and hope in the future which only youth can have." The first lady's effort to preserve harmony within the assembly was a rehearsal for the roadblocks she would confront in the United Nations. Compromise for the sake of holding together a vital coalition was a lesson neither she nor Murray would forget.

Pauli Murray's mentors at Howard University: Caroline Farrar Ware (top left) taught history, 1941. (*Library of Congress Prints and Photograph Division*) Howard Thurman (top right) taught religion; William H. Hastie (bottom left) and Leon A. Ransom (bottom right) taught law, circa 1940s. (*Scurlock Studio Records, Archives Center, National Museum of American History, Behring Center, Smithsonian Institution*)

15

"He Really Didn't Know Why Women Came to Law School"

Life in Washington, D.C., was complicated for blacks. Few public accommodations in the nation's capital were integrated, and Pauli Murray, accustomed to "the comparative freedom" of New York City, was repulsed by the segregated restaurants, movie theaters, and playhouses. Campus life, on the other hand, was a scintillating amalgam of people and ideas. Among the faculty were talented refugees from Europe, as well as prominent black artists and activists. The College of Liberal Arts faculty boasted such luminaries as the philosopher and writer Alain Locke, who was the first African American Rhodes scholar; the political scientist and diplomat Ralph Bunche, who would become the first person of color to win the Nobel Peace Prize; and the celebrated poet Sterling Brown, who would teach the future Nobel laureate novelist Toni Morrison, actor Ossie Davis, and writer LeRoi Jones, who would later take the name Amiri Baraka.

Murray was drawn to and embraced by the social historian Caroline Ware, the theologian Howard Thurman, and jurists Leon Ransom and William Hastie. Ware, a New Englander from a prominent white family of Harvard graduates, had come to Washington when her economist husband, Gardiner Means, joined the New Deal as an adviser to Agriculture Secretary Henry A. Wallace. In spite of Ware's first-rate credentials—she was Phi Beta Kappa, held a doctorate from Radcliffe College, and had several critically acclaimed publications to her credit—no history department at a research university would appoint her to a full-time tenure-track position because she was a woman. So she took a job in the federal government with the Consumer Division of the Office of Price Administration. Ware joined the Howard University faculty in 1942. Shortly thereafter, she met Murray when Murray audited her American constitutional history course.

Ware, whom Murray dubbed "Skipper" because of the way she "whizzed around blind corners and up and down narrow roller-coaster roads" in her convertible, became Murray's closest friend on the faculty. It was to Ware and Means's seventy-acre farm in Vienna, Virginia, that Murray retreated on weekends and school breaks. The Farm, as it came to be known, was a "sanctuary for city-weary students . . . and leaders of various humanitarian causes." Murray loved to gather around the fireplace in the common room of the Ware-Means home for spirited conversation just as much as she enjoyed cuddling up in a corner with a mystery novel.

Ware's upbringing as a Unitarian with abolitionist roots and the discrimination she suffered as a female historian in the academy fostered her lifelong commitment to social justice. Long before NAACP attorneys argued in the *Brown* case that segregation was detrimental to the psyche of black children, Ware asserted that "segregation laws," which "compelled her to sit in a separate car," robbed her of the "enriching experience" of her friends. A talented woman denied the distinguished history professorship she deserved, Ware encouraged Murray's exploration of the "parallels between racism and sexism." They would examine the intersection of sex and race inequality for the next forty years, eventually serving together with Eleanor Roosevelt on President John F. Kennedy's Commission on the Status of Women and as cofounders of the National Organization for Women.

Murray's relationships with Howard Thurman, Leon Ransom, and William Hastie lacked the social intimacy of her friendship with Ware, yet each was vital to Murray's development. Thurman, a professor in the School of Religion and dean of Rankin Chapel, was one of the nation's most influential theologians. A charismatic Baptist minister, he had led the first African American delegation to visit Mahatma Gandhi in India. Thurman taught a captivating blend of social ethics, Christian mysticism, and Gandhian philosophy. Murray would seek his counsel as she wrestled with the responsibilities of student leadership during her law school career.

Ransom and Hastie were Murray's favorite law professors. Ransom was warm and easygoing outside of class, but inside he drilled his pupils "unmercifully." Hastie, "cool and detached," unnerved opponents with his brilliance. Both men pushed Murray to excel.

Howard had a downside, despite its cultural richness and academic excellence. University policy constrained women's behavior and opportunities. On weekdays, women who lived in the dorms had a seven o'clock evening curfew, unless they got permission to go to the library—in which case, the deadline was eleven o'clock. Those who ventured into courses where the students were predominantly male faced ridicule from professors and classmates.

Aileen Clarke, a self-confident New Yorker, was the only woman in an international relations class taught by Professor Eric E. Williams, who would become the first prime minister of Trinidad and Tobago in 1962. An Oxford-educated scholar, Williams announced on the first day, "This is Political Science 183. . . . It is a course which has a great deal of work in it. There will be all kinds of papers, and I expect everyone . . . to be a dedicated student. . . . And if there is anybody in this class that is not prepared to do this, I would suggest that they leave now and sign up for home economics." Furious, Clarke not only kept her seat, she changed her major to political science. It was the first step in a pathbreaking career that would include stints as a labor organizer, the first female member of the Equal Employment Opportunity Commission, and the first and only (as of 2015) African American president of the National Organization for Women.

Murray's experience was similar to Clarke's. Like many institutions of its kind, the law school at Howard was a male bastion. There were currently no women on the faculty, although Ollie M. Cooper, the registrar, who was an HU law school graduate, had taught a course between 1925 and 1930 without pay or recognition. Murray was one of two women to enroll in the class of 1944, and the only woman to complete the first year. Often seen "trudging alone by herself carrying a huge armful of books," she stood out from her male peers and the stylish female undergraduates. She wore no makeup. She kept her hair short and unprocessed. Her clothes were drab and worn. She often wore pants, which school administrators deemed inappropriate attire for "nice" young women.

Murray, who had been reared in a family that placed no restrictions on women and where women were expected to be self-reliant, had graduated from a women's college and worked under women supervisors in the WPA. She had little awareness of sex bias. But her consciousness was awakened the first week of her first semester when Professor William Robert Ming Jr. told his class that "he really didn't know why women came to law school, but that since" they had, "the men would have to put up with" them. Drowned out by the louder, aggressive males, Murray seldom got the chance "to recite" in class.

She was deeply hurt when Ransom, whom she adored, told her she could not attend a "smoker," which was a gathering at his home for first-year male students sponsored by the campus chapter of a legal fraternity. Murray could not fathom how Ransom could risk his life fighting for civil rights in southern courtrooms yet host an event for students that excluded her. That he made light of women's exclusion, when she approached him about the issue, moved her to think of civil rights as an issue that went beyond race and class.

In a letter to the fraternity's president, Murray raised the question of equal opportunity for women. "I have no right to quarrel with the policies of your fraternity, if the objective of the fraternity is purely social and has no interest outside of that field of relationships," she wrote. "If, however, the objectives of the legal fraternity are professional in character, then I have a deep concern over the exclusion of women law students from your membership." According to the National Bar Association, there were only fifty-nine black women attorneys in the United States. Given this small number, Murray said, it was ill-advised to use "the same policies of exclusion" in membership "which are applied against us by the majority group."

The fraternity refused to revise its membership policy. Murray responded by outperforming her peers in class. She had "entered law

Pauline Redmond, circa 1934, worked for the Cook County Welfare Department and headed the Chicago Urban League Youth Activities Department before she came to Washington, D.C., to work for the federal government. Redmond's empathy, activism, and training—she held a bachelor's degree in sociology from the University of Chicago and a master of social work from the University of Pittsburgh—was the foundation of her lifelong friendship with Pauli Murray. *(Special Collections Research Center, University of Chicago Library)*

school preoccupied with the racial struggle and single-mindedly bent upon becoming a civil rights attorney." But she would graduate "an unabashed feminist" and take on sex discrimination—or Jane Crow, as she called it—"as well."

Murray's closest allies and confidantes were socially conscious women on campus and in the community. In addition to Ware, Murray befriended Ruth Powell, an undergraduate sociology major from Milton, Massachusetts, who was sitting in at segregated eateries by herself when they met. Murray also became close with Pauline Redmond, a social worker from Chicago and a friend of Eleanor Roosevelt's who worked in the National Youth Administration with Mary McLeod Bethune. Murray also reconnected with Corienne Robinson Morrow, an old friend from New York, who now worked in the Race Relations Division of the Housing and Home Finance Agency.

Murray's friends, her faculty mentors, a campus culture politicized by debate over war and civil rights, and the influx of war veterans fed her activist impulse. In the spring of 1942, she and Redmond coauthored a hard-hitting essay, "Negro Youth's Dilemma," condemning racial discrimination in the military, the defense industry, and other government programs. Their piece appeared in *Threshold,* the official publication of the U.S. committee of International Student Service.

Eleanor Roosevelt was on the ISS executive board, and it was she and the Roosevelt administration that Murray and Redmond had in mind when they penned the closing lines: "It is difficult for the Negro to locate the battlefield. Is it Java or Sikeston—Luzon or Alexander, Louisiana?" By comparing battle sites in Indonesia and the Philippines with Sikeston, Missouri, the scene of a lynching, and Alexander, Louisiana, where twenty-eight black soldiers were beaten and shot, Murray and Redmond highlighted the hypocrisy in the nation's fight for democracy abroad and its undemocratic domestic policy. To protect Redmond, who was a federal employee, from reprisal, they agreed that their provocative essay would carry only Murray's name.

Malvina ("Tommy") Thompson, circa 1941. The private secretary and principal conduit to Eleanor Roosevelt for thirty years, she was fiercely protective of the first lady. The access Thompson granted Murray demonstrated her interest in, and concern for, the young activist. *(Associated Press)*

16

"Many Good Things Have Happened"

Pauli Murray's participation in the International Student Assembly was a warm-up for her role as co-organizer of a student boycott campaign against a local restaurant in the spring of 1943. This campaign was set off by the arrest in January of three Howard University students. Sophomores Ruth Powell, Marianne Musgrave, and Juanita Morrow entered a United Cigar Store, ordered hot chocolate, and refused to leave without service. After the police came and directed management to serve the women, the staff overcharged them for their beverages. When the students refused to pay the extra charge, the police took them to jail, where they were searched and tossed into a cell already occupied by women inmates. No charges were filed, and after several hours, the police released them to the custody of HU dean of women Susie A. Elliott.

Word of the three students' arrest and incarceration spread across the campus, releasing "a torrent of resentment." Because the administration encouraged them to work with "established" groups rather than engage in "individual" protest, the women took their grievance to the NAACP campus chapter. They also went looking for the woman law student said to be experienced in civil rights.

The day Ruth Powell met Pauli Murray, Murray was walking jauntily to class, barely visible behind the stack of thick law books she carried. Her singular focus and her total disregard for the holes in her socks signaled to Powell that there was "nothing superficial about Pauli in any way." Because Murray could not find affordable housing off-campus, Dean Susie A. Elliott, who happened to be Murray's cousin, allowed her to live in the "powder room" on the first floor of Sojourner Truth Hall, the women's dormitory. In this space, which included a sink and a toilet, Murray set up a small bed, a bookcase, and a makeshift desk. After Powell, Morrow, and Musgrave discovered that Murray lived close by, they routinely took the passageway connecting their side of the dorm to Murray's room on the lower level. No matter how early they arrived, Murray was "sitting at her typewriter halfway through some project, always open to discussion." Powell, who "made more trips than anybody," observed that Murray "was an extremely sensitive person." She had "the heart of a poet, the mind of a high-powered attorney, and the soul of Saint Francis." Their freewheeling dialogue, laced with strong cigarettes and stronger coffee, laid the groundwork for a boycott campaign against the Little Palace Cafeteria.

Little Palace was situated in the center of the black community. Yet Mr. Chaconas, its Greek immigrant owner, served only whites. The cafeteria's strategic location and the stream of "unsuspecting" Howard students who wandered in and were turned away made it a logical choice for the first demonstration. As chair of the NAACP Campus Chapter Direct Action Committee, Powell took responsibility for recruiting students for the boycott. Murray served as the student legal adviser and liaison to the faculty.

On Saturday, April 17, 1943, nineteen students, twelve of whom were women, walked into the Little Palace in groups of threes and fours and requested service. Upon being denied, they took their trays to a table, sat down, and read or did their homework silently. The remaining students formed a picket line outside in the rain. The police came, but they made no arrests since the protest was lawful. Forty-five minutes later, Chaconas closed the cafeteria. When he opened on Monday morning, the picketers returned. On Tuesday, he began serving blacks.

While the mainstream press essentially ignored the boycott, Murray assumed that Eleanor Roosevelt had read about it in the black press and heard what school administrators thought about it from two of her friends—HU president Mordecai Johnson and dean Howard Thurman. Eager to share a student perspective on the demonstration and its aftermath, Murray forwarded her own lengthy account. "Many good things have happened since I talked to you last August," she wrote to ER.

Murray had not forgotten the concern for racial reconciliation the first lady had expressed after Waller's death. With that in mind, Murray and Powell made sure that no students carried "Don't Patronize" signs outside the restaurant. Their placards had less confrontational slogans, such as "Our Boys, Our Bonds, Our Brothers Are Fighting for YOU! Why Can't We Eat Here?," "United We Win," and "There's No Segregation Law in Washington D.C.—What's Your Story, Little Palace?"

Having "induced" the owner of Little Palace "to change his policy from 'white only' to all races," Murray and the students were "now pursuing a policy of reconciliation and cooperation." Chaconas had lost one-third of his white patrons, and the students were trying "to help him maintain his trade," Murray reported.

The boycott also opened the door to new relationships with white college students in the district. Howard students had invited American University students to a chocolate ice cream hour and a "discussion on Inter- and Intra-racial Relationships." In return, AU students hosted a Student Christian Fellowship hour and tea for HU students. On Easter Sunday, a week after the boycott, the HU and AU choirs gave a joint concert at the National Archives. The all-white AU choir performed despite opposition from some of its members and the school's board of trustees. "It was wonderful, Mrs. Roosevelt," Murray boasted. "It was real democracy in action."

Murray and her faculty advisers recognized the need for student leadership training, and they set about planning a one-day institute "to discuss techniques of organization, of securing and using factual information, of working with community organizations, of lobbying, methods of creative publicity, and analysis of various techniques of pressure." Murray invited ER, Caroline Ware, Anna Arnold Hedgeman, Ted Poston, Frank S. Horne (the race relations adviser in the Housing and Home Finance Agency), and Lillian Smith, the white liberal activist and writer who had just published an essay of Murray's in the journal *South Today* and who would become a friend and mentor.

Activism stirred Murray's creative juices. Along with news clippings about the boycott, she sent ER the essay "An Alternative Weapon," which she'd coauthored with Henry Babcock. Babcock was a conscientious objector and, like Murray, a member of the Fellowship of Reconciliation. Their essay was a passionate call for "full and equal opportunity . . . and justice for all—particularly sharecroppers, domestic workers, migratory workers, Negroes, Jews, Orientals, and other neglected groups."

Murray also enclosed a version of the poem "I Just Want to Eat, Mister," which she'd dedicated "to the brave band of Howard University students who held the picket line at Little Palace Cafeteria and to the Little Greek, Mr. Chaconas, who promised to try our way." This piece revealed a side typically not visible in Murray's self-assured prose. Only Thurman, Murray's spiritual adviser, and close friends, like Powell, Ware, and Redmond, saw the private strain of leadership this stanza captured.

> *Oh God, I'm cold. It's sleeting out here,*
> *And it's raining, too; I've got an hour to walk.*
> *Hope I can stick it out.*
> *They think I'm strong*
> *They elected me as a leader,*
> *But I'm cold, Lord, and I'm hungry.*

Murray's compassion for Chaconas found expression in the poem as well.

> *But I don't know, Lord.*
> *He's a little man. He's a Greek, He has no country,*
> *And sometimes I think I don't have a country, too—*
> *Now Lord, what must I do—*
> *I don't want to run him out of business—*
> *But I can't let the kids down.*
> *I've got thirty minutes to go.*
> *And I'm cold,*
> *I'm hungry,*
> *I'm wet—*
> *Lord, you be the judge—*
> *Tell us both what to do—*

That Murray wanted to share her poetry with the first lady signaled a growing trust in the friendship. For Eleanor Roosevelt, who loved poetry and Murray's favorite poet, Stephen Vincent Benét, Murray's poem was a pleasant surprise. It "is well done," the first lady wrote back.

Prior commitments prevented ER from participating in the training institute; however, she did invite Murray and the recently married Pauline Redmond to tea on May 31 at the White House. At Murray's request, her seventy-three-year-old adoptive mother, Pauline Dame, was added to the guest list.

．　．　．

LAW SCHOOL and the Little Palace boycott were not the only commitments on Murray's agenda. She was active in the March on Washington Movement, under whose auspices she had organized the silent demonstration to protest Odell Waller's execution. MOWM was still pressing Franklin Roosevelt on civil rights, even though he had issued Executive Order 8802, which prohibited racial discrimination in the national defense industry, and A. Philip Randolph had suspended the march. Murray joined the activists who drafted a program of demands at the MOWM policy conference in Detroit, on September 26–27, 1942. They called for the elimination of the poll tax and discrimination in federal jobs and job training programs, integration of the armed forces, eradication of racial bias in the media, employment of black reporters at white newspapers, special initiatives to address black women's employment problems, and passage and enforcement of laws guaranteeing civil rights and due process.

MOWM's bold agenda, Randolph's use of the Gandhian phrase "civil disobedience," and his insistence that MOWM leadership and funding come exclusively from African Americans worried some liberals. After stories about the conference appeared in black newspapers, the black conservative Warren H. Brown accused the black press and black leaders of "sensation-mongering," undermining the national morale in wartime, and fostering anti-Americanism.

Murray forwarded the MOWM conference proceedings and a pamphlet on civil disobedience to the White House after she learned that Eleanor Roosevelt had said that Brown's criticism was "temperate" and "that there are times when the Negro press is unwise." Murray admired the black press, and she took issue with Brown and ER. "Some of us thought" Mrs. Roosevelt's "statement on the Brown article . . . while sincere, was unfortunate," Murray wrote in the cover letter for an information packet she asked Malvina Thompson to give the first lady.

. . .

THE FAIR EMPLOYMENT PRACTICES COMMITTEE had been on shaky ground since its inception, in 1941. It lacked the power to enforce its judgments, and employers regularly defied its recommendations. Several members had resigned in frustration.

It bothered Murray that FDR had not appointed a woman to the committee. Plans were under way to appoint new members, and Murray, radicalized by her law school experience and her friendships with women activists, wired ER.

> UNDERSTAND COMPLETION APPOINTMENT SIX-MAN FEPC COM-
> MITTEE EXPECTED MOMENTARILY. CONVINCED GRAVE ERROR
> IF WOMAN MEMBER NOT INCLUDED. WOMAN WOULD BALANCE
> TENSIONS AND HELP OVER TACTLESS SITUATIONS. SURE YOU
> UNDERSTAND. PLEASE DO WHAT YOU CAN TO HELP ON THIS
> ISSUE. BELIEVE CAROLINE F WARE FRIEND OF MISS HILDA SMITH
> FITS ADMIRABLY BUT PRESENT ISSUE APPOINTMENT OF WOMAN
> NOT PARTICULAR PERSONALITY.

ER's long-standing affiliation with the women's trade union movement gave her an understanding of women's employment needs. She regularly lobbied the president and administration officials about the needs of women workers. When Franklin Roosevelt reconstituted the FEPC, one of the six appointees was a woman, Sara E. Southall, supervisor of employment and service for the International Harvester Company.

. . .

MEMORIAL DAY, MAY 31, 1943, marked Murray's first social visit to the White House. To have gotten such an invitation filled her with pride and a sense of history. Her undergraduate friends were so thrilled that they gave her a bouquet of roses for ER.

The closer the time drew to Murray's five o'clock appointment, the more apprehensive she became. Aunt Pauline was too ill to go, and Murray almost did not make it herself. Two hours before she and Pauline Redmond were due at the Executive Mansion, Theodore "Tee" Coggs, Pauline's husband, arrived. The Coggses had not seen each other since their marriage, right before he left for army training camp. Tee had only a weekend pass, and Pauline announced that she intended to stay with him.

Murray would not consider going to the White House alone, and she could not imagine passing up the opportunity to have tea with the first lady. ER had invited them together—and together Murray was determined to go. She called the White House, talked her way through the switchboard operators to Tommy, and explained the situation. Tommy conferred with ER and added Tee to the guest list.

Just when Murray thought all was well, Tee, a newly commissioned lieutenant, announced that he was not going to the White House. His trousers were crumpled, and he had no change of clothes. He insisted that presenting himself to the first lady in a "wrinkled" uniform would be disrespectful and reflect poorly on the army, in particular the black troops. Murray realized that she had no choice but to have Tee's pants pressed. She phoned Tommy again to say they were delayed and ask if they might still come. Tommy rescheduled the group for five-thirty.

With Lieutenant Coggs dressed in a crisp uniform, the trio drove the couple's 1933 Chevrolet at breakneck speed to the White House. They arrived at the gate just in time, but had inadvertently left their admission cards at home. They had to wait for security clearance from the first lady's office.

Finally, Murray and the Coggs couple were escorted to the south portico, where they joined ER and Tommy for the next hour and a half. The first lady graciously accepted Murray's wilted roses, which were now a reflection of how drained she felt. Only after Murray inhaled the fragrant white cups of the "big magnolia tree planted by Andrew Jackson" and the honeysuckle blossoming in the adjacent garden did she relax.

While the Coggses basked in their love for each other at this "mini-reception," Murray noticed the first lady's "sensible Red Cross shoes" and thought that someone practical enough to wear these round-toed, thick-heeled lace-ups would certainly appreciate the saga of near calamities that had delayed their arrival. Murray recounted the day's events, and ER burst into "spontaneous laughter."

The memory of that afternoon lingered with both women. ER recalled the pleasant "tea for a few guests and dinner on the porch" in her column. Murray waxed enthusiastic about the first lady's warmth to relatives. "She asked me of my future plans and seemed to approve," Murray wrote to Aunt Pauline. "You would have thought I was talking to either you or Aunt Sallie, the way she talked to me."

The debris looters left at Orkin's store on 125th Street was typical of what Pauli Murray saw after the Harlem riot on August 2, 1943. One southern newspaper held Eleanor Roosevelt "morally responsible" for the violence erupting around the country. *(Bettmann/CORBIS)*

17

"Forgive My Brutal Frankness"

For Pauli Murray, tea with Eleanor Roosevelt in the White House was an all-too-brief break from the demands of being a full-time law student and a full-time activist. Murray's unrelenting schedule and the backlash about her affection for a second-year female student took a toll on her health in the spring of 1943. Before the end of the semester, she was underweight, experiencing digestive and menstrual disturbances, and alternating between "periods of crying and cheerfulness." She spent a week in the Howard University infirmary before going to stay with Caroline Ware and her husband.

In the sun and fresh air at the Farm, Pauli tried to get over the campus gossip and a doctor's threat to have her placed under "mental observation" at the city hospital. Although she was worn-out and malnourished, she sensed that the doctor's warning had as much to do with her sexuality as it did with her physical health. Pauli's "emotional attachments" to women troubled her sister Mildred, too, on many levels. One, Mildred, like their mother, Agnes, had become a nurse, and her medical training taught that homosexuality was a mental disorder. Two, the "terrific breakdowns" Pauli suffered when a "love affair" ended weighed heavily on Mildred, for she was the sibling closest to Pauli and usually called upon to serve as caregiver. Three, Mildred was a member of a tightly knit circle of African American middle-class professionals in Washington, D.C., and she worried that Pauli's presence at Freedmen's Hospital, where she worked, would reignite old rumors of the "mad Murrays."

Pauli knew she had the support of Aunts Pauline and Sallie and a small circle of friends. She also knew that most people neither understood nor accepted her "pattern of life," she confessed in a heartfelt missive to Aunt Pauline.

> This little "boy-girl" personality as you jokingly call it sometimes gets me into trouble. And to try to live by society's standards always causes me such inner conflict that at times it's almost unbearable. I don't know whether I'm right or whether society (or some medical authority) is right—I only know how I feel and what makes me happy. This conflict rises up to knock me down at every apex I reach in my career and because the laws of society do not protect me, I'm exposed to any enemy or person who may or may not want to hurt me.

Convinced that she had "done nothing of which to be ashamed," Murray considered transferring to the University of Michigan or dropping out to pursue a career as a journalist. But Leon Ransom, whose faith in Murray had not wavered, insisted that she had "legal genius." He wanted her to finish at Howard, and he arranged for her to take her final exams over the summer.

Murray went to Durham to continue her recovery, but the war and escalating racial tensions made it difficult to rest. On June 7, she wrote to ER about two matters, making no mention of her health or the difficulties at school. One topic was the first lady's ten-year-old grandson, William Donner Roosevelt, who'd accidentally shot an eleven-year-old playmate with a .22-caliber rifle. Murray, a pacifist who believed in "wearing a rose instead of carrying a gun," said of the incident, "We cannot expect to put guns in the fathers' hands and not have little children follow unconsciously in their footsteps."

The other matter had to do with conversations she had with African Americans who had relatives in the military. One mother with "four sons in the Army" had told Murray, "My oldest son was born in the last war. And they no more than grew up when this war has taken them." It was a lament Murray heard many times over—"sorrow, despair, praying for peace."

Up until now, Murray's appeals to the first lady had been about labor and civil rights. This time the issue was peace. "I'm almost praying for an internal collapse of the Axis powers, so we can stop all this bloodshed," Murray wrote. "The civilian casualties—heart failure, nervous strain, utter weariness and heartaches—women and men—are mounting. . . . We cannot build a new world out of bullets and blood. . . . Forgive my brutal frankness, but you've always been able to count on my search for truth. . . . I must speak out against war."

Eleanor Roosevelt shared Murray's loathing for war, and she had close ties to Carrie Chapman Catt and Jane Addams, cofounders of the Woman's Peace Party. But the first lady did not share Murray's unqualified commitment to pacifism. "It was very sad to have this accident happen to our grandson and I hope it will not upset him too much," ER said of the shooting. "I do not think his having a gun is tied up with the war. He belongs to a family which goes hunting and has been taught to shoot as a sport." ER differed with Murray on the war as well. "I do not feel quite as you do," the first lady asserted. "I shall be happy and deeply relieved when peace comes, but I do feel we can build a better world on the ashes of war if we are intelligent enough and do not allow any people to be so low in morale that they are willing to accept a gangster like Hitler."

· · ·

RACIAL HOSTILITIES REACHED the boiling point in the summer of 1943. The reports of the indignities black troops suffered—segregated accommodations, inadequate provisions, and abuse by whites on and off military bases—were hard for Murray to bear. She had thirteen male relatives and a number of Howard University classmates in the armed forces. Some of her female friends—for example, Ruth Powell and Dovey Johnson—would be among the first African Americans to serve in the Women's Army Auxiliary Corps. Their safety, the harassment of black defense industry workers, and the unofficial hate strikes orchestrated by whites opposed to integrating lunch and restroom facilities kept her on edge.

Animosity toward blacks turned violent. In Mobile, Alabama, whites armed with bricks and makeshift bats attacked black workers at a shipyard. Clashes between blacks and whites in Detroit, where migrants from the South had come in record numbers for defense industry jobs, led to the deployment of six thousand federal troops. Seven hundred civilians and police officers were injured; nearly three dozen died. White mobs attacked black passengers in cars, then set the vehicles on fire. Blacks retaliated by looting white businesses. Property damage estimates were in the millions. Troops would remain in Detroit for six months.

In Los Angeles, after Hispanics attacked a sailor, the story spread that Mexican Americans were plotting a war against the military. For four nights, sailors and soldiers hunted down, stripped, and beat Mexican Americans and anyone else dressed in suits with broad-shouldered jackets and baggy pants that tapered around the ankles. *Time* magazine described the zoot-suit riots as "the ugliest brand of mob action since the coolie race riot of the 1870's." ER perceptively attributed the riots to a "question" that "goes deeper than just suits. It is a racial protest," she told the press, "with roots going a long way back."

Tempers also flared in Durham, North Carolina, where a white police officer struck a sixteen-year-old black girl for refusing to give her seat to a white passenger on a public bus. Authorities in Beaumont, Texas, declared martial law after whites, armed with hammers, axes, and guns, ransacked the black section of town. The accusation that a black man had raped a young white mother whose husband was at work set off the rampage. Dozens were injured, hundreds arrested, and two men—one black, one white—died.

Few public officials acknowledged that racial prejudice, competition for jobs and housing, and overcrowding had triggered the violence. Some blamed the NAACP, Mexican American gangs, drug use, and the Axis powers for instigating unrest. FDR's opponents blamed the first lady. Not only had she supported Odell Waller's appeal, the Tuskegee Airmen, and the recently established Women's Army Auxiliary Corps, she'd lobbied the administration to integrate federal housing for defense industry workers. After African Americans moved into the Sojourner Truth housing development in Detroit and riots ensued, a Mississippi newspaper, the *Jackson Daily News,* published an editorial titled "Blood on Your Hands" that indicted ER for "personally proclaiming and practising social equality at the White House and wherever she went."

FDR's reluctance to denounce racial violence, the rumor that his administration had established a "white cabinet" on Negro affairs, and a hostile encounter with a white physician prompted Murray to send Marvin H. McIntyre, the president's appointments secretary, a no-holds-barred statement on the racial crisis. She copied the first lady.

The racial problem, Murray told McIntyre, was the result of two competing forces: "a determination on the part of Negroes not to continue acceptance of second-class citizenship, and . . . an equally determined feeling on the part of a minority of whites . . . that the Negro must stay in an inferior social and economic position despite whatever sacrifices or contributions he may be making to the war effort." This would inevitably lead to more violence, Murray warned, adding, "Only yesterday, here in Durham, a member of my family was refused treatment by the head of the Medical Department, Duke University clinic after having been referred to him by our family physician. The reason given was 'You're in the wrong pew; I'm not going to have anything to do with Eleanor Roosevelt movements.'"

Murray gave McIntyre an earful to share with the president. She wanted the administration to protect blacks living in "lynch-mob areas," to convene an interracial conference on the Negro problem, and to authorize a "thorough and complete study" of race relations. She saw no hope in the two-party system, and she called for "the formation of a new liberal party" that embraced minorities, labor groups, and socialists.

Murray did not reveal that it was she whom the doctor had denied medical treatment or that her nondeferential demeanor and her association with the first lady were the likely reasons he'd implied that she belonged to an Eleanor Club. These alleged clubs encouraged African American women to retaliate against whites, leave domestic work, and demand social equality. Their motto was said to be "a white woman in every kitchen." The FBI found no evidence to substantiate the existence of Eleanor Clubs, yet stories about them were widespread. These stories appeared to be rooted in white hostility toward ER's support for civil rights, her friendships with blacks, the unconventional way she defined her role as the president's wife, and the exodus of black women from low-paying jobs in domestic service to lucrative employment in the defense industry.

On August 2, 1943, the false rumor that a white police officer had killed a black soldier in Harlem sparked a rampage that ended in the deaths of six people, hundreds of arrests, countless injuries, and untold property damage. Black Harlemites hurled bricks and bottles at the police and shattered the windows of white-owned stores, bars, and restaurants, looting all manner of merchandise.

The day after the riot, Murray, having come to New York, "tramped" through the rubble and glass-strewn streets, surveying the damage. She watched the police scatter crowds and gather up black soldiers for detention at the armory, "ostensibly for their protection." She stopped to talk with black and white shopkeepers, police officers, community leaders, young men in zoot suits, soldiers, and even looters. As she approached a butcher shop, she saw "a woman carry . . . a whole leg of meat and a man hugging a ham under his arm" as they ran away.

What Murray saw disturbed her. Her concern deepened when she saw that the looting was selective. Black-owned businesses were untouched and the shelves of white-owned establishments wiped clean. Her frustration spilled out in the poem "Harlem Riot, 1943" and the essay "And The Riots Came . . ."

Murray's irritation with the president's "mealy-mouthed" comment on the Detroit riot a month after it happened spawned another poem, "Mr. Roosevelt Regrets." She mailed it to ER shortly before its publication in the August 1943 issue of *The Crisis*.

MR. ROOSEVELT REGRETS
(Detroit Riot, 1943)

Upon reading *PM* newspaper's account of Mr. Roosevelt's statement on the recent race clashes: *"I share your feeling that the recent outbreaks of violence in widely spread parts of the country endanger our national unity and comfort our enemies. I am sure that every true American regrets this."*

What'd you get, black boy,
When they knocked you down in the
   gutter,
And they kicked your teeth out,
And they broke your skull with clubs
And they bashed your stomach in?
What'd you get when the police shot
   you in the back,
And they chained you to the beds
While they wiped the blood off?
What'd you get when you cried out to
   the Top Man?
When you called on the man next to
   God, so you thought,

And you asked him to speak out to save
  you?
What'd the Top Man say, black boy?
"Mr. Roosevelt regrets . . . ."

• • •

ELEANOR ROOSEVELT ARRIVED in New York City by train the day after
the Harlem riot. She had come to visit a naval training station for women
in the Bronx. Her "heart sank" when she learned about the disturbance
that threatened the fabric of her beloved city. She pleaded with New
Yorkers not to "be stampeded," or "believe everything that people tell us
without proof."

While upset, ER was not surprised. She knew that whites were fighting "unwelcome change" and that blacks were increasingly unwilling to
accept the status quo. When she read "Mr. Roosevelt Regrets," her pithy
response to Murray was "I have your poem dated July 21st. I am sorry
but I understand."

Ruth Powell, student activist (second from left), Eleanor Roosevelt (third from left), and two unidentified students participate in a panel entitled "What Can the Negro Do to Better Race Prejudice in America?" at Cook Hall, Howard University, Washington, D.C., January 14, 1944. Powell and Pauli Murray would seek ER's counsel after school officials directed students to call off the boycott of a local eatery that had refused to serve blacks. *(Moorland-Spingarn Research Center, Howard University Bulletin, and Howard University Archives)*

18

"I Count You a Real Friend"

By midsummer in 1943, the racial situation had become a powder keg. Franklin Roosevelt's advisers thought it best to extricate the outspoken first lady from the domestic scene. Eleanor Roosevelt wanted to visit the troops, and the administration swiftly approved a request she'd made months earlier. She went on two goodwill tours during Pauli Murray's last year of law school. The first of these began in August with stops in Australia, New Zealand, and nearly two dozen Pacific Islands. The second trip took her to Aruba, Brazil, British Guiana, Cuba, Guatemala, Jamaica, Panama, Puerto Rico, Trinidad, Venezuela, and the Virgin Islands in March 1944. She saw hundreds of thousands of armed service members, and she made a point to visit the black troops.

ER's days started at a six o'clock breakfast with the enlisted men, followed by visits to service personnel at Red Cross facilities, military bases, hospitals, and social halls. Hundreds of the wounded awakened to find the first lady, clad in a crisp Red Cross uniform, leaning over their beds, offering solace like a relative. She shocked Calvin Johnson, a nineteen-year-old African American soldier stationed in Brisbane, when she walked up to him in the canteen and asked if she could taste his ice cream. While Johnson stood there staring with his "mouth hanging open, not knowing what to do," ER "gently" took his cone, bit it, and gave it back. Her friendliness eased his loneliness and blunted the animosity of white soldiers. "Mrs. Roosevelt made me feel like a man again," Johnson recalled decades later. "I will never forget her."

The first lady rarely finished her rounds before midnight. She typed "My Day" on her portable typewriter between appointments or just before bed. She came home from the Pacific thirty pounds lighter, physically exhausted, and depressed by what she'd seen of war.

On January 14, 1944, ER was between tours when she joined a student panel sponsored by the Freshman Advisory Committee at Howard University. The Engineers, a contingent of soldiers in training, met her and stood guard outside Cook Hall. Inside, half a dozen students flanked the first lady at the speakers' table. HU president Mordecai Johnson and several members of his staff took seats in the audience.

Among the topics the panel addressed was the role of education in promoting better race relations. To ER's delight, the students led the way, hashing out how to combat prejudice and discrimination through job preparation and by monitoring their own behavior. At the close of the meeting, Leon Petty, chairman of the Freshman Advisory Committee, presented the first lady with a bouquet of roses. She graciously accepted the flowers and issued a challenge: "I know that this will be a difficult thing for you to do, but it is necessary for you as Negroes to excel other people, for you are always on the spot."

• • •

THE NOTION OF USING EXCELLENCE as a weapon was not a new idea for Murray. Her personal motto was "Don't get mad, get smart." Getting smart, by acquiring the legal skills to destroy segregation through the courts, was the reason she had come to law school. Her answer to the sex prejudice that threatened her ambition was to earn the highest grade point average in her class, thereby persuading her classmates to elect her—a woman—class president and chief justice of the Court of

Peers, which was the governing body of the Law Students' Guild and a quasi–honor society.

Even as Murray battled sexism in the classroom, she fought racial segregation in the community, co-organizing a second student boycott in the spring of 1944. The target this time was the John R. Thompson Restaurant, a "moderately priced" eating place in downtown Washington, at 1109 Pennsylvania Avenue. Unlike Little Palace, the cafeteria near Howard that Murray and the students had picketed the year before, Thompson's was close to the White House. Such a location increased the risk of an altercation with the police and a political backlash.

In preparation for the boycott, Murray and Powell mobilized the campus chapter of the NAACP and the support of other student organizations. Those who participated underwent "rigorous" training in "picketing and public decorum" and signed a pledge Murray and Powell drafted, agreeing not "to indulge in retaliatory remarks or actions." Those who felt they could not withstand the hazards of a picket line volunteered to stay home and do other jobs, "such as making signs and posters." Only Murray, the group's legal adviser and designated representative, was authorized to speak.

Using the meticulously scripted Little Palace boycott as a model, well-dressed students in preselected groups of "twos and threes" entered Thompson's at "ten-minute intervals" starting at four o' clock on Saturday afternoon, April 22, 1944. They requested service and took seats at empty tables when denied. While they silently read and did homework, another group picketed outside. Their signs said, "We Die Together—Why Can't We Eat Together?" and "Are You for Hitler's Way (Race Supremacy) or the American Way (Equality)? Make Up Your Mind!"

The demonstration produced mixed responses from passersby. One woman spat at the picketers. Some white soldiers shouted their disapproval. Members of the Women's Army Corps and the Women Accepted for Volunteer Emergency Service cheered. When white customers were asked if they were willing to eat in the same restaurant with blacks, seven out of ten were in favor or indifferent.

There was a startling turn of events when six African American soldiers, "smartly dressed and wearing corporals' and sergeants' stripes, filed into the restaurant, requested service, were refused, took seats at empty tables, pulled out *PM* newspapers, and began to read." Their silent presence was a stark contrast to the white military men eating and socializing at nearby tables. It was a scene so disconcerting that a couple of white military policemen asked the black soldiers to leave. The men did not budge. The soldiers brought the number of protesters inside Thompson's to fifty-six. The police came to monitor the situation, but they made no arrests.

The military policemen left and returned with a white lieutenant, who pleaded with the black soldiers to vacate the premises "as a personal favor so the Army won't be embarrassed." Overhearing his appeal, Murray interjected, "If the Army was afraid of being embarrassed, it should request *all* military personnel to leave." In the face of this unseemly standoff and the weight of Murray's argument, the MPs ordered all uniformed personnel to leave Thompson's. By eight o'clock that evening, the restaurant had lost 50 percent of its customers, and the manager got permission from corporate headquarters to serve everyone.

The students were jubilant. They had begun with the goal of forcing Thompson's to open its dining room service to blacks. They achieved that *and* pressured the army to remove all its personnel, not just blacks, from a segregated establishment.

This "victory," as Murray described it, did not allay her apprehension about her relationships with university officials. This was her second stint as co-organizer of a student boycott, and the demonstration had taken place near the White House. While she had won the admiration of fellow students, school administrators believed she was wasting her talents. They also saw her propensity to challenge authority, her budding feminism, and the whispers about her sexuality as negative influences on the other students, in particular the women.

Matters reached an impasse when President Johnson, a Baptist minister known for his powerful oratory and uncharitable treatment of those who disagreed with him, ordered the students to "suspend all activities" until he and his cabinet could clarify school policy on student boycotts. Murray admired Johnson. The first black president of Howard, he was highly regarded as a civil rights spokesman and had been educated at Morehouse College, the University of Chicago, and Harvard University. But his directive stunned her. Two days after the initial demonstration, when Thompson's refused to serve a black student, she thought it imperative to return. Furthermore, she and the students were planning to target other restaurants as well.

Murray soon learned that the protest had raised the ire of the District of Columbia Appropriations Committee in the Senate, which was responsible for 60 percent of the university's funds. At the reins of this committee was Mississippi senator Theodore G. Bilbo, an avowed segregationist who advocated the deportation of blacks to Africa, opposed anti-lynching legislation, and applauded Hitler's racial views. Johnson understandably feared Bilbo's wrath.

Murray was at a crossroads. She was as committed to desegregating Thompson's as she was to the well-being of Howard. Uncertain as to the best course of action, she sent ER a detailed narrative of the events leading up to the students' disagreement with President Johnson. Murray also enclosed a copy of the student pledge and various clippings. "Since I count you a real friend," she wrote to ER, "I thought it wise to be as open and frank as possible."

Murray had heard "second-hand," most likely from Howard Thurman, of the first lady's concern about the demonstration, and she urged ER to talk with campus leaders, such as HU Student Council president Jane Bowles and NAACP Campus Chapter president Ruth L. Harvey. "Freedom of action for student groups without Administration approval or interference, so long as such action is conducted in a lawful and proper manner and the proper safeguards have been taken to effect good public relations" was analogous, Murray insisted, with the faculty's right to academic freedom. She wanted desperately to resume the boycott, yet the potential damage to Howard's budget and its reputation gave her pause.

Despite Murray's determination, the campaign fizzled and end-of-the-semester requirements took precedence. The first lady did not meet with the students; however, she did invite Murray and her aunts Pauline and Sallie to tea at the White House on May 30. When Aunt Sallie fell ill, Murray asked permission to bring her sister Mildred in Aunt Sallie's place. Murray wanted Mildred to accompany Aunt Pauline, who was seventy-four and arthritic. Murray also requested that Ruth Powell be added to the guest list.

With arrangements for her next White House visit and graduation confirmed, Murray felt as if she were walking on air. That she had earned a law degree was more than a personal triumph. Her graduation marked the centennial year of Grandmother Cornelia's birth as "a slave in a small southern village." Murray also had sharper tools with which to battle discrimination.

19

"The Flowers Brought Your Spirit to the Graduation"

In the weeks before Pauli Murray's White House visit, she wrestled with whether to ask Eleanor Roosevelt for help with a personal matter. Murray had applied for a Rosenwald fellowship to pursue graduate study in labor law at Harvard Law School. The faculty at Howard University School of Law had a "tradition" of sending their best students to Harvard for advanced study, and Murray assumed that she, the top student in her class, would go to Harvard as others had done. Furthermore, Dean Hastie, who'd suggested she apply for the Rosenwald, had indicated that he expected her to join Howard's law faculty upon completion of her studies at Harvard.

Murray knew Harvard admitted African Americans to its law school on a token basis. Its black alumni dated back to the 1860s, and nearly half of the law professors at Howard were Harvard graduates. Murray was astonished to find that Harvard's centuries-old admissions policy barred women of any race as students. Still, she applied anyway, buoyed by Hastie's faith in her ability and the challenge of breaking precedent. She was encouraged even more after notice of her Rosenwald award arrived. Previous Rosenwald fellows included such distinguished scholars, artists, and writers as W. E. B. Du Bois, Marian Anderson, Langston Hughes, and Zora Neale Hurston.

Murray's joy at being named to the 1944 fellows class was squashed by twenty-five words in a letter from Professor Thomas Reed Powell, who chaired the Harvard Law School Committee on Graduate Studies: "Your picture and the salutation on your college transcript indicate that you are not of the sex entitled to be admitted to Harvard Law School." Murray brooded for weeks, enduring the "stinging gibes" of her classmates who saw her predicament as "a source of mild amusement rather than outrage." She envied a former classmate, now at Harvard, whom she had bested several times in courses they took together. Howard University School of Law founder Charles Hamilton Houston, SJD '23; Hastie, SJD '32; and Ransom, SJD '35 were the only African Americans who held this particular Harvard degree. She ached for the opportunity to become the first woman to earn the doctorate of juridical science from Harvard.

Unable to let the matter rest, Murray contacted Malvina Thompson ten days before the White House tea. "There's a limit to the demands or requests, or appeals that one can make on kind people, and the President and Mrs. Roosevelt are extremely kind people," Murray wrote. "Thus I don't have the nerve to send either of the enclosed notes to them directly. I'm sending them to you, because if I should be lucky enough to come to the White House on May 30th, I don't want to come battering Mrs. R. with problems—I just want her to feel free from racial requests, or any other kind."

Murray's packet included a letter to ER, indicating that she had won a Rosenwald fellowship for graduate work in labor studies at Harvard and that its law school had rejected her application because she was female. "Seems to me I've done nothing but worry you since you've been in the White House, but that's my history," Murray offered in apology. "Dean Hastie and Dean Ransom are kidding me to death about it, but down underneath all the kidding, it hurts not to be able to go to Harvard," she conceded. "I'm not expecting any answer, but I just thot [*sic*] that you'd like to know what I've been doing all this three years and why it is such a keen disappointment."

Murray saw Tommy as an ally. And Tommy, as Murray anticipated, gave the correspondence to ER, who passed it on to the president. While the first lady had not attended college, she knew from professional women friends and visits to campuses across the country that many schools denied women opportunities they rightfully deserved. ER nudged her husband, who'd graduated in 1904 from Harvard College, to write Harvard University president James B. Conant about the law school's admissions policy on Murray's behalf. FDR obliged his wife again.

"Dear Jim," FDR wrote in the cover note, to which he attached Murray's correspondence, "Here is a letter that I really do not know how to answer. Wholly aside from Radcliffe College, I always had an idea that women were admitted to many courses. Or perhaps this young colored lady wants to become an undergraduate freshman. I do not want to start you on a new dormitory program but perhaps you might ask one of your Deans to drop me a line."

FDR frequently employed humorous remarks and anecdotes as diversionary tactics when faced with difficult issues. Whether he or Harvard officials took the matter seriously, ER and Murray were grateful for his inquiry.

· · ·

ON MAY 30, Murray took her sister Mildred, Aunt Pauline, and Ruth Powell to the White House. The black servant who ushered them into the Blue Room was as excited as they were about their get-together with the first lady. Murray made sure they arrived on time and were "in position" before ER walked in. They were anything but calm. Ruth and Mildred "gawked" at the elegant chandelier hanging over the marble-topped table in the center of the oval-shaped room. Aunt Pauline "tried to re-copy the poem she had scribbled . . . but was so nervous she gave up." Murray "got caught feverishly writing" a request for the first lady's autograph for a niece.

Determined not to spoil the festive mood, Murray did not mention Harvard. The group had tea, toast strips, and a pleasant conversation in the presence of six guards "posted around the room watching every move." Even with this phalanx, "Ruth came out with a piece of toast" and some "crumbs" that "she shared with the girls in the dorm." Murray took home ER's autograph and "a bronze-colored [paper] clip found on the doorsill of the White House."

· · ·

JUNE 2, 1944, was a red-letter day for Murray and the 149 graduates, seven of whom were law students, receiving degrees and certificates at Howard's commencement. Philip Murray, president of the Congress of Industrial Organizations, and Charlotte Hawkins Brown, founding president of the Alice Freeman Palmer Memorial Institute, received honorary doctorates as well. No law student was more decorated than Murray. The Rosenwald fellowship and a citation from the student council recognizing the successful boycott campaign she had co-organized crowned her list of honors—until the arrival of a bouquet of posies and an accompanying card from Franklin and Eleanor Roosevelt. The first lady was out of town, but she had remembered Murray's graduation.

Eager to share her pride in this day, Murray dashed off a thank-you note and several mementos annotated with messages addressed to "Mrs. R." She inscribed a name card,

> *Pauli Murray*
> *School of Law '44*
> *A sharecropper was lost—*
> *I hope a "statesman" has been gained.*
> *It is the ideal.*

On another card, she jotted,

> *With deep appreciation*
> *And hope for all of us who love humanity.*
> *Pauli*

Next to her name in the commencement program, Murray scribbled, "With the wish that this career may be dedicated to making the life of the 'common man' a greater realization of the human personality at its best." On the back of the program, she wrote, "The flowers brought your spirit to the graduation platform and made the whole ceremony a thing of beauty for the 149 of us. Afterward they were placed in Frazier Hall to grace the dinner for Dr. Charlotte Hawkins Brown and Philip Murray. We all love you Mrs. R."

Murray also enclosed an open letter to the class of 1944 that was part peace offering to HU president Mordecai Johnson and part personal testimony. She characterized the two-page, single-spaced statement typed on legal-size paper as a "reaction of one of the candidates" to Johnson's baccalaureate address. Murray acknowledged at the outset that she'd gone to the ceremony "prepared to be skeptical about any 'militant' pronouncements" he made. Yet he "put his finger on the conflict . . . in her soul" when he urged graduates to go into poor southern communities to work for justice, forgoing lucrative opportunities in regions where they could live relatively free of racial discrimination. Johnson's plea went to the crux of a dilemma Murray felt deeply: whether to go home to the South, where her legal skills were badly needed and where she could care for her elderly aunts—as an unmarried daughter was expected to do—or to go where "the air is freest."

Johnson's language, especially his repeated use of the word "love," moved Murray. He spoke of the "necessity for the North to love the South as it did not do in 1865," for northerners to cast away "the stigmas" they placed on southerners, and for blacks "to try to love, understand and learn to work with the disinherited, misunderstood, and poverty-crushed white people in the South, who had never owned slaves even though they might act now as if they did." After citing the alarmingly low number of black professionals in the South, Johnson issued what every Howardite knew to be his "pet thesis": "Why don't you put your degree in your back pocket or hand it to your Mother and go down into Brasses Bottom, Mississippi, where you are needed most. If men like Bilbo and [Mississippi congressman John E.] Rankin refuse to see the needs of our beloved Southland because of their blindspot on race and the artificial barrier called 'race supremacy' why don't you go down there and become the true spokesman of those people?"

Johnson's battle cry for "Brasses Bottom, Mississippi," a phrase he'd coined to describe small rural towns in the Deep South, seemed different on this occasion to Murray. He looked tired, and "his face grew almost purple with the intensity of his feeling." She believed he was speaking from the heart, and she responded in kind with a series of pointed questions in her open letter to her fellow graduates.

> Shall we move into the relatively freer areas where we may have a little breathing space for ourselves and our children, or shall we go back down into "Egypt," so to speak, and rescue our people both white and black? Shall we go to Chicago or Harlem to come back Congressmen from black districts, or shall we go down into Mississippi and come back Congressmen and Senators in Bilbo's and Rankin's places?
>
> Shall we leave the South to those who have demonstrated they do not know how to save it, or shall we return to our native land or the land of our grandparents and win it over for democracy inch by inch, with books and ballots, and tolerance and understanding, and love and generosity in place of bullets and the instruments of violent conflict? Can we attract trained young white graduates from the great Universities to come down and join forces with us across the great void, so that together we can demonstrate to a hungry and yearning world a delayed post-war reconstruction and rehabilitation program which would bind up the wounds that have festered for eighty years?

Murray had no answers, and she would not tell others to do what she would not do herself. She would fight prejudice and discrimination until her last breath, but she could not endure the "dank and suffocating malaria of racial intolerance and oppression" in the South. The Petersburg bus and Odell Waller cases were still on her mind when she sent Virginia governor Colgate Darden notice of her graduation. "A live lawyer was far more danger to his system," she recalled she told him, "than a dead sharecropper."

．．．

HAVING READ THAT the president was not well and that the first lady was being pummeled with letters from angry white housewives who had lost their black maids, Murray composed a humorous report for ER about the White House bouquet and the people it serendipitously touched. Murray had "shouted 'Oh My God!' and run in the opposite direction" when she'd seen the flowers in the law school's main office. Once she'd recovered from the surprise, she decided to share them "with all the graduates, by putting them on the graduation platform." Murray told the first lady that she had "removed the identification card" because she was "too self-conscious to let the public" know that the Roosevelts had sent them to her. In truth, she loved the attention the bouquet sparked on campus and in the black press.

Murray lent the flowers to school officials for "the honorary dinner for Mrs. Charlotte Hawkins Brown and Philip Murray." A faculty member who did not know that the flowers belonged to Murray tried to give them to Brown before she left. Brown marveled at the lovely bouquet, took a handful of sprigs, and inquired about the card identifying the sender.

Murray heard about the mix-up the next day and "hot-footed it back to campus" to pick up the remaining flowers, which she divided into small bunches for family, friends, the Episcopal Church of the Atonement, at which she worshipped, and a local hospital. She kept the bright purple ribbon that adorned the basket for herself.

As Murray had hoped, her report on the bouquet made ER smile. "I was much amused by your letter and enjoyed the details of what I thought a very simple act on my part!" the first lady replied. For Murray, ER's "simple act" was a graduation-day gift "more powerful than an army of liberation."

Franklin Roosevelt delivers a radio address the day after he asked Congress for $70 billion, most of which would support the war effort, Washington, D.C., January 11, 1944. He was a few weeks shy of his sixty-second birthday, but his appearance fueled reports that he was suffering from heart disease and cancer. *(Franklin D. Roosevelt Presidential Library)*

20

"So at Last We Have Come to D-Day"

After commencement, Pauli Murray turned her attention to a question that held the attention of the nation: Would Franklin Roosevelt run for a fourth term? Murray's first consideration was the president's health. Photographs of his sallow face and press accounts of the ailments that sapped his strength made her uneasy. Even Eleanor Roosevelt's explanation of his bronchitis as "the weariness that assails everyone who grasps the full meaning of war" was not reassuring.

Like many activists who cut their teeth with groups such as the Workers Defense League, the March on Washington Movement, and the Fellowship of Reconciliation, Murray had become a socialist. She had never voted for FDR; yet she thought she might if he ran again—and if she did not have "to vote the Democratic ticket." While she could not abide the conservative Democrats who controlled Congress, she felt an affinity for the Roosevelts and the New Deal.

Murray labored over a draft of her opinion on the fourth-term issue before sending it to the White House. Setting aside her difficulties with the Democratic Party, she made the case for FDR's reelection. "I believe your great success as incumbents of the White House has been because, not a single man guided the country, as in Lincoln's time, but a whole family," she wrote in a letter addressed to the president and first lady. "Many people who normally would not vote for the Democratic party, have cast their votes for you, Mr. President, because they wanted to keep *both* you and Mrs. Roosevelt in the White House." This sentiment—that the Roosevelts were a team—was especially strong among African Americans. The black White House staff, observed seamstress and maid Lillian Rogers Parks, privately referred to ER as "the unofficial Vice-President."

Murray also proposed a form of government that would allow voters to split their ticket and give proportional representation to minority interest groups, such as blacks, labor, and socialists. Under such an arrangement, she could vote for Roosevelt for president and socialist candidates for other offices.

. . .

HAVING STATED HER OPINION on the fourth-term issue, Murray returned to the question of what to do about Harvard. No matter how hard she tried to hide it, the school's decision pricked a wound that was still tender. She had been rejected once again because of an accident of birth. Rather than race, which was the justification used by the University of North Carolina, the issue was now sex.

Determined to go to graduate school and unwilling to give up on Harvard, Murray decided on a two-pronged strategy: she would appeal Harvard's rejection *and* apply to the Boalt Hall of Law at the University of California, Berkeley. She reasoned that she could start school at Berkeley and transfer to Harvard after it lifted the ban on women students.

The law school at Berkeley interested Murray for a number of reasons. It had a distinguished reputation; it had a full complement of faculty, unlike several schools of comparable stature whose professors were on leave in war-related assignments; and it was located in a politically liberal city known for its teeming diversity, spawned in part by the influx of people who'd come to work in defense industry jobs.

For the next month, Murray prepared to move to California, organized her appeal to Harvard, and worked on a long, stirring poem that chronicled the black experience from Africa to present-day America. She entitled this ambitious piece "Dark Testament." One of her favorite verses spoke to the power of faith.

> Hope is a crushed stalk
> Between clenched fingers.
> Hope is a bird's wing
> Broken by a stone.
> Hope is a word in a tuneless ditty—
> A word whispered with the wind,
> A dream of forty acres and a mule,
> A cabin of one's own and rest days often,
> A name and place for one's children
> And children's children at least
> Hope is a song in a weary throat.

After Lillian Smith agreed to publish the poem in *South Today*, Murray sent an excerpt to ER and asked for her blessings and a favor. "When you read it, will you tell me whether it remains sufficiently objective not to hurt the white people of the South. With your comment, I'll be ready to turn it loose. I've held it for a year, just to be sure. Even so I still resist a stronger ending. It is the fragment of a longer poem which a legal career has interrupted."

Stephen Vincent Benét's epic poem *John Brown's Body* was the inspiration and prototype for "Dark Testament." ER loved *John Brown's Body*, and she enjoyed reading it aloud to friends, family, and schoolchildren. Murray's work impressed her. "Thank you for letting me read your poem," replied the first lady. "It is a fine poem—not too bitter." This was reassuring feedback for Murray, as the poem's initial title had been "Dark Anger" and several editors had said the tone was too strident for publication.

When ER learned of Murray's plans to go to law school in California, she contacted her friend Flora Rose, who had retired to the Bay Area after an illustrious career as cofounder and head of the Cornell University Department of Home Economics. "This will introduce Miss Pauli Murray, whom I have known for several years and who has just graduated from Howard University in Washington," wrote the first lady. "She wishes to study further, in Berkeley, and I know that she could profit greatly by your advice. I hope you will find it convenient to see her."

. . .

MURRAY HEARD, as did most Americans, of the D-Day invasion of Europe by Allied forces via radio broadcast the morning of June 6, 1944. This maneuver, code-named Operation Overlord, was an amphibious invasion of the beaches at Normandy, France. The largest such operation in history, it involved more than 10,000 aircraft, 5,000 vessels including warships, and 150,000 Allied troops. The magnitude of the effort was breathtaking, and the casualties were grave. More than 200,000 Allied and German troops were killed or injured in the campaign.

That evening, Murray gathered with friends to hear the radio broadcast of FDR's six-and-a-half-minute prayer for the troops. The text had been disseminated by news agencies in advance so that listeners could "recite the words" as the president spoke. "Almighty God," he began, "our sons, pride of our Nation, this day have set upon a mighty endeavor, a struggle to preserve our Republic, our religion, and our civilization, and to set free a suffering humanity. Lead them straight and true; give strength to their arms, stoutness to their hearts, steadfastness in their faith."

The faces of family, friends, and classmates flashed across Murray's mind as the president acknowledged the loss of life and the grief that would inevitably follow: "Some will never return. Embrace these, Father, and receive them, Thy heroic servants, into Thy kingdom. And for us at home—fathers, mothers, children, wives, sisters and brothers of brave men overseas—whose thoughts and prayers are ever with them—help us, Almighty God, to rededicate ourselves in renewed faith in Thee in this hour of great sacrifice."

"So at last we have come to D-Day," the first lady said in her column the next day. She had been "waiting for" and "dreading" word of the invasion. Now that it had come, she was neither excited nor relieved, for D-Day marked the "beginning of a long, hard fight." ER urged Americans on the home front to do their part, "no matter what these jobs may be." Doing one's job, she said, meant that employers and employees alike must avoid "unauthorized and unwarranted strikes" that might endanger "the boys over there" and the overall war effort.

Murray pronounced ER's D-Day column "eloquent." Nevertheless, she believed that doing one's job meant more than preserving harmonious labor relations in the war industry. It meant fighting for democracy and against racism at home and for freedom and against oppression abroad, as the *Pittsburgh Courier,* one of the most widely read black newspapers, had called for in its Double V campaign.

21

"This Harvard Business Makes Me Bristle"

A week after graduation, Murray received a packet from Franklin Roosevelt's private secretary Grace G. Tully. That packet contained a response from Harvard dean George H. Chase to the president's query about Murray's application. "The problem is comparatively simple," Chase wrote to FDR. "Miss Murray would be very welcome as a graduate student in Radcliffe College and I have asked Mrs. Cronkhite, Dean of the Radcliffe Graduate School, to send her the necessary application blanks. Under arrangements recently made with Radcliffe College, Radcliffe degrees *are* really Harvard degrees." While Chase's explanation may have satisfied the president, Murray saw it as a diversion from the real issue: Radcliffe had no curriculum in law, and enrolling there would not allow her to earn the equivalent of a graduate law degree from Harvard.

Harvard's rejection, the mounting casualties among friends—such as former WEP teacher Neil Scheinman Russell, who died on the battlefield in Europe—and word that an agent from the Federal Bureau of Investigation was asking questions about her on Howard University's campus prompted a pensive letter from Murray. "Dear Mr. Roosevelt," she began, "Tomorrow is Father's Day, and as I ponder over the sentiment of this day, I wish to send you greetings. My own father who died a tragic death would be pleased to have me do this, I think." Murray thanked FDR for his "intercession" with Harvard president Conant and she asked for his understanding as well. "Most of my letters to you during the past six years have been caustic, critical and perhaps impertinent by turns. Perhaps you never even got them. But Mrs. Roosevelt did. Now, without having reviewed that file of letters, I wish to apologize for those impertinent sections but not for the spirit in which they were written."

Murray felt guilty about her Harvard ambition in the wake of her friend's death. "If Neil could come back from that grave in Italy and speak to me," she told FDR,

> I believe he would say, "Pauli, don't waste your time trying to gain prestige, which is about all Harvard would give you that you can't get elsewhere; don't keep butting your head against brick walls; but identify yourself with the future, the common people, the little people who need you, so they won't let happen to our children what has happened to us. Harvard . . . does not recognize that in death there is no sex and that a man or woman's soul is judged by what he did with his talents, not his accident of birth."

Hoping, perhaps, that the president would intercede with the bureau, she lamented, "I've taken plenty of punishment for my ideals, and you and the FBI know it too."

· · ·

FRANKLIN ROOSEVELT WAS FOCUSED on the Allies' advance through Italy and France and the deadly battle against the Japanese in the Pacific when Murray notified Harvard that she intended to appeal the "ruling that women are not entitled to attend the School of Law at Harvard University." She offered multiple reasons for her "request" for reconsideration.

Some of her reasons had to do with "personal factors," such as her personality, which she described as a "'male slant'" on things; the sex discrimination she faced as an aspiring attorney; the predominance of Harvard alumni among her professors at Howard; and the time-honored practice of Howard sending its best students to Harvard Law for advanced study. Other reasons were rooted in such "social factors" as the movement of women into nontraditional arenas, including law, and the determination of talented women to earn the coveted law degree from Harvard. If Harvard did not admit her, she cautioned school officials, it would stain the school's "liberal" reputation and embolden, rather than discourage, prospective women applicants.

Among those to whom Murray distributed copies of her appeal were four Harvard men she held in high esteem: Franklin Roosevelt, William Hastie, University of Wisconsin Law School dean Lloyd K. Garrison, and

Associate Supreme Court Justice Felix Frankfurter. FDR was a symbolic father. Hastie was an academic mentor. Garrison, the great-grandson of abolitionist William Lloyd Garrison, had met and befriended Murray at a Howard University School of Law banquet, where he was the featured speaker. Frankfurter was a cofounder of the American Civil Liberties Union, for which Murray would one day serve as a board member.

Murray's classmates thought it futile to contest Harvard's decision. Eleanor Roosevelt, by contrast, offered encouragement, and it was with her that Murray shared her feelings. "I'm sorry, Mrs. Roosevelt but this Harvard business makes me bristle, fume and laugh by turns. I wish I could forget about it, but I guess there were times when the women suffragists wished the same thing a quarter of a century ago."

Harvard's administrators and FDR may have looked upon Murray's appeal as unmerited or even ridiculous. ER, on the other hand, appreciated the young woman's spunk. "Dear Pauli," the first lady wrote, "I loved your Harvard appeal." That ER addressed her missive to "Pauli" instead of "Miss Murray" signaled a growing ease in the friendship. It was precisely the kind of acceptance and endorsement Murray craved.

PART IV

STANDING UP TO
LIFE'S CHALLENGES,
1944–45

First Lady Eleanor Roosevelt pinning the Soldier's Medal on Private Sam Morris (left), April 5, 1943. In February, he had rescued several people trapped in a burning packing plant in Seattle, Washington. *(Bettmann/CORBIS)*

22

"You Wouldn't Want to Put Fala in Here"

While Democratic Party leaders awaited word of Franklin Roosevelt's campaign plans in the summer of 1944, Eleanor Roosevelt was writing columns and books, speaking to a wide array of groups, visiting wounded veterans, sponsoring relief projects, and raising funds for charities, such as the Wiltwyck School for Boys, on whose board she served. No matter what her schedule, she made time for her grandchildren. On one occasion, as she was about to have tea with guests in the White House, she paused respectfully for a cortege led by "a black dog, followed very solemnly by a five-year-old boy with a flag twice as big as himself. It was evidently meant to be a very solemn occasion," she told readers, "so we all waited for the procession to pass." Sometimes, she engaged the children in her work. One morning when she had to leave Hyde Park before her overnight guests awakened, she had a young grandson escort them to the president's library and "see them off at 10 o'clock to their train."

Meanwhile, Pauli Murray, who had been admitted "with enthusiasm" by the Boalt Hall of Law at the University of California, Berkeley, began her fourth cross-country trip. She was ambivalent about leaving the East Coast, and it consoled her to have her sister Mildred as a traveling companion. Mildred had taken a nursing position at the Veterans Hospital in West Los Angeles, where she would become one of the first African American nurses on the staff.

During the trip, they suffered one mishap after another. Mildred's tiny white Chevrolet, stuffed with enough utensils and canned food to fill "a full-sized trailer," repeatedly broke down. Their decision to pick up two young white males headed to Denver—one was a civil air patrolman; the other was trying to get to a military base before his brother shipped out—made the car even tighter. After driving for two days, they stopped in Hiawatha, Kansas, to rent two cabins and rest. When the woman checking them in realized that Pauli was African American—Mildred was fair-skinned enough to pass—she refused them lodging. After they got to Denver and dropped the men off, they were forced to stay there for four days because Mildred had lost her gas-rationing book and they had to secure a replacement. The sisters finally rolled into Los Angeles on July 8. It took them a week to find a place to live. Pauli planned to work and stay with Mildred until school started in the fall.

On her third day in Los Angeles, Murray sent ER a letter. Having "just finished *This Is My Story*," which covered ER's life from childhood to FDR's gubernatorial campaign, Murray wrote, "Understand so much now why I have been drawn to you. My own mother whose memory I have idealized through the years (she died when I was three) was born one year later than you. And many of your comments on childhood sorrows and joys are familiar to me." Like ER, Murray had lost her parents as a young girl and had been reared by elderly kin. Murray's father, William, and ER's father, Elliott, were both bright, winsome men who suffered from illnesses for which they were institutionalized and whose lives ended tragically. Murray's grandfather Robert was blind by the time she joined his household. Nonetheless, he nurtured her intellect in much the same way that ER found inspiration in her aunt Anna Roosevelt Cowles, who, despite curvature of the spine in her youth and deafness, and arthritis in adulthood, was one of the most confident people ER knew.

Murray cringed at the thought of all the letters she had "fired at the First Lady since 1938." She had wondered if ER was "too fragile" to withstand the vitriol of critics like Senator Bilbo. But ER's memoir revealed her to be as strong as "fine-tempered steel." Moreover, Murray had learned "something as a writer" from the first lady—that "simplicity and directness" could be beautiful as well as effective.

"We're a great people, Mrs. R.," Murray noted. "If we can just straighten ourselves out, we'll really live up to the faith other nations have placed in us." "Los Angeles is a confusing place at first but I think the people are gay and free," ER wrote back. "I feel just as you do about the country as a whole. It is a wonderful place when you see it as you did."

The trip also turned Murray's thoughts to race relations in the postwar period. Although her previous proposal to evacuate blacks from the South for their protection had offended ER, the harmonious relations between blacks and whites in the sparsely populated Rocky Mountain region impressed Murray, and she returned to the issue of resettlement. "You resisted this idea once, but won't you reconsider the possibility of helping Negro families to resettle on vacant western lands—if they desire," Murray asked. "If Negroes could spread out, become homesteaders, the prejudice of slums and cities would not be so great. . . . Please think it over again—there'll be a need for some plan—many plans in the post-war era."

White hostility toward black workers in crowded cities and the growing alienation among blacks worried Murray. "Mrs. R., the Negro soldiers are so bitter," she said. "And Negroes themselves are bitter. There are too few of us who feel American and too many of us who feel hyphenated. . . . I know that you cannot solve the world's problems by yourself, (altho I sometimes write you as if I expected you to)."

Murray's suggestion that blacks move voluntarily to small towns in the West appealed to ER. She had never "opposed" the voluntary "scattering of Negro people in different parts of the country," she wrote back. In fact, she "openly advocated" this and thought it "would be a great thing for the returning soldiers."

. . .

MURRAY FOLLOWED REPORTS OF Franklin Roosevelt's health closely. Hoarseness, sinusitis, bronchitis, influenza, intestinal upset, and a cyst "the size of a hen's egg" removed from the back of his neck forced a cutback in his work schedule. Murray had no knowledge of the "unsteadiness of his hand as he lit his cigarette" or his labored breathing. Even so, she was concerned about the dark circles underneath the president's eyes and his emaciated appearance in newsreels and press photos.

Rumors that FDR was ill and would not seek another term were widespread. Pronouncements about the president's sound health from his personal physician, Vice Admiral Ross T. McIntire, failed to silence gossip that he might not run. Finally, at a press conference on July 11, Franklin Roosevelt released a letter confirming that he would accept the nomination for an unprecedented fourth term "if . . . so ordered by the Commander in Chief of us all—the sovereign people of the United States." He yearned to return to his "home on the Hudson River," yet he would gladly serve if the American people so willed. The president's skillful declaration not to "run in the usual partisan, political sense" outmaneuvered his foes.

FDR's announcement prompted a letter from Murray. "You are to be commended particularly on your concept of a non-partisan candidacy and an acceptance only as a mandate of the people," she wrote. "There is no one of us who should not appreciate your longing to return to private life, and I do hope the issue will be decided in November in such a way that will bring hope, courage, strength and peace to you and your family, and to all of us."

· · ·

MURRAY HAD ARRIVED in California too late to take the bar exam. She and Mildred survived for the first month on money Pauli made as a special correspondent for *PM.* Her poetry had been published in *South Today, The Crisis, Opportunity,* and the *Carolina Magazine,* and she was beginning to find an audience for her prose in African American newspapers and leftist periodicals. Committed to presenting both the facts and the emotional truth, her writing foreshadowed the genre that would become known as literary journalism.

In addition to writing for *PM,* a newspaper based in New York City whose contributors included I. F. Stone and Ernest Hemingway, she landed a summer job reporting for the *Los Angeles Sentinel,* an influential black weekly whose goals were to expose discrimination and empower black Los Angelenos. Among the issues Murray would cover were the racially segregated blood banks at the Red Cross and the Los Angeles Railway's refusal to hire African American conductors.

In August, two pieces of mail appeared in Murray's mailbox. One was a reassuring note from ER that read, "I am glad to know your sister is going to work at the Veterans Hospital and delighted to have the news about Harvard." (The medical school faculty had voted to admit women students into the class of 1945, and Murray had passed this information along to the first lady.) The other item was an eviction notice dated August 20, 1944, and addressed to "Mrs. Mildred M. Fearing and Pauli Murray."

> We the property owners of Crocker Street wish to inform you the flat you now occupy at 5871 S. Crocker Street is restricted to the white or caucasian race only.
>
> We are quite sure that you did not know of this restriction or you would not have rented the flat.
>
> We intend to uphold these restrictions, therefore we ask that you vacate the above mentioned flat, at the above address, within 7 days or we will turn the matter over to our attorney for action. Thank you.
>
> Yours truly,
> South Crocker Street Property Owners

Pauli and Mildred had rented this apartment from a black real estate agent in a shabby, multifamily building at the edge of a white neighborhood. They were grateful to have found this place, in spite of the fact that they had no hot water. There was a housing crisis in Los Angeles, and it worsened as hundreds of thousands poured into the city to work in the defense industry. Restrictive covenants forbade the sale or rental of property to anyone other than whites in many parts of the city. At least seven thousand black defense industry workers were reportedly sleeping in cars, depots, the corridors of apartment buildings and condemned structures, ten or more to a room, and in "hot beds," where those getting up were immediately replaced by others.

The font in the unsigned notice looked so familiar that Murray wondered if someone had removed the key from under her doormat, entered the apartment, and used her typewriter. She sent the notice with a cover letter to ER that said, "I wish you could see this 'restricted' palace. Why,

Mrs. Roosevelt, you wouldn't want to put Fala in here. It looks like a barn, is one block from an industrial neighborhood and less than six blocks from Central Avenue district, the heart of Negro Los Angeles."

The lighthearted reference to FDR's beloved Scottish terrier downplayed Murray's fear and anger. But she and Mildred resolved not to move. With police protection, the support of black property owners, and the *Sentinel*'s exposé on racially restrictive covenants, they faced down the South Crocker Street Property Owners.

The shortage of decent and affordable housing was an ongoing concern for ER, and she knew that the threatening notice Pauli and Mildred had received was an all-too-common experience for blacks. The first lady could hardly contain her anger. "That rent notice made me boil!" she wrote back.

· · ·

FALL SEMESTER AT UC BERKELEY was fast approaching when the letter from Harvard Law School acting dean E. M. Morgan arrived, informing Murray that the admission committee had decided not to change its admissions policy until the war was over and the school "returned to normal conditions." Her friend Lloyd Garrison had forewarned her of an "indefinable male egoism" at Harvard. That egoism would keep the ban against women law students in place until 1950, and Harvard would not enroll its first African American woman law student, Lila Fenwick, until 1953. Unable to admit that she had lost her appeal, Murray said in a postscript to ER, "Definitely plan to enter U. of Cal. in October."

23

"This Letter Is Confidential"

As the 1944 presidential campaign heated up, so did criticism of Eleanor Roosevelt. Sometimes rumors set off attacks against her, as did the rumor that she wanted to quarantine returning soldiers because she thought them unfit "to associate with workers at home." Of this allegation, she said, "The story does me no harm. The people who spread it are evidently too stupid to realize that my only concern would be that such a story would hurt the men themselves."

Sometimes what ER wrote stoked sentiment against her. A case in point was her advocacy for a peacetime national youth service program for men *and* women. Such a program, she argued, would ensure the nation's preparedness, encourage civic participation, and expose young people to one another early in life, thereby promoting ethnic tolerance. The first lady's stance on youth service proved to one reader that she had grown "wilder in her attempts to force American youths to follow the pattern of life she wants to dictate to them." That ER favored youth service was bad enough. That she wanted to include girls in the program was unconscionable.

The first lady was a campaign veteran, and she took most criticism in stride. To the reader incensed by the notion of a national youth service program that would send boys, as well as girls, away from home, ER replied, "No one is more conscious than I am that many a girl, when she finishes high school, will not want to leave home, and that her family, as well, will not want her to go from under their direct supervision." On the other hand, "some girls might feel they wanted to see something of their own country beyond their immediate surroundings." No matter what the reader thought about youth service, "the essential thing," the first lady maintained, was "to increase our participation in government."

The attacks against ER concerned Pauli Murray, and she tried to deflect them. She told the first lady that she liked "the idea of a year's participation in government by young people. If the American people would only know and feel responsible for their government, it would make your job and that of the President so much easier." Murray also tried to humor ER with stories Mildred heard from wounded veterans at the hospital. One joke the troops told one another went, "You know, we could get this old war over with any day now, but we're afraid that we might get Eleanor caught in the crossfire, so we have to take it easy."

Murray came to the first lady's defense publicly after a letter she sent to an Alabama woman sparked controversy. The woman had complained that ER lacked "complete knowledge of the Negro situation in the South, particularly in the small towns where there are almost as many Negroes as whites." ER had replied, "Much that is said about my attitude on the Negro question is distorted and exaggerated by people who are opposed to my husband and me, and by those who have deep-rooted prejudices. I have never advocated social equality." Social equality, she explained, was "what you have among friends." This was different from equality before the law, which ER advocated. Once the first lady's letter was released to the press, political enemies made hay of what sounded like an anti-integration statement by the nation's most influential white liberal.

Murray published an editorial, "Social Equality Needs Definition," in the *Los Angeles Sentinel,* hoping to clarify for African Americans what ER had meant. "The Negro is not interested in" enacting laws that dictate "who selects him as a friend or invites him to a private home or develops an intimate relationship with him," Murray opined. "Nobody wants legislation to regulate such personal and individual matters." Legal equality—specifically, equal access to all public accommodations, fair housing and employment, and freedom of movement and association without discrimination—was the constitutional right for which blacks and ER were fighting.

The flap over her statement rattled the first lady, and she shared her frustration with Murray in a candid missive. This was the first time ER asked Murray to guard a letter.

October 3, 1944

Dear Pauli:

I will be glad when election is over and I can assure you that though I do think it would be better for the country if the President was to continue in office for the next few years, I shall be equally happy if he is out because as far as my personal feelings go, I would like nothing better than to be free to do as I choose during the next few years.

Social equality to me does not mean at all what it seems to mean to certain people. I do not think you can legislate about the people with whom you have friendly relations and those people are your social equals. I think it is all important that every citizen in the United States has an equal opportunity and that is why I have emphasized the four basic things we should fight for.

A number of people have been asking me to make a statement on segregation. I do not want to do it until we have achieved the four basic citizenship rights because I do not think it wise to add any antagonism that we do not have to have. Besides, I think if I made such a statement now it would be felt I was doing it purely for political reasons and I am much more interested in having good race relations than I am in the political situation.

In addition to this, I think that there will be a time which will come very soon after the war . . . , for those of us who really care that this question . . . be settled without bloodshed, . . . will have to stand up and be counted and that will be the time when to make such a statement would have some effect and some meaning.

I believe, of course, that all public places should be open to all citizens of the United States, based entirely on behavior and ability to pay as individuals. I do not think this has anything to do with social equality which is concerned with one's personal relationships. I might be quite willing to sit next to someone in a streetcar or a bus whom I would not want in my own house but that person would have just as much right in the streetcar as I had and we should be judged entirely on our behavior. But any statements such as I am making in this letter will be much more effective when no campaign is going on and should only be made after we get our four basic rights accepted, unless the situation becomes such that in order to help people to be patient we have to give them the feeling that there are people with them who will help them, which may save us from bloodshed.

This letter is confidential and not for publication and that is said because of the way in which people have been publishing all I have written lately!

> Very sincerely,
> Eleanor Roosevelt

· · ·

BECAUSE MURRAY WOULD BE IN Los Angeles until October 1, she had not yet made contact with ER's friend Flora Rose. Eager for the two to meet, the first lady shared an excerpt of a note she'd received from Rose. "Your young friend Pauli Murray has not gotten in touch with me as yet but if she does I shall be so glad to see her and talk with her," Rose had written. "There is so much which intelligent and educated colored people have ahead of them to do for their people at this time. Furthermore, there is so much the colored people are doing with their increased opportunities which are against their own interests it makes me heartsick at times."

Murray promised to call on Rose, but Rose's language made Murray bristle. "It does worry me when people talk of 'my people' or 'their people,'" she explained to ER. "If we start thinking about Americans it helps to dissolve some of the superficial differences. I find so many well intentioned 'white' people using that phrase, and it always irritates me. Forgive me, I know your friend means nothing by it, but if you feel as I do, I wish you'd convey the idea to somebody about it."

In her youth, ER might not have understood Murray's feelings. Now, thanks to a diverse network of friends and associates, the first lady's consciousness had been raised. "You are right we should think about Americans," she responded. "I think both Miss Rose and I do. It is curious how thoughtlessly we use words."

The railway station (above) and the pier (below) at Port Chicago naval munitions base, in California, were destroyed by an explosion in July 1944. Like Thurgood Marshall, Pauli Murray held the navy's "policy of discrimination and Jim Crow directly responsible for this incident." *(U.S. Naval Research Center)*

24

"The Whole Thing Has Left Me Very Disturbed"

In October 1944, Pauli Murray covered the court-martial of fifty African American seamen on Yerba Buena Island, in San Francisco Bay, for the *Los Angeles Sentinel*. The Port Chicago Fifty, as the group came to be known, were charged with conspiracy and mutiny for refusing to load ammunition after a cataclysmic explosion at the Port Chicago Naval

Magazine. Of the 230 navy personnel and civilians who died, 88 percent were black. This disaster accounted for 15 percent of all the deaths suffered by black military personnel in World War II. The court-martial of the Port Chicago Fifty was the first "mass trial" of the war.

Located on the Sacramento River thirty miles northeast of San Francisco, Port Chicago was built shortly after the United States declared war on Japan. The weapons loaded at this installation were indispensable to the war in the Pacific. The demand for munitions was so great that Port Chicago operated around the clock in eight-hour shifts. Approximately 125 seamen worked each shift.

The navy had accepted African Americans, albeit reluctantly, "for general service" in 1942. Secretary of the Navy W. Frank Knox and Secretary of War Henry L. Stimson were opposed to integrating the armed forces. Thus, blacks lived and trained in segregated facilities and were assigned to labor battalions or as stewards. Even after Doris "Dorie" Miller, a twenty-two-year-old black messman from Waco, Texas, pulled the wounded captain of the USS *West Virginia* from the line of fire during the attack at Pearl Harbor and downed several Japanese planes using a machine gun for which he was not allowed to be trained, the navy refused to place blacks in combat or supervisory positions.

Of the fourteen hundred black seamen stationed at Port Chicago, not one, Murray discovered, was a commissioned officer. Yet all of the seamen loading munitions ships were African American. The danger and difficulty of their assignment; the lack of opportunity for advancement, transfer, or recreation; and racial hostility on the base and in the adjacent town fostered resentment and low morale.

Neither the seamen nor the white officers who supervised them had been trained to handle explosives. The loading process was harrowing. After the munitions arrived at the pier in railroad boxcars, the men broke the containers open with crowbars and sledgehammers. They then rolled, lifted, or passed the matériel to ships, where it was stacked in layers. Some bombs weighed as much as two thousand pounds. The pressure to load the weapons as quickly as possible increased the hazard.

The ill treatment of African American seamen at Port Chicago was an old problem. The year before, they had written a letter protesting conditions on the base, but nothing came of their complaint. On July 17, 1944, the inevitable happened. Shortly after ten o'clock in the evening, the ten-thousand-ton SS *E. A. Bryan* and the seventy-five-hundred-ton SS *Quinalt Victory* exploded while seamen were loading an assortment of shells, depth charges, and bombs. Two horrific blasts, approximately seven seconds apart, illuminated the sky in a golden-orange display of fire, smoke, and debris that reached several thousand feet. The blaze glowed for about ten minutes, then turned black. The explosion, which had the power of five thousand tons of TNT, was as intense as a small earthquake. Tremors were felt fifty miles away.

Everyone at the pier died instantly. The hulls of the big ships were shattered. The locomotive, boxcars, and pier were blown to bits. Seamen in the barracks were thrown from their bunks and hit by hot flying metal and broken glass. The wreckage seared the neighboring town, where some residents lost their homes, businesses, or eyesight.

The cleanup was as traumatic as the explosion. Authorities called in an army demolition team to remove unexploded weapons. Surviving seamen helped tend the wounded and gather up the floating heads, unattached limbs, and disfigured torsos of their comrades. Only fifty-one bodies could be identified. The survivors suffered from flashbacks, sleep disturbances, heart palpitations, extreme nervousness, and hypersensitivity to sound. None received counseling. All, including those injured, were denied survivor's leave.

The navy transferred the men to the nearby Mare Island Naval Ammunition Depot and soon ordered them to resume loading munitions ships. Once they realized that conditions at Mare Island were essentially the same as those at Port Chicago, the seamen requested another work assignment. Their request was denied.

Terrified of another detonation and angry about how they were being treated, the seamen refused to load munitions. After efforts to get them to resume loading failed, the commander threatened to have them tried for mutiny and sentenced to death. Most returned to work, but fifty men, presumed by navy officials to be the leaders of the work stoppage, were charged with mutiny and conspiracy.

Murray cringed when she heard the prosecution characterize the seamen as depraved cowards. She sympathized with twenty-five-year-old Freddie Meeks, who said, "I am willing to be governed by the laws of the Navy and do anything to help my country win this war. I will go to the front if necessary, but I am afraid to load ammunition."

The defense argued that the men's refusal to load munitions was the result of paralyzing fear caused by the explosion, their injuries, the gruesome cleanup, and the imminent threat of another disaster. Of the seamen's mental health, Dr. Cavendish Moxon, a San Francisco psychoanalyst said, "When men are shocked by an explosion into a serious state of panic, they are not free to undertake new risks or even normal activities until they have been helped to overcome their nervous and mental upset." To court-martial the seamen, Moxon maintained, was like punishing "a neurotic for being unable to overcome his panicky fears."

Present in the courtroom with Murray were NAACP counsel Thurgood Marshall and Edna Seixas, an African American woman affiliated with the Berkeley Interracial Committee. Marshall, who was gathering information for an appeal, said of the case, "This is not fifty men on trial for mutiny. This is the Navy on trial for its whole vicious policy towards Negroes—Negroes in the Navy don't mind loading ammunition. They just want to know why they are the only ones doing the loading!" Seixas, the mother of a serviceman killed in Italy, sat through the entire trial. She was not allowed to speak to the seamen, but "her silent presence and kindly gaze" made them feel less alone.

On October 24, 1944, after thirty-two days and fourteen hundred pages of testimony, the all-white military court took little more than an hour to find the seamen guilty of mutiny and conspiracy. They were demoted and sentenced to prison. Ten received a fifteen-year sentence, eleven got ten years, twenty-four got twelve years, and five received eight years. They were to be dishonorably discharged after serving their sentences.

· · ·

"THE WHOLE THING has left me very disturbed," Murray wrote to the first lady after the trial. For the men to be relegated to loading munitions because of their race and then punished after the explosion for refusing to resume loading seemed to Murray doubly unfair.

Edna Seixas wrote to Secretary of the Navy James V. Forrestal, who had succeeded Frank Knox, and asked for leniency in view of the "terrible disaster" and discrimination the seamen suffered. While she acknowledged that the work stoppage was "untimely," she argued that the men's actions had broader significance. "I see not only 50 frustrated men and boys asking for a chance to do more than one dangerous assignment for their country," Seixas said, "but all of the Negro people asking to do their part not only as burden bearers, but to share in all the work of the armed forces commensurate with their individual skills and training."

Murray sent a copy of Sexias's letter to ER, who read it "with extreme interest" before passing it on with a note to FDR that said, "Please read because I do think something might be done to make it a little easier." The first lady could see "how, in following the letter of the law, these men were considered guilty." Even so, she sympathized with them and wished "the verdict could have been different." ER also sent Secretary Forrestal the pamphlet *Mutiny? The Real Story of How the Navy Branded 50 Fear-Shocked Sailors as Mutineers,* which had been prepared under the auspices of the NAACP Legal Defense and Educational Fund. She urged him to read the document and apply "special care" in this case.

On November 15, 1944, Rear Admiral Carleton H. Wright reduced the sentences of forty of the seamen, citing extenuating circumstances, their youth, and their prior good service records. Nonetheless, their felony convictions would stand and they would be ineligible for veteran's benefits. The Port Chicago disaster would weigh into President Harry S. Truman's decision to issue Executive Order 9981 on July 26, 1948, abolishing segregation in the United States armed forces. On December 23, 1999, fifty-five years after the incident, President Bill Clinton would pardon eighty-year-old Freddie Meeks.

Pauli Murray, graduate law student (third from the left), with the International House Panel, University of California, Berkeley, 1945. Murray recalled years later that each "had suffered from exclusion and rejection" because their African, Asian, Hispanic, Jewish, or immigrant ancestry assigned them to "an unpopular or despised group." *(The Schlesinger Library, Radcliffe Institute, Harvard University and the Estate of Pauli Murray)*

25

"I Shall Shout for the Rights of All Mankind"

In October 1944, Pauli Murray started classes at the Boalt Hall of Law at the University of California, Berkeley. Because the pool of male students had evaporated with the war and few women were pursuing advanced law degrees, she was the sole graduate student. Berkeley was a college town, and race relations there, compared to Los Angeles, were relatively calm. The rolling hills and mild temperature of the Bay Area were a welcome change from the hurried life and cold winters in New York City and Washington, D.C., where she'd spent the last three years. The students, especially the residents of International House, where Murray

lived, were a rainbow of ethnic groups and nationalities. Daily life reso-
nated with a chorus of languages.

International House was a complex of four residences located at
the edge of campus, and it was there that Murray forged close friendships with five students in House Number Three. Her roommates were
Mijeyko Takita, a second-generation Japanese American who had been
interned for three years at a relocation camp in Arizona, and Eva Schiff,
a Jewish refugee from Germany whose extended family died in the Holocaust. Murray's other new friends were Jane Garcia, a fifth-generation
Mexican American whose dark skin sparked confusion and hostile reactions from whites; Lillian Li, a naturalized Chinese American who was
treated like a new immigrant even though she had lived half her life in
the States; and Genevieve Tutell, a white American raised in China and
ostracized by the Chinese because she was different.

Over the requisite "coffee and cigarettes," Murray and her friends had
thought-provoking, "heart-to-heart" discussions about the similarities
and differences in their "minority status." These talks, which became as
important as the degrees for which they were studying, inspired them
to organize a panel to share with campus groups what they had learned.
They were convinced that "friendship and peace can exist among individuals from different countries." "The real crux," Murray wrote to Eleanor Roosevelt, "is how to make our personal experience that of nations."

Murray's friendships at International House spawned an eloquent
essay, "American Credo," which appeared in *Common Ground,* a literary
quarterly that promoted cultural understanding. Encouraged by Howard
Thurman's and Bayard Rustin's efforts to adapt Gandhian principles to
the U.S. civil rights struggle, Murray pledged, in her piece, to fight segregation not with force but with "persuasion" and "spiritual resistance."
"When my brothers try to draw a circle to exclude me, I shall draw a
larger circle to include them," she wrote. "When they speak out for the
privileges of a puny group, I shall shout for the rights of all mankind."
This moving essay found a broad and receptive audience that included
a black soldier stationed "somewhere in the Marianas Islands" and ER,
who "liked it very much."

Living on the West Coast brought immediacy to the Allied victories
in the Pacific and the impending meeting of the United Nations charter
conference in San Francisco. Being "released from the 'racial struggle'
temporarily" and allowed to shift her focus to international relations
gave Murray new energy. In addition to the required coursework and the

International House panel, she took a seminar with the eminent jurist Hans Kelsen on the Dumbarton Oaks Conference, at which the plans were formulated for the organization that would be named, as FDR had suggested, the United Nations. She also co-organized a speaker series on the San Francisco conference, whose purpose was to draft a charter that outlined the goals, membership, and governance structure of the new agency.

Like Murray, ER was studying the Dumbarton Oaks proceedings and the plans for the San Francisco meeting. She envisioned the U.N. as a "place where anything which troubles the world can be brought out and aired."

Eleanor Roosevelt's daughter, Anna Boettiger (far left); the first lady (center, in long black veil); and her son Brigadier General Elliott Roosevelt (partially hidden at right, in military cap) at Franklin Roosevelt's burial service at the Rose Garden, Hyde Park, New York, on April 15, 1945. Pauli Murray stayed close to the radio, following the funeral rites in her "mind's eye." *(Bettmann/CORBIS)*

26

"I Pray for Your Strength and Fortitude"

For Pauli Murray, April 1945 brought disappointment and shock. First, there was Eleanor Roosevelt's April 5 letter declining the invitation to visit International House. "I will be in San Francisco for just one day," wrote the first lady, "and I know from past experience that when I am with the President it is too difficult to make separate engagements." Then came the news of Franklin Roosevelt's death on April 12.

Murray had been apprehensive about the president's health for more than a year. Her suspicions were confirmed when he began his March 1 address to Congress after the Yalta Conference with a surprising reference to his physical disability. "I hope that you will pardon me for the unusual posture of sitting down during the presentation of what I want to say," he began, "but I know that you will realize it makes it a lot easier for me in not having to carry about ten pounds of steel around on the bottom of my legs and also because of the fact that I have just completed a 14,000-mile trip." FDR was well "the entire time," he insisted, and he had come home from the meeting with Winston Churchill and Joseph Stalin "refreshed and inspired." He even brought the House to laughter with a quip: "The Roosevelts are not, as you may suspect, averse to travel; we seem to thrive on it." Nonetheless, the president's sagging body and the occasional slur in speech overshadowed his genial façade.

Grief blanketed the nation as word of his death spread. Men and women wept openly on the streets. FDR's allies and rivals issued statements of sympathy. When word of his death reached the House of Commons of the United Kingdom, Prime Minister Winston Churchill said, "It is not fitting that we should continue our work this day but that we adjourn to the memory of this great departed statesman." Governor Thomas Dewey, the former Republican candidate for president, said, "Every American of every shade of opinion will mourn the loss of Franklin Roosevelt as a human being of warm human qualities and great capacities."

Newspaper editors from coast to coast recounted the president's steady stewardship through the Depression, the war, and preparations for the U.N. conference. The *New York Times* said, "Men will thank God on their knees a hundred years from now that Franklin D. Roosevelt was in the White House, in a position to give leadership to the thought of the American people and to give direction to the activities of their Government in that dark hour when a powerful and ruthless barbarism threatened to overrun the civilization of the Western world and to destroy the world of centuries of progress."

African Americans were devastated. "Negroes cried publicly without embarrassment and these tears came from tenant farmers in Mississippi as well as penthouse dwellers in Harlem," reported the *Pittsburgh Courier.* Howard University president Mordecai Johnson spoke for millions when he declared, "Since Abraham Lincoln, no man has so laid hold upon the hearts of the people, and no man's death has so greatly grieved them." Mary McCleod Bethune, one of four blacks among some two hundred guests invited to the president's White House funeral, lamented, "Little people, the common people, will miss him as no other group is capable. He has been the unyielding champion of minorities for a fair chance in the race of life. His works will live forever."

The president's death was a double loss for African Americans, for it also meant, as the *Courier* explained, "the removal of Mrs. Roosevelt from the social life of the Nation." Unlike FDR, who was "necessarily

restrained" by political considerations, ER spoke "for the rights and privileges of Negroes," even when the president's advisers viewed her remarks
as unwise. Maethelda Morris wrote in the *Washington Afro-American*
that an era had closed for a "noted champion" of democracy. The *Philadelphia Afro-American* published a twelve-page extra edition, featuring
photo tributes and stories about Franklin *and* Eleanor Roosevelt. The
front page appropriately bore two headlines: "America Loses Greatest
First Lady" and "World Mourns FDR."

Although Murray had visited ER in New York City and the White
House, she had never met the president. Murray had lived her "entire
adult life . . . under the Roosevelt Administration," and it was hard for
her to imagine the executive government without FDR. She had come
close to voting for him for the first time in 1944, but the designation of
Harry Truman as his vice presidential running mate instead of Henry
Wallace, whose "tough western idealism" she admired, had held her back.

Despite Murray's differences with FDR, she felt a sense of loyalty to
him, which she poured into a letter the day he died.

April 12, 1945

Dear Mrs. Roosevelt:

We have just heard. There is not one I've seen who has not
expressed a physical illness over the disaster which has befallen each
individual American today.

We are still unwilling to believe it although it has been verified for
us. At this crucial period just before the Conference the President
gave his life to bring about, we know what his leaving us means.

But because he would be the last person to have a people give in
to despair, I've been trying hard to find some purpose and meaning
in his going at this particular time. I believe this calamity had to
come to us. We have escaped the national sorrow under which the
people in the rest of the world have labored—invasion, bombing
out, suffering. While death has touched the homes of individual
Americans, this thing touches all of us in a personal way. The President's going will unite the American people in an equality of sorrow
which will cleanse and purify us, I believe.

It is now up to us, each one of us, to carry on, to do each small
task with greater dedication, simply because we have been robbed of
our symbol and Top Man. The greatest tribute we can pay to him
will be to make real the things he died for—because he is no less a
war casualty than the boy in the foxhole.

I know that these are empty words today, but I can't help believing that the hearts of the American people and the people of the

world will be shaken from their moorings over this thing, and that as Americans the only way we can repay the debt we owe to him and to you, or to ease your loss, is to take individual responsibility for giving our best to our country and to mankind.

I only hope that we will be given a kind of collective vision and insight, and that an entire people through a sorrow which is not unlike that of losing the firstborn son, will rise to meet the test which is upon us.

For a long time, we have known that no other man could quite fill the requirements of leadership. Now God—or death—has removed that man. History will not be able to record that Roosevelt lost the peace. If we lose it this time, it will be lost by the American people. This is the task we face—this is the dedication we must make.

I pray for your strength and fortitude, because we all need you more than ever now.

Am I presumptious [*sic*] to believe that the President would have preferred to go as he did—in harness.

Just
Pauli

Murray's missive was among the thousands of condolences the first lady received and that Tommy gathered in clothes baskets for safekeeping until they could be answered. It would be two months before Murray heard back. In short order, ER had to fly to Georgia, accompany the president's body to the Capitol by train, plan the funeral, and move out of the White House. Her grief, unbeknownst to the public, was compounded by the revelation that FDR's old flame Lucy Page Mercer Rutherfurd was with him when he died, and that ER's daughter, Anna, had helped her father keep the rekindled affair secret. Notwithstanding her private troubles, the first lady cast a reassuring image to the nation in her black shoulder-length widow's veil.

Just as the hearse bearing Franklin Roosevelt's coffin left Warm Springs, Graham W. Jackson Sr., the black bandleader who had been preparing to perform for the president the day he died, stepped forward with his accordion. With tears streaming down his face, he played "Goin' Home," a Negro spiritual often sung at funerals. Millions lined the railroad tracks from Georgia to New York to wave farewell to the president's flag-draped casket. A mournful hymn sung by the Rowan County Pleasant Grove Baptist Church Choir was heard as the train passed through nearby Salisbury, North Carolina, and in Washington, D.C., a unit of black soldiers marched in the funeral procession. FDR was laid to rest in the Rose Garden of his Hyde Park estate on April 15.

Jackson and the black Baptist choir had paid their final respects in song. Murray paid hers with the poem "The Passing of F.D.R.," which she sent to ER. "We wish the great love and concern we have felt for you this week-end could spread over the earth and become man's universal concern for his brother," Murray wrote in a cover note. "If [Stephen Vincent] Benét were here, he could say what needs to be said. Since he isn't here, this is what I have been thinking about the President these past two days."

"*PRESIDENT ROOSEVELT IS DEAD*"
New York Times, dateline April 12, 1945

A lone man stood on the glory road,
Peered through the shadows,
Made sure he was alone—at last,
Then drank a new-found solitude,
Drank long and deep of the vast
Breath of lilacs and honeysuckle.

He stumbled a pace,
Groped about in the April twilight
As one who feels his legs beneath him
For the first time,
Tests them on solid earth
And finds them worthy of a good sprint.

The man laughed, a golden laughter,
Rich and deep as a Georgia sunset,
Lifted a foot and kicked a pebble,
Shouted and sang, danced up and down,
As do all free things
Finding themselves free.

His shoulders spread like an eagle's wing
Freed from some killing weight, and so
Putting one foot down before the other
He strode with a whistling gait.

And then his face, miracle of light,
Gay and soft as a child's
Retrieving a beloved toy,
Turned toward the going sun,
Turned to the hills and the long road upward.

It is such a common thing to see
A man walking a road in Georgia twilight,
But if you had been watching
Or held your ear to the ground long enough,
You would have known this man
Walked as few had done before him.

There was the sound of marching in his step—
A world marching,
There was the patter of children's feet,
There was earth music, a million-voiced hymn,
And a great prayer thrust up in many tongues,
A small dog's barking, a small lad's tears,
And the silence of a world aged with grief.

Oh, bare your breast to the grindstone, brothers,
Let the heart's filings fill this crack in time,
For a lone man walks on the glory road,
Waits for the final gun,
The last exploding cannon,
When a man can walk in Georgia twilight,
Shouting as all free things do
Finding themselves free.

27

"The Problem Now Is How to Carry On"

After Franklin Roosevelt's funeral, Eleanor Roosevelt packed to move out of the White House. Although she had come to Washington reluctantly, she had grown confident in her role as first lady. For twelve years, she had been the president's emissary, assiduously reporting what she observed, lobbying fiercely for causes close to her heart.

She had also learned to take pleasure in life in the White House. When the weather permitted, she dined on the sun porch near the flowers. On her last night in the Executive Mansion, as she stared through her bedroom window at the "little red light" atop the Washington Monument, she told herself, "If Washington could be steadfast through Valley Forge, we could be steadfast today in spite of anxiety and sorrow." The next morning, ER, accompanied by sons James and Elliott, daughter Anna, and Tommy, said good-bye to the White House staff. She left, without looking back.

ER resumed "My Day" on April 17, 1945, five days after FDR passed. "Perhaps, in His wisdom, the Almighty is trying to show us that a leader may chart the way, may point out the road to lasting peace, but that many leaders and many peoples must do the building," she wrote. "It cannot be the work of one man, nor can the responsibility be laid upon his shoulders, and so when the time comes for peoples to assume the burden more fully, he is given rest."

Despite her husband's death, ER would discover an upside to being alone. No longer the president's wife, she could say and do as she pleased. And she intended to do just that as a private citizen and a journalist. Having written "My Day" for a decade, she felt she had earned her stripes. Finally free to write without constraints, she wanted her work judged "on its own merits."

. . .

FOR PAULI MURRAY, a political landscape without the Roosevelts in the White House was a somber reality made even more unsettling by her reservations about the new president. Harry Truman was a senator from Missouri when he replaced Henry Wallace as Franklin Roosevelt's vice president on the 1944 Democratic ticket. While many Americans were hopeful about Truman, his reputation for congeniality and plain speaking did not ease suspicions about him among African Americans. Indeed, his friendly relations with Senate conservatives, and his native connection to a state whose admission into the Union was part of a compromise that permitted slavery within its borders, made Murray leery. She was not alone in her misgivings.

Demps Whipper Powell, a ninety-four-year-old black Civil War veteran said to have marched with General William Tecumseh Sherman through Georgia, was so upset about Truman's ascendance to the presidency that "he refused to complete his dinner" when he heard the news. J. Mercer Burrell, a black attorney who had served in the New Jersey state legislature, said he feared that "the delicate balance in international affairs" and domestic "race relations" were at risk "with Harry S. Truman of Missouri becoming President."

The *Courier,* which had endorsed FDR's rivals in the 1940 and 1944 presidential elections, had warned Roosevelt's supporters to pray for his health after Truman joined the Democratic ticket. That warning proved prophetic. Truman took the oath of office eighty-three days after Roosevelt's fourth inauguration.

Murray's uneasiness about Truman extended to his wife, Elizabeth "Bess" Truman. In contrast to Eleanor Roosevelt, Bess Truman shunned the public glare and made no plans to hold frequent press conferences. Murray was desperate to keep the lines of communication open between the White House and blacks, and she raised the issue with ER. "Negroes, as with Labor, will have to get used to the idea that two friends over long years, and a confidence built out of a growth of understanding their problems, are not to be in the White House," Murray wrote. "Your long years of liaison work helped over many a tense point, and you not only grew in your own understanding of our problems, but you and Mr. Roosevelt taught people like me to grow. . . . The problem now," Murray continued, "is how to carry on, to build a working relationship with the Truman administration." Toward this end, she encouraged ER to host a meeting between Bess Truman and a "small group of our leading Negro women."

. . .

GIVEN THE CRITICISM ELEANOR ROOSEVELT had endured as first lady, she was not about to impose her views upon her successor. She did, however, enter the fray over the Fair Employment Practices Committee, the existence of which was due to expire on June 30, 1945. The House Rules Committee had blocked the bill that authorized funds and gave the FEPC permanent status, and Senate conservatives promised a filibuster.

ER was unwilling to let the committee die, and she told readers, "This bill would give us a permanent group in the government whose function it would be to see that, as far as employment goes throughout this country, there is complete equality of opportunity and treatment for all." The consequences would be grave should Congress not act affirmatively, she insisted. "If we do not see that equal opportunity, equal justice and equal treatment are meted out to every citizen, the very basis on which this country can hope to survive with liberty and justice for all will be wiped away."

ER's remarks pressured President Truman into publicly releasing his June 5 letter to House Rules Committee chairman Adolph J. Sabath, urging a floor vote on the bill. At a news conference, Truman echoed ER's sentiment when he said, "Discrimination in the matter of employment against properly qualified persons because of their race, creed or color, is not only un-American in nature, but will lead eventually to industrial strife and unrest."

After the president's conference, Murray told ER, "I feel you are as much responsible for that statement as any other single human being." Democratic Party leaders apparently agreed, and they tried to persuade ER to run for public office or to accept a political appointment, such as U.S. secretary of labor or U.S. delegate to the San Francisco U.N. Conference. She rebuffed the idea of a public office for the time being. What she wanted and intended to do was pursue her writing and settle her husband's estate.

. . .

BY MAY 8, 1945, Victory in Europe Day, the day after Germany's unconditional surrender, Murray faced a series of personal challenges. She was suffering from chronic appendicitis. Her money was running out. She had neither finished her master's thesis nor taken the bar exam. And Aunt Pauline wanted her to come home.

Adding to Murray's concerns over the summer was news of a secret weapon. On August 6, 1945, a Boeing B-29 Superfortress bomber, the *Enola Gay,* dropped a nuclear bomb on Hiroshima, Japan. Over seventy-five thousand people died instantaneously, and hundreds of thousands were injured and would eventually die. U.S. forces dropped a second atomic bomb on Nagasaki on August 9. Japan surrendered on August 15. Murray prayed for the families of American service personnel wounded and killed, and for the civilians, among whom were the grandparents of Mijeyko Takita, one of her roommates.

The use of a nuclear weapon prompted Murray to make a proposal. "Have you ever considered the idea of a Department of Peace as a part of the Cabinet, with a Secretary of Peace to do a job of intercultural interpretation on the international scene?" she asked ER in a letter. "The Departments of War and State are primarily concerned with military and political arrangements, but you and I know that peace is composed of human understanding as well as power and politics. . . . I have often thought of you as our first woman President (Please don't protest—I'm not alone in this thought), or our first Secretary of Peace," Murray went on, waxing enthusiastic. "You are fitted by training and experience for either."

Murray's ideas seemed impractical to ER. "I have never considered the idea of a Department of Peace as part of a Cabinet," she replied, "as I do not believe in augmenting the existing departments, but I wish the State Department could be made to do more along these lines." On the question of holding public office, she told Murray, "You are sweet to feel as you do about me, but nothing would induce me to run for any office, or to accept an appointment to any office. Aside from my own personal feelings about public life, I feel that women have not yet succeeded in establishing themselves well enough to have a large public following and without that, no one could do a good job."

The notion that women, and especially Eleanor Roosevelt, could not garner the wherewithal or following to perform well in public office was one Murray did not share. In fact, the master's thesis she was writing argued for women's right to equal opportunity in employment.

PART V

FASHIONING
NEW LIVES,
1945–52

Mary McLeod Bethune (far left) recognizes Pauli Murray (front row, third from right), Maida Springer (immediately left of Murray), and Women of the Year honorees at the National Council of Negro Women headquarters, Washington, D.C., 1946. Murray was cited for her contribution to "the field of public service," and Springer, an official in the International Ladies' Garment Workers' Union, for her work as "the first American Negro woman to represent labor abroad." *(National Archives for Black Women's History, National Park Service)*

28

"Just Know How Cherished You Are to So Many"

In the fall of 1945, Pauli Murray finished requirements for the master of laws and passed the California bar exam. The publication of her thesis, "The Right to Equal Opportunity in Employment," in the *California Law Review* marked several milestones. It was her first publication in a law review journal; it was the first essay ever published in a law review by an African American woman; and it was the first law review essay on the subject of sex discrimination and employment.

Now that Murray had the master's degree and the bar exam behind her, she pondered her next step. Her preference was to pursue a doctorate, preferably at Harvard—if not there, then at the University of California, Berkeley. In either case, her financial circumstances made further schooling impractical. Her second choice was to join the Howard University

School of Law faculty or the NAACP Legal Department. But the refusal by Howard's administration to appoint Leon Ransom to the deanship following Hastie's departure provoked Ransom's resignation and "created an untenable situation" for Murray. She was devoted to Ransom and had lobbied the board of trustees on his behalf. In addition, the NAACP had no vacancy and no funds with which to increase its legal staff.

After discussing her situation with Eleanor Roosevelt, Murray contacted Associate Supreme Court Justice Frank Murphy about the possibility of working on his staff. She had interviewed him for the *Los Angeles Sentinel,* and he had been impressed with her. But there were no openings in Murphy's office, and his assurance that there would be a post for a person with Murray's talent would bear no fruit.

There was the possibility of going back to the Workers Defense League. However, Murray knew from her experience with the Waller campaign that a job with the WDL would be unbearably stressful. The cases were always tragic, the obstacles maddening, and the workload overwhelming. She eventually took a temporary position with the local branch of the American Civil Liberties Union, where she worked to restore the status of Japanese Americans who had been forced or duped into renouncing their citizenship.

Murray wanted to remain out west, yet she felt obliged to live near Aunt Pauline. By Thanksgiving, she had resolved to return east. Her belongings were packed and her train ticket booked when she met Robert W. Kenny at her swearing-in ceremony to the California bar, on December 8, 1945. Kenny was a liberal Democrat, an advocate for fair employment legislation, and California state attorney general. Having just read Murray's groundbreaking law review article, he offered her a temporary post as deputy attorney general on the spot. Until she passed the civil service examination, her appointment would be subject to the return of employees on military service leave. Murray accepted Kenny's offer in spite of the shaky terms. In doing so, she became the first black deputy attorney general for the state of California.

· · ·

BY THE TIME MURRAY RECEIVED a note of congratulations from ER, the former first lady was in London for the first United Nations General Assembly. President Truman had nominated ER to the U.S. delegation, and the Senate had confirmed her just before Christmas. Senator Theodore Bilbo, who cast the only vote against her, declined to talk about the

Eleanor Roosevelt, age sixty-one, U.S. delegate to the United Nations (left), confers with unidentified associates at the first meeting of the U.N. General Assembly, London, January 1946. Honored to be appointed to the delegation, ER "felt a great responsibility to the youth who fought the war" and to women. *(Franklin D. Roosevelt Presidential Library)*

reasons for his opposition—except to say they were so numerous "that he was writing a book about them."

Notwithstanding the Senate's strong endorsement, some senators and members of the delegation felt ER was too outspoken, too liberal, and poorly prepared in foreign policy. She worried privately about the challenges of the job, but she accepted the assignment believing she could offer at least two things: "a sincere desire to understand the problems of the rest of the world and our relationship to them" and "a real goodwill for all peoples."

ER spent most of the five-day voyage to England aboard the *Queen Elizabeth* in her cabin, studying the details of the agenda, and conferring with fellow delegates and representatives of the State Department. She was the only woman in the six-person delegation, and her personality and status as Franklin Roosevelt's widow made her the most popular delegate. Reporters clamored for interviews and press conferences with her. A crowd lined the walkway outside the meeting hall to say hello when she arrived and to shake her hand when she left.

Determined not to fail, ER worked hard to make friends. At first, she invited women delegates to tea in the sitting room at her hotel. This proved so helpful that she began hosting daily get-togethers "with other nations' representatives at luncheon or dinner for a few hours." To her delight, she found that delegates tackled "a common problem with better results than when they were meeting officially as a committee." ER quickly emerged as the leading advocate for human rights. She presented an open letter to the assembly on behalf of the women representatives that called for the inclusion of women in civic and international affairs, and she led the fight against repatriation and punitive treatment of refugees.

The assembly debate over the fate of war refugees motivated ER to visit the camps for displaced persons. In Germany, she saw children so paralyzed by physical and psychological deprivation that they could not cry. She came home anxious for the U.N. to make amends for the wrongs done and for the United States, which had not suffered widespread devastation and displacement of its people, to take a leadership role in Europe's recovery. "The whole of Europe is hungry but worse than that, all Europe is without any social structure," she said at a rally for the United Jewish Appeal. "We cannot live in an island of prosperity in a sea of human misery."

"I had a most interesting time in London and learned a great deal which I hope to be able to get over to as many people as possible," ER wrote to Murray. "After my visit to Germany, which was horrible, I realize that we must keep the peace at all costs." Troubled by news of Murray's health problems, ER added a postscript: "Hear you haven't been well. Don't work too hard. I'll be in S[an] F[rancisco] in late March and I hope you come see me."

· · ·

MURRAY WAS INDEED UNWELL. She had acute appendicitis and a hormone imbalance that doctors would eventually diagnose as a thyroid disorder. While she had neither the funds nor health insurance to pay for treatment, she was relieved to have an explanation for the "perpetual motion" and mood swings that had periodically disrupted her life.

Murray's health concerns extended to Aunt Pauline, who became so sick in April that Murray had to go to Washington, D.C., to have her admitted to Freedmen's Hospital. Aunt Pauline improved after several weeks, but while Murray was away from California, the civil service exam was given and she was bumped from her post. She had been on the job for less than three months.

Murray regrouped by reminding herself that ER had comforted a grieving nation and represented the United States at the U.N. less than a year after her husband's death. Following ER's example, Murray pushed her woes aside to focus on the needs of others. She pitched the idea of a Waste No Food Campaign similar to the wartime scrap drives for iron, rubber, and paper to California governor Earl Warren. She testified at the Senate confirmation hearing for William Hastie, whom President Truman had nominated for the governorship of the Virgin Islands. A deafening silence filled the room when Murray stepped forward, looked Mississippi senator James Eastland, an avowed segregationist, "straight in the eye," and proudly listed Hastie's achievements. Her statement, along with testimonials from Lloyd Garrison, Norman Thomas, and U.S. Secretary of the Interior Julius A. Krug, defeated a smear campaign led by Senate conservatives. Hastie's supporters carried the day, and he would become the first African American governor of the Virgin Islands on May 7, 1946.

The disappointing turn of events in Murray's career and the first anniversary of FDR's death prompted a heartfelt letter on April 9, 1946.

> Dear Mrs. Roosevelt:
>
> I have been thinking of you this morning. Perhaps it was because I was playing the hymn "O God Our Help in Ages Past," one of Mr. Roosevelt's favorites. Perhaps because it is April and Spring and near the Eastertide. Since I'm not quite sure when we'll be able to see each other, may I say a few little words of friendliness?
>
> I want you to know how many of us, the world over have admired your courage and strength of spirit during the past year. . . .
>
> Your stepping into harness and representing the American people at the London UNO [United Nations] conference gave many of us reassurance that at least one delegate would represent our point of view. Your acceptance of continued public responsibility in the face of many shocks to a spirit as sensitive as yours has been a kind of yardstick by which we have measured our own small contributions. We have known that you moved in high places where history is made and that you often knew many things which you could not speak of, so that we have known the continual strain under which you have labored.
>
> We have also noted with amusement your insistent humility about your own role. Someday you will realize that when you were in the White House, we felt we had a team of Presidents. One official and one unofficial. None of us were under the slightest illusion as to the fact that your personality swung the vote in favor of FDR on three occasions. . . .
>
> As you reflect this week, just know how cherished you are to so

many people, first and foremost because of your own greatness of spirit and only secondarily because of the wise and understanding heart which you shared with Franklin D. Roosevelt. . . .

I say all these things despite the fact that I often differ with you on some issues. It is because of people like you that I still cling to the democratic ideal—symbolized by the American family. It is possible to have every political shade from Republican to "revolutionary pacifist" (that's me) within the same blood ties and yet move forward toward a common ideal. . . .

I do appreciate your interest in my health. . . .

> Fondly,
> Pauli

Pauli Murray, age thirty-six, former deputy attorney general for the state of California and lawyer with the American Jewish Congress, 1946. She would soon set up her own law practice. *(Bettmann/CORBIS)*

29

"Glad to Hear the Operation Was Successful"

Pauli Murray returned to New York City in the spring of 1946. It seemed unwise to go back to California, where there was virtually no chance the attorney general could rehire her. Fortunately, she got work with the American Jewish Congress Commission on Law and Social Action. This position allowed her to focus on civil rights, but it did not give her the experience in legal practice she wanted and needed.

Nine months into the job, Murray had an emergency appendectomy at Sydenham Hospital. The day of the surgery, April 8, 1947, Eleanor Roosevelt and Dr. Peter Marshall Murray (no relation to Pauli), the renowned African American surgeon scheduled to perform the procedure, were at the Howard University Board of Directors meeting. Dr.

Vaughn C. Mason, Dr. Murray's thirty-one-year-old associate, operated in his absence.

Seven years earlier, Pauli had hidden her institutionalization in the psychiatric ward of Bellevue Hospital from ER. This time, however, she disclosed the details of her hospitalization at Sydenham. Her doctor had found "an enlarged and enflamed appendix . . . , an ovarian cyst . . . , and one other little maladjustment which needed suspension," but the surgery went well, she reported to ER. Within twenty-four hours, Murray was walking in the hospital.

ER was "glad to hear the operation was successful," and she sent a pot of African violets to brighten Murray's hospital room. Though ER hoped Murray would "take a good long rest," she agreed to send a reference letter to Sydenham Hospital, where Murray had applied for a position in the outreach program. ER also opened a new door in their friendship. "Once I get settled in the country," she wrote, "if you are still in New York City, perhaps you would like to come to Hyde Park for a day or two of peace and quiet?"

Murray considered it an honor to have visited ER in the White House and at her New York City apartment. On the other hand, an invitation to stay overnight at Val-Kill, ER's country retreat, was truly special. Family and good friends regularly gathered there, as did world leaders with whom she wished to talk in a relaxed setting. Such an invitation meant one had significance in ER's personal life. It pained Murray to take a rain check, but she had decided not to return to the commission and she had to find a job as soon as possible.

. . .

MURRAY WAS ONE OF the brightest and best-trained civil rights attorneys in the nation, irrespective of race or sex. Still, no job offers in government, private practice, or the academy came her way. She found herself on the outside of a profession where Ivy League credentials, prestigious clerkships, influential friends, and personal appearance marked one's fate. The sentiment among most lawyers and their clients was that African Americans and women were ineffective attorneys because they had little if any access to the social networks necessary to launch and sustain a successful career. Given this attitude, Murray, a black woman, was suspect on two counts.

The rejection she faced and the black-and-white polka-dot dress she wore to interviews—it was the only business attire she had—were constant reminders of the disparity between her and the well-heeled men who dominated the New York legal community. Whether the firm was white- or black-owned, large or small, the response was always the same: hiring a black woman lawyer, no matter how smart, was too big a risk to take. Everywhere Murray went, the doors were closed. "Being a woman in the field of law is as bad as being a Negro and the combination is pretty awful," she lamented in a letter to Aunt Pauline.

Out of desperation, Murray took a job as a law clerk in a firm owned by Carson DeWitt Baker, a prominent black attorney who would become a municipal judge. Like scores of talented female attorneys regularly denied access to positions as associates and forced into clerkships, she was overqualified, underpaid, and overworked. Male partners and senior associates treated Murray as an "errand girl" with "no authority." Moreover, the humiliation extended into the courtroom.

One particularly demeaning incident occurred at a hearing where a white male witness for the prosecution identified Murray, rather than her client, as the prostitute with whom he had had sex. Murray fumed silently, while the court clerks snickered. Making matters worse was the judge's refusal to dismiss the charge, even though the witness had failed to identify the defendant. To preserve her self-respect and set the terms of her work conditions, Murray struck out on her own. She would run her own firm—no matter how hard the financial struggle.

. . .

MURRAY'S PREMATURE RETURN TO the workforce complicated her recovery, and she was rehospitalized in late April. Despite her doctor's insistence that she rest, she could not resist the opportunity to offer tactical support to Bayard Rustin and George Houser, co-organizers of a two-week interracial bus campaign into the upper South for the Congress of Racial Equality. The goal of the April 9 to 23, 1947, campaign, which they christened the Journey of Reconciliation, was to test the 1946 Supreme Court *Morgan v. Virginia* decision that outlawed segregation in interstate bus travel.

Irene Morgan, the defendant in that case, was a black twenty-seven-year-old mother of two who boarded a Greyhound in Virginia, bound for Baltimore to see her doctor. Ill, Morgan refused to give up her seat to a white couple. Virginia authorities convicted her for resisting arrest and violating a state law requiring segregated seating. Thurgood Marshall handled Morgan's appeal to the U.S. Supreme Court, and the justices ruled in a six-to-one decision that the statute was unconstitutional.

Rustin and Houser, young staffers at the Fellowship of Reconciliation, were responsible for nurturing CORE. Like FOR, CORE was an interracial organization of activists whose goal was to use the Gandhian principles of nonviolence and civil disobedience to advance civil rights. Unwilling to allow bus companies traveling south to ignore the *Morgan* decision, Rustin invited Murray to join a small group of "veterans" to plan a bus campaign.

Rustin and Murray had first learned about each other in the early 1940s, when he was organizing CORE chapters around the country and she was leading student boycotts at Washington, D.C., restaurants. They were both supporters of A. Philip Randolph and active in the March on Washington Movement. They found it a heady experience "thinking through each possibility" together.

The planning group selected sixteen bus riders, eight blacks and eight whites, all men. The decision to exclude women on the ground that their presence would fan fear and hatred of interracial relationships bothered Murray; nonetheless, she gave the project her blessings. Some prominent civil rights leaders were skeptical of the bus campaign. Thurgood Marshall called the project "insane." Murray, by contrast, saw a connection between the bus ride and her earlier efforts. "You will recognize the same techniques we used in Washington in the restaurant situations in 1943 and 1944," she noted in the cover letter attached to the project description that she forwarded to ER.

At the same time Murray was mentoring a new generation of activists, she was juggling the demands of private practice and caring for Aunts Pauline and Sallie, who had moved in with her in her Brooklyn apartment. Having two elderly relatives underfoot was a jolt for Murray. She had been on her own for nearly two decades. Living in a large city was a major transition for her aunts, too. They had left lifelong friends and a home where they had "flower gardens, shade, fruit trees, and space to move about, to come to a strange city and be confined to three boxlike rooms."

• • •

THE TWELVE MONTHS FOLLOWING Franklin Roosevelt's death in April 1945 brought challenge and change for Eleanor Roosevelt as well. No sooner than she'd moved out of the White House, she began the process of turning Springwood, her husband's ancestral home, over to the federal government, as the president had requested in his will. She would purchase Val-Kill and nearby acreage from the president's estate for herself. The transfer of Springwood to the government marked the end of her role as a political wife. Her expanding duties at the U.N. as head of the Commission on Human Rights, her leadership in the Democratic Party, and her membership on the boards of the NAACP and numerous educational and humanitarian organizations signaled the beginning of an autonomous life and a unique place in world affairs.

In August 1946, the demands of ER's schedule endangered her life. Sleep-deprived, she dozed off at the wheel of her Lincoln sedan on the Saw Mill River Parkway, north of New York City, colliding with two cars, hitting one head-on, and swiping the other on its side. She hit her head on the steering wheel and broke her two front teeth "about halfway up." Her eyes were "black and blue." Four people suffered lacerations and chest injuries.

ER took responsibility for the accident and confessed to the authorities and the press that she had fallen asleep. After the court revoked her license for six months, she put the situation in perspective. "I am a little sad about this, since it takes away one of the things that I enjoy, but I recognize fully the justice of punishment for endangering other people," she wrote in her column. "And while I hope that some day the license may be restored to me, I shall certainly not ask for any special consideration. I can only be grateful that no one was permanently injured in the accident."

One outcome of the mishap pleased ER. Her dentist repaired her "protruding" front teeth with porcelain caps, which altered her profile and softened her smile.

Maida Springer, manager, Pauli Murray for
New York City Council Campaign, circa 1950.
The campaign slogan was "Good Government
Is Good Housekeeping." *(Kheel Center for Labor-
Management Documentation and Archives, Martin P.
Catherwood Library, Cornell University)*

30

"I Hope to Follow the Roosevelt Tradition"

On March 12, 1947, Harry Truman called for economic and military aid to Greece and Turkey. Fearing chaos and the spread of communism, Truman told a special session of Congress, "It would be an unspeakable tragedy if these countries, which have struggled so long against overwhelming odds, should lose that victory for which they sacrificed so much." His speech troubled Pauli Murray, and she turned to Eleanor Roosevelt for an explanation. "My superficial understanding of it is that it implies President Truman has no faith in the slower processes of the United Nations and is setting a dangerous precedent. . . . Does the President's speech demonstrate good faith?" Murray asked.

ER was uncomfortable with Truman's initiative, too. She thought it unfair for the United States to aid Greece and Turkey and ignore the need for food relief in Yugoslavia and Poland. She would have felt better about the president's proposal had the United States given aid "for relief and rehabilitation on a purely non-political basis" and then worked through the U.N. "in deciding what should be done on any political or policing basis to keep Greece and Turkey free from all outside interference."

Nine days later, Truman signed Executive Order 9835, establishing a loyalty review program that would remove disloyal employees from the federal government. He hoped to allay fears of Soviet expansion and silence the charge that he was soft on communism. ER characterized the president's program as a "repressive" measure that could harm innocent people. To her, loyalty reviews were antithetical to the democratic values of freedom of speech and freedom of association.

In the spring of 1948, ER's relationship with the president reached a crisis point after he and the State Department announced the Proposal for Temporary United Nations Trusteeship for Palestine. This signaled a reversal in the State Department's support for partitioning Palestine into Jewish and Arab states. The change in policy upset ER. She offered to resign, but Truman would not accept her resignation. It was an election year, and the president was eager to avoid a public rift with the influential Democrat leading the U.N. commission mandated to promote and protect human rights. When word of ER's potential departure from the U.N. leaked, Murray insisted she stay on. "They need a mind and personality which transcends legal technicalities and you have that," she said.

Shortly after the State of Israel was established, Pauli Murray and Maida Springer went to a fund-raising rally organized by the International Ladies' Garment Workers' Union to celebrate "the birth of a new democracy." From there, they went to Greenwich Village for dinner with ER, Tommy, and Lorena Hickok, the newspaperwoman who became ER's intimate friend in the 1930s. "Mrs. R. sat at the head of the table with the golden light shining on her face," Murray observed, and Hickok, who suffered from diabetes, inquired about Aunt Pauline, who was also diabetic. "It was different from the many meetings we have had, where race was the red-hot issue," Murray reported to her adoptive mother. This time the discussion was about "history in the making."

. . .

IN THE SUMMER OF 1948, Eleanor Roosevelt asked two lawyers—her son Franklin D. Roosevelt Jr. and a family friend, Harry S. Hooker—to help Murray after she was admitted to the New York State bar. Hooker promised to keep Murray "in mind." Franklin offered to refer cases to Murray without a forwarding fee. His response, while positive, lacked his mother's personal touch. Even so, Murray felt an affinity with him. They were cohorts. She was thirty-seven, he thirty-three. Both were attorneys who had become involved in New York politics.

When Franklin ran for his first term as U.S. representative from the 20th District, Murray canvassed for him, partly because of her affection for his parents, and partly because he ran on the Liberal Party ticket. (In subsequent elections, he would run as a Democrat.) The Liberal Party was an independent political organization that backed anti-Communist progressives, supported liberal Democrats and Republicans, and occasionally ran its own candidates for office. Franklin defeated the Democrat backed by the party machine.

In 1949, Murray agreed to run as the Liberal Party candidate for the New York City Council from the Tenth Senatorial District, in Brooklyn. Her opponents included a Democrat, a Republican, and an American Labor Party candidate. Given that three-fourths of the voters in Murray's district were working-class whites, and that she had little money and no experience in elective politics, the challenge seemed formidable. However, the possibility of forging a multiracial coalition was too sweet for her to pass up.

Maida Springer, who had been one of the first black women to run for the New York State Assembly, signed on as campaign manager. Her presence brought an understanding of local politics and organizational know-how to the team. Operating on a budget of less than eight hundred dollars, Murray, Springer, and a small army of volunteers canvassed the district, shouting until they were hoarse. They so annoyed one woman that she dumped a bucket of cold water on them from her apartment window. The "little blue-and-white fliers" they handed out featured a fashionably coiffed image of Murray with a brief description of her "qualifications and platform." Her platform "called for more traffic lights . . . , cleaner streets, . . . frequent collection of garbage, keeping libraries open daily, more schools and playgrounds, and adequate housing for the aged and middle-income residents."

When Murray's opponents accused her of not understanding the needs of working people, she fired back. "I think it is more important to the people," she told a *New York Post* reporter, "that I worked longer as a dishwasher, waitress, elevator operator, typist-stenographer, switchboard operator and newspaper reporter than as a practicing attorney."

The enthusiasm her candidacy generated and a twenty-five-dollar donation from Eleanor Roosevelt raised Murray's expectations. "I have drawn so much inspiration from you through the years," Murray wrote to ER. "If successful in the campaign, I hope to follow the Roosevelt tradition and be the kind of public servant who transcends party labels and whose talents will be devoted to the entire community." Mindful that she was a long shot, on another day Murray asked, "Please use your nicest prayer rug for me, preferably Eleanor blue."

During the campaign, Murray learned that Harvard's administration had decided to admit women to its law school, and she prepared to apply again. Her correspondence file with school officials was now six inches thick, and her desire to study there had not waned. But after the "crowds at her nightly Brooklyn meetings" mushroomed, and the *New York Post,* the Americans for Democratic Action, and the Citizens Union endorsed her, Murray reconsidered her Harvard plans. She had agreed to run for city council, and she was committed to serving, if elected. Furthermore, to have the stamp of approval from a liberal newspaper, a political organization cofounded by ER, and "a prestigious nonpartisan body" was a serious matter. "I've waited years to get into Harvard Law School," she said in an interview. "I can easily wait two more until I finish my first Council term."

Only Springer knew how disappointed Murray was on election night when she came in second to the Democrat. She had won 17 percent of the electorate, bested her Republican and American Labor Party rivals, and doubled the Liberal Party vote from the previous election. Her supporters were certain she had a future in elective politics. Democrats tried to lure her to their ranks.

ER must have been pleased to see Murray move toward the political center. While she had not joined the Democratic Party faithful, she was inching away from the radical left. Unlike Franklin, who was reelected to the House, and later ran unsuccessfully for New York State attorney general and governor, Murray did not have the stomach to run for political office again.

31

"I Couldn't Wait to Give You One of the First Copies"

On March 26, 1949, the marriage between Pauli Murray and Billy Wynn was annulled. They had been legally married just over eighteen years. Until now, Murray had not had the funds to file for an annulment. Yet many of her friends, including Eleanor Roosevelt, had no prior knowledge of the marriage. Having closed this chapter in her life, Murray began work on a study of U.S. laws on race and color for the Methodist Church. The impetus for the project came from the head of the Women's Division, Thelma Stevens, and other white women activists, who wanted to open church-related programs to all races. The goals of the study were to provide a reference book for lawyers, lawmakers, and the public, and to identify the extent to which American law sanctioned or prohibited racial segregation.

Murray was convinced that a comprehensive compilation of laws on race and color would "carry an intrinsic argument against" segregation. Intellectually, this study was a continuation of the research on state statutes she had started in Leon Ransom's civil rights seminar at Howard University School of Law. Emotionally, the work gave her another vehicle through which to channel her activism, without the organizational politics that so often frustrated her.

As the sole full-time researcher for the project, Murray spent the next year combing reference books and identifying, hand-copying, and then typing every statute she found. It was tedious labor. To combat fatigue and renew her spirit, she "developed a ritual" of pausing briefly at St. Paul's Chapel on her way to the library. She found solace in reading the Universal Declaration of Human Rights, the statement on human equality drafted by the U.N. Commission on Human Rights under ER's leadership. For Murray, this statement epitomized "the best of Christian-Judaeo-Democratic culture," and she felt a philosophical connection between it and documents she had coauthored, such as the resolutions on human rights at the 1942 International Student Assembly.

It was not until President Truman sent the military into South Korea without a declaration of war that Murray interrupted her work to reach out to ER. The United States and the Soviet Union had partitioned Korea into two zones of control at the end of World War II. The Soviets backed the government in the north. The United States backed the south. Intent on unifying the country under Communist rule, the North Koreans invaded South Korea in June 1950, with military support from the Soviets. This incursion proved "beyond all doubt," said Truman, "that Communism has passed beyond the use of subversion . . . to armed invasion and war."

North Korea's aggression and the president's response disturbed Murray. "I think of you in these troubled times," she wrote to ER, "and I know how heavily the world situation weighs on you. I know of no single individual who has done more toward trying to bring about world peace and understanding, and though we stand resolute against further aggression, we do so with heavy hearts." ER would side publicly with Truman in this instance, despite previous differences with him. She would also urge the Soviets to honor their commitment to the U.N. by exerting their "influence over the Northern Koreans in peace."

When Murray finished typing her manuscript, the twelve-inch-high copy included pertinent sections from state and local statutes, the U.S. Constitution, federal legislation, executive orders, administrative regulations, and U.N. documents. It was "the first effort to bring together under one cover the laws of the forty-nine American jurisdictions in the field of race." The official title was *States' Laws on Race and Color and Appendices: Containing International Documents, Federal Laws and Regulations, Local Ordinances and Charts.*

Murray picked up the first copies at the publications office of the Methodist Church on March 5, 1951. The sight of the yellow, 746-page book that bore her name in bright green letters filled her with pride. She had an impressive record of published poems and essays, but this, her first book, was special. *States Laws'* was a compelling documentary of the nation's efforts to regulate race relations. In it, Murray revealed that there were laws forbidding the integration of public transportation, hotels, places of employment, housing, hospitals, military units and installations, prisons, recreational facilities, and schools all over the country. Thirty states restricted intermarriage. Mississippi made it illegal "to publish or distribute" literature that promoted racial equality. Oklahoma authorized separate telephone booths, and Arkansas mandated separate tax rolls and voting booths.

Murray raced to ER's office three days later with the book. "I couldn't wait to give you one of the first copies that came off the press so I delivered it myself," she said in an attached note. "If you think it worthwhile I hope you'll call attention to the book in your column and radio program. Let me know what you think of it. I hope I'll get to see you before too long."

The Methodist Church intended to distribute the book in states where it had affiliates. However, interest was so strong that the American Civil Liberties Union made copies available to law libraries, black colleges, and progressive organizations across the nation. Thurgood Marshall dubbed it "the bible" for civil rights attorneys. The New York County Lawyers' Association *Bar Bulletin* called it "a primary source useful to public and private agencies charged with . . . building better inter-group relations."

. . .

A FEW WEEKS AFTER the book's release, the Women's Division held a celebration and invited representatives from several professional groups to accept first editions. Among these representatives were Dorothy Kenyon, one of the first women judges in New York; Francis J. McConnell, a Methodist bishop who had supported the Odell Waller campaign; Ben Frederick Carruthers, a Romance languages specialist with the U.N. Commission on Human Rights; and Paul North Rice, head of the Reference Department at the New York Public Library.

Murray did not attend the celebration because she was at Freedmen's Hospital, in Washington, D.C. She had pushed herself to the point of exhaustion again. Maida and Aunts Pauline and Sallie stood in for her at the book party. Murray's month-long hospitalization gave her time to read. Among the books she devoured were *This I Remember,* ER's second autobiography, which covered her life as a political wife up to Franklin Roosevelt's death in 1945; *Roosevelt and Hopkins,* Robert E. Sherwood's study of the relationship between the president and his close adviser; and *Roosevelt in Retrospect,* a biography by John Gunther, whose description of ER's efforts to get her husband to intervene in the Waller case confirmed a sincerity of heart Murray had sensed all along.

Moved by the revelation that FDR had written Governor Darden at ER's urging, and that ER had pressed the president past his convictions, Murray opened the next missive with a nickname of her own creation. "Dear 'Mrs. Rovel'—I hope you don't mind my using that term just once. For the past six months I've been so saturated with the life of the Roosevelts—*This I Remember,* Gunther's book, *Roosevelt and Hopkins*—that it's difficult for me to be formal. . . . I understand so many things better about those hectic years 1940–1944 than I did then."

When Murray learned that ER had a "nasty" virus, she urged her "to take care" and, once out of the hospital, sent a "sprig of lilacs." Of her "own health situation," Murray wrote that she was experiencing eye trouble and rapid weight loss. "Today it was 99, about five to eight pounds under normal. The various tests will take about two or three weeks, I'm told, but the tentative indications point toward some glandular disorder which has been a recurr[ence] over a period of fifteen years and has continuously obstructed my progress." Murray yearned to say more; alas, this was not the time. "Someday I wish I could tell you the story of my family," she said. "I think you'd understand a lot of things."

• • •

NOW THAT THE *States' Laws* project was done, Murray went back to her law practice. Increasingly ambivalent about her profession, she considered other options. When she expressed a desire to work for the U.N., ER contacted David Morse of the International Labour Organization in Geneva. "I have known Miss Murray for a long time and she is a very brilliant girl," ER wrote. "If she has the necessary qualifications for the position, I think you would find her a very useful member of your staff." Notwithstanding this endorsement, Morse turned Murray down. "I guess this just isn't my year," she admitted to ER.

As an antidote to Murray's disappointment, Eleanor Roosevelt invited her to the Park Sheraton Hotel on June 13, 1951. ER had an apartment there. Murray took Maida Springer with her. As was often the case, ER had several guests join them. She was usually careful to avoid spending so much time with one person that others felt slighted. But at this gathering, Springer observed, ER became so engrossed in a conversation with Murray about her employment situation, the presidential campaign, and U.S.-Soviet relations "that she had to quickly make amends" to the other guests.

Dorothy Kenyon, lawyer, testifies before the Senate Foreign Relations Subcommittee in response to Joseph McCarthy's charge that she was an instrument of communism, Washington, D.C., 1950. A lifelong champion of human rights and civil liberties, Kenyon and Pauli Murray would collaborate on briefs for the NAACP and ACLU. *(Associated Press and Prints and Photographs Division, Library of Congress)*

32

"I Have to Stand or Fall with the People Who Know Me"

In March 1952, Pauli Murray applied for a research assistant position with the Codification of Laws of Liberia Project at the Cornell University School of Industrial and Labor Relations. The goal of this three-year project was to provide technical support to the Republic of Liberia. The prospect of joining a community of experienced scholars, gaining expertise in international law, and earning a steady salary excited

Murray. Her academic credentials and prior experience with *States' Laws on Race and Color* made her uniquely qualified for this job—or so she thought.

Instead of being offered the position, however, Murray was engulfed by the suspicion that tainted liberal activists as tensions escalated between the United States and her former ally the Soviet Union. These tensions—or the Cold War, as it came to be known—set off a crusade against communism that cast doubt on the loyalty of many Americans. And no one did more to fan the hysteria than Wisconsin senator Joseph R. McCarthy.

According to McCarthy, a broad spectrum of individuals and groups were knowingly and unknowingly supporters of the Communist front. Many of these alleged subversives were in the U.S. State Department, and countless others were fomenting insurrection in other government agencies, the movie industry, academia, and the labor, civil rights, and peace movements.

One of the first individuals McCarthy targeted was Dorothy Kenyon. A New Yorker from a white upper-class family, Kenyon had been elected to Phi Beta Kappa at Smith College, from which she'd graduated in 1908, and she had earned a law degree at New York University in 1917. Devoted to liberal and anti-fascist causes, Kenyon had served as a municipal court judge, deputy commissioner of licenses, and U.S. delegate to the U.N. Commission on the Status of Women. She also "had a penchant for wearing large floppy hats and colorful dresses," Murray recalled.

Kenyon's public-service career came to a halt in 1950, after McCarthy accused her of being "affiliated with twenty-eight Communist-front organizations." At her own insistence, Kenyon testified before the Senate Foreign Relations Subcommittee, denying under oath that she was a Communist. She had worked for "little people and civil liberties," she asserted, and she might have joined or lent her name to some organizations now under suspicion. However, she had not "knowingly identified with any organization, or persons, holding subversive views." Kenyon was eventually cleared of the charge, but she would receive no further political appointments.

The attack on Kenyon was an omen for Murray, for whom Kenyon was an icon. Though they came from different backgrounds, they had a good deal in common. They were intellectually gifted liberal activists. They had chosen a profession dominated by men. And they could be combative when challenged (Kenyon had called McCarthy "an unmitigated liar"). In 1946, when Murray had found the doors of New York

City law firms closed to her, Kenyon had urged her "to stick it out." When *States' Laws on Race and Color* was released, Kenyon had come to the book party.

Another harbinger of the political climate was the rising number of attacks on liberal faculty members. In the state of Washington, where the legislature set up its own Un-American Activities Committee, the University of Washington dismissed three professors for refusing to answer questions about their political affiliations. These attacks would extend to high school teachers and staff members suspected of Communist ties.

Because the Liberian project was funded through a contract with the State Department, which McCarthy had already attacked, Cornell officials wanted to avoid the controversy that had befallen liberals like Kenyon and the schools in Washington State. Martin P. Catherwood, the dean of the school, and Milton R. Konvitz, the project director, asked Murray "if there was anything" about her background "which might be open to question, with reference to the issue of loyalty."

Murray said she was "an outspoken critic of the American government on the issue of civil rights," that she was not and had never been a member of the Communist Party USA, and that she had not "knowingly joined" any group that was a Communist front. She did indicate that from 1936 to 1938 she had belonged to a group opposed to the Communist Party USA, known as the Communist Party (Opposition), that she had renounced the CPO, and that whenever Communists "infiltrated or were attempting to dominate" groups in which she worked, she "actively" opposed them.

Murray's background frightened Catherwood, and he asked her to submit a document "for the record, should some question arise" about her loyalty. Since he provided no guidelines about the kind of information he wanted or needed, she tried to guess which issues to discuss. She drafted a brief description of her published writings and the organizations with which she had been associated. She submitted a copy of her application for admission to the New York bar, which included a detailed background check.

After reviewing Murray's file, Konvitz informed her that Dean Catherwood thought "a recommendation from someone . . . more conservative" than her current references would be beneficial to her candidacy. Taken aback by this request, Murray replied "that as a person of limited means and minority status," she had few opportunities "to come into intimate association with the kind of" people he wanted. Rather than "produce a casual reference who would satisfy the requirement of 'conservative' persuasion," she said, "I have to stand or fall with the people who know me."

Murray had been an activist for nearly two decades, and the House Un-American Activities Committee now considered several groups with which she had been associated to be part of the Communist front. HUAC defined the Communist front as a network of people and organizations whose goal was to advance the cause of communism. Because this network allegedly camouflaged its agenda by hiding behind appeals to humanitarian causes, such as peace and human rights, HUAC published the *Guide to Subversive Organizations and Publications* to expose them.

The May 14, 1951, edition of the *Guide* was a 161-page inventory that listed the Southern Conference for Human Welfare, which Eleanor Roosevelt cofounded, and the CPO, to which Murray briefly belonged, alongside the Communist Party USA. Similarly cited were the Negro People's Committee for Spanish Refugees, from which Murray had resigned, in protest over the efforts of Communists to influence policy, and the China Aid Council, for which FDR's mother, Sara, had once been honorary cochair.

When Murray learned that school officials were uneasy about her background, she volunteered to undergo a loyalty review. They declined on the ground that she was not a employee of the school. Neither Murray's impeccable qualifications nor her impressive references, among whom were ER, Lloyd Garrison, William Hastie, Thurgood Marshall, and A. Philip Randolph, outweighed the concern Cornell officials had about her affiliations. Even a separate statement from ER, indicating that she had known Murray and of her work for "several years" and that Murray was "devoted to the cause of democracy," fell on deaf ears.

In May, Konvitz informed Murray that neither he nor any of his fellow administrators doubted her "qualifications" or her loyalty. All the same, "they felt they ought not to take any chances by inviting the possibility of bad public relations, which might arise out of embarrassing questions" about her past. Of his dilemma, Konvitz told ER, "I share with you a very favorable impression of Miss Murray's character and her devotion to American democracy. I have shown your letter to Dean Catherwood of our School of Industrial and Labor Relations but it is not at all certain that we will be in a position to proceed with her appointment as I had hoped."

Murray viewed Konvitz as "the unhappy go-between," for he had been Thurgood Marshall's assistant general counsel at the NAACP and personally knew most of her references. While Konvitz made no mention of political considerations, ER sensed that fear and guilt by association were at the heart of the school's decision. Indeed, Murray's experience confirmed ER's belief that HUAC and the loyalty review program did more harm than good.

The freedom to "think and to differ" was more important to the "survival of democracy than banning or punishing those who espoused unpopular views within the bounds of the law," ER said at an Americans for Democratic Action conference. "The day I'm afraid to sit down with people I do not know—because five years from now someone will say: 'You sat in the room and five people were communists, you are a communist'—that will be a bad day," she warned. Of Kenyon's integrity and the allegations McCarthy made against her, ER wrote in "My Day," "If all of the Honorable Senator's 'subversives' are as subversive as Miss Kenyon, I think the State Department is entirely safe and the nation will continue on an even keel."

· · ·

ELEANOR ROOSEVELT INVITED MURRAY to lunch at the U.N. on May 8, 1952, to lift her spirits. This time Murray brought along Maida Springer's twenty-two-year-old son, Eric, a second-year law student at New York University. ER was "absolutely furious" about the Cornell situation, Murray reported later to Caroline Ware. ER had insisted that Murray not give up: "One has to go on with one's life, one cannot stop, no matter what."

ER was also concerned about another friend embroiled in controversy. Edith Sampson, an attorney who was the first black delegate to the U.N., had purportedly told an audience in Copenhagen that the reports of racial violence in the U.S. were "exaggerated stories, spread only by the 'enemies of America.'" William Worthy, a CORE activist who had risked his life as a bus rider with Bayard Rustin, was in the audience. That Sampson had dismissed the "race riots, physical aggression against Negroes, or the pall of fear under which millions of Negroes in the South are obliged to live" made him angry. Worthy characterized Sampson's speech as "dishonest" and "revolting" propaganda in a provocative essay entitled "In Cloud-Cuckoo Land" that appeared in *The Crisis*.

Given Murray's support of CORE and the bus riders, her knowledge of racial violence in the South, her loyalty to ER, and her professional friendship with Sampson, who belonged to a small circle of black women with advanced law degrees (Sampson held a master of laws from Loyola

University Chicago School of Law), it must have been hard for her to take sides. Perhaps, for this reason, the usually outspoken Murray attached a copy of Worthy's essay without comment to a thank-you note to ER that read, "It was wonderful to have lunch with you and Eric is 'tickled as a dog with two tails.'"

PART VI

DRAWING CLOSER
AS FRIENDS,
1952–55

Pauli Murray (front row, sixth from the right, in black-and-white top) and James Baldwin (back row, second from the left) were the first African American writers admitted as fellows to The MacDowell Colony, Peterborough, New Hampshire, in August 1954. Other literary artists pictured are: Sol Stein (back row, far left) and, in the front row, Virginia Sorensen (second from left), Peter Viereck (fifth from left), Elizabeth Shepley Sergeant (fifth from the right), Gordon Reevey (third from right) and Sara Henderson Hay (second from right). *(Milford Historical Society)*

33

"I Could Write in Privacy Without Interruption"

Unable to challenge the rejection from Cornell and the "shadowy inference" its officials raised about her background, Pauli Murray turned to a project in the fall of 1952 that gave her a chance to say who she really was. That project was a memoir of the Fitzgeralds, her fiercely devout and patriotic maternal ancestors, who were the "earliest and most enduring" of all her "past associations." The idea of writing a family memoir had been incubating since her college days. Stephen Vincent Benét, with whom Murray had shared sketches a decade earlier, had recognized her work as "the germ from which a remarkable novel or a remarkable story might come." He had insisted that she "do some more" and that she tell her story "from the inside and with sensitiveness and truth."

Despite Benét's encouragement, Murray put the book on hold to go to law school and start a legal career. Not until the difficulties with Cornell did the desire to write overtake her. One day, she "rolled a sheet of paper into the typewriter" and pecked out a sentence that began a four-year journey of research and writing.

Pressed for time and money, Murray suspended her law practice and took a job with the New York City Welfare Department as a caseworker. She wrote before and after work and on weekends. Once she'd completed an outline and several chapters, literary agent Marie F. Rodell and Harper & Brothers editor Elizabeth Lawrence Kalashnikoff helped Murray secure a book contract and a residential fellowship at The MacDowell Colony, in New Hampshire. Of her time there, Murray would say with delight, "I could write in privacy without interruption."

The MacDowell was the oldest residential retreat for writers, composers, and visual artists in the United States. Joining Murray in the 1954 fellows class was writer James Baldwin. Fourteen years younger than Murray, Baldwin was a native New Yorker with large, arresting eyes. He was "dedicated to becoming a great artist," and he regularly missed the socially expected communal dinner. Murray, who often took supper to Baldwin in his cottage, usually found him tearing "himself to pieces over his typewriter." Together, they would occasionally venture into town to see a movie or have a beer.

Baldwin had already published his first novel, *Go Tell It on the Mountain,* a semiautobiographical account of his boyhood in Harlem. He was working on *Notes of a Native Son,* which was a collection of personal essays about race, and *Giovanni's Room,* a novel whose main character, a young white man, wrestles with his homosexuality, an experience Baldwin knew firsthand.

Murray's writing, like Baldwin's, drew on life experience, but she would not explicitly raise issues of sexual orientation beyond references to her childhood tomboyishness. Multiple factors influenced her reticence. In contrast to Baldwin, who in 1948 had moved to France, where he found a measure of social and artistic acceptance, Murray lived in a milieu where politicians and religious leaders denounced homosexuals as criminally prone degenerates. The reputations and careers of people she knew and admired, such as Bayard Rustin, had been tarnished by revelations of homosexual relations. And she knew that lesbians, like gay men, had no protection against harassment and baseless charges of disloyalty.

The political climate was not the sole reason Murray wrote or spoke only with trusted friends and family members about her sexuality. She had been studying the medical literature for years, and she had yet to find an explanation for homosexuality she could accept. She was attracted to women and she considered herself normal. If, according to science, being homosexual meant one had a psychological disorder and was, therefore, not normal, then she would reject this categorization.

Murray's family background also played a role in her decision to be circumspect about her sexuality. She was a devout Episcopalian reared by elderly kin with Victorian values. Whereas Aunts Pauline and Sallie had accepted Murray's relationships with women, some relatives and friends did not. Moreover, the thought of adding to the rumors about her parents' deaths, which had marked the Murrays as mentally unstable, was something Pauli could not bear.

. . .

WHILE MURRAY RETREATED at the colony, Eleanor Roosevelt was coming home from the U.N. assembly meeting in Paris "the long way." She started in the Middle East, stopping in Lebanon, Syria, Jordan, and Israel, visiting historic and religious sites, humanitarian projects, and a cross-section of people. From Israel, she flew to Pakistan, where she toured a maternity ward sponsored by the All-Pakistan Women's Association. From Pakistan, she went to India, where Prime Minister Jawaharlal Nehru and his sister Vijaya Lakshmi Pandit, who headed the Indian delegation to the U.N., welcomed her.

In India, ER addressed parliament, met with women's groups, and visited a school Mahatma Gandhi had established for the untouchables, who, in accordance with the caste system, were excluded from society. She met with students at the University of Bombay against the advice of officials, who feared protesters would insult her. She fielded questions about discrimination, attitudes toward communism, and censorship in American universities with confidence and ease.

Because ER's father, Elliott, had promised they would see India together, this leg of the trip held special significance. ER yearned for him when she reached the famous Khyber Pass, connecting northern Pakistan with Afghanistan. She was only ten when he died. Still, she remembered his stories of "going through this pass on Indian hunting trips." She also went to the Taj Mahal, his favorite site, three times. Each time, she "hated to leave."

Despite the blurriness, Pauli Murray adored this snapshot she took of her "three" aunts—(left to right) Sallie F. Small, Eleanor Roosevelt, and Pauline F. Dame—in the yard at Val-Kill, Hyde Park, New York, on August 15, 1952. ER was "happy to have the picture" as well. *(The Schlesinger Library, Radcliffe Institute, Harvard University, and the Estate of Pauli Murray)*

34

"We Consider You a Member of the Family"

On August 15, 1952, Eleanor Roosevelt treated Murray and her aunts Pauline and Sallie to lunch at Val-Kill and a tour of Franklin Roosevelt's birthplace. Dining with them at umbrella-shaded tables in front of a "beautiful blue pool" were Tommy; Ruth, the wife of ER's grandson Curtis Roosevelt; Anne Roosevelt, the pregnant wife of ER's son John; and three Roosevelt grandchildren. ER and Tommy heaped generous helpings of fish, corn on the cob, salad, buttered bread, peaches, and cake on plates, which the children carried to the adults. The dinnerware was a practical combination of silver serving dishes and paper plates and cups.

Aunt Pauline and Tommy chatted about teaching. Aunt Sallie and Anne Roosevelt discussed "raising and training" children. Murray and ER "talked politics." ER thought the Republican candidate for president, former five-star general and commander of Allied forces Dwight David Eisenhower, unbeatable. Just the same, she was convinced that Illinois governor Adlai E. Stevenson II was the best man for the job. His intelligence and "liberal civil rights record" impressed Murray, too, and she would soon join New York Volunteers for Stevenson.

After lunch, ER drove Murray and her aunts to the entrance of the library and museum, where a guide took them on a tour. They admired FDR's collection of model ships and stuffed birds; the Dresden china, chandelier, and mantelpiece in the Dresden Room, the cozy room where his mother, Sara, read and wrote her letters; and the family library, from whose window the president had addressed his neighbors on the eve of his elections.

All of the furnishings, including his spartan boyhood room, with its small brass bed and school diplomas, had been restored. Near the bathtub was his wheelchair. Hanging in a clothes chest was the presidential cape. His felt hats rested on an upper shelf. Fala's blanket, collar, and leash lay on a chair.

Murray and her aunts exited the house and crossed the lawn to the Rose Garden, where a "white plain marble monument, eight feet long, four feet wide and three feet high," marked the president's grave. Its inscription read:

FRANKLIN DELANO ROOSEVELT
1882–1945
ANNA ELEANOR ROOSEVELT
1884–19

Fala's resting place, behind the monument near a sundial, was covered by a "flat marker level with the ground."

Their final stop was the Presidential Library. There they saw Franklin's and Eleanor's christening gowns, the "little kiltie Scottish plaid suit" the president "wore when he was six," and a collection of photographs that documented his life from childhood to Yalta. Murray was an avid diarist, and she was fascinated by the January 30, 1882, entry Franklin Roosevelt's father, James, made in his diary: "My Sallie gave birth to a bouncing baby boy today—he weighed 10 pounds at birth."

Upon returning home, Murray and her aunts composed a letter for family and friends, capturing the high points of their visit. The most emotional moment for Murray was when she took a photograph of ER flanked by Aunts Pauline and Sallie in their Sunday best on the lawn. Of that snapshot, Murray wrote to ER, "It's not the best picture because I was so nervous taking it, my camera shook, but it rests on our mantelpiece with other numerous pictures of the family, and in our spiritual way, we consider you a member of the family."

35

"I Was Deeply Moved That You Counted Me
Among Your Close Friends"

On November 4, 1952, Dwight Eisenhower became the thirty-fourth president of the United States. Although he pledged to strengthen the United Nations in his inaugural address, he did not reappoint Eleanor Roosevelt to the U.S. delegation. His decision worried her supporters, many of whom saw her as the agency's most influential advocate and voice of goodwill.

ER's departure compounded Pauli Murray's disappointment over Adlai Stevenson's defeat. He had carried the black vote nationwide; and in Harlem, where Murray canvassed, he garnered 83 percent of the vote. That the new president was a war general who seemed unwilling to call Senator McCarthy on his red-baiting tactics disheartened Murray even more.

The day after Eisenhower's inauguration, Murray was thumbing through the February 1953 issue of *Ebony* magazine when she discovered ER's essay "Some of My Best Friends Are Negro." The cover featured a photograph of ER and Mary McLeod Bethune seated together. Inside, Murray was mentioned and pictured alongside Walter White, Bethune, musician Josh White, U.N. delegates Channing Tobias and Edith Sampson, and Nobel Peace Prize laureate Ralph Bunche.

ER admitted in this candid piece that she had had no significant contact with African Americans or any awareness of racial discrimination until she was in her mid-teens. Not until adulthood did she develop genuine friendships with blacks and relate to them as "social equals." "One of my finest young friends," she boasted, "is a charming woman lawyer—Pauli Murray, who has been quite a firebrand at times but of whom I am very fond. She is a lovely person who has struggled and come through very well." Of Murray's growth in the fourteen years they had been friends, ER wrote, "I think there were times when she might have done foolish things. But now I think she is well ready to be of real use. My relationship with Pauli is very satisfying."

ER's upbringing made it difficult for her to address people by their given names, and her status made friends reluctant to call her Eleanor, she told readers. To bridge the social gap, she encouraged young and "really close friends" to call her "Mrs. R.," and she pushed herself to use their first names. ER probably did not know that Murray's first name was actually Anna, and so called her Pauli, as she preferred.

That ER spoke so honestly about their friendship in *Ebony*, a glossy, photo-rich African American–interest magazine with more than five hundred thousand subscribers, pleased and amused Murray. "I howled when I read that line about the 'firebrand,'" she wrote to ER. "I had always thought of myself as a 'spearhead' but never a firebrand. Anyway, I was deeply moved that you counted me among your close friends and delighted that you thought of me as Pauli—as naturally as it should be."

. . .

WHEN MURRAY'S LETTER ARRIVED, ER was in the midst of packing and saying good-bye to her colleagues at the U.N. "I am glad you liked the appellation," she replied. "Of course I count you among my close friends." Leaving the U.N., where she had friends and work of tremendous import, made ER sad. The days had been arduous, the victories hard to come by, but cherish them she would.

On December 10, 1948, in Paris, after the assembly had adopted the Universal Declaration of Human Rights, for which she had so diligently labored, ER had hosted a champagne reception for a small circle of colleagues. Later, as she was about to exit the Palais des Chaillot, she gave in to unbridled joy. ER "ran, gathered momentum, and then slid down" the hall's empty, black marble floor, "her arms outstretched in triumph." It was so much fun that ER "did it again," she wrote to her niece and namesake Eleanor Roosevelt II.

In addition to losing her U.N. post, ER lost her incomparable assistant, collaborator, and confidante of thirty years. Malvina Thompson died of a brain hemorrhage on April 12, 1953. She was sixty-one. Her death coincided with the eighth anniversary of Franklin Roosevelt's death from the same illness. ER had attended a memorial ceremony at

FDR's grave site earlier and arrived at Tommy's bedside just before she passed. "Her standards were high for me, as well as for herself," ER said of her beloved friend in "My Day." To Murray, she wrote, "I will miss her terribly and I know you will as you were very fond of her."

Murray was indeed fond of Tommy and had frequently praised her in letters to ER. Tommy had faithfully routed Murray's materials to ER, scheduled their social visits, and been present at most of their gatherings. To be sure, the friendship between Pauli and Eleanor could not have flourished without Tommy's supportive hand.

Left to right: attorneys George E. C. Hayes, Thurgood Marshall, and James M. Nabrit on the steps of the U.S. Supreme Court after the NAACP's historic victory in the *Brown* case, Washington, D.C., May 17, 1954. "For those of us who are restrained Episcopalians," Pauli Murray wrote to Eleanor Roosevelt, "this decision has had the effect of a good old time 'conversion,' with shouting and singing." *(Associated Press)*

36

"I Know How Much This Decision Means to You"

Pauli Murray spent the first half of 1954 tracing her maternal ancestors, the Fitzgeralds, through census, tax, and property records from Chester County, Pennsylvania, to Orange County, North Carolina. On May 17, she was at the typewriter mulling over chapter 10 of her memoir when Aunt Sallie burst into the room with news of a landmark decision by the U.S. Supreme Court. The high court had ruled unanimously in the case of *Brown v. Board of Education of Topeka* that racial segregation of the public schools violated the Equal Protection Clause of the Fourteenth Amendment. NAACP chief counsel Thurgood Marshall had represented the plaintiffs.

Murray was ecstatic. The *Brown* decision confirmed what she had known all along—that black segregated schools were inherently unequal to white schools. "I think I can now understand for the first time how my great-grandfather felt when he, a former slave, read the Emancipation Proclamation," she said in a letter to the editor published in the *New York Times*. "I could not let the event of the United States Supreme Court decision grow colder without making some personal contact with you," she wrote jubilantly to ER. "I know how much this decision means to you, how it is an individual as well as a national triumph, and how much you have done to bring it about. . . . I'm writing a book called *Proud Shoes* which Harper and Bros. will publish if I ever finish it. Another Supreme Court decision like May 17th and I'll never finish it. I'll be too happy! I think, however, you're going to like it."

Murray's happiness was sweetened by her connection to several people involved in the *Brown* case. She knew Chief Justice Earl Warren from her days in California, when she was acting deputy attorney general and he was governor. She had known Marshall since the 1930s, when she'd sought his help in challenging the University of North Carolina's whites-only admissions policy. The team of lawyers who helped Marshall shape the *Brown* brief included George E. C. Hayes and Spottswood W. Robinson III, with whom Murray had studied at Howard University School of Law.

She was astonished to learn later from Robinson that the NAACP defense team had used an essay she wrote in Leon Ransom's civil rights seminar as background for the case. In that essay, "Should the Civil Rights Cases and *Plessy v. Ferguson* Be Overruled?," Murray had argued that segregated schooling placed black children "in an inferior social and legal position." Finding "no legal precedents to rely on," she had drawn on the work of social scientists to demonstrate that segregation did "violence to the personality of the individual affected whether he is white or black."

Representative of this kind of work was the research of Mamie Phipps Clark and Kenneth B. Clark, who began their research on discrimination and children's identity development as graduate students at Howard in the psychology department. Their experiments with black and white dolls, which demonstrated black children's preference for white skin, had grown out of Mamie's 1939 master's thesis, "The Development of Consciousness of Self in Negro Pre-School Children." The Clarks made an impression on Chief Justice Earl Warren, who said in the court's opinion, "To separate them [black children] from others of similar age and qualifications solely because of their race generates a feeling of inferiority as to their status in the community that may affect their hearts and minds in a way unlikely ever to be undone."

The significance of the moment prompted Murray to propose that the NAACP award the Spingarn Medal to Eleanor Roosevelt and Lillian Smith for paving the way for the *Brown* decision. But to do so would require the association's board to open the competition, presently reserved for blacks, to whites. Changing the policy was precisely what Murray asked the board to do. To deny the award to these women on racial grounds was "rubbish," she protested. ER and Smith had stood firm in the face of criticism about their friendships with African Americans, their support of civil rights, and their uncompromising writings. "If legalities must be observed," Murray told ER, "then any one of us would be willing to donate a drop a blood (Smile). . . . Not that you need a Spingarn," she added, "but it would do our souls good to give it to you."

· · ·

ELEANOR ROOSEVELT WAS APPEARING on the *Tex and Jinx* television talk show the day the Supreme Court announced the *Brown* opinion. She was "delighted" that the ruling "wiped out segregation in the schools." She was especially pleased that the decision was unanimous, for this made it hard for segregated school districts to find hope in a dissenting opinion. Because the ruling removed "one of the arguments offered by totalitarian states against democratic states," ER believed the *Brown* ruling strengthened the United States' standing in the world community. On the question of interracial marriage, that hot-button issue that so inflamed segregationists, she said, "One can no longer lay down rules as to what individuals will do in any area of their lives in a world that is changing as fast as ours is changing today."

ER loved Murray's reaction to the *Brown* decision so much that she shared it in "My Day." "I have been thinking more and more of how some of my friends, to whom the Supreme Court decision on segregation was a matter of great personal concern, are feeling now that it is over," she wrote. "I would like, therefore, to give you a little quotation from a letter sent me by a brilliant young Negro woman lawyer. She tells me she is writing a book which will be published, if she ever finishes it, and adds, 'Another Supreme Court decision like May 17 and I will never finish it. I will be too happy!' "

Writer Langston Hughes (front right) appears with his attorney, Frank D. Reeves (front left), before the Senate Permanent Subcommittee on Investigations, Washington, D.C., March 1953. The questions raised, directly and by innuendo, frightened Pauli Murray. *(Associated Press)*

37

"I Cannot Live with Fear"

Pauli Murray's elation over the *Brown* decision was dampened by the ongoing hearings of the Senate Permanent Subcommittee on Investigations, chaired by Joseph McCarthy, and by the growing number of State Department and military personnel, intellectuals, artists, and labor, civil rights, and peace activists denied work because of alleged ties to subversive groups. Hundreds of entertainers and artists had been suspended, fired, or blacklisted. Eventually, 214 witnesses would be summoned to testify in public before McCarthy's subcommittee. Some 395 would be questioned in closed session. Among those prominent figures interrogated were cartoonist Herbert Block, Pulitzer Prize–winning composer Aaron Copland, writers Dashiell Hammett and Lillian Hellman, and artist Rockwell Kent. The writer Langston Hughes was summoned, too.

Hughes, who testified in closed testimony on March 24, 1953, and in public two days later, retained Murray's friend Lloyd Garrison and

NAACP attorney Frank D. Reeves as his counsel. The purpose of the hearing, Senator Everett Dirksen stated at the outset, was to determine if books by certain authors, purchased with government funds and placed in libraries abroad by the State Department and the International Information Administration, promoted American culture and values. While subcommittee members never clarified for Hughes what they considered an acceptable representation of American culture, they deemed his writings un-American, pro-Communist, and anti-Christian.

Roy Cohn, chief counsel for the subcommittee, alternated in a closed session between asking Hughes if he was or had ever been a Communist and calling him an "undeviating follower of the Communist party." Cohn hounded Hughes about the meaning of two poems, "Goodbye Christ" and "Put Another 'S' in the USA," published twenty years earlier. Cohn grilled Hughes about his affiliation with the League of American Writers and about the trip he took with twenty-two black artists and intellectuals to the Soviet Union in 1932 for a film project on African American life.

Hughes denied in open and closed sessions that he was a Communist. He did admit that communism had seemed promising when he was a young man frustrated by segregation, that some of his early writings had appeared in Communist periodicals, and that he had been associated with the International Labor Defense campaign to free the Scottsboro Boys, which had been headed by William L. Patterson, a Communist. Now that Hughes was "older" and could "see social progress accelerating itself more rapidly" in the recent Supreme Court decisions and the work of the Fair Employment Practices Committee, communism had no appeal for him.

Hughes confirmed that he had written the poems the subcommittee cited, but he rejected Cohn's interpretation of certain passages. "A portion of a poem," said Hughes, like "a bar of music out of context[,] does not give you the idea of the whole thing." Because the poems Cohn singled out were misconstrued and "not very representative" of his writings, Hughes said, he agreed that they should not be in American libraries abroad.

Cohn, a homosexual who would die of AIDS thirty-three years later, badgered some witnesses into admitting that they were homosexual and demanded that they name others. Cohn did not explicitly ask Hughes about his sexuality; however, he was asked about his relationship status. This indirect question about the personal life of the fifty-one-year-old, never-married writer created an aura of suspicion.

Murray admired Hughes. Like him, she had migrated to New York

City in the 1920s and immersed herself in a social milieu that fueled her activism and writing. They were friendly, and their paths had crossed several times. The Harlem Suitcase Theatre, which Hughes had cofounded with Louise Thompson, the wife of William Patterson, gave a benefit performance for the Negro People's Committee for Spanish Refugees when Murray was acting secretary. She had contributed a short story and poem to Nancy Cunard's *Negro* anthology and "protest poetry" to a special issue of the journal *Voices*. Hughes played an influential role in both projects. Murray had also worked with groups that had Communists, former Communists, and socialists as members. She had even considered joining Hughes and the group of blacks who went to the Soviet Union. Only lack of funds and the need to finish college had stopped her from going.

Hughes was not the only influential African American Murray knew and admired whose loyalty was questioned. The New Jersey Anti-Communist League had accused Democratic Party stalwart Mary McLeod Bethune of subversive affiliations the year before. Dorothy Boulding Ferebee, a physician who had treated Murray at the Howard University infirmary and had succeeded Bethune as president of the National Council of Negro Women, was summoned by McCarthy's committee. And Nobel laureate Ralph Bunche would be interrogated for twelve hours by the International Organizations Employees Loyalty Board. Murray shuddered at the thought of what could happen to her if the loyalty and reputations of people as well liked as Hughes, and as politically connected as Bethune, Ferebee, and Bunche, could be impugned. That Caroline Ware, Murray's friend and mentor, was denied permission to travel to Chile by the International Organizations review board intensified her fear.

"Most of these investigations seemed to do more harm than good," Eleanor Roosevelt said of the government's loyalty reviews. "If we continue the Congressional investigations . . . , we are going to find ourselves living in an atmosphere akin to that of Communist countries, for we are using the very weapons which those countries use." Of the accusations about her old friend, ER insisted, "Mary McLeod Bethune would meet the Devil and confront him with Christ and I feel quite sure that she and Christ would triumph." Of Bunche, with whom she had worked closely at the U.N., ER asserted that his extraordinary service to the nation left "no question" about his loyalty.

ER was opposed to communism, as well as such measures as the McCarran Internal Security Act. This bill, passed by Congress over President Truman's veto, stripped away the rights of free speech and freedom of assembly for persons suspected of being Communist or fascist sympathizers. The fear fostered by this legislation and by governmental bodies, such as the House Un-American Activities Committee, troubled ER. "I have always thought," she said in her column, "that a strong democracy should stand by its fundamental beliefs and that a citizen of the United States should be considered innocent until he is proved guilty."

. . .

FOR MURRAY, the McCarthy hearings were "like garbage thrown upon the shining surface of the Supreme Court decision." That the questions witnesses faced were often based on misinformation, outright inaccuracies, and "derogatory material" unnerved her. "As a serum against fear," Murray committed herself to writing "one letter of personal faith each day to some friend or person." One of her first letters went to Ralph Bunche, for whom she prayed as if he were a relative.

Murray had long believed that she was under surveillance. Her suspicions were confirmed when a librarian at Howard University told her that "operatives" of the Federal Bureau of Investigation had come to campus "looking for pictures" of her and her friend Pauline Redmond Coggs, who now lived with her family in Milwaukee. Furious at being investigated "behind one's back," Murray made a "bold" decision. She sent J. Edgar Hoover a brief "personal history" and a recent photograph to avoid "misidentification." Murray informed the director that a background dossier was available from the appellate division of the New York State Supreme Court and that her fingerprints were already on file with the bureau. Her knees nearly buckled at the post office the day she mailed the registered letter, return receipt requested.

Despite Murray's assertive stance with the FBI, she was experiencing intense anxiety. She knew that her activism, writings, and sexuality made her a likely target for McCarthy's subcommittee. She was worried about her health and about her brother William, who was a patient at St. Elizabeths psychiatric hospital in Washington, D.C. He had had "an experimental lobotomy several years ago and it left him balanced but without any initiative."

"I cannot live with fear and the doctor has just told me I have a nervous heart," Murray wrote to Pauline Coggs, whose personal and professional experience gave her a profound understanding of Murray's emotional struggle. Murray and Coggs had made a pact a decade earlier to talk each other through the mood swings from which they both suffered and which Coggs referred to as manic depression. "I call it a frightened heart," Murray continued. "It has been frightened all of my life because of race. Now it is frightened because of something deeper than race—the atmosphere which threatens one's integrity—an atmosphere of fear."

The day after Murray wrote to Hoover and Coggs, she reached out to ER. That day, June 6, 1954, was the tenth anniversary of D-Day. "Since the Supreme Court decision and the McCarthy hearings I have felt the need to be in close personal touch with dear friends who have my kind of faith in America and who are unwilling to turn our country over to the apostles of fear," Murray said. "So reflecting, I wrote to Pauline Coggs and I thought you might like to read my letter. It seems to me that we should now make this day F-Day, or Faith-Day. I'm hoping this letter to Pauline may in some small personal way start a chain reaction."

By sharing the Coggs letter with ER, Murray did something she had not done before. She lifted the veil that covered a bold persona, admitting that she was under a doctor's care for anxiety and that her brother William had been lobotomized.

Frank Horne (left) and Corienne Robinson Morrow
(right), veteran staffers in the Race Relations Division of
the Housing and Home Finance Agency, circa 1950. After
they were accused of being security risks and fired, Pauli
Murray wrote to Eleanor Roosevelt, "There appears to be
not one person in the United States who is *not* suspected
of being a disloyal, indiscreet, security-risk American!"
(Amistad Research Center, Tulane University)

38

"Some Fear-Mongers May Feel That Even President Eisenhower Might Be a Security Risk"

Pauli Murray tried to keep her focus on the victory of the *Brown* decision. Yet it was difficult for her to hold the fear of an FBI investigation at bay. At times, she felt as if the "flesh was literally shaking off" her bones. By June 1954, she was anemic and fifteen pounds below normal weight. She suffered from heart palpitations, insomnia, and a persistent dry cough. She had smoked a pack and a half of cigarettes a day for twenty-five years, and her anxiety intensified the addiction.

Murray's longtime physician, Dr. May Chinn, diagnosed "an overactive thyroid" and recommended surgery to remove a nodule. This diagnosis was a breakthrough, for now Murray had a medical explanation for her nervous energy, mood swings, persistent weight loss, and irregular heartbeat. She canceled a much-anticipated luncheon with Eleanor Roosevelt and confessed that she was "'a panty-waist' about operations." But it would be "a blessing," Murray believed, if the procedure relieved the "disturbances" that had periodically disrupted her life.

The day before the surgery, Murray lay in her hospital bed reading Lillian Smith's latest book, *The Journey.* Smith had finished it while recovering from breast cancer surgery. *The Journey* was an autobiographical reflection on the South, in which Smith revealed a vulnerable side of herself that Murray had not seen. Struck by Smith's openness, Murray lingered over the passage that read, "But how hard it is, when we are struggling with fears, to think beyond ourselves and the present moment. Even the most responsible of us is not in a learning mood on those days, days which sometimes stretch into years, years when the quiet voice of reason is drowned out by the cries of the terrorized child within us."

Murray put her reading aside when flowers and a get-well note from ER arrived. ER was preparing for her first trip to the Soviet Union, and she hoped to find Murray "well and strong" upon her return. Murray scribbled a letter, explaining the procedure she was about to have. She also asked ER to come see her at Freedmen's Hospital and to write to Lillian Smith, as she had "lost a great deal of tissue."

ER promised to "drop in" on Murray "if at all possible" and to make contact with Smith. ER admired Smith and considered her a friend. ER had lobbied Franklin Roosevelt to lift the U.S. Postal Service ban on *Strange Fruit,* Smith's 1944 debut novel about an interracial romance. Like Murray, ER found the psychological insights in *The Journey* fascinating. In fact, she was reading it aloud to her friend the Broadway producer John Golden, who was almost blind.

. . .

WHILE MURRAY WAS IN THE HOSPITAL, she received a letter signed by J. Edgar Hoover's secretary, Helen Gandy. The letter stated that no record in FBI files indicated that a representative of the agency had inquired about Murray at Howard University and that "such a request might well have been made by a representative of some other Government agency."

Whether the bureau was currently investigating Murray or had previously sent an agent to Howard is difficult to ascertain. The FBI records on her contained reports of uneven accuracy from informants dating back to the early 1940s of her affiliation with groups that either the U.S.

attorney general or the House Un-American Activities Committee cited as subversive. According to an internal office memorandum, informants said Murray was an active member of the Socialist Party, the National Lawyers Guild, and the national committee of the Civil Rights Defense Committee; that she was involved in the Workers Defense League; that she subscribed to the Socialist Workers Party weekly, the *Militant*, in 1943; and that she was a delegate to the January 1944 National Council for a Permanent Fair Employment Practices Committee conference in Washington, D.C.

There is little doubt that Murray's activism, political writings, and friendships with liberal activists, including Lillian Smith and ER, both of whom the bureau surveilled, attracted FBI attention. Hoover intensely disliked ER, and the thirty-five-thousand-page file the bureau created on her at his direction would become the largest assembled for an individual prior to the 1960s.

Eager to push her fear aside, Murray took the bureau's disclaimer at face value. After the surgery, she propped herself up in her hospital bed and typed a four-page, single-spaced appeal to ER on behalf of an old friend, Corienne Robinson Morrow. Morrow, an administrative staff member in the Race Relations Division of the Federal Department of Housing, had been suspended in March without pay by a loyalty review board, despite two decades of meritorious service. The basis stated for the suspension was the charge that she had been a member of the Young Workers League and a probationary member of the Communist Party in Chicago in 1925–26. As part of its investigation, the board also raised questions about the loyalty of Morrow's husband, Captain Edward Morrow. An army review board had accused him of belonging to subversive groups, Murray wrote.

As far as she was concerned, Corienne Morrow was an unheralded civil rights hero upon whom many "front men" relied "to negotiate with difficult and uneducated officials on race relations." (Among these unnamed front men were Morrow's supervisors, Robert C. Weaver, an economist, and Frank Horne, both of whom had been members of FDR's unofficial Negro Cabinet.) Because of Morrow's status as a female assistant, her male superiors customarily took credit for her behind-the-scenes work. Fair housing advocates regularly bolstered legal arguments against restrictive covenants with Morrow's research, which showed that blacks "received less housing value for the housing dollar they spend than other groups."

Almost fifty and suddenly unemployed, Morrow and her husband lost their home. Unlike Mary McLeod Bethune and Ralph Bunche, who were defended by powerful friends when they were accused of Communist affiliation, Morrow had no one except Murray, who took the matter to ER.

The charge that Morrow was a Communist was "ridiculous," Murray told ER. Morrow was "a violent anti-Communist" and a member of the Americans for Democratic Action, the liberal anti-Communist organization ER had cofounded. Frustrated, Murray said, "I would not doubt that some fear-mongers may feel that even President Eisenhower might be a security risk."

What Murray did not write was that she thought Morrow's suspension was about more than alleged Communist affiliation or her advocacy for desegregated housing. Murray believed, she confided to Pauline Redmond Coggs, that the board suspected that Morrow's marriage was a deception and that both she and her husband were homosexual. Coggs, who lived in Washington, D.C., and worked in the federal government, had possibly met Corienne in a social or professional setting. The circle of blacks at the administrative level in the federal government was small and tight-knit. It is unclear if Coggs had met Edward Morrow, about whom not much is known. He was a native of Huron, South Dakota, who had graduated from Yale University in 1931, the only black student in his class. He had worked as a journalist in Harlem. It is clear that Coggs knew of Corienne as a friend of Murray's, and the worry Murray expressed about her own vulnerability as a lesbian and the possibility of an investigation by the FBI gave Coggs the impression that Corienne was lesbian as well.

Since the publication of the 1950 Senate report *Employment of Homosexuals and Other Sex Perverts in Government* and President Eisenhower's 1953 Executive Order 10450 on security requirements for government employment, loyalty boards had charged thousands of government workers and military personnel with engaging in "behavior, activities, or associations" that made them security risks. "Sexual perversion," one of the behaviors for which one could be dismissed, included homosexuality. Thus, homosexuals and those accused of having homosexual tendencies were said to be morally prone toward criminality and communism, and could be dismissed summarily without the right to appeal, even when the allegations came from anonymous sources.

Because the executive order permitted review boards to investigate an employee's "illness, including any mental condition," sexuality, and political background, it locked the door to federal employment against

Murray. Not only was she a committed liberal activist, she was a lesbian with a record of hospitalizations precipitated by thyroid disease, bouts of malnutrition and exhaustion, and the stress of an unrelenting battle against discrimination on multiple fronts. Still, her conscience demanded that she try to help Morrow.

. . .

WHILE MURRAY ALTERNATED BETWEEN resting and working on Morrow's appeal, ER went to the fiftieth reunion of the Harvard College class of 1904. She addressed the group on "women's achievements" as a leader in her own right, as well as the wife of the most famous class member. Following her talk, ER joined Franklin Roosevelt's classmates at a baseball game and then for dinner at the Fogg Art Museum. It was a delightful weekend, and she "wished so much" that her husband "could have been there."

39

"*What I Have to Say Now Is* Entirely Personal"

P auli Murray was so preoccupied with her health and a gravely ill relative that she did not know Eleanor Roosevelt had postponed her trip to the Soviet Union. The visa for the journalist *Look* magazine assigned to accompany ER had been delayed. With a month to do as she pleased, ER decided to go see Murray at Freedmen's Hospital. When ER walked into her room at four o'clock in the afternoon on June 30, 1954, Murray grinned liked the Cheshire cat.

Word of ER's presence spread like wildfire, kindling excitement among the hospital staff members and patients. Doctors and nurses who had never reviewed Murray's medical chart suddenly decided she required immediate attention. As soon as her doctor, Arthur F. Burton, got out of surgery, he came to her doorway in his green uniform and stared at the famous visitor, who placed her arms around Murray's shoulders as Murray pranced up the hall "like a little happy elf." ER's visit was an expression of her affection for Murray, and it was the perfect curative for low spirits.

Adding to Murray's delight was a fortuitous meeting between ER and Corienne Morrow. Morrow's father was also a patient at the hospital, and she had come to take him home. When Morrow stopped to look in on Murray, she bumped into ER. Murray introduced them.

On Independence Day, four days after ER's visit, Murray penned a four-page letter with the words "PERSONAL AND CONFIDEN-TIAL" capitalized and underlined at the top of the first page. In her missive, Murray spoke of "the deep residuum of love" people had for the former first lady and the late president and her belief that ER was destined for the presidency. With an "army of trained New Deal–Fair Deal babies who have now come to maturity—as I believe I have done"—and a bright, young running mate like Adlai Stevenson, Murray wrote, "you could toss off the problems of State in the same way that your 'school-teacher' soul tossed off the Russians in the Commission on Human Rights."

Halfway through her letter, Murray described a family secret known to only a handful of friends, such as Ruth Powell, who had accompanied Murray to Saint Elizabeths Hospital to visit her brother William. It had taken Murray sixteen years to share this story with ER. "What I have to say now is *entirely personal,*" Murray began.

> My reasons for behaving as I have done over the years, of being an unreconstructed rebel, of searching in many places for the answers to my life, is due in large part to the double tragedy of my parents— whose ages and the ages of whose children largely correspond to those of the Franklin D. and Eleanor Roosevelt family. My mother (whose picture you saw) died in 1914 when I was just over three, from what was diagnosed as a cerebral accident. However, a rumor arose at the same time that she committed suicide because she was in her seventh pregnancy, my father was hopelessly mentally ill (he had had typhoid and brain fever several years earlier) and . . . under these conditions she could not face bringing an additional child into the world. Three years later my father was hospitalized in Crowns-ville, and six years later he was murdered by a guard there. Two of my own siblings have been hospitalized in mental institutions, and the fear of insanity has hung over all six of us, despite evidence of stamina and intellect. This double tragedy has cast a shadow over a very fine, potentially creative family, and we have not known how to handle it. We have been afraid that the tragedy of our own lives would be handed on to our descendants, and the trauma of this has caused each of us in turn to trim our souls (what a slip, I mean our sails) and never hope for any recognition in accordance with our respective abilities.
>
> Living under this cloud, I never dared to apply for a government job—and of course, you saw what happened to my Cornell application in 1952. Since then, I have been systematically trying to find answers to my family's medical problem which has kept us all so unhappy and held down our potential.
>
> Now that I have found a partial answer to the emotional thyroid storms which have tipped me over at every important step in my life—and somehow you have been aware of them—I want to see if

I can do something further to straighten out our lives and leave us free to do good work in the world. We are now all 40 or over, we are all in good physical health . . . , we have been blessed with a heritage of long-livers and good minds over a period of several generations, and we do have a contribution to make to our country and to the world. I am said to have my father's brilliant mind, and I have often thought that had he lived in my generation when medical science and psychiatry had advanced further than it had now, and when he might have had more consideration based upon merit rather than racial status, we all might have avoided the near-tragedies which constantly beset us.

Murray's postscript—"Do not try to answer this except to acknowledge receipt of it, so that I know you got it"—discouraged a response. Thus, it is difficult to know what ER thought. What is known is that she had a personal connection to the issues Murray raised. ER had lost her mother and then her father before she became a teenager. ER knew the strain of a relative's illness, as her father, Elliott; brother Gracie Hall; and paternal uncles Valentine and Edward Hall had suffered from alcoholism, a disease shrouded in shame the way mental illness was. ER had seen and lobbied against the deplorable conditions under which shell-shocked World War I veterans were housed at Saint Elizabeths Hospital, the same facility where Murray's brother William was now institutionalized. And while ER might not have fully understood how a thyroid disorder affected Murray's functioning, she had periodically experienced what she referred to as "Griselda moods," and her symptoms—emotional withdrawal, weight loss, inability to concentrate—resembled depression.

ER followed Murray's request to reflect "prayerfully" without comment on her personal history. But she felt compelled to squash Murray's speculation about the presidency. "You have one idea which you must get out of your head," ER wrote back, "namely that I should run for political office. I am much too old for that and in any case the American people are not yet ready to have a woman as President or Vice-President. I am glad they are not because I would feel very inadequate to fill the role at the present time."

It was inconceivable to Murray that ER was too old or not prepared to run for office. At seventy, she averaged no less than forty lectures a year, and she was well versed in world affairs. She continued to write a daily column, plus numerous articles, and books. And her influence as a spokesperson for progressive causes was undeniable.

Murray agreed not to raise the presidency issue again.

Nevertheless, she refused to stop pushing the NAACP to change its selection criteria for the Spingarn Medal. She thought it philosophically inconsistent and morally wrong for the nation's premier civil rights organization to deny Eleanor Roosevelt or Lillian Smith consideration for its most prestigious award. The association "can now well afford to make its highest honor to . . . any citizen regardless of race, color or sex," Murray wrote to NAACP board chairman Channing Tobias, "so long as the merit is one of contribution to human rights." Despite Murray's appeal and the board's high regard for ER and Smith, it refused to change the eligibility requirements for the Spingarn award.

Eleanor Roosevelt with granddaughter Sara "Sally" Roosevelt (left), whom Pauli Murray and her niece Bonnie Fearing met at Val-Kill the weekend a category 4 hurricane struck New York State, October 15–17, 1954. ER's "indomitable courage" in the face of this ferocious storm was an "example" that would inspire Murray for years to come. *(Franklin D. Roosevelt Presidential Library)*

40

"What a Wonderful Weekend It Was"

Pauli Murray had hoped for a measure of emotional calm after thyroid surgery. What she experienced instead were vision problems and a "laugh-and-cry-loss-of-memory-mean-pick-a-fight-with-everyone stage" that lasted through the summer of 1954. The side effects of the operation and her medications, along with a relative's death, increased her anxiety. Too disoriented to write, Murray longed to get away to a quiet place in the mountains. "If it would not be too much trouble," she asked Eleanor Roosevelt, "may I hibernate up there for a few days? The idea is to look at nature and not at the typewriter."

ER welcomed Murray's request for respite at her country cottage. She also told Murray that she could bring her twenty-one-year-old niece, Bonnie. Bonnie, who had just graduated from Catholic University, had always wanted to meet ER, and Pauli decided to make the weekend trip a graduation gift.

On Friday, October 15, 1954, at five o'clock in the afternoon, Pauli and Bonnie met ER at her New York apartment for the drive up to Hyde Park. The first reports of Hurricane Hazel had come the day before from Haiti, where a curtain of wind and rain had killed hundreds. From there, Hazel made her way up the Atlantic seaboard of the United States, uprooting trees, toppling houses, breaking power lines, and blowing debris along transportation routes.

Thousands in the Carolinas were left homeless and exposed to contaminated water and broken sewer lines. In Virginia, a battleship washed ashore in the James River. In the District of Columbia, the Potomac overflowed, and at Mount Vernon, George Washington's estate, a century-old pecan tree was destroyed. In Delaware, a woman was hurled to her death in front of a trolley car. By the time Hazel reached New York, her wind gusts were averaging one hundred miles per hour. A Brooklyn couple "stepped on a live wire" and perished. A nineteen-year-old girl riding the Staten Island Ferry vanished after a wave "swept over its front lower deck."

ER seemed unconcerned about Hazel's havoc and the U.S. Weather Bureau's warning of hazardous conditions. She napped in the front seat, while her driver, William White, "sped along the parkways, trying to outrun the storm." Murray and Bonnie crouched together in the backseat, terrified.

When they reached Val-Kill, there was no electricity or water. Unruffled by this inconvenience, ER guided her guests to their upstairs bedroom by candlelight. Before Pauli and Bonnie could unpack, ER called out, "Hurry up, girls, put your things down. We have an engagement at Bard College and we don't want to keep them waiting." ER had promised the students she would read to them from her favorite works. Bard was over an hour away under normal conditions, yet she fully intended to keep her commitment.

ER and her guests took off, with White navigating the car through small streams and around fallen branches. At times, the wind and rain made it difficult for them to see more than a few feet ahead. At the college, they found an upended tree blocking the entrance, so they abandoned the car and trudged to the meeting hall by foot.

The students, having assumed that ER would not come in such a storm, were surprised when she and her party arrived. She quickly took a spot on the floor in front of the burning fireplace, with the students and her guests around her. She read excerpts from *Winnie-the-Pooh*, T. S. Eliot, and James Stephens. Her calm manner gave no hint of the danger she and her companions had braved to get there. Her reading so dazzled Murray that she concluded that the tortuous journey had been worth this moment.

The next morning, Pauli and Bonnie were roused by a knock at their bedroom door and the appearance of a pink-faced "apparition" framed by a "towel-turbaned" head. It was ER, offering a practical suggestion. "There's a swimming pool around by John's house and nobody uses it this time of year," she said. "I just came back. I took my soap and towel down with me, rubbed myself all over with the soap, looked up and down the road to see that nobody was coming, and I just went right down in the pool and took my bath. If you hurry, you can do the same. Just be sure nobody's looking."

Murray and her niece were incredulous. What would happen if the neighbors, who included the Vanderbilts and Morgenthaus, saw two unfamiliar black women bathing in the Roosevelt family pool? Too shamefaced to admit how nervous ER's proposal made them, Murray and Bonnie donned their robes, gathered soap and towels, and slunk toward the pool.

Their hope of going unnoticed was dashed when ER's daughter-in-law Anne "came out and stared" at them "in utter bewilderment." They explained that they were following ER's instructions, whereupon Anne led them to the pool, and the family's large dog happily joined them. No sooner had they dipped their toes into the water than they spotted a delivery truck coming toward them. They scurried back to the cottage and were relieved to find the lights and hot water restored.

Later, over lunch, everyone chuckled at seven-year-old Sally Roosevelt's tale of seeing Grandmère bathe in the swimming pool and Anne's account of the confused, bathrobed strangers wandering through her backyard. Murray would never forget "what a wonderful weekend it was."

41

"You Might . . . Comment from the Special Woman's Angle"

After her Val-Kill visit, Pauli Murray learned that her editor "was very disturbed at the direction the book had taken." This was troubling news, yet Murray was not surprised. She knew that "something was wrong, but could not pinpoint the problem. It seems," she told her friend Caroline Ware, "that I got bogged down with factual and historical material, and had my characters in the background instead of the foreground." Having identified the problem, Murray started over, rising every day at four and working until noon. Her family soon emerged center stage in the narrative.

Rewriting so consumed Murray that she did not contact Eleanor Roosevelt for a year. By the time Murray wrote to ER, her editor had approved the first half of the book, and the Housing and Home Finance Agency had dismissed Corienne Morrow and her supervisor, Frank Horne. Of the agency's nine hundred employees, Morrow and Horne were among the highest-ranking of the small number of blacks. Clearly, they had been singled out. Although agency officials gave "budgetary considerations" as justification for this action, civil rights leaders charged that the real goal was to remove two capable, Democratic advocates of housing integration from the federal government. (Morrow and Horne were replaced by two black Republicans, Joseph Ray, a real estate agent from Louisville, and Joseph Rainey, a former magistrate from Philadelphia.)

Because Morrow was a woman and without Horne's political connections, Murray forwarded a packet of background information to ER and a letter that said, "You might . . . comment from the special woman's angle." Morrow was "one of the top-level women in federal service" and among a handful of experts in "the complicated field of federally-aided housing." A role model for African Americans and women, she had worked her way up from an entry-grade secretarial job to a senior civil service position. If she could be dismissed in violation of civil service guidelines after twenty-one years, Murray declared, "the outlook is discouraging indeed."

The firings angered ER. She was a longtime supporter of open and fair housing, and she detested political intimidation. She knew Frank Horne from his work in the Negro Affairs Division of the National Youth Administration. And thanks to Murray's introduction, ER had a personal interest in Morrow as well.

Joining a chorus of critics, such as Charles Abrams, an urban planner and anti-discrimination activist who claimed the firings were motivated by Republican-affiliated real estate groups opposed to housing integration, ER spoke out in her column. "There are very few Negroes employed at their level and yet Negroes are among those needing better housing in almost every city in this country." In view of the fact that HHFA funding had actually increased by approximately $2.8 million dollars, the "budgetary reasons" officials gave seemed invalid and the dismissals "highly unfair." ER reprimanded HHFA director Albert M. Cole and his staff for asking Congress "to go slow" on integrated housing. "This should not be the policy in any national agency," she insisted.

ER also put the spotlight on Morrow, closely paraphrasing Murray's description of the situation:

> Dr. Horne's case is being publicly fought. Mrs. Morrow's is just mentioned in passing now and then but it is of special interest to women because she worked her way up from a very low income bracket to an administrative position and she has been a symbol to many of her people both of the success and opportunity which Negro women might have in government service. She has almost 21 years of career service behind her and she is the senior in period service of all racial relations functionaries in the Housing and Home Finance Agency. Her annual salary was $10,065 when she was released. This makes her case important to a very great number of women, and I think should be brought to the public and followed very carefully.

Encouraged by ER's advocacy, the National Council of Negro Women and several civil rights groups took up Morrow's cause. The pressure forced the commission's hand. "You're a real darling," Murray wrote to ER after Morrow's reinstatement. "Among the many reasons why we love you—and we number billions—is your personal commitment to the many causes of humanity and the time you take with each cause whether it be one person or a nation."

Pauli Murray takes a break at a rummage
sale sponsored by a local Unitarian church
in Hancock, New Hampshire, November 11,
1955. On the back of this snapshot, she wrote,
"To Mrs. Roosevelt, with great affection."
(Franklin D. Roosevelt Presidential Library)

42

"I Cannot Afford to Be a Piker"

On October 26, 1955, Murray's eighty-five-year-old adoptive
mother, Pauline Dame, died of a heart attack. Aunt Pauline had
been the central maternal figure in Murray's life since she was
three. Murray was devastated by the loss, and the memory of her aunt's
final hours compounded her grief.

Murray had rushed home from The MacDowell Colony in response
to her aunt's complaint of vision problems. To Murray's surprise, Aunt

Pauline had prepared a birthday meal even though Murray's birthday, November 20, was three and a half weeks away. Her aunt seemed to sense that it would be their "last ceremonial meal together."

Before daybreak, Aunt Pauline developed chest pains and breathing difficulties. After trying unsuccessfully to reach her personal physician, Murray arranged for another doctor to come to the house. He relieved Aunt Pauline's discomfort with medication and urged her to go immediately to a hospital. Murray soon discovered that no hospital would admit her aunt without her physician's authorization, and Murray could not reach him until midmorning.

The next hurdle was getting an ambulance. In spite of Murray's repeated calls, even with the doctor's authorization, they waited for hours. Her worst fear surfaced when Aunt Pauline, gasping between breaths, murmured, "I don't think I'll live to get to the hospital. I've got death rattles in my throat."

The possibility that this beloved mother-aunt, who was a devout Episcopalian, might die without a priest to deliver Holy Communion horrified Murray. She made a string of desperate calls to the church. Unable to reach a priest, she offered to read the "Order for the Visitation of the Sick" from their well-used copy of *The Book of Common Prayer*. Aunt Pauline nodded her approval, and Murray began, slowly reciting "the psalms and all the prayers," replacing all masculine pronouns with the feminine form: "O Lord, look down from heaven, behold, visit, and relieve this thy servant . . . defend her in all danger, and keep her in perpetual peace and safety."

The ambulance finally arrived. As the attendants carried Aunt Pauline out of the house, she pointed to a hatbox that contained her "burial undergarments." Once in the hospital and resting comfortably, she sent Murray home, then "slipped away peacefully" during the night.

Hearing the sacred text appeared to have consoled Aunt Pauline, yet Murray believed she had violated two family customs. One called for elders to lead their younger kin in prayer. The other called for priests, who were by definition male, to give the last rites. Murray felt that she had let her aunt down. Not having finished the family memoir intensified Murray's sorrow.

Aunt Pauline was the third close relative of Murray's to die in an eighteen-month period. Another maternal aunt, Maria Fitzgerald Jeffers, and a paternal uncle, Lewis Hamilton Murray, had passed earlier. These deaths and Lillian Smith's life-threatening illness deepened Murray's emotional reliance on Eleanor Roosevelt. Murray steadied herself during the memorial service for Aunt Pauline with memories of ER's "fortitude" during FDR's funeral.

After the burial, Murray divided the funeral spray ER sent into two bouquets, placing one bunch on Aunt Pauline's grave and giving the other to a next-door neighbor whose wedding Aunt Pauline had planned to attend. Murray thought it appropriate that ER's flowers grace her aunt's grave site and the wedding festivities of a family friend. ER *was* family and "even more precious" now that so many elders were gone.

. . .

EAGER TO RESUME WORK on the memoir, Murray went to Vassar College, in Poughkeepsie, New York, to confer with Lillian Smith and Helen Lockwood. Smith was lecturing at Vassar and undergoing treatment at Memorial Hospital. Lockwood chaired the English Department. Both were enthusiastic about Murray's writing, and the visit with them temporarily lifted her spirits.

During the drive back to the colony, Murray thought she glimpsed ER in the front seat of "an Alice-blue colored car." Fueled by the possibility of spending a moment in the presence of ER's warmth, she "chased" the vehicle until it disappeared on the Saw Mill River Parkway. As Murray made her way to New Hampshire, alone and heavy of heart, she kept saying to herself, "If Mrs. R. has the courage to do these things, I cannot afford to be a piker." When she told ER about the car she had followed on her way back to New Hampshire, ER replied, "You are very brave always so I think you have no need to fear."

. . .

MURRAY WAS RELIEVED to be back at The MacDowell Colony, where the solitude and the natural beauty of the terrain comforted her. As she walked the well-worn paths of former and current colonists, she paused periodically to bask in a stand of pine or a maple grove and to admire the ever-present deer, birds, chipmunks, and squirrels. This communion with nature and the desire to honor Aunt Pauline's life renewed Murray's determination to finish *Proud Shoes*. She plunged into the manuscript. She also began reading a biography of Susan B. Anthony that deepened her connection to the "marvelous tradition" of feminist activism.

Two weeks after her aunt's death, Murray posed for a "little snapshot" of herself, dressed in pants, galoshes, a beanie cap, and a sweater topped with a short jacket and an ascot wrap. She was underweight again, but she liked the photograph. It reminded her of how she had looked the first time she saw the first lady at Camp Tera, twenty-one years earlier. "It's my most natural self, I think," she wrote to ER, who pronounced it "delightful."

. . .

AFTER THE CIVIL SERVICE COMMISSION ordered the Housing and Home Finance Agency to reinstate Morrow, agency officials abolished her position and offered her a secretarial job at less than half her previous salary. Neither Murray nor Morrow had the "heart" to ask ER to "to do anything else," although Murray continued to keep ER informed.

The week before Christmas, Murray sent ER a chapter of her memoir as a gift. This particular chapter explored a painful issue—a longing to be white—that manifested itself in color prejudice among blacks. Several of Murray's relatives were passing, distancing themselves from their darker-skinned kin in order to escape discrimination, shame, and the stigma of inferiority associated with being black. Aunt Pauline's marriage to Charles Morton Dame, a "blond, blue-eyed" Howard law school graduate, had dissolved when he decided to pass for white and she refused to do the same. Under no circumstances—not even for love—would she renounce her heritage as an African American and a Fitzgerald. "This is an inside story which you can appreciate, having seen pictures of my family," Murray said in her cover letter to ER.

Whether or not ER understood the dynamics of within-group color prejudice, the story fascinated her. "If the rest of your book flows as smoothly," she said, "you are sure to have success with it."

As Murray's attachment to ER grew stronger, she increasingly spoke of the familial bond she felt. "Did I ever tell you," Murray boasted, "I was christened *Anna* Pauline, a first name that carries with it a very high standard to meet—two high standards, in fact." The standard-bearers to whom Murray was referring were her paternal grandmother, Annie Price Murray, and ER, whose first name was also Anna.

PART VII

FIGHTING FOR
A JUST WORLD,
1956–59

Pauli Murray (right) confers with an unidentified supporter at an Adlai Stevenson campaign event, New York City, 1956. "Civil rights cannot be dealt with with moderate feelings. It involves a passion for justice and for human decency, and if Mr. Stevenson has not felt this passion, then he does not belong in the White House," Murray told the columnist Doris Fleeson, who was a Stevenson loyalist. *(The Schlesinger Library, Radcliffe Institute, Harvard University, and the Estate of Pauli Murray)*

43

"There Appears to Be a Cleavage"

By February 1956, the presidential campaign was in full swing, and Eleanor Roosevelt was backing Adlai Stevenson's second bid for the Democratic nomination. Pauli Murray had endorsed the governor in 1952. She was inclined to support him again. However, his cautious response to the *Brown* decision and the Supreme Court's subsequent rulings in a number of desegregation cases gave her pause.

If enforced, *Brown* promised to transform social relations in the South, and the reaction of segregationists was predictably hostile. The general assembly of the Commonwealth of Virginia moved to provide state funding for private schools. Louisiana legislators passed a law that banned the state's athletic teams from playing opponents whose rosters included African Americans. Authorities across the South posted fresh "White Only" and "Colored Only" signs at bus and railroad stations, boldly defying the Interstate Commerce Commission's ban on segregated interstate transportation.

Mississippi governor James P. Coleman threatened to close the state's colleges rather than admit black students. He was not alone in his resolve. On March 12, Georgia senator Walter F. George took to the Senate floor and read a manifesto opposing racial integration on behalf of some one hundred southern members of Congress. The *Brown* ruling, George and his colleagues argued in their statement, was "a clear abuse of judicial power" and an encroachment on states' rights. Although they publicly advised against "disorder and lawless acts," their vow "to use all lawful means" to reverse *Brown* and to "prevent the use of force in its implementation" emboldened those intent on disobeying the high court through violent measures.

It was ironic that Murray happened to be writing a chapter on Reconstruction in her memoir. The "parallels" between that tumultuous period after emancipation and the current backlash against integration pained her. Tears spurted from her eyes onto the typewriter as she chronicled the quest of former slaves for full citizenship and the furor of whites determined to stop them. "*Proud Shoes* is every much a story of 1956 as it is of 1866," she told Corinne Morrow. When Eleanor Roosevelt read Murray's chapter draft, she too found the similarities "sad but true."

· · ·

VEHEMENT OPPOSITION TO INTEGRATION made wooing southern conservatives without alienating blacks and liberals an impossible task for Stevenson. As governor of Illinois and as the Democratic presidential candidate in 1952, he had established solid liberal credentials. But he stunned many of his allies when he did not speak out after the August 28, 1955, murder of Emmett Louis Till, a fourteen-year-old black boy accused of flirting with a white woman in Money, Mississippi. Matters worsened after Stevenson told a gathering of black leaders at the Watkins Hotel in Los Angeles that he wanted "to proceed gradually" with integration so as not to "upset the habits or traditions of generations overnight."

Thus, he would not enforce the law with troops and set off another civil war. The governor's relations with African Americans suffered another setback when he declined to endorse the Powell amendment. This measure, proposed by a fiery black congressman from New York City, Adam Clayton Powell Jr., denied funds to states with segregated schools.

Incensed by Stevenson's remarks, Roy Wilkins, who had succeeded Walter White as chief executive of the NAACP, lashed out at a birthday observance for Abraham Lincoln in Springfield, Illinois. "To Negro Americans 'gradual' meant either no progress at all," Wilkins argued, "or progress so slow as to be barely perceptible." George Meany, president of the powerful American Federation of Labor and the Congress of Industrial Organizations, was irritated too, and he accused Stevenson of "running away" from the *Brown* decision.

As the Democratic Party's left wing pulled away from Stevenson, ER found herself in the unenviable role of go-between. She regretted his remarks in Los Angeles; even so, she thought black activists and the press had overreacted. Eager to de-escalate tensions, she issued a statement from the governor's Chicago campaign headquarters, imploring people to consider the evidence. "The record," she offered, "should speak more loudly than words because it was created not only by words but by deeds." She told civil rights leaders that she agreed with the governor's concern about changing "mores faster than people can accept it."

To Murray, Stevenson's remarks and ER's defense of him signaled that civil rights had become "secondary to winning the White House." Murray registered her disappointment in a letter on February 16, 1956.

> Dear Mrs. Roosevelt,
>
> . . . There appears to be a cleavage in your point of view and that of Negro leaders whom you have known and worked with over many years in harmonious relations and fundamental agreement. This difference may be more fundamental than you realize. If so, it would be tragic for all of us. You have also indicated your perplexity at the present confusion and misunderstanding surrounding Mr. Stevenson's statement. Because I fear further misunderstanding among people whom I am sure are in agreement on principle, I urge you at your earliest possible free moment to counsel informally with leaders in this field whose opinions you respect and in whom you have trust and confidence.

Among those Murray recommended ER consult were Ralph Bunche, Lester Granger, Frank Horne, Maida Springer, Channing Tobias, and

Robert Weaver. Murray excluded herself on the grounds that she had no "close association with public leadership" and, therefore, had "no place in such a discussion." She did offer to help, if asked.

It is somewhat curious that Murray disqualified herself from the discussion, given her admiration for Stevenson, her strong opinions about his campaign, and her extensive background in civil rights. This decision, perhaps, recognized the difficulties she experienced working in groups, her bumpy relationships with male civil rights leaders, and her desire not to attract further attention from the FBI.

ER offered her opinion of these matters a week later.

February 22, 1956

My dear Pauli:

I had a long talk with Ralph Bunche yesterday and I don't think that fundamentally there is any cleavage between my point of view and that of Mr. Stevenson and that of the really wise Negro leaders. I did not like Roy Wilkins' hotheaded statement which I thought poorly thought out, nor did I like the garbled reporting of what Mr. Stevenson said in Los Angeles. Unwittingly Mr. Stevenson used the word "gradual" and this means one thing to the Negroes but to him it was entirely different. However, Mr. Stevenson's record remains remarkably good and he certainly was courageous in the statements he made in the last campaign. I think so far he has made no really deeply felt statement on the situation but I don't think that is because of any political reactions that might come. I simply think that he is waiting for the time when he thinks it will be of most value. However, the more he seems to be under attack by the Negroes, the less possible it is for him to make such a speech because he will be accused of doing so in order to get the Negro vote.

The only thing on which Stevenson and I differ with some of the Negro leaders is in the support of the Powell amendment. His feeling is that aid should not be withheld from the states that need education most in order to improve. He also realizes there are many other ways, probably more effective, which can be used to influence the South on desegregation of schools if you have the money. It seems to me obvious that if a state was flouting the Supreme Court or if it passed legislation to make all its schools private, it could not receive money, but if it is within the power of the Executive to allocate it, he could use that to influence the recalcitrant Southern states.

I have just come back from a trip to Florida, Georgia and South Carolina and I don't think that putting children in a classroom together is all that has to happen. Many things have to be improved—housing, economic conditions, and the right to vote and protection in that right. It will probably take a generation or so before a colored child can hope to be receiving equal education even if long before that time it sits in the same schoolroom. In the meantime, if the Powell amendment gets through in the House, the Republicans will call the bill up in the Senate, immediately the Southern Senators will filibuster and no other bill will come through. The Republicans will then say: "Look at the Democratically controlled Congress which did nothing." Truman used that very effectively in the last campaign.

I think it is a mistake for the Negro leaders to be tearing down Stevenson who is after all the only real hope they have, the President having told Mr. Powell that he would make no statement on whether the Executive would refrain from allocating funds where schools were segregated. Yet the papers and the Negro leaders have not attacked the President. Why this discrimination?

I think the courage being shown by the [Aubrey and Anita] Williams and the [Clifford and Virginia] Durrs and people like them in Alabama just at the present time is really something quite extraordinary and I hope it will get recognition and praise from the Negro leaders, though I would not like the praise to be voiced just now because I think it would make life harder for the courageous Southerners.

Affectionately,
Eleanor Roosevelt

Neither ER's testy defense of Stevenson nor her warm closing swayed Murray. She still wanted a forceful, unambiguous endorsement of *Brown* and the principle of racial integration from the governor. Of her disagreement with ER about Stevenson's position, Murray confided to Corienne Morrow, "Much as I love and admire her, I have never for one moment been under illusions as to the limits of her extension of herself on these issues. She has reached her hand across the line as far as any human being can do—considering her political commitments." Murray observed, "She is a regular Democrat, and as fond as she is of me, I shall never forget her article in . . . *Ebony*, entitled 'Some of My Best Friends Are Negroes' (the editor's title, not hers) in which she characterized me as a 'firebrand' (which I am and proud of it) and that I had done some 'foolish' things in my youth (which I did, but not the ones to which she was referring)."

. . .

BY THE SPRING OF 1956, Murray had nearly finished the memoir. She also learned that the New York City Commission on Intergroup Relations had hired Morrow as a research associate. (Her old boss Frank Horne had been named executive director.) Murray credited her own perseverance and Morrow's good job fortune in part to ER's "encouragement and understanding." In spite of an unwieldy schedule and innumerable personal commitments, ER had diligently responded to Murray's drafts and generously recommended Morrow to Mayor Robert F. Wagner Jr. for the commission post.

Just as Murray began the final revision, doctors diagnosed her last maternal aunt, seventy-nine-year-old Sallie F. Small, with advanced liver cancer. It had been less than six months since Aunt Pauline's death. Murray was awash in "troubles."

The strain of another loss on Murray worried ER, and she invited Murray to Val-Kill for an overnight stay. Unfortunately, Aunt Sallie took a turn for the worse, and Murray missed the appointment. The mix-up was "providential," she later wrote to ER, as her aunt passed on May 19, the day she was to come to Hyde Park.

"I am so sorry to hear about your Aunt's death but I am sure you are consoled by the fact that she is relieved from pain," ER wrote in condolence. "Nonetheless this is a very sad time for you and I can understand the great sense of loss you must feel now that two of your very dear ones are gone. I have already written giving you another date but, under the circumstances, I will understand if you feel you can't come in. Do take care of yourself."

Aunt Sallie had "clung to life" long enough to see *Proud Shoes* go to press. After each hospital visit, Murray went home "to the typewriter," hoping to stay the grief. Now that the book was done, depression set in. She had little interest in returning to private practice. "Cut adrift" from the family elders, who were the pillars of her childhood, Murray found that her friendship with Eleanor Roosevelt became her anchor.

Eleanor Roosevelt and Autherine Lucy, the first black student admitted to the University of Alabama (right), at a civil rights rally in Madison Square Garden, New York City, on May 24, 1956. ER had called on the school to admit "not one student but ten." *(Bettmann/CORBIS)*

44

"You're a Bit of a Firebrand Yourself"

Unsettling events in the state of Alabama distracted Pauli Murray from thoughts of her loss. In Montgomery, the December 1, 1955, arrest of Rosa Parks, a local NAACP leader and seamstress who refused to give her seat to a white passenger, had set off a bus boycott led by the young, charismatic Reverend Dr. Martin Luther King Jr. In Tuscaloosa, some ninety miles north, a reserved yet strong-willed twenty-six-year-old native, Autherine Juanita Lucy, was admitted to the University of Alabama's graduate school under court order. The youngest of nine children, she was a graduate of the historically black Miles College.

Lucy's first day on campus was uneventful. Some students tried to make her feel welcome by sitting close to her. Others wished her well as they passed by. Only a somber gray mist and the band of reporters and police escorting the attractive newcomer around campus hinted at the storm to come.

Over the weekend, a white mob hammered the campus with chants of "Keep 'Bama White" and "Hey, hey! Ho, ho! Autherine's gotta go." Before it was over, the mob had swelled to a thousand, raised a Confederate flag, and burned a cross. On Monday, when Lucy returned to school, she faced a barrage of eggs, rocks, sticks, and racial epithets. As she braved the walk from one building to another, protesters stepped into her path. She heard someone behind her shout, "Let's kill her!" When university officials permanently expelled Lucy, purportedly for her own protection and the security of the campus, she was too exhausted to continue. It would be three decades before the authorities overturned the expulsion and Autherine Lucy Foster reenrolled. She would graduate with a master's degree in 1992, alongside her daughter Grazia Foster, who received a bachelor's degree.

Eleanor Roosevelt was following the developments in Alabama, too. She invited Rosa Parks to tea, and after five hundred students signed a petition supporting Lucy, ER praised them. "They must have known that their names would be published and that there would be feeling against them," she said. "It takes courage to act on one's belief in the dignity of man."

On May 24, 1956, ER joined Lucy, Reverend King, Rabbi Israel Goldstein, Congressman Adam Clayton Powell, A. Philip Randolph, and Roy Wilkins on the podium at a civil rights fund-raiser in Madison Square Garden. Before an audience of sixteen thousand, ER called on state and federal officials to obey the court order and protect "the Negroes' right to vote" in southern states.

Notwithstanding the turmoil in Tuscaloosa, there were white Alabamans in whom ER and Murray put their faith. In Montgomery, Virginia Durr, a cofounding member of the Southern Conference for Human Welfare, and her husband, Clifford, a lawyer and civil liberties activist, had worked with E. D. Nixon, the local NAACP branch president, to post bail for Rosa Parks. Aubrey Williams, a former executive director of the National Youth Administration, was also part of the interracial coalition supporting Parks and the bus boycott.

There were others working for justice across the South without fanfare and little support. In Louisville, Kentucky, Superintendent Omer Carmichael orchestrated the peaceful integration of the public schools. Mindful of the resistance whites like him faced, Murray sent Dr. Carmichael a note, applauding his "courage" and "intelligent planning." Then she brought Carmichael to the attention of ER, who followed Murray's example by sending him a personal letter. Not content to convey her admiration privately, ER publicly compared the "outstandingly good job" Carmichael did in Louisville with the situation in Clay, Kentucky, where a "crowd of unsmiling men" had turned a black mother and her two children away from a white school.

. . .

SEPTEMBER 1956 WAS DOUBLY SPECIAL for Murray. *Proud Shoes* came off the press, and she had lunch with Eleanor Roosevelt. Murray handed an advance copy to ER, in place of Aunts Pauline and Sallie, who were now gone. Recognizing the significance of Murray's gesture, ER wrote afterward, "I am very happy that our date coincided with the launching of your book. No one could wish you more luck with it than I do."

ER promised to review *Proud Shoes,* which she sent with *Killers of the Dream,* Lillian Smith's penetrating critique of southern racism, to Adlai Stevenson. ER's wish to have the governor read these books evidenced her uneasiness about his relations with African Americans. Her concern was well founded. Black voters in key states were reportedly leaning toward President Eisenhower and the Republicans. As the election approached, the *Pittsburgh Courier* ran a front-page feature under the headline "We're for Eisenhower." An editorial in the *Philadelphia Afro-American* said, "We like both Ike and Adlai" but added that Eisenhower "should be re-elected."

ER campaigned fiercely to preserve the Democratic base. She told the NAACP and the Americans for Democratic Action—both had endorsed New York governor W. Averill Harriman for the Democratic nomination because he'd pledged to support the Powell amendment and uphold the *Brown* decision—that Stevenson's appeal for moderation was not a retreat from integration. "What moderation really means is that you face all the realities of a situation," she argued. Gradualism, moreover, "doesn't mean you do nothing, but it means that you do the things that need to be done, according to priority."

In an effort to keep conservatives from abandoning the Democratic Party, ER crafted a civil rights platform that embraced the principles of racial justice and obedience to the law but omitted specific reference to the *Brown* decision. "I do not think it is necessary to say a specific thing when you have said quite clearly that you accept the law of the land," she told reporters.

For progressives like Murray, a Democratic platform that did not mention *Brown* was a bitter pill to swallow. She was convinced that a second term for the Eisenhower-Nixon administration would be disastrous for the nation. Even so, she could not be silent about what she believed to be Stevenson's halfhearted support of *Brown* or his attempted rapprochement with segregationists. She found his speeches uninspiring and his call for gradualism insulting, given the violent resistance in the South. Only after a soul-searching discussion with Lloyd Garrison did she join the Committee on Registration and Voting in Special Areas of Stevenson's New York campaign.

When Powell announced at a news conference in the White House that he was endorsing Eisenhower because Stevenson had snubbed him and waffled on school desegregation, Murray pleaded with the governor to show that he had "the moral leadership and vision necessary to advance integration on all fronts during the next four years. . . . You *have* the support of those to whom a rational appeal makes sense," she said. "You need to *get* those who respond to an appeal from the heart." Murray took the bold step of sharing an excerpt from a speech by Garrison, as an example of the kind of "tone" she thought helpful. To make sure Stevenson got her message, she copied ER, who promptly forwarded the letter to the governor. Thus, Stevenson received Murray's letter twice.

While neither Murray nor ER budged on their feelings about Stevenson's political strategy, ER did appreciate Murray's feedback. ER knew the governor's penchant for abstract rhetoric was a problem. Yet she had defended him when a critic called him an "egghead."

. . .

ON OCTOBER 31, Murray attended a Women's Luncheon for Stevenson in New York City, where Eleanor Roosevelt gave a rousing address. In a letter dashed off the next day, Murray exclaimed, "One of the reasons we 'firebrands' (your own term) love you so is that when you're 'riled up,' you're a bit of a firebrand yourself. . . . I gloried in you. You had the indignant fire of one who has labored a lifetime to build values of peaceful solutions to international problems, and could see it slipping away because of stupidity, dishonesty and downright apparent lack of integrity. . . . You are a constant inspiration to us more obvious 'firebrands.' "

In spite of Stevenson's efforts to broaden his appeal, he lost the election. Eisenhower won 57 percent of the popular vote and the electoral vote in forty-one states. Even in the Democratic stronghold of New York City, where Murray had campaigned, the president made significant inroads with African Americans.

Left to right: Sylvia L. Ravitch, trustee, New York Urban League; Lloyd K. Garrison, attorney and former president, National Urban League; Pauli Murray; and Frank Horne, executive director, New York City Commission on Intergroup Relations, celebrate the release of *Proud Shoes* in New York City on October 17, 1956. Eleanor Roosevelt declared Murray's family memoir a testament to "the courage and the great strength of the Negro people who have slowly forged ahead, both in the North and South." *(Library of Congress Prints and Photographs Division)*

45

"You Caught the Feeling I Had in Mind"

Proud Shoes was a personal and literary milestone for Pauli Murray. The *New York Times* called it "a gallant book" by "a writer of uncommon gifts," who "proves that the work of Grandfather Fitzgerald and all those like him was not ended." Langston Hughes, who had recently published the travel memoir *I Wonder as I Wander,* "loved" Murray's book and suggested that they organize a literary event that featured authors of newly published autobiographies. After reading Murray's memoir during a trip to California, Eleanor Roosevelt responded, "I have finished *Proud Shoes,* a fascinating story, told with restraint and deep feeling." Mindful of the doubt and hardship Murray overcame to complete the book, ER added, "What courage!"

It had taken two decades for the entry Murray scribbled in her diary on July 18, 1933, to blossom into the family saga at the core of *Proud Shoes*. For its title, she had borrowed a phrase from Stephen Vincent Benét, who first urged her to write the story. The dedication—"To Caroline [Ware], Edmund [Ziman], Marie [Rodell] and the Memory of Pauline Fitzgerald Dame"—was a tribute to Murray's mentor, psychiatrist, literary agent, and mother-aunt, respectively.

Using data gathered from census, church, court, business, and military and school records; family diaries, letters, and legends; personal interviews; photographs; and sites where her ancestors once lived, Murray constructed a narrative that gave the reader two views of the American experience. One was a close-up of the Fitzgeralds from the early 1800s to the beginning of the twentieth century. The other was a wider-angle portrayal that positioned her family within a larger cultural mosaic.

Against the historical backdrop of slavery and Reconstruction, Murray cast multidimensional portraits of her great-grandfather Thomas Fitzgerald, a manumitted mulatto from Pennsylvania, and his wife, Sarah, a "blue-eyed, black-haired" white woman from Delaware whose parents never forgave her for running away to marry a black man. Their son Robert, a Civil War veteran who went to the South to teach ex-slaves, was Murray's grandfather. Robert and his wife, Cornelia Smith, the daughter of a white North Carolina lawyer and a part-Cherokee slave, became the central characters in *Proud Shoes*.

Having grown up in her grandparents' home listening to family legends, Murray had conceived the book as a story for her nieces and nephews. Over time, her motivation for the book expanded. What began as the history of one black family grew to include an account of the Civil War and Reconstruction in a North Carolina community. What started out as a conventional work of nonfiction developed into a novelistic narrative. Writing it had soothed the wounds of suspicion Cornell officials and FBI surveillance had raised about Murray's "past associations" and loyalty.

Proud Shoes was technically and emotionally the most difficult writing Murray had ever done. It required her to portray her ancestors—slave, free black, and white—with their accomplishments, disappointments, and contradictions in full view. To do this meant broaching the provocative issues of racial passing, the color-caste system among blacks, the accepted rape of black women by white men, and voluntary interracial liaisons between black men and white women. It also demonstrated that a family heritage of racial pride and achievement, rather than Communist subversion, had inspired her intellectual fervor and social activism. Murray's personal identification with her characters was so complete that for months after visiting the ancestral home place, she unintentionally substituted 1854 for 1954 in her correspondence.

On October 17, 1956, Harper & Brothers released *Proud Shoes*. It was a 276-page book whose tan dust jacket carried handsome pictures of Murray and her grandparents. In addition to a blurb from Lillian Smith, the cover bore an endorsement from the black writer and intellectual J. Saunders Redding: "What a story! It is history and it is biography, and neither history nor biography is sacrificed to the drama which is itself superb."

For Murray, the joy of holding the published memoir in her hand was second only to the reception it received. A telegram from Lillian Smith made her heart sing. "You have done a beautiful job on the book," Smith wrote. "There is distinguished writing in it and it is at times deeply moving and at other times delightfully entertaining. A truly impressive documentary. I am proud of you and happy." The *San Francisco Chronicle* applauded Murray's "effective use of fictional techniques," noting that "many sections do indeed read practically like a novel." The *Akron Beacon Journal* said the memoir was history "told with an uncanny newness." The *New York Post* dubbed it "a Civil War story as moving as *Gone with the Wind* or *Andersonville*." The New York Public Library placed *Proud Shoes* on the "Books to Remember" list, and the *New York Herald Tribune* named it one of the "Outstanding Books of 1956." For several months, the memoir sold "100 copies per week."

ER introduced Murray's memoir to her readers as a work "anyone interested in the problem of civil rights in this country will find stimulating and enlightening. It is written with a sensitive feeling for the past as well as the present." Of the characters' tenacity, ER noted, "This is an American story about American people. The roots of the family lay in slavery and then came the long hard years of freedom which were never really freedom. Yet there was a tremendous pride handed down from the day when the children, who were almost white, knew they belonged, as blood relatives of the family, in the big plantation house and that they were free."

Murray's description of the "intangibles" her grandparents gave her so touched ER that she excerpted a passage in "My Day":

They had little of the world's goods and less of its recognition, but they had forged enduring values for themselves which they tried to pass on to me.

I would have need of these resources when I left the rugged security of Grandfather's house and found myself in the maze of terrifying forces which I could neither understand nor cope with. While my folks could not shield me from the impact of these forces, with their own courage and strength they could teach me to withstand them.

Murray was bowled over by ER's praise. "Your review was perfect—you caught the feeling I had in mind when I wrote the book," she wrote back to ER, "and your quote was my favorite passage!"

The string of positive reviews helped blunt the criticism of Jane Speights, who wrote in the Mississippi *Clarion-Ledger and Jackson Daily News,* "The cause for miscegenation is herewith presented by a writer who has been actively associated with the cause of civil rights. . . . With this background, it is perhaps too much to expect a fair appraisal of her family history from the author." Speights coupled the innuendo about Murray's motives with a rebuke of her sources and methodology: "Built on a thin framework of Robert's reminiscences to his small granddaughter, the book is fleshed out with the most inaccurate generalities." In view of these alleged weaknesses, Speights concluded, "a book such as this can serve no useful purpose."

Frank Hains, literary editor for the newspaper, sent Murray's publisher a letter vouching for Speights's "objectivity." She was "an intelligent and perceptive woman" from Ohio, he insisted, who "had done reviews for Columbus newspapers before coming South." Murray forwarded his letter and the review to ER. "It's amazing," Murray remarked, "how differently two people can react to the same printed word."

Left to right: Ray N. Moore, head, Stanford L. Warren Library; Pauli Murray; John Hervey Wheeler, president, Farmers and Mechanics Bank and civil rights activist; and Lyda Moore Merrick, founder, *Negro Braille Magazine,* in Durham, North Carolina, circa 1956. Murray was the featured author at the library's American Heritage Series. *(North Carolina Collection, Durham County Library)*

46

"I Never Cease to Marvel at the Greatness of Your Humanity"

In the fall of 1956, Pauli Murray got a "professional opportunity" she had thought she would never have. Lloyd Garrison recommended her for a position in the litigation department of his law firm. Paul, Weiss, Rifkind, Wharton and Garrison was a venerable practice whose character was rooted in the experience of its cofounders. John F. Wharton, a Christian, and Louis S. Weiss, a Jew, had been classmates at Columbia Law School. When no law firm would hire them on the same staff, they set up a practice together in 1923, defying the custom of religious segregation.

Their firm, from its inception through its succeeding mergers, welcomed attorneys like Walter Pollak, who took on controversial clients, such as the nine black boys falsely accused of raping two white women in

Scottsboro, Alabama. It was the first prominent white practice to hire an African American attorney, William T. Coleman, in 1949, and the first to name a woman partner, Carolyn Agger, in the early 1950s. It set another example by hiring Murray as an associate attorney.

Ten years earlier, no white or black firm in New York City would hire a black woman. It mattered not that Murray held law degrees from Howard University and the University of California, Berkeley, or that she was the first African American appointed to the post of deputy attorney general for the state of California. Therefore, her new job called for a celebration. In the absence of the customary meal Aunts Pauline and Sallie would have prepared, Murray marked the occasion by savoring a note of congratulations from Eleanor Roosevelt that included an invitation to tea.

· · ·

A WEEK BEFORE HER VISIT with ER, Murray attended a family reunion in Baltimore, where her adolescent niece Rosita mentioned that she wanted to meet Eleanor Roosevelt. "It's too bad you won't be in New York next Saturday," Murray chuckled, "since I am having tea with Mrs. R." Murray gave no further thought to the matter until the high schooler called at a quarter past six the following Friday morning and announced, "Aunt Pauli, Daddy sent me the money and I have bought a new dress for the occasion. Would you meet me at 7:51? I'm taking the Congressional out this afternoon."

Murray promptly got permission to bring her spunky niece, and they arrived at ER's East Sixty-second Street apartment on the afternoon of December 1, 1956. Seated around the living room in rapt conversation with ER were Israeli minister of foreign affairs Golda Meir; Justine Wise Polier, a human rights activist and the first woman judge in New York City; and several Protestant leaders. ER paused long enough to introduce Pauli and Rosita, and then she returned to the discussion, which focused on the Suez crisis and the treatment of Jews in Egypt.

Because this powerhouse gathering so mesmerized Rosita, it shocked her when ER began "emptying the ashtrays, putting back the chairs" after the dignitaries left. To see the former first lady feed "bits of cookies" to her Scottish terrier Mr. Duffy struck the teenager as odd. Rosita's "eyes popped even wider" as she watched the most admired woman in the world "calmly munching nuts from a dish" and "in deep conversation about the fate of aid to education, the NAACP, [Adam Clayton] Powell, the Negro vote, etc." with her aunt Pauli.

"I never cease to marvel at the greatness of your humanity," Murray wrote to ER after the visit. "I shall never forget the picture of you sitting—in a moment of respite from world problems—dutifully writing *nine* autographs for a fourteen-year-old!" When asked what she planned to do with her bounty, Rosita had said, "One for my billfold; one for my scrapbook; one for my boy friend; one for my best girl friend; and one for my sister. I'll save the other four for special events."

Murray always left visits with ER inspired, but this moment was special, she explained. "By contact with such youngsters you are projecting the greatness of your spirit into the future many decades. She's one of my favorite nieces and I think the exposure to current history she got at your home will have a significant effect upon her life."

47

"Our Friendship Produced Sparks of Sheer Joy"

P
auli Murray moved into her quarters at Paul, Weiss, Rifkin, Wharton and Garrison shortly after the November 1956 election. Her accommodations in the firm's Madison Avenue office, which boasted more than sixty attorneys and an army of clerks and secretaries, dwarfed the one-woman operation she had run for four years. The change was so dramatic that she felt like a "sandlot player catapulted overnight into major league baseball."

Being a middle-aged African American woman in this setting made Murray a "triple minority." Although she was the second black attorney the firm had hired, she was the only black associate on the legal staff at the time, for William Coleman had taken a position with another firm. All the other associates, except two white women who would soon leave, were white males under thirty, and the senior partners were ten to fifteen years younger than Murray. That she worked in the litigation department on "corporate mergers, bankruptcies, mechanics' liens, and the like" upped the ante, given that her experience and passion were in labor and civil rights law.

Despite the circumstances, Murray was motivated to succeed. She had "earned the right to be delivered from the civil rights struggle long enough to become a top notch lawyer. If I can do well here," she told Caroline Ware, "it will mean much to those who come behind me, particularly the gals in the profession."

Murray spent the first year boning up on tax law and acclimating herself to the firm's culture. As a junior associate, she was at the bottom of "the totem pole" and relegated to doing research for the partners. She neither interacted with clients nor appeared in court. The workload was heavy and the demands unremitting. She spent so much time in the library that she had to change the prescription for her eyeglasses. "I've been so busy trying to clean the rust off my legal equipment that I haven't had time to wish you New Year's greetings," she wrote to Eleanor Roosevelt on January 20, 1957.

Murray especially wanted to make a favorable impression on her department head, Simon H. Rifkind, a Russian émigré who was a former federal district court judge. Though he "was rumored not to think too highly of women lawyers," Murray resolved to counter his prejudice by producing excellent work. She admired Rifkin's trial skills and his efforts to secure aid for Holocaust survivors. That Franklin Roosevelt had appointed Rifkin to the bench enhanced his judicial aura in her eyes.

In addition to demonstrating her competence, Murray had to negotiate an ambiguous code of office etiquette. Since she was not one of the "girls," as the secretaries were called, or one of the "boys" who made up the majority of the legal staff, she had no one after whom to model herself. Typical of the "awkwardness" she experienced was the interaction one day when she and Rifkind approached the elevator to leave the office. Murray stepped aside in deference to the judge's status and waited for him to board. Rifkind, "the essence of courtesy" in his social interactions with women, stood back and waited for Murray. While they remained frozen in front of the elevator "staring foolishly at one another," several passengers loaded and the doors closed.

Lloyd Garrison, having joined the firm after a stint in the federal government and a decade as a law school dean and professor, tried to bolster Murray's confidence. He knew how hard it was to enter corporate law at midlife. He advised Murray to use the criticism of her work as a "grindstone to sharpen" her skills. She took his counsel to heart.

Murray found an ally and more in Irene Barlow, the office manager. An organizational whiz whose winsome personality had earned her the unofficial title "the managing partner," Barlow was a tall, attractive Brit with blue-green eyes. She had come to the United States when she was six with her mother and four older sisters. Renee ("pronounced to rhyme with Jeannie"), as family and close friends called her, had worked her way through high school and finished her college degree at night, after she'd joined the firm. Ridiculed as a child for her "threadbare hand-me-down clothing" and Yorkshire accent, she determined to open the door to others who had been marginalized because of their nationality, ethnicity, religion, poverty, or sexual orientation. Consequently, the clerical staff Barlow hired was one of the most diverse among the city's law firms.

Barlow's "job kept her on the go, moving unobtrusively through the corridors, untangling snafus which interrupted the flow of paperwork, hustling messengers on their rounds, putting out brushfires of revolt in the stenographers' pool, mediating between lawyers and secretaries, solving problems of space, or, on occasion, offering a kind word to an associate who had just been humiliated by an irate partner." She had a way of defusing conflict and provoking "spasms of laughter" with English colloquialisms. "Now don't get up in the boughs" was a favorite of Murray's. "Oh, blast" was as close as Barlow came to cursing.

Barlow sensed the loneliness and apprehension behind Murray's proud façade and invited her to lunch. During their first meal, they discovered that they were both devout Episcopalians. They would later learn that they were close in age. Murray was forty-six, Barlow forty-two. As children, both had lost parents (Renee's father had abandoned the family after she was born) and moved away from their birthplaces. Each had a thirst for knowledge that had fueled a hard-won battle for education. By Easter, they were going to St. Bartholomew's Church together for noon services on their lunch break.

Barlow walked like a gazelle balancing several tasks at once, whereas Murray moved as if she had been "shot out of a cannon," jumping "from thought to thought." While Barlow never disclosed "firm confidences," she cheered Murray on, urging her to dress and speak gracefully and to be "less the rough diamond and more the sophisticate." In spite of the difference in personality and style, "our friendship produced sparks of sheer joy," Murray would write in her autobiography. Their common religious heritage gave the "relationship a special quality" Murray had not known. She likened their bond to that of Damon and Pythias, friends in a Greek legend whose trust and loyalty were so deep that they risked their lives for each other.

Barlow's beauty and her "strong-willed, creative, traditional-on-the-outside-and-revolutionary-on-the-inside" spirit captivated Murray. Of their feelings for each other, Murray later recalled, "I think she loved me as much because she saw me as identified with the 'despised and rejected' of the earth as because of whatever qualities I had which she admired. I loved her because of her steadfastness, her loyalty, her quiet support and the many things she did (without my ever knowing it) to save me heartache."

This relationship proved the most satisfying of Murray's adult life, as it gave her acceptance and the embrace of family again. Barlow's mother, Mary Jane, who took to mending Murray's "neglected clothing," relieved the void left by the loss of Aunts Pauline and Sallie. Though Murray and Barlow never lived in the same apartment, together they opened a bank account, owned a car, vacationed, lunched with ER, and would eventually share the same burial plot. When they were unable to see each other, they spoke by phone, and they sprinkled their letters with pet names, such as "Barney Google," "Ms. Marple," "darling," and "mushroom." Barlow sent care packages of vitamins and named Murray executor of her will. Murray kept Barlow's portrait on her mantelpiece with the family photos, which included the snapshot of ER with Aunts Pauline and Sallie. The "gift of this friendship," Murray confided in her journal, "is to have been blessed beyond riches."

Left to right: Soviet premier Nikita Khrushchev, translator Anna Lavrova, and Eleanor Roosevelt at his vacation home near the Black Sea, Yalta, Ukraine, on September 28, 1957. ER would earn the New York Newspaper Women's Club Best Series of Articles Award for the "My Day" columns she wrote during the tour. *(Bettmann/CORBIS)*

48

"You Can Say We Had a Friendly Conversation, but We Differ"

In March 1957, Eleanor Roosevelt went to Morocco at the invitation of Sultan Mohammed V. She embarked on this trip with several goals in mind. She hoped to promote better relations with the United States. She was eager to see how Morocco was faring, now that it was no longer a French protectorate. She wanted to visit Casablanca, which had been the site of the 1943 conference between Franklin Roosevelt and Winston Churchill. And she intended to investigate the situation of Moroccan Jews, whose right to emigrate to Israel had been suspended after Morocco's independence.

ER arrived with a party that included her son Elliott; his wife, Minnewa; ER's personal physician, David Gurewitsch; and his daughter Grania. From Casablanca, the group went to Rabat, Fez, and Marrakech, stopping at historic sites, the Jewish quarter, and model projects along the way. One day their car hit a rock, and they were forced to picnic under a weeping willow tree. When the *caid,* the village leader, learned of the mishap, he sent "a beautiful orange and black Berber rug" and "two cushions to lean against 'for the ladies.' "

Everywhere ER went, she saw the need for economic development and a better standard of living. The longing of Moroccan Jews to leave deepened her support for emigration and the young nation of Israel.

Murray had not been abroad, and she was uneasy whenever ER was on foreign soil. ER's trip coincided with Murray's growing interest in Africa. This interest was stirred in part by Maida Springer's work with African labor leaders and her attendance at Ghana's independence celebration a few months earlier. The example of these two friends and a curiosity about the cultural links between African Americans and Africans would eventually lead Murray to Africa.

· · ·

ER BELIEVED, as did Murray, that it was important to learn as much as possible about political ideologies one disagreed with. For this reason, ER jumped at the opportunity to go to the Soviet Union in September 1957 as a reporter for the *New York Post.* She took Maureen Corr, an Irish immigrant who had succeeded Malvina Thompson as her personal secretary, and David Gurewitsch, who spoke fluent Russian. In addition to touring well-known places, such as Lenin's tomb, the Kremlin, the Winter Palace, and Moscow University, ER ventured beyond the typical tourist sites. She told representatives of Intourist, the government's travel bureau, that she "wanted to get as far away from Moscow as possible."

Determined to see the country through the eyes of its people, ER made her way to Tashkent and Samarkand, two of the oldest cities in central Asia. She met with the esteemed Committee of Soviet Women. She talked to people in their homes, schools, and at state and collective farms. At one hospital, she and Gurewitsch put on white surgical garb and entered an operating room. There, a young woman, "under local anesthesia" with an open abdomen, "nearly fell off the table in her eagerness to shake Mrs. Roosevelt's hand."

The highlight of the trip was undoubtedly ER's three-hour interview with Premier Nikita Khrushchev. The short, portly premier, known for his brashness, sat down at a large table to talk with the deceptively cool former first lady through her interpreter. This was Khrushchev's first major interview with a Western journalist, and he discussed a range of issues, such as the proliferation of atomic weapons, the treatment of

Soviet Jews, the violation of the Yalta agreement, and the requirements for peaceful coexistence. He "flared up" when ER raised the issue of Israel's security and the Soviet sale of arms to Syria, but she held her own. When the premier asked, at the end of their meeting, if he could say they "had a friendly conversation?" she replied, "You can say we had a friendly conversation, but we differ."

ER observed that women's work in the Soviet Union included much of what Americans thought of as men's work, from "street-cleaning and section-hand work on the railroads" to all kinds of farm labor. She thought some features of the Soviet education and health care systems were commendable. Nonetheless, she found the low standard of living, government censorship, and regimentation of daily life unacceptable. "I think I should die," she wrote upon reflection, "if I had to live in Soviet Russia."

Elizabeth Ann Eckford (center front, in sunglasses) and anti-integration protesters outside Central High School, Little Rock, Arkansas, September 4, 1957. This scene and news accounts from *New York Post* reporter Ted Poston, a friend of Murray's, caused her to question her decision to go into corporate law. *(Bettmann/CORBIS)*

49

"The Chips Are Really Down in Little Rock"

On September 4, 1957, a crowd of angry whites cornered a slight African American girl near the entrance to Little Rock's Central High School. Fifteen-year-old Elizabeth Eckford and the eight black students who arrived later were soon to be known as the Little Rock Nine. They had registered to attend the all-white school because its curriculum and state-of-the-art physical plant were among the best in the nation. They also lived close to Central, and it was far superior to the city's segregated black schools.

The day before the students showed up, truckloads of National Guardsmen cordoned off the school. White supremacists were heading toward Little Rock from all over the state, Governor Orval Eugene Faubus claimed, and he had called up the troops to keep the peace. If black students entered Central, he warned, "blood will run in the streets."

In the wake of the governor's actions, Little Rock city school superintendent Virgil T. Blossom asked black parents not to accompany their children to Central. Should there be violence, said Blossom, "It will be easier to protect the children if the adults aren't there."

Fearing the worst, Daisy Lee Gatson Bates, the thirty-seven-year-old president of the Arkansas State Conference of the NAACP, who was the principal adviser to the students and their families, arranged for an interracial escort of ministers to accompany the students to Central. On September 3, she notified the parents by telephone to have their children meet the ministers at eight-thirty the next morning. After a day of nonstop preparations, Bates fell asleep, forgetting to send word to the Eckfords, who had no telephone.

The following morning, Elizabeth Eckford said a prayer with her family and took the bus. The day promised to be a scorcher; the sun was blinding. Wearing sunglasses and a black and white dress she and her mother had made for the occasion, Eckford walked the block from the bus stop to Central alone, her notebook tucked against her chest. Four hundred white protesters and a phalanx of guardsmen waited at the schoolyard. Jeers erupted as she approached. A woman spat on Elizabeth's new dress. The guardsmen, whom she turned to for protection, offered none and blocked her path with bayonets.

Eckford tried to enter the building three times before turning to walk back to the bus stop. The hostile horde followed her there, where she sat down on a bench—petrified. Tears streamed from behind her glasses as she waited for a bus. When the other students arrived, the crowd turned them away, too. News photos of the scene shocked the nation.

The snapshot of Eckford and the throng of demonstrators must have reminded Murray of the night a group of white men surrounded her at the entrance to the Norfolk, Virginia, train station. She was only eight. Aunt Pauline, whom the men assumed to be white, had gone to the ticket counter unnoticed and inadvertently left Murray in the whites-only waiting room. Murray, an olive-skinned child, was "out of place," and her presence provoked a swarm of menacing stares. Like Eckford, Murray was cornered and "too frightened to scream." Fortunately, Aunt Pauline returned before she came to harm. They quickly boarded the train and took their seats in the black section.

On September 24, the day after a thousand protesters converged on

Central High with makeshift weapons, forcing the Little Rock Nine away for a second time, President Eisenhower sent one thousand paratroopers from the 101st Airborne Division to Little Rock. He also federalized the Arkansas National Guard. The decision to deploy troops was difficult for Eisenhower. He had tried to negotiate with Faubus, and he had urged civil rights leaders, much to their irritation, to have "patience and forbearance." But after the governor refused to obey the court order and quell the violence, Little Rock mayor Woodrow Mann asked for federal troops. The president had no recourse, he told the nation in an address telecast from the White House. As commander in chief, he was obligated to uphold the law and to take action against "mob rule."

. . .

BY MAY 1958, when Ernest Gideon Green graduated from Central, the first black student to do so, Murray could hardly keep her mind on her job. She found it disconcerting to be in her elegant Madison Avenue office, combing through law books, drafting background papers, while black students in the South risked their lives to get an education. She jumped at the chance to support the Little Rock Nine when a disagreement between them and the NAACP arose.

The association had taken the unprecedented step of awarding the Spingarn Medal to the students as a group (all previous medals had been given to an individual), and they were thrilled—until they learned that Daisy Bates, their counselor and chief strategist, was not a corecipient. An incredulous Melba Pattillo asked, "How can they draw a line like that? Yes, it was rough on us but she went through things which seem humanly impossible." Carlotta Walls declared, "Mrs. Bates and the nine of us are all one. Without her, we're like a head without a body. She should have been included." Ernest Green put it simply, "Mrs. Bates is more deserving than the rest of us."

Bates had not only coordinated every move the students made, she'd gone with them to Central and to meetings with authorities. They gathered at her home before and after school to fortify themselves. She and her husband, L. C. Bates, faced death threats all year. They risked foreclosure on their home, as subscriptions and advertising revenue for the *Arkansas State Press,* the weekly newspaper they owned and published, plummeted. Their sacrifice and support meant so much to the students that they unanimously agreed to refuse the award unless the NAACP named Bates as well.

When Murray heard about the controversy, she insisted that the

NAACP make amends for snubbing the person who'd engineered the desegregation of Central High. She believed that Daisy Bates was as vital to the school integration movement in Little Rock as Martin Luther King was to the bus boycott in Montgomery. "Just as a baseball fan cannot think of the last decade of the Dodgers without thinking of Jackie Robinson or the New York Yankees without thinking of their manager, Casey Stengel, it is impossible," Murray wrote to the Spingarn Award Committee, "to think of the Little Rock Nine without thinking of their manager, Daisy Bates." Not to acknowledge Bates as a corecipient was a slap in the face to the parents who had entrusted their children to her and to the local branch of the NAACP, for which she served as president. Murray must have also wondered, given her previous experience with male leaders in the NAACP, if the fact that Bates was a woman had influenced the committee's actions.

Sentiment for honoring Bates ran strong. The stories about the controversy that appeared in the black press left no doubt as to the sympathies of most editors. The campaign for Bates made an impact. For the first time since establishing the award, the committee changed its vote and unanimously agreed to name Daisy Bates as a corecipient.

· · ·

IN JUNE 1958, Daisy Bates and the Little Rock Nine took a four-day holiday to New York City, compliments of Local Six of the Hotel and Club Employees Union. The reception they received from Governor Harriman, Mayor Robert Wagner, and local civic groups was a welcome contrast to the antipathy they confronted at home. Local Six honored them with its annual Better Race Relations Award. Fourteen hundred people came to a luncheon for them that the Utility Club hosted at the Waldorf-Astoria. Area youth bands feted them with a parade. The group visited the United Nations, the Statue of Liberty, Coney Island, and Broadway, where Lena Horne and Ricardo Montalbán greeted them backstage before a production of the musical *Jamaica*.

On June 15, Bates and the students spoke at a rally sponsored by the NAACP at Brooklyn's Concord Baptist Church. Murray squeezed into the packed balcony, where she could "see every movement and expression of the platform guests." Ted Poston, who had lived with the Bateses while covering the story for the *New York Post*, introduced the students. Their maturity and courage moved Murray. She found it remarkable that after a year of unrelenting abuse, they appeared to be typical teenagers.

Fourteen-year-old Carlotta Walls, the youngest girl, credited Rosa Parks as her inspiration. Gloria Cecilia Ray, fifteen, had an aptitude for science. Elizabeth Eckford remained resolute, notwithstanding her encounter in the schoolyard. Sixteen-year-old Thelma Jean Mothershed had rarely missed a day of school, even though she had a heart condition. Fifteen-year-olds Melba Pattillo and Minnijean Brown were fans of the handsome young crooner Johnny Mathis. Fourteen-year-old Jefferson Allison Thomas, the youngest of the boys, loved to run track. Terrence James Roberts, fifteen, professed an interest in social work and law. Ernest Green, sixteen and the only senior, enjoyed playing jazz on his saxophone.

Murray was especially interested in Daisy Bates, whose petite stature belied her strength. No matter how many times white classmates had hit, cursed, shoved, kicked, tripped, spat on, or otherwise attacked her charges, Bates had counseled them not to retaliate. Her account of what the children had endured brought Murray and everyone else to tears. The audience responded with a $1,100 donation to the NAACP for expenses related to the case.

Murray managed to have a private conversation with Bates, during which she described the campaign to run her and her husband out of town and to shut down the *Arkansas State Press* before school resumed in the fall. White supremacists had stuck a burning cross in the Bateses' yard, hurled bricks through the window of their beautiful ranch home, threatened advertisers, beat up carriers, and confiscated their newspapers. The couple had already lost $10,000 in advertising revenue.

Eager to help, Murray came up with "a perfectly mad idea" of replacing the lost revenue by getting a thousand people to purchase four inches of ad space at ten dollars each. Those who bought space could have their names published or have the space left blank or use "a catchy pseudonym." Murray sent a ten-dollar check for ad space, and then she wrote to ten people, asking them to do the same. "The chips are really down in Little Rock," Murray warned ER. "May I count on you?"

· · ·

THE SOVIET PRESS had peppered ER with questions about Little Rock during her tour. Now that she was home, she joined the fray and sent a check to the *Arkansas State Press* "for an advertising space at the request of Miss Pauli Murray." ER profiled Daisy Bates and the students in "My Day," paraphrasing a section of one of Murray's letter.

This group has made a very fine impression here. The dignity and gallantry of Mrs. Bates is easy to see, and the young people carried themselves with dignity, too. It is good to know that one of these children graduated from school, making the honor roll for several successive months, and another one won a prize for a biology exhibit.

In looking at the group, you wonder why anyone would have wanted to keep them out of an American school or to do them harm. It is to be hoped that their courage will make it easier for other children to follow in their footsteps.

ER condemned the people who harassed the students, and she praised those, black and white alike, who refused to back down. She was convinced that there were Arkansans ready and willing to integrate the schools. All they needed to step forward was strong leadership from the federal government. ER's frustration with the president led her to goad him in her column. "I think instead of sending troops," she wrote, "I wish President Eisenhower would go down to Little Rock and lead the colored children into the school." No matter what segregationists believed or wanted, "the world has changed," she asserted. "The old doctrine of equal but separate cannot hold any longer."

. . .

ON JUNE 21, 1958, barely a week after the Little Rock Nine's trumpeted visit to New York City, Federal District Judge Harry J. Lemley granted the Little Rock School Board's request to postpone integration for two and a half years. Lemley acknowledged that the black students had a constitutional right to attend Central, but he said the pandemonium besetting the city proved that the time was not right.

Two days following Lemley's ruling, Lester Granger, Martin Luther King, A. Philip Randolph, and Roy Wilkins went to the White House and asked President Eisenhower to articulate and implement "a clear national policy" supporting school integration. When Pauli Murray read that the president had given the men no indication that he would aggressively back the *Brown* decision, she put pen to paper again.

In a testy proposal to NAACP board chairman Channing Tobias that she copied to ER, Murray urged the organization to mobilize "economic resources to aid the victims of economic reprisals in the South" and to develop "cooperatives, credit unions and other organizations of economic advancement." What was needed, she argued, "is a 'United Negro Appeal' similar to the fund-raising drives of the 'United Jewish Appeal.'"

Despite the efforts of supporters around the country, the *Arkansas State Press* folded the next year, the Bateses left town, and state officials closed the Little Rock public schools to avoid integration. During the 1958–59 school year, approximately 3,500 black and white Little Rock high school students were shut out of the public schools. Most black students, having little means to travel to other cities for schooling, did little if any academic work. White students had the option of attending private alternative schools, which were segregated, as well as commuting to schools outside the district. The schools would reopen for the 1959–60 term, but the Bateses would not return to Arkansas until 1965. Daisy Bates resurrected the *Arkansas State Press* in 1984, and it would survive until 1997. Fifteen years after Murray proposed the concept of a United Negro Appeal to the NAACP, a group of activists would establish the National Black United Fund to create and sustain economic institutions within African American communities.

THE TEST OF OUR PROGR...
WE ADD MORE TO THE ABUNDANCE
WHO HAVE MUCH; IT IS WHETHER W
ENOUGH FOR THOSE WHO HAV

FRANKLIN D. ROOSEVELT

Entertainer and activist Harry Belafonte with Eleanor Roosevelt at the
World's Fair, Brussels, 1958. The housing problems he faced in New York
City, like the eviction notice whites served Murray and her sister Mildred in
Los Angeles fourteen years earlier, made racial discrimination a personal issue
for ER. *(Franklin D. Roosevelt Presidential Library)*

50

"Discrimination Does Something Intangible and Harmful"

While Pauli Murray was earning her stripes in corporate law, Morris Milgram, her old friend from the Workers Defense League, was starting a new career as a housing developer. His recent projects, the Concord Park and Greenbelt Knoll housing subdivisions near Philadelphia, were the first privately funded and racially integrated developments for middle-class families in the nation.

Murray's friendship with Milgram and one of his investors, her former Howard University School of Law professor William Hastie, gave her a personal connection to the venture. In fact, Milgram credited his work with Murray on the Odell Waller campaign and her epic poem "Dark

Testament," which he had read in full to audiences around the country at least fifty times, as the inspiration for his decision to devote his life to building integrated housing. The cycle of poverty that entrapped the Wallers and Davises and the legacy of slavery Murray chronicled in her poem convinced Milgram that housing segregation played a central role in the creation and maintenance of a racial caste system in the United States.

After Murray sent Eleanor Roosevelt an *Ebony* magazine feature about integrated housing that mentioned Milgram's enterprise, ER promised to visit Concord Park and Greenbelt Knoll "sometime soon." On July 3, 1958, she met with Milgram and Murray at her New York City apartment. There, over lunch, Milgram laid out an ambitious plan for a new project, Modern Community Developers, Inc. MCD was a for-profit corporation whose goal was to provide technical, practical, and, where possible, financial assistance to developers seeking to build integrated housing around the country.

ER was so taken by Milgram's passion, intelligence, and winning personality that she agreed to join the MCD board and to mention the project in her column. She also made a rare request of her own. A young friend of hers was having trouble finding an apartment, and she asked Milgram and Murray if they could help. ER was so incensed about her friend's situation that she shared her feelings with readers.

"I am sure that every New Yorker was shocked the other day to read that Harry Belafonte and his charming wife and baby were finding it practically impossible to get an apartment in New York City except in what might be considered segregated areas or in a hotel," she wrote. "I have long been saying that in the North we have only one step to take to meet the Supreme Court order of non-segregation in schools, and that is non-segregation in housing. In New York State we have the laws necessary to achieve non-segregated housing if we saw that they were diligently respected."

Belafonte was a native New Yorker and a consummate entertainer whose popularity spanned the globe. ER had seen him mesmerize audiences from off-Broadway theater houses to the American pavilion at the 1958 World's Fair in Brussels. That landlords in his hometown turned him away because of his race was unconscionable to her.

"I can think of nothing I would enjoy more than having Mr. and Mrs. Belafonte as my neighbors," she continued. "I hope they will find a home shortly where they and their enchanting little boy can grow up without feeling the evils of the segregation pattern. Discrimination does something intangible and harmful to the souls of both white and colored people."

Belafonte's case was proof positive that housing discrimination transcended regional and class boundaries. Although he would eventually purchase the thirteen-story building on West End Avenue where he had been denied an apartment, the impact of his ordeal worried ER so deeply that she invited him and his family to move into her apartment. Belafonte "thanked her profusely" and declined. To accept this offer, he explained, would have meant "walking away from a battle" he had to face.

ER profiled Milgram in her column, citing his successful track record as a developer of integrated housing projects in Philadelphia. She highlighted the importance of MCD, which would allow him to share his expertise and foster desegregated housing at a national level. Like Milgram, who practiced what he preached by moving into one of his housing developments, ER was ready to move into an integrated complex. "Now I am waiting to have someone announce the construction of apartment houses here in New York City on an open occupancy basis," she wrote. "I have tried to find one in the area in which I would like to live, but so far have been unsuccessful. I hope before long to hear of such a development."

Housing discrimination was on ER's mind the night she saw *A Raisin in the Sun,* Lorraine Hansberry's prize-winning play about an African American family's struggle to move into an all-white neighborhood. ER had already read the script, and the production touched her. "This play has been praised by all the critics so it does not need my praise to add to its popularity," she opined in her column. "But I would like to thank both the author and Mr. Poitier for an evening that had real meaning, and I hope meaning that will sink into the conscience of America."

51

"There Are Times When a Legal Brief Is Inadequate"

Between the fall of 1958 and the summer of 1959, Pauli Murray learned about two cases that persuaded her that corporate law was not her calling. The first, which was detailed in a story Ted Poston broke in the *New York Post,* was about two black boys in Monroe, North Carolina. Nine-year-old James Hanover Thompson and seven-year-old David "Fuzzy" Ezzelle Simpson were charged with sexual assault and sentenced indefinitely to the Morrison Training School for Negro Delinquent Boys for playing a kissing game with seven-year-old Sissy Marcus. Marcus was white. Her father vowed to kill the boys and lynch their parents. The boys were beaten and threatened with castration while incarcerated.

The lengthy sentence and the fact that the authorities denied the boys advice of counsel and visitation by their mothers for six days triggered a flood of telegrams and letters from around the world. Only after national press coverage, public outrage, and the efforts of Robert Williams, president of the Monroe chapter of the NAACP, and Conrad Lynn, a civil rights attorney from New York, were the children released. Lynn, who asked Eleanor Roosevelt to help, later recalled that she had cried when he told her about the children. She then called Eisenhower and insisted that he "put a stop to the persecution." The president, in turn, called North Carolina governor Luther Hodges, and the boys, who had served three months, were released to their mothers.

The second incident took place in Poplarville, Mississippi, where a gang of masked, white-gloved men abducted Mack Charles Parker, a twenty-three-year-old black truck driver, from jail and murdered him.

Parker was awaiting trial for the kidnapping and rape of a pregnant white woman. Although his accuser had picked him out of a lineup, she was not certain that his vehicle was the one used in the kidnapping, and she wavered on whether Parker looked or sounded like her attacker. Parker went to his death claiming his innocence. Nine days after his abduction, his battered and bullet-ridden body surfaced in the Pearl River near Bogalusa, Louisiana.

Parker's murder came on the heels of the tenth anniversary of the Universal Declaration of Human Rights. "What made the recent miscarriage of justice in a Mississippi case particularly sad," said ER, was that Parker "was kidnapped from his jail cell and lost his life without even going to trial." The chance of a fair trial, had Parker lived, was doubtful. There were men in the community intent on meting out their own punishment, and the sixty-three-year-old trial judge, Sebe Dale, was a white supremacist. Though the FBI identified several white suspects in an in-depth report to the local authorities, no one was indicted for the murder.

The Parker lynching and Murray's inability to help the North Carolina boys drew her into a state of despair. It had been seventeen years since Odell Waller's execution, and the judicial system was still failing African Americans. Furthermore, the financial security and prestige of being a corporate attorney brought her little personal gratification. She craved a creative outlet.

Murray retreated as often as she could to The MacDowell Colony. There, she channeled her emotions into a series of prayerful poems. "For Mack C. Parker" was a meditation on "The cornered and trapped, / The bludgeoned and crushed, / The hideously slain" victim of lynching. "Collect for Poplarville" was an entreaty for "that most difficult of tasks— / to pray for them, / to follow, not burn, thy cross!" Murray revised and sent "Dark Testament," her homage to Stephen Vincent Benét's epic poem *John Brown's Body*, to Eleanor Roosevelt, along with "Psalm of Deliverance," a poem she dedicated to the black schoolchildren of the South. ER found Murray's poems "strong and stirring and disquieting, as they should be."

· · ·

BY THE SPRING OF 1959, Murray was beginning to believe that practicing law put her in conflict with her true calling as a poet. "There are times when a legal brief is inadequate to make the point," she wrote to ER. As a lawyer, Murray was bound by the facts, but as a poet, her job was to respect the truth. And this required that she write about "the 'shape of things to come' long before people . . . are able to comprehend them," as her role models Countee Cullen and Benét had done.

While Murray pondered her options, she continued to work at the firm, write poetry, and contribute wherever she could to civil rights. She reviewed and recommended changes in a book contract for Martin Luther King. She monitored developments with the Bateses in Arkansas. She followed civil rights legislation at the federal and state levels, and she reached out to one of the most influential men in government.

Murray had watched Senate majority leader Lyndon Baines Johnson engineer passage of the 1957 civil rights bill. This bill, the first such legislation in eighty-two years, authorized the creation of a civil rights division in the U.S. Department of Justice and a commission on civil rights with investigatory power. The bill made voting rights violations a federal offense and empowered the U.S. attorney general to prosecute voting rights abuses.

Johnson was now considering two new civil rights proposals. One, his own bill, called for a federal conciliation commission that would be an advisory body without enforcement power on school desegregation. The other measure, advanced by Florida governor Thomas LeRoy Collins, would establish administrative commissions within the states to plan and oversee desegregation.

Murray favored the Collins proposal, but she forwarded a critical summary of both bills to ER. She also wrote Majority Leader Johnson a pointed letter, urging him to seize the moment. "If you would use your genius for drafting a Wagner-type 'charter of civil rights' as was done in the Wagner Labor Relations Act, you would go down into history and probably up into wherever you want to go. But piecemeal legislation won't do it," she warned. "You've got to approach fundamental solutions. The time is ripe and you are at the helm of the Senate. What are you going to do about it?"

Eleanor Roosevelt (second from left), the camel Duchess, granddaughter Nina (third from right), and unidentified Israeli hosts in the camel market, Beersheba, Israel, 1959. It amused ER that people at home seemed more curious about Duchess than other aspects of the trip. *(Courtesy of Werner M. Loval)*

52

"That Granddaughter Must Be a Chip off the Venerable Block"

Eleanor Roosevelt and her sixteen-year-old granddaughter, Nina Roosevelt, took a month-long trip abroad in March 1959. They stopped in Italy, Iran, Israel, France, and England, visiting historic sites and humanitarian projects. They met socially with foreign leaders and diplomats. They spent time in Iran with ER's daughter, Anna, and her husband, James A. Halsted, both of whom were working at the newly established Pahlavi University Medical School, in Shiraz.

Nina, the eldest daughter of ER's youngest son, John, and Anne Lindsay Clark, was a shy, serious girl. An avid reader like her grandmother, Nina buried her head during the long flight to Rome in *The Ugly Amer-*

ican, a popular novel about American arrogance in Southeast Asia by Eugene Burdick and William Lederer. ER's reading material included Michel Del Castillo's novel *Child of Our Time,* which was based on the author's internment in a Nazi concentration camp.

ER had never traveled alone with one of her granddaughters, and she was eager to introduce Nina to her favorite places. In Rome, they lingered at the Pantheon. At St. Peter's Basilica, they admired Michelangelo's *Pietà.* In Iran, they walked through the tombs of ancient Persian kings and dined with the shah in the Marble Palace. In Israel, they saw the Dead Sea Scrolls, attended Easter rites in Jerusalem, and admired "sapphire blue" fish while riding a glass-bottomed boat in the Red Sea.

The day they arrived at the Cathedral of Notre Dame in Paris, the sun gave the medieval rose windows a "special brilliance." In London, they made a beeline to Grosvenor Square to see the bronze statue of Franklin Roosevelt, depicted standing with a cape draped over his shoulders. It was fitting that the architects had placed "fountains and the benches" nearby, ER told her granddaughter, for the president "always liked to have people around him."

Nina kept "close watch" on her grandmother throughout their journey. Indeed, at times, she felt compelled to take control of the schedule. "People forget that she's 74," Nina told a reporter. "They'd have her climbing any number of stairs or walking miles over cobblestones unless I put my foot down." Nina's concern was justified. On more than one occasion, she had to stop ER from nodding off to sleep by tapping her on the foot. This was quite "awkward" when they were in conversation with others or when ER was standing up.

Murray was always interested in ER's foreign travel, and this trip, which included visits to historic and religious sites Murray longed to see, had special significance. She was also fond of Nina and her family. They were living next door to Val-Kill in Stone Cottage, when Murray met them over lunch.

Murray giggled when she read the news story about the baby camel Nina bought in Beersheba, Israel. Nina had planned to bring Duchess back to Hyde Park. However, the U.S. Department of Agriculture blocked the camel's entry because it came from a region thought to be plagued by hoof-and-mouth disease. Disappointed, yet determined to make the best of circumstances, Nina donated Duchess to a poor Bedouin.

In Murray's view, Nina had found the perfect solution. She had not only helped a needy person, she'd outmaneuvered the Eisenhower administration. "It is not yet clear from the news stories," Murray wrote tongue-in-cheek to ER, "whether it was the CAMEL which might be subject to hoof-and-mouth disease or the ADMINISTRATION! That granddaughter must be a chip off the venerable block."

· · ·

ELEANOR ROOSEVELT INVITED MURRAY to lunch at her New York City apartment on May 15, 1959. Murray took Renee Barlow, whom she had introduced earlier in a letter as "a former YWCA gal and an Episcopalian who adores you and would just like to sit and look at you while we chatter—or, on the other hand, she deeply needs your guidance as to what a sincere Anglo-American can do in this present crisis to be effective."

It is not known if Murray said in words that she and Renee were partners, but ER may have sensed that they were more than coworkers for several reasons. First, Murray exuded an air of happiness friends had not seen prior to her relationship with Renee. Second, in nearly twenty years of correspondence, Murray had not indicated a romantic interest in men. She had taken only female relatives and friends to private gatherings with ER, except for Maida Springer's son Eric and longtime friend Morris Milgram, who was married. (Murray would later take her brother and nephews to Val-Kill.) Third, ER had close friends who were lesbian, such as the former newspaper reporter Lorena Hickok, and who lived in partnerships that resembled marriage, as did the progressive activists Esther Lape and Elizabeth Read. Furthermore, Murray had come to rely on ER's acceptance, and she must have believed that ER would embrace Renee as well.

One topic they discussed that day was the local hospital workers strike. A week earlier, more than three thousand cooks, housekeeping and laundry workers, nurses' aides, orderlies, and porters had gone on strike against six private hospitals in New York City. These workers were not guaranteed minimum wage and were excluded from unemployment insurance coverage and disability benefits. Conditions were so bad, union officials charged, that many workers needed welfare assistance to survive. Although these employees were vital to the care of patients and the work of the technical, administrative, and medical staffs, management refused to consider their grievances or recognize Local 1199 of the Retail Drug Employees Union.

Murray had been jailed twenty-five years earlier for picketing with workers who'd organized a chapter of the American Newspaper Guild at the *New York Amsterdam News.* She could not resist the invitation to join the Citizens' Committee for a Just Settlement of the Hospital Strike. Among its influential members were her old allies A. Philip Randolph and Bayard Rustin, along with the theologian Reinhold Niebuhr, distinguished jurists Grenville Clark and Telford Taylor, Councilman Stanley Isaacs, and Gardner Taylor, pastor of the Concord Baptist Church. The committee urged union recognition, arbitration of "all economic issues," and that upon "union recognition, the union waive its right to strike."

ER generally opposed unionization of workers in critical areas, such as hospital work, public safety, and publicly owned utilities. In this case, the conditions hospital workers faced and management's rigidity persuaded her to side with the workers. "It seems to me," ER said in frustration, "that this whole situation has been very stupidly handled by the refusal of the heads of the hospital to meet with their employees from the very beginning." The stalemate would last for forty-six days before management and the employees reached a settlement.

PART VIII

LIGHTING THE PATH
FOR NEW ACTIVISTS,
1959–62

Left to right: President Kwame Nkrumah of Ghana; African American scholars W. E. B. Du Bois and his wife, Shirley Graham Du Bois; and an unidentified man at reception following Nkrumah's inauguration, July 1, 1960, in Accra, Ghana. Pauli Murray had arrived five months earlier, brimming with hope for the newly independent nation-state. *(W. E. B. Du Bois Papers, Special Collections and University Archives, W. E. B. Du Bois Library, University of Massachusetts Amherst)*

53

"Nothing I Had Read or Heard Prepared Me"

Late in the fall of 1959, Pauli Murray accepted a three-year appointment as senior lecturer in the new Ghana School of Law, in Accra. She had learned about the position from an advertisement Maida Springer brought back from Africa. Murray had not taught since her days with the WPA Workers' Education Project. She had hoped to teach after she finished the master of laws at the University of California, Berkeley, but no offers had come her way. Most law schools, except those that were all female or all black, would not hire women or black faculty. Even Howard University, which had no women faculty when Murray was a student in the early 1940s, currently had only one female instructor, Cynthia Straker, who doubled as the law librarian.

Given the bleak prospects for a career teaching law, Murray had gone into private practice, running her own office, until Paul, Weiss, Rifkind, Wharton and Garrison hired her as an associate attorney. Corporate law had paid well, yet the work left Murray unfulfilled. At forty-nine, she returned to teaching because it offered steady income and reconnected her with a family tradition that had begun with Grandfather Robert. Unlike Murray's job at the firm, where she felt like "a desk lawyer in an assembly-line practice," rarely interacting with clients, teaching engaged her directly with people.

Springer's work as an international representative for the AFL-CIO and her friendships with African leaders piqued Murray's interest in Africa. Murray had met the Kenyan labor activist Tom Mboya and the future president of Tanzania Julius Nyerere at Springer's home. The fact that Ghana was the first sub-Saharan African colony to achieve independence (from Great Britain, in 1957) gave Murray a sense of high purpose. As a teacher, she would both witness and be a partner to history in the making.

On February 3, 1960, Murray sailed out of New York City on the SS *Tatra*. It was her first trip abroad. In addition to her beloved Shetland sheepdog, Smokey, she brought a donation of law books from the attorneys at the firm, a cache of Savarin coffee from the clerical staff, and a basket of fruit from Eleanor Roosevelt.

Before the *Tatra* reached Ghana, it docked in Monrovia, Liberia. Eager to set foot on the continent, Murray disembarked. "Nothing I had read or heard prepared me," she recalled later, for

> the flies and insects swarming over the smoked fish sold on the ground in the native markets; the naked children with protruding stomachs wading through cesspools of muck; a child with large tumors growing out of his neck begging in the street; the furnitureless mud shacks with dirt floors and roofs of straw pieced together with old tarpaulins or discarded fragments of rusty tin; the mangy, half-starved dogs creeping along the gutters . . . ; and the half-comatose, scurvy-ridden old people dozing in the sun and looking like breathing corpses.

Murray found the poverty in Ghana just as staggering. While the countryside was reminiscent of the American rural South, the language gap, the frustratingly slow pace of life, the shortage of basic supplies, and the isolation from family and friends made her homesick. Having to drive on the left side of crowded roads flanked by open ditches on both sides made getting from one place to another an obstacle course. However, these problems paled in comparison to the physical challenges.

Murray suffered intermittent attacks of malaria. The heat made her so uncomfortable that she sometimes showered "three times a day." Even Smokey had problems acclimating. He developed pneumonia after Murray "cut his hair short to relieve him from the heat and ticks."

Murray's adjustment was further complicated by an "entrenched custom" that required foreign professionals to hire African male cook-stewards. Because she had grown up in the American South, where blacks were once enslaved and where many were still relegated to domestic service in white homes, the thought of employing an African servant, and the subservience expected of them by their mostly foreign or white employers, offended her. But an endless procession of job applicants eventually convinced Murray to set her objections aside, and she hired Yaredi Akare.

Yaro, as Akare asked to be called, was a twenty-eight-year-old Ghanaian with "an angry-looking gash" on his left cheek, a tribal scar. He belonged to an ethnic group from one of the poorest regions in northern Ghana, referred to as the Frafra people, who marked their babies with a cut on the cheek to distinguish them from other Ghanaians. The Frafra had low status in Ghanaian culture, and Yaro's "dignity and lack of obsequiousness," despite the discrimination he faced, earned Murray's respect and trust.

In her journal and round-robins to family and friends, Murray chronicled her daily routine and included observations of political events, such as the ratification of Ghana's constitution and the election of the nation's first president, Kwame Nkrumah. That the country had no functional bar underscored the significance of her job: to prepare the first generation of homegrown attorneys.

At the law school, Murray held the distinction of being the sole American, one of only two women, and the instructor of what her colleagues deemed the most "politically controversial" course in the program: constitutional and administrative law. Her training differed from that of the other faculty, who included a former judge from the Republic of Tanganyika, a former senator from the Union of South Africa who'd opposed the apartheid government, a Ghanaian trained in England, and an Englishman who served as the school's director. There were few library facilities and no curricular materials. Her students were all male. Most worked full-time and had no previous college training.

To introduce the core concepts of constitutional government, Murray mimeographed lecture notes and case materials on legal-size paper that she fastened into packets "with bright-blue covers." She adopted an American-style discussion method that required students to study the readings in advance, so they could talk about them in class. She changed the seating in the room to a rectangle, making it possible for students to see one another when they spoke. She also made a practice of bringing up hot-button issues near the end of each session.

Although Murray's teaching strategy initially befuddled her students, they soon embraced it. They asked for additional time and readings to study landmark U.S. civil rights cases. Their debates often became so animated that they "switched from English to their own vernaculars."

Joseph Musah, one of the youngest and brightest students, began the course skeptical of his American professor. He soon changed his mind. "We used to accept without questioning whatever the lecturer told us," he admitted to Murray. "Through your class we have now learned to inquire." Musah's experience with Murray would serve him well. He would later earn a master's degree at Yale University, return to his homeland after Nkrumah was ousted, and serve in the national government as an elected and appointed official.

Front left to right: Michigan governor G. Mennen Williams, Adlai Stevenson, Eleanor Roosevelt, and Michigan senator Patrick V. McNamara in Michigan, 1960. During Stevenson's bid for the presidency, ER was his most influential friend and supporter. *(Franklin D. Roosevelt Presidential Library)*

54

"It Is a Bit of a Pest to Have to Keep Still"

On February 1, 1960, Ezell A. Blair Jr., Franklin E. McCain, Joseph A. McNeil, and David L. Richmond, students from the historically black North Carolina Agricultural and Technical College, entered F. W. Woolworth's, took seats at the lunch counter, and asked to be served. Woolworth's, like most white-owned restaurants in the South, did not serve African Americans at its counters, so the men—who came to be known as the Greensboro Four—sat in silent protest while the white patrons ate. The following day, twenty-nine students showed up. By the end of the week, more than two hundred students, including whites from local colleges, joined in. By April, sit-ins and other forms of nonviolent protest had spread across the South.

Murray saw these sit-ins as the fruit of the seeds she and her fellow Howardites had planted twenty years earlier in their campaign against segregated eateries in Washington, D.C. She saw the North Carolina students' courage, and the growing number of black and white activists who joined them, as evidence that the civil rights movement was gathering steam.

Eleanor Roosevelt was also inspired by the students' bravery and the nonviolent-protest strategy espoused by Reverend King and the Congress of Racial Equality. She made her sympathies known by lending her name to a full-page ad with the heading "Heed Their Rising Voices," published in the *New York Times* and paid for by the Committee to Defend Martin Luther King and the Struggle for Freedom in the South. She criticized a Georgia court for sentencing King to Reidsville State Prison Farm on the trumped-up charge of violating his probation for a minor traffic offense. She applauded Senate majority leader Lyndon Johnson in her column for his efforts to bring a civil rights bill to the floor for discussion.

ER's advocacy so angered some southerners that her address to an integrated audience of two thousand at the predominantly black Gibbs Junior College, in Saint Petersburg, Florida, provoked a bomb threat. The auditorium had to be evacuated for thirty minutes before she could resume her talk. Two years earlier, segregationists had bombed a tree less than three hundred yards from a church in Guilford, North Carolina, where ER had spoken, and the Ku Klux Klan had threatened to attack the Highlander Folk School in Monteagle, Tennessee, on the day she was to participate in a workshop on integration. ER had not backed down in North Carolina or Tennessee, and she would not be silenced in Florida. Undaunted, she insisted, "If I blew up, it wouldn't change one iota of what inevitably is going to happen."

Like Murray, ER was also returning to the classroom. She had always loved teaching. She was good at it. And she had hated giving up her job at the Todhunter School for girls when FDR became president and she first lady. Not surprisingly, she was delighted to accept an appointment as visiting lecturer for a seminar on international relations and the law at Brandeis University. She would commute to the Boston area to teach and serve as host for *Prospects of Mankind,* an educational television series produced by WGBH. This monthly program, which featured a discussion among influential thinkers and leaders, plus the Brandeis seminar, fed her need to be engaged in world affairs.

At seventy-five, ER had no plans to curtail her schedule or be silent about what mattered to her. Only a collision with a car slowed her down.

Temporarily sidelined at home, she reported to Murray in frustration, "I managed to get behind a car which was backing up so I was knocked down and some ligaments in my foot were torn. This necessitated my canceling most of my engagements for a week, so that I could keep off the foot. It is a bit of a pest to have to keep still but perhaps I needed the rest and this was the only way I could take one!"

. . .

INJURY ASIDE, ELEANOR ROOSEVELT weighed in on the 1960 presidential campaign by chairing the Draft Stevenson Committee. The governor, having lost in 1952 and 1956, refused to seek the Democratic nomination outright. However, if nominated, he told ER, he would run. She seconded Stevenson's nomination at the Democratic National Convention and lobbied delegates into the wee hours. In the end, she could not woo enough delegates to his camp. She went home disappointed and without endorsing the dashing forty-three-year-old nominee, Senator John Fitzgerald Kennedy of Massachusetts.

ER knew that Kennedy had the personal drive, financial resources, and political organization to run for president. Yet she did not believe that he had the experience, intellect, or commitment to the principles she thought necessary to serve as the nation's chief executive. Kennedy had not distinguished himself since his election to Congress, first as a representative in 1946, then as a senator in 1952. Moreover, his cautious approach to civil rights, his unwillingness to denounce Joseph McCarthy, and the disagreements his father, Joseph P. Kennedy, had had with the Roosevelt administration (which eventually resulted in his resignation as ambassador to England), caused ER to doubt the senator's integrity.

John Kennedy knew that Eleanor Roosevelt's support was indispensable for the general election, and he sent a string of emissaries to speak on his behalf. She finally agreed to meet him privately at Val-Kill on Sunday, August 14, 1960. This day held double significance for ER. It marked the twenty-fifth anniversary of the Social Security Act, which was a legislative landmark in Franklin Roosevelt's administration. It was also the day of her thirteen-year-old granddaughter Sally Roosevelt's funeral. Sally, Nina's younger sister, had fallen off a horse four days earlier at summer camp, passed out climbing a mountain the next day, and died of a brain hemorrhage in the ambulance on the way to the hospital. The child's death "was a great blow to all of us," ER lamented in a letter to Murray. "It is hard to realize that she was taken from us so quickly."

Understandably in no mood for small talk, ER laid out what the senator needed to do to get her support: utilize Stevenson in the campaign and as a resource on foreign affairs; reach out to the governor's supporters; and show African Americans that a Kennedy administration would be serious about civil rights. Only by solidifying the liberal base, she maintained, could he carry the populous Democratic strongholds of California, Illinois, and New York. Kennedy thanked her and pledged to address her concerns.

ER endorsed the senator after their meeting, but she did not offer to stump for him. Though he was a charming man with "a quick mind" and "hospitable to new ideas," she reported in "My Day," he was also "hard-headed." He would have to prove that he was a man of conviction before she would travel with the campaign.

· · ·

"I THOUGHT OF YOU with deep affection and sympathy when I read of young Sally's death," Murray wrote to ER as soon as the news reached her in Ghana. Murray had fond memories of Sally, a charming little girl, regaling a lunch party at Val-Kill with her account of ER's bath in the family swimming pool the morning after Hurricane Hazel.

As far as the presidential campaign, Murray knew that Stevenson was a poor campaigner, but she felt that his intelligence, values, and knowledge of world affairs made him far superior to Kennedy. Furthermore, the senator's lukewarm embrace of civil rights, refusal to condemn McCarthy, and selection of Texan Lyndon Johnson as his vice presidential running mate made the Democratic ticket unpalatable to Murray. She had long suffered the economic and emotional costs of racial segregation and political persecution, and she had no patience with a candidate who was either unclear or afraid to say where he stood on these critical issues. Murray's brief response to ER's endorsement spoke volumes: "I see you've finally come out for Kennedy. No comment."

55

"I Hope You Were Not in Danger"

In Ghana, Pauli Murray found herself countering criticism of U.S. race relations and foreign policy at gatherings of the American Women's Association of Accra and the First Conference of African Women and Women of African Descent. This was a new experience, as she was more accustomed to calling out U.S. shortcomings in these areas. Fearing that the United States and European nations might underestimate the desire for power and autonomy in the new African nation-states (seventeen would emerge from colonialism in 1960), Murray warned in an opinion letter she shared with friends that "the Africans, too, are seeking to make themselves great in the eyes of the world. They aspire to be the 'third force' and a world leader toward peace. This is the meaning of their nationalism and Pan-Africanism. They seek only what they believe we have achieved, but they want it on their own terms."

Murray's concerns struck a chord with Eleanor Roosevelt, who wrote back, "Africa is certainly pinpointed for all of us today, and the Soviets are making a great play to gain the favor of the new states who have been admitted to the U.N. I hope you were not in danger at any point!"

ER's apprehension was justified, for danger was knocking at Murray's door. Relations between the United States and Ghana had been tense ever since a struggle for power erupted between Patrice Lumumba, prime minister of the newly independent Congo, and rival forces supported by Belgian colonial interests and U.S. intelligence. Ghana's president, Kwame Nkrumah, criticized the United States for its alliance with the colonial powers. Reprisals against native dissidents, Europeans, and Americans escalated. Not even the distinguished diplomat Ralph Bunche, who was overseeing operations for the U.N. in the Congo, escaped harassment.

Nkrumah had initially favored Murray's appointment to the law school, thanks to Maida Springer, who had sent him copies of *States' Laws on Race and Color* and *Dark Testament and Other Poems,* as well as a letter of introduction praising Murray as a brilliant lawyer with "a sense of history, the love of teaching and the ability to challenge searching young minds." However, Murray's nationality and her assertion of American democratic values quickly put her at odds with Ghanaian officials.

Murray proved to be all Springer had promised and more. Indeed, Murray's course on constitutional law, her opposition to the Ghanaian government's preventive detention act, which allowed authorities to imprison those labeled as national security risks for up to five years, and her support for Joseph Danquah angered Nkrumah. Danquah, the founder of Ghana's first daily newspaper, had run against Nkrumah for the presidency and had spent a year in prison under the preventive detention program.

The emergence of a one-party government increasingly intolerant of free speech virtually ensured that Murray would come under surveillance. Her suspicion that she was being watched was confirmed when half a dozen uniformed members of the Criminal Investigation Department showed up in her class. Murray felt a sense of déjà vu as she battled the denial of civil rights and civil liberties on African soil. Determined not to shrink in fear, she took a deep breath and taught the class as she had always done. The investigators never came back. Nevertheless, she knew her days in Ghana were numbered.

· · ·

SHORTLY AFTER MURRAY'S BRUSH with security agents, Yale Law School professor Fowler V. Harper visited Ghana to lecture on the American judicial system. He was awed by what Murray had accomplished despite limited resources, underprepared students, and the government's hostility toward Americans. A civil rights and civil liberties advocate, Harper was also convinced of two things: that Murray was an extraordinary teacher and that she would be deported. He urged her to come to Yale and study for the doctor of juridical science, a degree that would qualify her to teach in an American law school.

Murray was unsure about starting a doctorate at age fifty, but she applied anyway. When the acceptance letter arrived, indicating that the school had awarded her a $5,000 fellowship, she had less than six months to finish the course she was teaching and a textbook she was writing with Leslie Rubin, a senior lecturer at the University College of Ghana. A Jew who had been the only colored member of the South African parliament, Rubin had suffered discrimination and had left his country in protest of apartheid. The text he and Murray were writing, *The Constitution and Government of Ghana,* became the first volume in the Law in Africa Series, published by Sweet & Maxwell of London.

As Murray prepared to return to the States, she tried to capture her feelings in the essay "What Is Africa to Me?" Coming to terms with her African heritage and the uniqueness of her African American background was at the heart of her quest. "I am beginning to understand that I am the product of a new history which began on African shores but which has not been shared by Africans, a history accompanied by such radical changes in a new environment that over time it produced a new identity," she wrote. "For me, the net gain of coming to Africa has been to reexperience imaginatively this break in continuity as well as to gain an appreciation for the peoples and cultures who remained on the African side of the historical divide."

At peace with who she was, Murray neither romanticized nor demonized Africa and its people. "Africans are no longer faceless peoples," she declared. "They have emerged as individuals who may be kind or cruel, honest or thievish, industrious or lazy, arrogant or gentle, as the case may be. And in this knowledge of real people, lingering ghosts of the past have been exorcised. I can face all the contradictions of my American background without ambivalence and return to my country with renewed determination to claim my heritage."

Tractors for Freedom Committee members (front, left to right) Eleanor Roosevelt; Walter Reuther, president of the United Automobile Workers; and Milton Eisenhower, president of Johns Hopkins University with (at rear) a delegation of Cuban invasion prisoners, Washington, D.C., May 22, 1961. ER hoped that an exchange of tractors with the Cuban government would save lives. *(Franklin D. Roosevelt Presidential Library)*

56

"Read That You Had a Bad Case of Flu"

On January 20, 1961, John Kennedy took the oath of office and became the thirty-fifth president of the United States. Eleanor Roosevelt had brought the full weight of her influence to his campaign after he had pledged to end segregation in federal housing and joined her at a civil rights conference in Harlem. She rallied African Americans and Stevenson supporters, raised funds, and appeared in political ads. "If I am right," she wrote optimistically in her column, "perhaps we are going to have someone who can draw from the people of the United States the greatness that underlies all their everyday concerns."

A warm atmosphere permeated the inaugural ceremony, despite the bitter cold and a six-inch carpet of snow. ER arrived early, swathed in a fur coat, hat, and blanket. Kennedy had offered her a seat on the podium with his family, in gratitude for her contributions to his campaign, but ER declined and sat with friends on a stand beneath the dais. It must have pleased her that Marian Anderson, who had been barred from Constitution Hall twenty-two years earlier, sang "The Star-Spangled Banner" before Kennedy gave his address. Hard of hearing, ER lifted her head as the newly sworn-in president began, "We observe today not a victory of party, but a celebration of freedom—symbolizing an end, as well as a beginning—signifying renewal, as well as change." Perhaps no line in his speech excited her more than his embrace of the U.N. as "our last best hope in an age where the instruments of war have far outpaced the instruments of peace." ER left the Capitol grounds buoyed by the president's call to service: "My fellow Americans, ask not what your country can do for you; ask what you can do for your country."

From Ghana, where she was working on the index and galleys for her textbook, Pauli Murray tracked developments in the new administration through press accounts and letters from home. She was not surprised by ER's optimism or that Kennedy had appointed her to the national advisory board of the Peace Corps. A new program whose goal was to send volunteers to teach and provide technical support to developing countries, the Peace Corps captured the spirit of the national youth service program ER had advocated during the New Deal.

In spite of Murray's reservations about the president, she was "glad" that ER agreed to serve on the Peace Corps board and to chair the politically sensitive Tractors for Freedom Committee, organized in April 1961 after a group of U.S.-backed Cuban exiles invaded the Bay of Pigs but failed to overthrow the Cuban regime. When President Fidel Castro offered to return the men in exchange for agricultural equipment, Kennedy established the TFC as a nongovernmental entity to raise funds for the equipment and to avoid the appearance of paying ransom. When Castro's demands escalated to include millions in relief, the TFC disbanded. The men would eventually be released in December 1962.

Murray took comfort in the fact that ER's support for the president did not dampen her willingness to challenge him. After only nine of the first 240 federal appointments went to women, ER met with Kennedy in the White House and handed him a three-page list of women qualified for high-level positions. "This is still a man's world," she said later at a press conference, and "men have to be reminded that women exist."

When the president's advisers proposed sending military aid, including U.S. troops, to Vietnam, ER aligned herself with a group that urged him to take the issue to the U.N., where people with different perspectives could come together, discuss the ramifications, and work toward mutual understanding. "Guns never really change ideas," she said. "We must have new ideas to fight those in which we do not believe."

ER's apprehension about the threat of nuclear war and the escalating tensions between the United States and the Soviet Union moved her to sign and reprint "A Declaration of Conscience and Responsibility" in her column. This statement, developed by the American Friends Service, took a stand against "the present drift towards war" and called upon the signers to engage in initiatives for peace.

The exclusion of women from the executive branch of government reinforced Murray's misgivings about the president. "He seems a little slow on the uptake in that department," she wrote to ER. "In fact, some of us gals have a slogan that in the Kennedy Administration we are trying to raise women to the status of Negroes! (This should amuse you.)"

Murray was anxious to see firsthand the changes stirring in the nation. She was also ecstatic about returning to school. "You'll be pleased to know that I have just been awarded a fellowship to do graduate law at Yale next year, and that I am going to try for my doctorate," she proudly announced to ER. "This 18-month experience suggests that I have teaching ability, so I think I shall move in that direction." Brimming with anticipation of their next visit, Murray added, "Seriously, I have thought of you often and hope that you are taking care of yourself. Read that you had a bad case of flu, and do hope that you are feeling fit again."

· · ·

ELEANOR ROOSEVELT HAD ALWAYS BEEN a hardy woman whose endurance astounded those around her. However, during the last year, a series of colds had sapped her energy, made her hoarse, and, at times, forced her to bed. Plagued by fatigue, she catnapped between engagements.

ER had aplastic anemia, a condition in which the bone marrow fails to produce adequate red and white blood cells and platelets. Along with exhaustion and recurring infections, this illness caused bouts of fever and chills, shortness of breath, dizziness, and a tendency toward bleeding. Still, she maintained a taxing schedule. "As one gets older," she told David E. Lilienthal, who had headed the Tennessee Valley Authority under FDR and chaired the U.S. Atomic Energy Commission under President Truman, "there are aches and pains, more and more, and if you pay much attention to them, the first thing you know you're an invalid."

In March, she accepted yet another presidential assignment when Kennedy named her to the U.S. delegation to the U.N. In this capacity, she appeared briefly at a meeting of the Commission on Human Rights. Although she had made plans to attend the plenary sessions, she had to stay home with her "two old legs in the air" she confided to Adlai Stevenson, who was now U.S. ambassador to the U.N.

News reports said ER had the flu, but this was not true. She "didn't want to talk about" her condition and "thought the flu a good excuse." The real culprit was phlebitis, an inflammation of the veins caused by the transfusions her doctors had prescribed to combat her fatigue and blood cell deficiency.

ER resolved not to become preoccupied with her condition or to alarm friends and colleagues. "I am delighted to hear about your fellowship and I look forward with joy to seeing you when you return," she wrote in a cheerful note to Murray, making no mention of her health. "I hope you will plan to come and stay with me, so do let me know when you arrive."

· · ·

IN JUNE, Murray and Smokey returned to the States. Their homecoming was marred by an encounter with a New Haven rental agent who refused to lease Murray an apartment because she was black. She eventually found a two-room apartment in an integrated housing complex five minutes from Yale Law School. This "space capsule," as she called it, housed "the personal effects of six large rooms in Ghana," plus the "equipment of a law office." Finding a place for everything was a feat. When Smokey claimed the corner where she studied for his "private office," she had to move her books to avoid a "territorial squabble."

Sixteen years had passed since Murray had finished the master of laws, and she had to learn how to be a student again. Preparing for class took her "three times" longer than the other students, most of whom were young men half her age. Twenty-five of the fifty graduate students were foreign nationals. Only two, she and Mary Ellen Caldwell, were women.

The complexion and gender of the law school faculty at Yale had changed little since 1931, when it graduated its first black woman, Jane Matilda Bolin. Murray's professors, all white men, were an esteemed group that included Eugene V. Rostow, school dean and critic of the Japanese internment program; Myres S. McDougal and Leon Lipson, specialists in international law; Filmer S. C. Northrup, philosopher and ethicist; Boris I. Bittker, expert in tax law; and Telford Taylor, former

U.S. prosecutor at the Nuremberg Military Tribunals. Thomas I. Emerson, a constitutional scholar and civil liberties activist, became Murray's adviser.

The law school student body, by contrast, was more diverse. There was a young crop of black civil rights activists. W. Haywood Burns and Clarence Laing would become law professors and assist in the defense of Angela Davis, the African American scholar and activist charged with—and eventually acquitted of—conspiracy, abduction, and the murder of a California judge during an attempted prisoner escape. Inez Smith Reid would have a distinguished career in government service that culminated in her appointment to the District of Columbia Court of Appeals. Marian Wright Edelman would champion the rights of minority, poor, and disabled children as founder of the Children's Defense Fund. Eleanor Holmes Norton would be elected delegate to the U.S. Congress from the District of Columbia and, before that, serve as the first woman chair of the U.S. Equal Employment Opportunity Commission. In that capacity, Norton would oversee the implementation of Title VII, a provision barring sex discrimination in the 1964 Civil Rights Act. She would credit Murray with "almost single-handedly" preserving the provision when it was imperiled by conservatives.

While Murray was acclimating herself to Yale, ER was experiencing negative reactions to the blood transfusions. Her condition worsened, yet her outlook and correspondence remained upbeat. "I was delighted to get a message from you and astonished to note that you are home," she wrote to Murray. "I do want to see you and I hope you will be in touch with me soon. At the moment I am resting in bed but I hope shortly to be back on my regular schedule." Murray would not realize for a year that ER's innocuous comments about her health masked serious illness.

Front, left to right: Margaret J. Mealey, executive director, National Council of Catholic Women; William F. Schnitzler, secretary-treasurer, American Federation of Labor and Congress of Industrial Organizations; and Eleanor Roosevelt, chair, President's Commission on the Status of Women, with John Kennedy and unidentified commission members (rear), February 12, 1962. This was the first meeting of the commission, whose work, ER explained, "is to find how we can best use the potentialities of women without impairing their first responsibilities, which are to their homes, their husbands and their children." *(Franklin D. Roosevelt Presidential Library)*

57

"I Am as Well as Anyone Can Be at My Age"

The demands of Pauli Murray's doctoral studies and Eleanor Roosevelt's commitments, which included canvassing on street corners and from the flatbed of a truck for the reelection of Democratic mayor Robert Wagner—who would win, in part, because of ER's efforts—prevented them from having a reunion in the fall of 1961. ER remained circumspect about her health, publicly rebuffing speculation by gossip columnist Walter Winchell that she was gravely ill. "I have no idea from what source he received this information," she said in her column, "but as far as I know I am as well as anyone can be at my age and am very active at the present time."

On December 14, 1961, John Kennedy issued Executive Order 10980, authorizing the President's Commission on the Status of Women. He did so in response to pressure from an array of women's organizations; Assistant Secretary of Labor Esther Peterson, the highest-ranking woman in his cabinet; and May Craig, the spunky Washington correspondent for Maine's *Portland Press Herald.*

Kennedy charged the PCSW "with the responsibility for developing recommendations for overcoming discriminations in government and private employment on the basis of sex and for developing recommendations for services which will enable women to continue their role as wives and mothers while making a maximum contribution to the world around them." Among the twenty-six commissioners were the U.S. attorney general; the secretaries of agriculture, commerce, labor, and health, education, and welfare; the chair of the Civil Service Commission; congressional representatives; senators; and leaders from business, education, and women's organizations. The commission's makeup and that the president had named ER as chair signaled that women's issues would receive unprecedented consideration.

Kennedy broke the ice at the commission's inaugural meeting by announcing that he had appointed the group for "self-protection" against May Craig's persistent queries about what he was doing for women. After a round of laughter and smiles, he said, "The other and more serious reason" for calling together this group "is that one-third of the country's labor force is made up of women whose 'primary obligation' is to their families and their homes, but whose work makes it possible to maintain that home and that family in many cases. We want to make sure," the president maintained, that women "are able to move ahead and perform their functions without any discrimination by law or by implication."

The PCSW went to work at its Maryland Avenue office after a tour of the White House and lunch. That evening, Vice President and Mrs. Johnson hosted a reception at their residence. The meeting ended the afternoon of the next day.

John Kennedy's charm held no sway with Murray. Yet she could not ignore the importance of the commission's charge or its stature. That ER, Caroline Ware, and National Council of Negro Women president Dorothy Height were part of this powerhouse ensured that the work would be of high quality and taken seriously. The group's plans called for subcommittees or study groups to tackle the broad areas of home and community, protective labor legislation, education, social insurance and taxes, civil and political rights, federal employment policies and practices, and private employment. Murray enthusiastically accepted ER's invitation to serve on the civil and political rights subcommittee.

Oregon congresswoman Edith Green and Marguerite Rawalt, an attorney who had been president of the Federal Bar Association and the National Federation of Business and Professional Women's Clubs, cochaired the fourteen-member subcommittee on civil and political rights. To this distinguished group of jurists, union leaders, academics, and civic leaders fell the politically charged task of examining barriers to women's participation in elective and appointed office, political parties, and jury service, in addition to the issue of women's constitutional rights.

Because Murray had more than twenty years of experience as a scholar and an activist in the areas of race and sex discrimination, the group asked her to draft an informational memorandum on women's constitutional rights that considered the feasibility of a constitutional amendment. To be working with the PCSW under ER's leadership and to be appointed tutor of law at Yale, which gave her junior faculty status, made Murray as excited as a "puppy with two tails," which was her favorite phrase for describing joy.

· · ·

AFTER THE COMMISSION MEETING, Eleanor Roosevelt went back to New York City, packed her clothes, and flew to Paris, where she taped a segment of *Prospects of Mankind.* From there, she flew to London, then to Israel, and on to the Swiss Alps. During this trip, she found it difficult to stay up late or walk for long periods. The steroid prednisone and periodic blood transfusions doctors had prescribed did not relieve her fatigue and discomfort.

Despite her condition, ER continued to host her television series and to write and advocate for social justice. One especially meaningful commitment involved chairing a citizens' committee that heard testimony from black and white civil rights activists victimized in the South by the unprovoked use of police dogs and tear gas, unreasonable bond, extended sentences, and solitary jail confinement. Murray, assuming all was well with ER, concentrated on her classes and the memorandum for the PCSW.

Pauli Murray, age fifty-one, and Eleanor Roosevelt, age seventy-seven, near the spot where Murray photographed ER with Aunts Pauline and Sallie a decade earlier at Val-Kill, Hyde Park, New York, July 14, 1962. It had been twenty-eight years since Murray first encountered ER at Camp Tera. *(The Schlesinger Library, Radcliffe Institute, Harvard University and the Estate of Pauli Murray)*

58

"Would You Please Bring Me a Glass of Lemonade?"

Pauli Murray was in the audience when Eleanor Roosevelt spoke at Yale Law School in June 1962. They had not seen each other in two years. Eager to hear firsthand about Africa and Yale, ER invited Murray to lunch at Val-Kill on July 14. A few days before Murray's visit, ER hosted 150 people for the annual Wiltwyck School picnic on her lawn. Wiltwyck, a residential facility for troubled boys between the ages of eight and twelve, was located on a three-hundred-acre estate in nearby

Esopus. Most of the youths came from poor or minority families, as did two of the school's famous alumni, heavyweight boxing champion Floyd Patterson and writer Claude Brown.

A tireless advocate and major fund-raiser for Wiltwyck, ER had served on the board for twenty years. During her tenure, the school had developed into a racially integrated treatment center whose teachers and counselors created a nonpunitive learning environment, provided outlets for therapeutic and wholesome play, and taught the boys to function responsibly. ER's friend Harry Belafonte took a special interest in Wiltwyck. He performed there, gave benefit concerts for the school at Carnegie Hall, and funded music lessons for the boys.

When a judge sent ten-year-old Floyd Patterson to the school, he could neither read nor write. He suffered from nightmares and paralyzing self-doubt. At Wiltwyck, he learned to read and write, make friends, and be at peace with himself. He also put on his first pair of boxing gloves, opening the door to a career that would include an Olympic gold medal and several professional boxing titles. Claude Brown was an eleven-year-old petty thief who regularly skipped school before he arrived at Wiltwyck. His relationship with the staff inspired him to finish high school, go to college, write a best-selling memoir, and become an advocate for juvenile justice.

Brown and Patterson would later dedicate their memoirs to ER and Wiltwyck. Like all the boys, they cherished the picnics at Val-Kill, where ER and her grandchildren served hot dogs, potato salad, hot buttered rolls, cupcakes, ice cream, and milk. Once satiated, everyone gathered around ER on the lawn to hear her read selections from Rudyard Kipling's *Just So Stories* collection. She loved these gatherings as much as the boys did, and she was as disappointed as they were that she was too weak to read to them on this occasion. The magician John Mulholland performed for the group, but the boys, unaware of ER's declining health, complained that they missed her reading.

· · ·

ON JULY 14, Murray arrived at Val-Kill with her brother Raymond; his wife, Margaret; and their three children—Robert, fourteen; Marcia, twelve; and Michael, nine. ER was waiting for them near the entrance to the Roosevelt estate "in her car surrounded by a throng and graciously" signing autographs. When Murray had brought Aunts Pauline and Sallie to a similar gathering, they had lunched in the yard with ER, a daughter-in-law, several grandchildren, and Malvina Thompson, before touring FDR's home and library. Since then, Murray's aunts, Tommy, and Sally Roosevelt had passed away. In remembrance, perhaps, Murray repeated the tour with her brother's family.

Joining Murray and her relatives for lunch were ER's ninety-two-year-old uncle David Gray, U.N. diplomats from Haiti and India, and "a swarm of children." Guests, served at buffet tables inside the cottage, took seats outside to eat. Once everyone had been served, ER prepared her plate and joined Uncle David and Murray, who were talking in the sitting room. Having forgotten her beverage, ER made a request that surprised Murray: "Pauli, if you are going into the next room for anything, would you please bring me a glass of lemonade?"

In all their years of friendship, ER had rarely asked a "personal favor" of Murray, and Murray was "overjoyed" that ER "felt close enough" to ask. Unaware that ER could barely get up once she sat down, Murray would later take comfort in the fact that she "had the privilege of performing this one tiny service for one whose whole life was a symphony of service to others."

After lunch, Raymond took the first and only snapshot of Murray and ER together. His snapshot, which captured their practical low-heeled shoes and short-sleeved bodice dresses, was symbolic of how far they had come since 1934. At midlife and still a firebrand, Murray was a distinguished writer, scholar, and lawyer. She was lean but no longer underweight, and she sprouted gray streaks near the front of her hairline. ER was a septuagenarian, her mane white and her midriff thickened. While she had remained true to her husband's legacy, she stood in no one's shadow. She was a torchbearer for American liberalism and the indisputable First Lady of the World.

One of the last things ER talked to Murray about was her campaign appearance in Harlem for a Democratic candidate, during which people rushed "to touch her" as she rode by in her open car. She had "felt like the fat lady in the circus," ER said, making light of the scene. She had rebuffed her grandsons' concerns about her safety, she explained, for it was more important to show people that someone cared.

As Murray and her family were leaving, she paused to watch ER walk into her cottage. Her shoulders were "slightly stooped," her footsteps measured. It was the last time Murray would see her friend.

Mourners at Eleanor Roosevelt's burial ceremony in the Rose Garden, Hyde Park, New York, on November 10, 1962. To Pauli Murray, who was among the invited guests, it seemed that "a great light had gone out of the world, and even nature was weeping." *(Bettmann/CORBIS)*

59

"We Shall Be Working Doubly Hard to Carry On"

On August 3, 1962, three weeks after Pauli Murray's visit to Val-Kill, Eleanor Roosevelt was rushed to Columbia Presbyterian Hospital with a temperature of 102 degrees, night sweats, and chills. Being in the hospital and having her blood pressure, pulse, and temperature taken around the clock made her restless and depressed. Doctors released her five days later, after her fever dropped.

In ER's growing mail pile was a memorandum from Murray to "all the new friends of Kwaku Baah," a young Ghanaian whom she had helped leave his country so he could attend Northwestern University on a fellowship and avoid arrest by the Ghanaian authorities. (Baah had been classified as a security risk because of his opposition to the government's preventive detention program.) ER was among the 135 donors who'd responded to Murray's appeal for Baah's travel fund. Two thousand dollars had been raised, and Baah had arrived safely in the United States. Enclosed with Murray's memo were a receipt, a copy of *Proud Shoes,* and a cover letter with an affectionate postscript: "Did anybody ever have the temerity—hutzpah—to tell you that you're 'a doll'?"

ER was happy to have another copy of Murray's memoir. "My uncle will want to read it too, for he was most interested to meet you," she wrote on August 29. ER had "had a miserable summer and spent a week in hospital," she admitted. "I am slowly getting stronger and learning not to be impatient with my progress. All lectures, except dinner speeches, are being cut down, so I am really trying to lessen my workload from now through December." This would be the last letter to Murray ER would sign in her own hand.

While she did curtail her commitments, ER still pushed herself beyond what her doctors and family thought wise. She continued to speak out on a range of issues, such as the influence of lobbyists on Congress, the need for prison reform, the obstacles to integration, the enduring Arab-Israeli conflict, the benefits of cultural exchange, and internal opposition to General Francisco Franco of Spain.

ER was also working on her final book, *Tomorrow Is Now.* "Staying aloof" was cowardice, she would write, "not a solution." Fear, she declared, "clouds the judgment" and "paralyzes action." No longer willing to obey unjust laws, ER called upon people of conscience to challenge injustice wherever they saw it, which was what Murray had done more than twenty years earlier when officials at the University of North Carolina rejected her application for admission and two Petersburg, Virginia, policemen arrested her and Adelene McBean for violating a state ordinance that required segregated seating on buses.

When the Franklin Delano Roosevelt Bridge, linking Lubec, Maine, and Campobello Island, New Brunswick, was dedicated, ER was too weak to attend the ceremony. Her son James went as the family representative. ER did fly to the island against her doctor's orders, although she could hardly walk. Her voice was but a whisper. Nonetheless, she stayed for over a week, recalling her husband's fondness for Campobello as a young boy and the pleasure she and her children had taken in the island's natural beauty. This trip and the stops ER made on her way home to see dear friends, such as Esther Lape, whom she had known since 1920, were undoubtedly a personal farewell.

ER was hospitalized again on September 26, the day her last column appeared. She had blood in her stool, and her fever reached 105 degrees.

. . .

WHILE DOCTORS RAN TESTS to determine the cause of ER's persistent high fever, Murray was hard at work on a presentation for the October 1 meeting of the President's Commission on the Status of Women, where ER expected to preside. Murray's presentation, "A Proposal to Reexamine the Applicability of the Fourteenth Amendment to State Laws and Practices Which Discriminate on the Basis of Sex Per Se," was an in-depth analysis of women's constitutional rights. Murray was anxious for ER's feedback. ER had once opposed the Equal Rights Amendment; however, her position had softened in recent years.

When Murray arrived for the meeting and learned that ER was in the hospital, she realized that the infections ER had dismissed, her weary appearance, and her request for a glass of lemonade were signs of serious illness. "The important thing," Murray wrote to ER the next day, "is that you take care of yourself and reduce, if not entirely eliminate, all pressures which retard your progress."

ER could no longer answer mail. Her personal secretary, Maureen Corr, sent Murray a note that said, "Mrs. Roosevelt is still in hospital but she read your letter and asked me to tell you how much she appreciated hearing from you."

. . .

MELANCHOLY HUNG OVER the 250 attendees at the conference hosted by the National Council of Women of the United States on October 11, 1962, at the Waldorf-Astoria. It was ER's seventy-eighth birthday. Murray, introduced as an author and a tutor of law at Yale, shared the dais with Esther Peterson; Rene Carpenter, the wife of astronaut M. Scott Carpenter; and Rachel Carson, the marine biologist and nature writer, whose latest work, *Silent Spring*, would help spawn the environmental movement.

Murray borrowed the title of her address, "Grace Under Pressure," from Ernest Hemingway, who had coined the phrase to explain what he meant by courage. It took grace under pressure, Murray said, waxing eloquent, for astronauts to brave the unknown and open a new frontier, for James Meredith to enroll as the first black student at the University of Mississippi under military guard, for Rosa Parks to refuse to give up her seat to white passengers on a Birmingham bus, knowing she would be arrested, and for Lillian Smith to write about the psychosis of white supremacy and align herself with the civil rights movement. As "women of conscience," Murray told the audience, "we must reject both extremes of being put on a pedestal and of being downgraded so that in neither case are we able to fulfill our highest potential." She closed her speech with a call to duty and an allusion to ER: "We have the responsibility for carrying on the great pioneering tradition of the valiant women who have gone before."

Murray went back to Yale and penned her last letter to ER the following day. It was part birthday greeting and part tribute to ER and their friendship.

October 12, 1962

Dear Mrs. Roosevelt:

Congratulations on three-score-ten and eight! I did not send you a greeting or attempt to reach you yesterday because the women assembled at the All-Women Conference (included a number of foreign delegates to the U.N. Commission on the Status of Women) sent you a joint greeting. Your spirit dominated our thoughts even though you were not there physically.

I know how difficult it is for you to have to stay in the hospital. Your life is and has been so filled with service to others that I suspect you are a most *impatient* patient (smile)!

Today is the 470th Anniversary of the discovery of our country. I realized what a young people we are when I stood on the shores of the Atlantic in Ghana, looking at Elmina Castle, built by the Dutch in 1481 (I believe). Your life span covers one-sixth of our history and the impact of your personality will be felt for generations to come. You have the gift in human relations which Marian Anderson has in vocal music—a gift so rare that it takes centuries to produce it.

For many years you have been one of my most important models—one who combines graciousness with moral principle, straightforwardness with kindliness, political shrewdness with idealism, courage with generosity, and most of all an ongoingness which never falters, no matter what the difficulties may be. Two generations of women have been touched by your spirit and, as Esther Peterson said yesterday, you are the very embodiment of a *woman of conscience* (the theme of our conference).

Yesterday was a red-letter day for me—marred only by your absence and that of Maida Springer (she was flying back from a conference in Costa Rica). It was the first time I have addressed a group of such distinguished women leaders, and remembering the long, stormy paths over which I have come, you more than most people can appreciate the growth from the "firebrand" days of the 1940's.

You probably saw the news item in *The New York Times* yesterday from Durham, N.C. about quiet successful integration; also about the young woman from Pittsylvania County in Southwestern Virginia who is the first Negro to be admitted to a branch college of the University of Virginia. (You will recall that Odell Waller came from Pittsylvania County.) It must be so gratifying to you, as it is to me, to see the fruit of so many of your labors.

I enclose a copy of my remarks and am writing the National Council of Women to send you those of the other three speakers. All of these women have grown up under your influence, for while you have not kept school records for many years, the world has been your classroom and the United States your teacher's desk and platform. You would have been proud of us all.

Know that while you are "laid up" we shall be working doubly hard to carry on, following in your footsteps, for you are our great pioneer of the Twentieth Century, linking us with the Nineteenth Century. I am presumptious [*sic*] enough to suggest that you amuse yourself by watching the "election returns" of your efforts, for almost every achievement of women active today is a spiritual vote for Eleanor Roosevelt, the First Lady of the World. I do not exaggerate. Don't bother to answer—I know how burdened Miss Corr must be. My love . . .

Pauli

. . .

ELEANOR ROOSEVELT KNEW that she was dying, and she did not want to die in the hospital. On October 18, doctors allowed her to go home, and photos of her frail, "stretcher-borne" body appeared with news reports that she was suffering from fever, anemia, and a lung infection. She refused water and food. She secreted in her mouth the pills nurses tried to get her to swallow. To no avail, friends and family members attempted to engage her by reading the newspaper aloud. The autopsy and later reevaluation of ER's medical records would conclude that she had a highly drug-resistant form of tuberculosis that had spread throughout her body.

"It is just so difficult to conceive of Mrs. Roosevelt being ill," Murray wrote to Maureen Corr. "She has always been a tower of physical and spiritual strength to so many of us. . . . Those of us who have been privileged to be near her and to feel the greatness of her spirit, her courage, simplicity, humility and kindness must stand firm and, . . . in our small way, . . . carry on the things she has taught us." Murray "kept a private vigil." With no way to communicate her love directly, she followed ER's "example of doing the things at hand." The memorandum on women's constitutional rights for the PCSW became Murray's personal memorial to her beloved friend.

On November 7, 1962, three days after a stroke that left her comatose, ER died at her New York City residence. Word of her passing prompted tributes and condolences from Premier Nikita Khrushchev, Queen Elizabeth, United Nations acting secretary-general U Thant, and other world leaders. President Kennedy ordered the Stars and Stripes to half-staff and issued a statement: "One of the great ladies in the history of this country has passed from the scene. Her loss will be deeply felt by all those who admired her tireless idealism or benefited from her good works and wise counsel."

Martin Luther King said in a telegram to ER's children, "Her life was one of the bright interludes in the troubled history of mankind." The headline of the *Baltimore Afro-American* read, "We Have Lost a Great Friend." "A hushed silence fell in Negro homes across the nation as families heard the sad but expected news that Eleanor Roosevelt, First Lady of the World, had died quietly in her apartment," wrote Ernestine Cofield in the *Chicago Defender.*

On Saturday, November 10, the funeral rites began with services in Hyde Park, at St. James Episcopal Church. This centuries-old church where ER had been a devoted member could accommodate but 250 people. Murray, Renee Barlow, and Renee's sister Doris joined a gathering of six hundred for the two-thirty p.m. graveside service in the Rose Garden of the Roosevelt estate. Among the mourners were President and Mrs. Kennedy; Vice President and Mrs. Johnson; President Dwight Eisenhower; President and Mrs. Harry Truman; U.N., New York municipal, and state government officials; members of Congress; Chief Justice Earl Warren; Marian Anderson; and many without portfolio or title.

Murray braced herself as the plain oak coffin, adorned with pine boughs from the nearby woods where ER had loved to walk, was brought into the garden. The "low-hanging dark clouds and intermittent heavy rains" magnified the sadness of Reverend Gordon L. Kidd's words:

"In the death of Eleanor Roosevelt, the world has suffered an irreparable loss" and "becomes one family orphaned."

At the end of the ceremony, the haunting melody of taps pierced the air. The gray mist gave way to a downpour. Pauli Murray walked away carrying the candle Eleanor Roosevelt had lit in her heart.

PART IX

SPEAKING TRUTH
TO THE END,
1963–85

Pauli Murray, tutor of law and doctoral student at Yale University, circa 1962. Despite her lifelong commitment to the NAACP and her groundbreaking work as an activist, lawyer, and writer, she was relegated to the sidelines by male civil rights leaders and never received the coveted Spingarn Award. *(Franklin D. Roosevelt Presidential Library)*

60

"Mrs. Roosevelt's Spirit Marches On"

Pauli Murray was among the 250,000 demonstrators who poured into the U.S. capital for the historic March on Washington for Jobs and Freedom on August 28, 1963. It was the centennial year of the Emancipation Proclamation, and Murray savored the moment by marching twice. The first time, she marched with her niece Bonnie Fearing Alexis and Patricia Roberts Harris, a fellow veteran of the 1943–44 Howard University student boycotts. After they reached the Lincoln Memorial, Murray turned around and went back to the starting point. This time she "fell in line" with the delegation from St. Mark's Church-in-the-Bowery, where she and Renee Barlow worshipped in New York City.

Like everyone who heard Martin Luther King's "I Have a Dream" speech that day, Murray was moved. Yet the treatment of the women activists who'd helped plan, raise funds, and organize MOW made her steam. A week before the demonstration, Anna Arnold Hedgeman, the only woman on MOW's administrative committee, had appealed to its all-male decision-making body in writing and in person for fair and visible representation of women. No women were slated to give major addresses during the rally at the Lincoln Memorial or to join the delegation scheduled to meet afterward in the White House with President Kennedy.

"The men seemed to feel that women were digressing and pulling the discussion off the main track," National Council of Negro Women president Dorothy I. Height recalled. March leaders justified their actions with the argument that they had more than enough speakers, that the program was already too long, and that women, by virtue of their participation in the sponsoring organizations, were represented. When told that Mahalia Jackson was on the program, the women had replied, "She's not speaking on behalf of women, or on behalf of civil rights. She's singing."

MOW national director A. Philip Randolph's decision to speak at the National Press Club forty-eight hours before the march made matters worse. Women reporters, barred from membership and from sitting alongside male reporters when they covered speakers at the club, demanded a change of venue.

Murray was unwilling to accept the argument that public criticism would undermine MOW, and she blasted Randolph in a letter that was printed in the *Washington Post and Times Herald*. She was outraged that Randolph had agreed to speak at the club and that several members of the march committee, including Reverend King, would be on the platform with him. "As one who has been a victim of both Jim Crow and Jane Crow," she wrote,

> I can give expert testimony that discrimination solely because of race and discrimination solely because of sex are equally insulting and do violence to the human spirit. It is as humiliating for a woman reporter assigned to cover Mr. Randolph's speech to be sent to the balcony as it would be for Mr. Randolph to be sent to the back of the bus. . . .

> At this crucial moment in our struggle, Mr. Randolph's accep-
> tance to speak before a professional organization which ignores and
> excludes half of the population (including half of the Negro popula-
> tion) can only be construed as a sign that Mr. Randolph and Com-
> pany are concerned with the rights of Negro men only and not the
> rights of all people.

Ever mindful of the example set by activists in the nineteenth century,
Murray asserted,

> It seems appropriate to call attention to the fact that in 1840 William
> Lloyd Garrison and Charles Remond, the latter a Negro, refused
> to be seated as delegates to the World Anti-Slavery Convention in
> London when they learned that the women members of the Ameri-
> can delegation would be excluded and could sit only in the bal-
> cony. Certainly we have a right to expect nothing less from men like
> A. Philip Randolph who act as spokesmen for human rights in the
> 20th century.

Although MOW's leaders refused to move to another site, they made a
number of conciliatory gestures. They issued a statement affirming their
commitment to women's equality and "the utilization of their abilities
and talents in the building of a free and democratic American society."
They decried "the fact that in the year of 1963 there could exist in the
United States any institution that would discriminate against women."
They added Dorothy Height to the White House delegation, invited the
wives of civil rights leaders to march to the platform in a group behind
the men, and asked Daisy Bates to give a short address. Bates, Marian
Anderson, and gospel singer Mahalia Jackson were the only black women
who would be part of the planned program. Entertainers Lena Horne
and Josephine Baker, an expatriate who flew in from France, would make
unscheduled remarks.

Randolph honored a handful of women during the rally by calling
their names. Murray was not among them. Some of the women hid their
discomfort behind forced smiles at one another. Murray, on the other
hand, was too angry to mask her feelings. She had answered Randolph's
first call for a march on Washington in 1941, raised black women's concerns at the 1942 Detroit policy conference, and battled sexism within the
civil rights movement for decades. "What you may not know," Murray
told Mary Ransom Hunter, daughter of her late beloved law school pro-

fessor Leon Ransom, "is that Mr. Randolph, while a great leader of the Negro cause, is medieval in his thinking about women."

. . .

TWO MONTHS AFTER MOW, Murray gave a speech entitled "The Negro Woman in the Quest for Equality" at a conference in Washington, D.C., called by the NCNW to consider women's role in the civil rights movement. "It was bitterly humiliating for Negro women on Aug. 28 to see themselves accorded little more than token recognition in the historic March on Washington," she told the audience. Just as troubling for Murray was the number of black women recently pushed out of leadership positions in local civil rights organizations and assigned to "secondary, ornamental roles."

The assertion by civil rights leaders, such as James Meredith, that women and children should not be placed in roles that put them at risk held no water for Murray. Decades before Meredith's enrollment at the University of Mississippi provoked violent outrage, prompting President Kennedy to order U.S. marshals and federal troops to the scene, Murray had been jailed for defying a Virginia statute requiring segregated buses and had co-organized two boycotts of segregated eateries in Washington, D.C. In neither case was law enforcement called in to protect her. Murray was not about to see women shunted aside or their contributions ignored under the premise that conditions were unsafe. "All Negroes," she maintained, "are born involved in the civil rights fight and exposed to its dangers."

Many of the women at the meeting shared Murray's sentiment. That male leaders had shown "no sign of remorse" or awareness of injustice made the women "take a hard look" at their treatment during the march and in the civil rights movement. Even so, Murray's public attack against Randolph had a chilling effect on her relationships with her allies and friends. In a smoldering missive, she told MOW deputy director Bayard Rustin that it might be easier for him to see "that women's rights were and *are* an integral part of the civil-human rights revolution" if he would get off his "lofty masculine heights and become a brother for a few minutes." Her indignation at the exclusion of women from visible, policy-making roles in the movement would lead her to resign from the executive board of the A. Philip Randolph Institute, for which Rustin served as executive director.

Pauli Murray and her close friend Maida Springer had words after Springer said she cared deeply about women's issues but "never in this life" would she oppose Randolph, whom she affectionately referred to as "St. Philip." This disagreement resulted in a long period of silence between them. Nonetheless, Murray would carry on, insisting "that human rights are indivisible and that it is shortsighted to assume that the issue of discrimination because of sex must await resolution of the issue of discrimination because of race."

. . .

ON SEPTEMBER 15, 1963, seventeen days after MOW, Robert Edward Chambliss, also known as Dynamite Bob, placed a bundle of explosives underneath the steps of Birmingham's Sixteenth Street Baptist Church. The bomb killed eleven-year-old Carol Denise McNair and fourteen-year-olds Addie Mae Collins, Carole Robertson, and Cynthia Wesley. NAACP field secretary Medgar Evers had been gunned down outside his Jackson, Mississippi, home, on June 12, and President Kennedy would be assassinated in Dallas on November 22.

Murray had lobbied the new president, Lyndon Baines Johnson, about the need for strong civil rights enforcement measures when he was Senate majority leader. She deemed it a positive sign that Johnson had urged Congress to move swiftly on the civil rights bill Kennedy introduced before his death. House conservatives tried to block the bill by stalling, and opponents in the Senate filibustered until a compromise garnered enough support to end debate.

Before the final vote, Virginia congressman Howard W. Smith, a Democrat and an avowed segregationist, introduced an amendment that added sex as a protected class in Title VII of the bill. Because Smith had used his power as chair of the House Rules Committee to prevent civil rights legislation from coming to the floor for a vote, liberals viewed his support for women's rights with cynicism. Smith's real motive, some believed, was to induce his fellow representatives to vote against the legislation by pandering to male chauvinism.

In any case, Murray was ecstatic about the inclusion of sex as a category in the bill, as were many of the activists with whom she had worked on the President's Commission on the Status of Women. The sex provision ensured that millions of employed women, irrespective of race or class, would be covered by the legislation.

At the last minute, Senate minority leader Everett Dirksen threatened to amend Title VII by eliminating sex as a category. In doing so, he mobilized a national network that included women in Congress, the federal civil service, and professional and social service organizations. Murray drafted a document titled "Memorandum in Support of Retaining the Amendment to H.R. 7152 (Equal Employment Opportunity) to Prohibit Discrimination in Employment Because of Sex," which was duplicated and dashed off to Dirksen, congressional leaders, and Attorney General Robert F. Kennedy.

Murray argued in the memorandum that "there were few, if any, jobs for which an employee's sex could be considered relevant" and that the sex amendment would strengthen the proposed civil rights bill, as well as the recently passed Equal Pay Act. "Title VII without the 'sex' amendment," she pointed out, "would benefit Negro males primarily and thus offer genuine equality of opportunity to only half of the potential Negro work force." "If it is true that slavery and all that followed has denied the Negro male his manhood," Murray said in irritation to a reporter for the *Washington Post and Times Herald*, "isn't it equally true that the view of a Negro woman as a sex object or a body to be employed in domestic labor has denied her her due respect?"

Murray also sent her document to Lady Bird Johnson, urging the first lady "to discuss the matter with the President." Murray was on edge until she received word from Lady Bird Johnson's social secretary that she had "checked this matter out" and "that as far as the Administration is concerned, its position is that the Bill should be enacted in its present form."

On July 2, 1964, President Johnson signed the historic Civil Rights Act into law at a ceremony in the White House. The president acknowledged the contributions of Reverend King, who was present as a guest, by giving him the first pen used to sign the bill. For Murray, there would be no souvenir pen or White House invitation, but she would forever cherish a note of appreciation from Marguerite Rawalt just the same. Rawalt, who had helped disseminate Murray's document, wrote, "To you comes a real measure of credit for the ultimate successful passage of Title VII of the Civil Rights Bill with the protection for women in employment. . . . Your memorandum and your thinking was [*sic*] really fine."

Murray summarized her behind-the-scenes work in a letter to Lloyd Garrison, who shared his great-grandfather's commitment to women's rights. "You'll be amused to know that I take a little credit for the retention of 'sex' in the fepc [Federal Employment Practice Committee] section of the Civil Rights Act of 1964," she told her old friend. "When it was endangered by the Dirksen maneuvers, some of us organized a quiet little campaign; I wrote a brief and got it into the White House, the AG's [attorney general's] office and a few other places. Mrs. Roosevelt's spirit marches on. Wouldn't she be pleased to know that one of the major areas of discrimination against women has been dealt with by Congress?"

Eleanor Roosevelt would have been pleased about the legislation. She would have also been delighted that Murray was finally a "registered but independent Democrat." Murray had come a long way from voting for socialist Norman Thomas in the 1932 presidential election, running for the New York City Council on the Liberal Party ticket in 1949, and campaigning for Democrats Harry Truman and Adlai Stevenson in the 1950s, to embracing the southern Democrat Lyndon Johnson in 1964.

Pauli Murray, age fifty-four, class marshal and first African American
to earn a doctorate in the science of law from Yale, New Haven,
Connecticut, June 14, 1965. This was her third law degree. *(Photo by
Louise E. Jefferson, Patricia Bell-Scott Collection)*

61

"I Have Been a Person with an Independent Inquiring Mind"

Twenty-one years after Harvard University rejected Pauli Murray's
application to study for a graduate degree in law, she completed
her three-volume, 1,308-page dissertation at Yale University.
"Roots of the Racial Crisis: Prologue to Policy" was a treatise on the
historical and legal origins of the American race problem. Now in pos-

session of the credential that assured most men of a faculty appointment at a premier law school, Murray faced the irony that only a handful of historically black law schools and not a single predominantly white law school employed a full-time African American woman professor. Shut out once again from the kind of position she rightfully deserved, she sought alternative means to support herself and use her legal talents.

Murray returned to New York. Renee and several good friends were there, but her dog, Smokey, soon died. They had been together for thirteen years. Murray soon adopted Doc from a local pound. He was a large mutt "with a clumsy gait" and a black-and-white coat. Murray jokingly referred to Doc on occasion as "Black-and-White-Together-We-Shall-Overcome."

She signed a contract with the Methodist Church to write *Human Rights U.S.A.: 1948–1966,* a monograph in which she assessed the history and future of the human rights movement. She worked as a consultant for the U.S. Information Service and the U.S. Department of Labor, doing research and writing reports. She served on the American Civil Liberties Union board of directors; the ACLU's vice chair, Dorothy Kenyon, was a liberal activist Joseph McCarthy had accused of Communist ties. In 1966, Kenyon and Murray coauthored the union's brief for *White v. Crook,* successfully challenging an Alabama statute restricting jury service to males and whites. They also planted the seeds for the ACLU Women's Rights Project, which blossomed later under the leadership of future U.S. Supreme Court justice Ruth Bader Ginsburg.

Ginsburg would pay homage to Murray and Kenyon by placing their names on the cover of the brief for *Reed v. Reed,* a 1971 precedent-setting case in which the Supreme Court struck down an Idaho law favoring the appointment of a man because of his sex over his ex-wife to act as the administrator of an estate, in this case their deceased son's. Murray and Kenyon did not help write the brief; however, Ginsburg, who coauthored the document, felt that their intellectual work had laid the ground for the high court, which held that the Equal Protection Clause of the Fourteenth Amendment protected women's rights.

Like Ginsburg, Betty Friedan, the author of *The Feminine Mystique,* found inspiration in Murray's work. Murray came to Friedan's attention in the fall of 1965 when Freidan read a *New York Times* feature about a conference hosted by the National Council of Women of the United States at which Murray had said that it might be necessary for women to march on Washington "to assure equal job opportunities for all." Friedan, who was not at the conference, contacted Murray, and they began a series of conversations with each other and others that resulted in the birth of the National Organization for Women in 1966.

Friedan became the face of NOW and its first president; Murray stayed out of the spotlight, drafting organizational documents imbued with her vision of an NAACP for women. She would fight for women's equality for the rest of her life, but her association with NOW's national board would be short-lived. Disagreement over the process by which NOW would come to endorse the Equal Rights Amendment, power struggles within the leadership, insufficient attention to poor and minority women's concerns, and the lack of appreciation shown her at meetings would lead Murray to resign within a year. She would publicly endorse the ERA in time, but would remain outside the national leadership structure.

· · ·

AT THE SAME TIME that Murray was working with Friedan and others to establish NOW, she was also employed as a consultant to the recently established Equal Employment Opportunity Commission. The EEOC, a federal agency authorized by Title VII of the Civil Rights Act of 1964, was empowered to investigate and adjudicate claims of discrimination based on race, color, religion, sex, or national origin in the hiring, firing, compensation, and treatment of employees. The commission was composed of five members, who were appointed to five-year terms by the president with the advice and consent of the Senate. Only three commissioners could be from the same political party. The EEOC general counsel, whose job was to facilitate implementation of the law and the agency's work, was also appointed by the president with the advice and consent of the Senate.

The agency opened shop on July 2, 1965, at 1800 G Street, NW, two blocks away from the White House. The first commissioners were an interesting group. Democrat Franklin D. Roosevelt Jr., a former undersecretary of commerce in the Kennedy administration, was named chair. Democrat Luther Holcomb, a minister and civic leader from Texas, served as vice chair. Democrat Aileen Clarke Hernandez, a former International Ladies' Garment Workers' Union organizer and deputy chief of the California Division of Fair Employment Practices, was the only woman. Republican Samuel C. Jackson, a lawyer and civil rights leader, was from Kansas. Republican Richard Graham, a former deputy director of the Peace Corps and a future cofounder of NOW, was from Wisconsin. Charles T. Duncan, a lawyer and former assistant U.S. attorney for the District of Columbia, was named general counsel.

Aileen Clarke Hernandez, president of NOW and former commissioner of the EEOC, Denver, Colorado, 1971. During her tenure at the EEOC, she and Richard Graham repeatedly challenged their fellow commissioners to address complaints of sex discrimination. *(Getty Images)*

Duncan, Jackson, and Hernandez were African American. No Hispanics were appointed to the EEOC, although President Johnson's advisers possibly assumed that Hernandez was Hispanic because of her surname. (She was the daughter of Jamaican immigrants and had married and divorced Alfonso Hernandez, who was Hispanic.)

The EEOC's first year was rife with difficulty. The agency was understaffed and besieged by more than eight thousand complaints, one-third of which dealt with sex discrimination. Guidance from Congress, with respect to the agency's power and limitations, ranged from inadequate to absent; and there was no consensus among the commissioners, the legislators, or the public on the issue of sex discrimination. Years later, Commissioner Holcomb, whose reluctance to act unnerved Hernandez, would admit that the agency's "number one objective" at the beginning "was racial discrimination in the workforce." Women's employment concerns were "second place."

Frustration with the EEOC's initial decision (Hernandez and Graham dissented) that permitted employers to continue the practice of segregating job advertisements into male and female positions led Murray to accuse the agency of violating Title VII of the Civil Rights Act. When it became apparent that the EEOC's hiring practices discriminated against women as much as, if not more than, the employers it was investigating, she drafted and disseminated a chart highlighting the concentration of women and blacks in lower-level, non-policy-making positions.

When EEOC general counsel Charles Duncan left, in the fall of 1966, to become corporation counsel for the District of Columbia, Murray, as well as her supporters, believed that she was uniquely qualified to fill the vacant post. She had coauthored the groundbreaking and frequently cited law review essay "Jane Crow and the Law: Sex Discrimination and Title VII" with Mary O. Eastwood, and she had co-orchestrated the battle to preserve sex as a protected category in the 1964 Civil Rights Act. Murray was elated when her name was sent to the White House. After years of watching her male peers move up the career ladder in the federal government, she felt that a high-level appointment was within her reach.

In a scenario eerily reminiscent of when she applied for a research position with the Cornell University Codification of Laws of Liberia Project, Murray was asked to document her "organizational affiliations" from 1930 to 1948 in her application materials. Clearly worried, she asked reviewers to consider several "factors" as they examined her record:

1. That I have been a person with an independent inquiring mind and that my major emphasis has been upon the fulfillment of individual capacities.
2. That my activist activities and writing during my youth were in furtherance of the sole objective to become an integral part of American life.
3. That as one whose immediate family has been the victim of violence, I have been particularly concerned with seeking alternatives to violence in social conflict.
4. That my employment record reflects the limited job opportunities for Negroes prior to World War II in areas outside of segregated institutions and menial occupations.
5. That admission to the New York Bar in June 1948 was evidence of . . . loyalty to the United States and its institutions since this issue was a key question in the exhaustive questionnaire which all candidates for admission are required to fill out.

Murray's apprehension was warranted. Despite the testimony of her colleagues, friends, and neighbors to her high character, loyalty, intelligence, and work ethic, and the fact that no FBI informants close to the Communist front said they knew her, could confirm that she had ever been a member of the Communist Party USA, or could furnish information about her, the profile presented to the White House was one of suspicion.

Murray was described as a highly educated black woman and a former member of the CPUSA with ties to multiple Communist-front groups. The FBI agents assigned to her investigation, who purportedly accessed Bellevue Hospital records and questioned staff members, said doctors had diagnosed her as a schizophrenic who stated upon admission that "she was a homosexual." These operatives further noted that she had married Billy Wynn in her twenties, that they had separated shortly after the marriage, and that her marital status was unclear. Her treatment in 1954 for a thyroid disorder—the symptoms of which may have led doctors to conclude that she was schizophrenic—and the fact that her marriage to Wynn had been annulled in 1949 were absent from the summary report.

The FBI file frightened White House officials. The problem, said one presidential aide, "was to determine how not to give Murray the job as General Counsel," as she had been working for "the Government on a consultant basis for some eight months." Given her first-rate credentials and references, the aide told FBI officials that the best he could do was to "challenge . . . her affiliation with Communist Party organizations, the circumstances of her admission and release from Bellevue Hospital, her unconsummated marriage and lack of annulment, and her two arrests and jail sentence."

When the White House backed away from Murray's appointment, she lamented in her journal, "This has been the most crushing blow of my entire career." At fifty-six, "no longer young" and yet to achieve a job commensurate with her training and experience, she felt like "a has-been." She was "not part of anyone's power structure." She did not have the backing of an established organization. Moreover, the realization that she belonged at the EEOC "as a Commissioner and not a staff member" compounded her frustration. It had been a mistake, she admitted on the page, to "try to be what I am unable to be well—a subordinate." She determined not to remain at the agency in any capacity.

Murray tried to analyze her career objectively. She had been a competent, though not an extraordinary, associate attorney at Paul, Weiss, Rifkind, Wharton and Garrison. Sexism and the fact that her "personality and talents were not geared to remain in that atmosphere" had complicated her efforts. She had been a successful law professor in Ghana despite the political challenges; and at Yale, she'd been a highly regarded doctoral student and junior faculty member. While her consultancy with the EEOC had not led to the coveted position of general counsel, by all accounts, she had done an outstanding job.

When Cornell University had refused to hire Murray on the grounds that her political background put the school at risk, Eleanor Roosevelt had offered unconditional support. Once it became clear that the school officials could not be persuaded otherwise, ER had insisted that Murray move forward with her life. In keeping with that advice, in the spring of 1967, Murray accepted an appointment as vice president for educational development at Benedict College, a historically black Baptist liberal arts school in Columbia, South Carolina. She prayed that this job would be a reprieve from "civil rights, women, politics."

Professor Pauli Murray, age fifty-nine, in her office at Brandeis University, Waltham, Massachusetts, September 25, 1970. She was the university's first full-time African American faculty member. *(Associated Press)*

62

"Mrs. R. Seemed to Have Been Forgotten"

Race riots had already erupted in New York, Los Angeles, Chicago, Cleveland, and Atlanta. Despair and unrest would reach a new level in 1968 after the assassinations of Martin Luther King, on April 4, and Robert Kennedy, on June 5. On February 8, in Orangeburg, South Carolina, thirty-five miles from where Murray lived, the police fired into a crowd of youths who were protesting a segregated bowling alley. Many of the demonstrators were students at the predominantly black South Carolina State College, and they had friends at Benedict College. In the wake of this incident, which came to be known as the Orangeburg Massacre, seventeen-year-old Delano Herman Middleton and eighteen-year-olds Samuel Hammond Jr. and Henry Ezekial Smith lay dead. More than two dozen were injured. Most were shot in the back. Louise Kelly Cawley, a twenty-seven-year-old expectant mother who was beaten by the police, miscarried.

State officials blamed outside agitators for the confrontation, declared a curfew, and called in the National Guard. Murray used the incident as an opportunity to teach students on her campus about the historical struggle against oppression. Jean E. Friedman, a young white history professor, would never forget Murray's commitment to nonviolent protest or her stirring recitation of the poem "Dark Testament," which moved the students to tears and beyond fear. At Murray's urging, the students organized a dignified memorial service "in the open air" on the college grounds.

. . .

MURRAY HAD NOT LIVED in the South for four decades, and her job did not bring the respite she craved. Adding to her worries about racial violence was the escalating hostility toward homosexuals that would lead to police confrontations, such as the 1969 Stonewall riots. Indeed, conflict seemed to be everywhere she turned, and the voice she longed to hear most was gone. Seeking the solace of Eleanor Roosevelt's spirit, Murray took her fourteen-year-old nephew, Michael Kevin Murray, on a pilgrimage to the Roosevelt summer home on Campobello Island, New Brunswick, in August 1968.

The first thing they saw as they entered the reception center was Douglas Chandor's portrait of ER. This painting, a montage of sketches—the first lady "holding her glasses . . . and knitting"—took Pauli back to moments when she had seen "these familiar movements." As she and Michael walked through the cottage, they marveled at "the baskets of canes by the front entrance" and "the huge horn used to communicate with boats in the bay and to call everyone to meals." Pauli basked in the warmth of the "wood fire burning cheerfully in the big old-fashioned kitchen range." She lingered at ER's "writing table" and her bedroom.

Heartened by the ambience at Campobello, Pauli and Michael decided to stop at the Roosevelt burial site in Hyde Park on the way home. She had not been to the Roosevelt estate since the funeral. She had not cried during or since that service, and this visit brought buried emotions to the surface.

Pauli would acknowledge her feelings over dinner with ER's former assistant. "Dear Maureen," Pauli later wrote,

I have been able to weep a little, which eases the ache, and am now able to think a little more clearly about some of the things I shared with you the other night.

First, over the past six years I have been shocked and amazed at how quickly Mrs. R. seemed to have been forgotten to the point of seldom hearing her name mentioned. Perhaps this has not been forgetfulness, but as if many people, like myself, locked their grief in their hearts and tried to carry on in circumstances so alien to the things for which she stood it would have been almost a desecration to mention her name.

The year ER died, Murray had asked Ralph Bunche to nominate ER for the Nobel Peace Prize. Murray raised the issue again, suggesting that Corr approach U.S. Supreme Court justice Abraham Fortas for help. This prize, Murray said, would spark "a kind of rebirth memorial" to ER, "reemphasizing her philosophy, her compassion, her embodiment of the principle that human rights are indivisible."

Murray felt "psychically close" to ER, and she believed "Mrs. R's spirit" was "troubled by all of the things happening today." Though ER "would frown upon anything which smacks of an Eleanor cult," Murray told Corr, "I do think the principles for which she stood must be kept alive and associated with her name. And since, above all things, she was the highest expression of womanhood I think women must take the initiative here." If the Roosevelt children were hesitant about carrying the banner of their mother's work, those "who loved her and whom she loved do have a responsibility here," Murray insisted.

. . .

CONVINCED THAT HER INTERESTS and temperament were better suited to teaching than administration, Murray resigned from Benedict College and accepted a faculty appointment in 1968 in the American Civilization program at Brandeis University. The academic reputation of Brandeis, ER's longtime association with the school, and its proximity to the culturally rich city of Boston and her adopted home of New York City enhanced its appeal in Murray's eyes. The five years she would spend there were "exciting, tormenting, satisfying, embattled, frustrated, and at times triumphant."

At Brandeis, Murray introduced courses on legal studies, women, and civil rights. She worked closely with Professor Lawrence H. Fuchs, who had cotaught a course on international relations and the law with ER. Murray helped lay the groundwork for the Afro-American Studies program. She also challenged school policies that discriminated against women students, faculty, or staff.

Murray's relationships with "impatient young Black Militants" on campus were difficult, for they seemed to her to have "little, if any, sense of history." She had spent decades fighting for racial integration, and their demands for "separate dormitories and cultural centers" and black studies programs staffed exclusively by black professors offended her. That Murray's office and personal files were housed on the second floor of Ford Hall, the building students occupied and threatened to raze during a ten-day demonstration, deepened her alienation. No less trying were the "white liberal colleagues" who "retreated in confusion and uncertainty."

Human rights remained the focus of Murray's academic and creative writing. She took great pride in the publication of her poetry collection, *Dark Testament and Other Poems*. This collection, which was dedicated "to the memory of Eleanor Roosevelt," contained "Mr. Roosevelt Regrets," "The Passing of F.D.R.," and a selection of poems inspired by political, spiritual, and personal issues.

Notwithstanding the breadth and impact of Murray's writings, an all-white tenure review committee at Brandeis questioned the "brilliance and conceptual power" of her scholarship, she wrote to her agent, Marie Rodell. After a battle, she was awarded tenure as a full professor. She became the first holder of the Louis Stulberg Chair in Law and Politics. Murray's brilliance and conceptual power had been and would continue to be hallmarks of her work.

It was certainly an honor to be appointed to a professorship endowed in the name of the president of the International Ladies' Garment Workers' Union. Then again, it was not a professorship at an American law school, which was the goal Murray and her mentors at Howard University Law School had set decades earlier. She was disappointed that Yale had not offered her a faculty appointment in the law school. She satisfied her goal by teaching part-time at the Boston University School of Law.

In 1978, twenty-two years after the publication of the hardcover of *Proud Shoes*, Harper & Row released a paperback edition that included an introduction and family photographs. Reissued on the heels of Alex Haley's *Roots: The Saga of an American Family*, a historical novel that told the story of his African ancestors, *Proud Shoes* received a new reception. This time, readers went beyond a preoccupation with interracial sex and marriage and found the Fitzgerald women, especially Murray, fascinating.

Nearly every review of *Proud Shoes* compared it with *Roots*. The *Nation's* Jack Hicks wrote that *Roots* "dwells . . . on African continuations," whereas "*Proud Shoes* traps the beast of slavery." Larry Swindell of the *Philadelphia Inquirer* said that *Proud Shoes* was "not a spinoff on *Roots* but a splendid forerunner."

Murray was happy about the commercial success of Haley's novel and the television miniseries it spawned. With adequate marketing, she had no doubt that her book would find a wide audience and that Katharine Hepburn would be perfectly cast as Grandmother Cornelia in a film adaptation.

· · ·

MURRAY CONTINUED TO RAISE the issue of sex discrimination in her writings and presentations to academic and civic groups. On June 19, 1970, at a hearing held by the U.S. House Committee on Education and Labor, she described the multilayered discrimination black women faced, using an impressive array of charts to compare salary and unemployment rates by race, sex, and age to supplement her testimony. From her days as a restaurant worker in college to her career as an attorney and educator, she had been paid less than, and denied the respect accorded to, her male peers. She had spent the first half of her life fighting for equal rights as an African American, only to discover that she would have to spend the second half fighting for equal rights as a woman. "If anyone should ask a Negro woman what is her greatest achievement, her honest answer would be," Murray told the committee, her voice laden with emotion, "'I survived.'" Three months later, she would testify before the New York City Commission on Human Rights, headed by fellow Yale Law School alumna Eleanor Holmes Norton. Unable to hold back the tears, Murray openly wept as she recounted the opportunities she had been denied.

Of her peers in the legal community, Murray perhaps most admired Thurgood Marshall. The feeling was mutual. For years, Marshall had informally solicited Murray's legal advice. Good-humored, he liked to open their dialogue with the refrain "I know what the law says, Pauli, but tell me something different." After Marshall was appointed to the Court of Appeals for the Second Circuit, he thanked Murray for her good wishes and said he hoped his "work on the Bench" would meet her "expectations."

Murray was emboldened by Marshall's subsequent appointments to the Office of Solicitor General, in 1965, and the U.S. Supreme Court, in 1967. Now an old hand at lobbying the White House, she wrote to President Richard M. Nixon in 1971 to say that she was ready and available to serve on the high court should he wish to nominate a woman. Murray knew she was an unlikely appointee. Still, she wanted to be considered. She believed that her nomination, whether successful or not, would at least raise the issue of women's representation on the court. Murray would never be nominated, and she would wait a decade to see the first woman Supreme Court justice, Sandra Day O'Connor, confirmed, on September 21, 1981.

Pauli Murray, age sixty-six, at her ordination, Washington National Cathedral, January 8, 1977. No path or training had been as arduous for her. *(Associated Press)*

63

"The Missing Element . . . Is Theological"

Murray took a series of actions in 1973 that baffled her friends and colleagues. She resigned from Brandeis, deposited a substantial portion of her personal papers at the Arthur and Elizabeth Schlesinger Library on the History of Women in America at Radcliffe College, moved back to New York City, and enrolled at the General Theological Seminary to study for holy orders. That she would leave the security of a tenured professorship in her sixties to prepare for the priesthood when the Episcopal Church had not approved the ordination of women seemed ill-advised and "self-destructive" to some of her supporters. For Murray, on the other hand, it was an act of faith and part of a lifelong quest for "authentic selfhood."

The seemingly abrupt decision to enter the seminary was not sudden at all. Murray's religious education had begun in childhood with family Bible readings, watching Aunts Pauline and Sallie serve as "prime movers" in St. Titus, their home church in Durham, and visits to church missions with her uncle the Reverend John Small. She was nine years old when the Right Reverend Henry B. Delany, the first African American bishop of the Episcopal Diocese of North Carolina, confirmed her. When she was seventeen and Delaney was on his deathbed, he blessed her and pronounced her "a child of destiny." Murray had come to believe that his words were "prophetic."

Before Murray could articulate a philosophy of human rights, she was channeling her thoughts and emotions into poetry and prose. She became an activist, and this had led to a career in law. But years of working as an attorney and, more recently, as a professor had not satisfied her desire to tackle the moral foundation of inequality. "The missing element in my training and experience," she announced to family and friends, "is theological."

Murray was fully aware of the roadblocks to priesthood. She had once stopped going to church for a year to protest its treatment of women. Unable to abandon an institution that had been central to her life, she returned to work with Renee Barlow and others for the inclusion of women in all church roles.

Despite decades of study and debate, the Episcopal Church had not sanctioned the ordination of women. Yet Murray had ministered the last rites to Aunt Pauline, technically violating church tenet. Murray would assume a ministerial role again in the weeks before Renee Barlow's death, on the morning of February 21, 1973.

On January 10, Renee was admitted to Columbia Presbyterian Medical Center, suffering from paralysis on her right side, blurred vision, and slurred speech. She had had a radical mastectomy seven years earlier. This time, doctors diagnosed an inoperable brain tumor. Renee was fifty-nine.

On learning that the prescribed steroid and cobalt treatments might permanently impair her sight, mobility, and mental functions, Renee gave Pauli power of attorney. Renee's physical decline proved to be as rapid as her cognitive deterioration. Pauli did her best to lift Renee's spirits, manage her affairs, and keep friends and family informed. The competence and grace with which Pauli performed her duties camouflaged her heartache. Her only refuge was often a hospital closet, where she could drop her cheerful countenance and her "uncontrollable sobs" were out of earshot. Pauli sat at Renee's bedside for sixteen days, "talking to Renee as if she were fully present." The night before Renee passed, Pauli read the Twenty-third Psalm to her, urged her to rest, and "kissed her goodbye."

A private service was held at Frank E. Campbell's Funeral Home on Saturday, February 24. Renee's oak coffin was draped in a purple pall and "flanked on each end by a tall vase of spring flowers." The public memorial took place on February 27 at Calvary Church, where Eleanor Roosevelt had been christened. Lloyd Garrison, who represented the law firm where Renee and Pauli had worked, and Beatrice Worthy, an African American who represented women personnel professionals in New York City, gave eulogies. The service closed with a stirring rendition of "We Shall Overcome" by the local choir. Because the officiating priest was available only for the public memorial, Pauli stood in his place, organizing both services and caring for family and friends from out of town.

Since the deaths of Aunts Pauline and Sallie and Eleanor Roosevelt, Renee had been "the closest person" in Pauli's life. Renee's passing meant the loss of "a Christian partnership of nearly seventeen years," in which Pauli "was never rejected." The death, eleven weeks later, of Renee's ninety-three-year-old mother, Mary Jane, whom Pauli regarded as extended kin, compounded her grief. Pauli's efforts to quiet her longing and anxiety by listening to recordings of Robert Schumann's Piano Concerto in A Minor and Arnold Schoenberg's *Transfigured Night*, which Renee had given her and loved, proved unsuccessful.

Pauli and Renee had worked side by side in the Episcopal Church, and it was to this institution that Pauli turned for consolation. God had brought them "together to comfort and help one another when each needed it most," and now that Renee was gone, Pauli felt compelled to continue the work they had begun. Until now, Pauli had not seriously considered the priesthood. However, the call to the ministry seemed insuppressible in Renee's absence.

• • •

RENEE HAD DESIGNATED PAULI as coequal beneficiary of her $10,000 life insurance policy. With the money bequeathed her, Pauli entered the General Theological Seminary in the fall of 1973. GTS was the first school of religious education established by the Episcopal Church in the United States. Murray was the oldest seminarian, the only African American woman in her class, and senior to many of her professors in age and professional standing. Undaunted by what some may have viewed as her advanced age or the fact that she would be "in limbo" until church policy changed, she brimmed with optimism. At the end of the first term, Murray gave the Right Reverend Paul Moore, bishop of New York, a copy of *Dark Testament and Other Poems* as a Christmas gift. Her hopeful inscription read, "With the prayer that someday you may be able to ordain me a Priest in our Church."

An undiagnosed hearing problem and Murray's background as a lawyer fueled the perception that she was "abrasive." After a fellow woman seminarian identified Murray's hearing problem and Murray acquired a hearing aid, she no longer interrupted others in class. Rumors of her impoliteness faded. However, Murray's calls for diversity in the student body and curriculum led to the charge that her interests were political rather than theological.

To one male seminarian, who complained that all the talk about discrimination dominated too much class time, Murray responded, "If you have to live with anger, I have to live with pain. I'll trade you both my pain, my sex, my race and my age—and see how you deport yourself in such circumstances. Barring that," she continued, "try to imagine for 24 hours what it must be like to be a Negro in a predominantly white seminary, a woman in an institution dominated by men and for the convenience of men, some of whom radiate hostility even though they do not say a word, who are patronizing and kindly as long as I do not get out of my place, but who feel threatened by my intellect, my achievements, and my refusal to be suppressed." Of their differences, Murray told him, "If I can't take your judgmental statements and your anger, I am in the wrong place. If you cannot take my methods of fighting for survival, then you have chosen the wrong vocation."

"Church politics," Murray wrote to Patricia Roberts Harris, a fellow Episcopalian who would soon join President Jimmy Carter's cabinet as secretary of housing and urban development, "is probably the ultimate in politics—and dealing with Bishops is like something almost 'out of this world.' They speak in double entendre."

The disapproval of her peers did not dampen the delight Murray took in the GTS experience. She excelled in her courses. For pastoral care training, she ministered to the sick and dying at Bellevue Hospital, where she had briefly been a psychiatric patient in 1940. She did her fieldwork at St. Philip's Chapel, the mission in Prince George's County, Maryland, where her uncle John had served as minister and where she, as a young girl, had played the organ for church services.

Murray would later recall her time at the seminary as "the most rigorous discipline I had ever encountered, surpassing by far the rigors of my law school training." It also proved to be a period of personal growth and healing, during which she would examine her "fears, insecurities, and unresolved problems." Through dialogue with others, intense study, and "constant self-examination," she grew in self-acceptance and came to terms with her childhood loss of her parents.

No matter what criticism came Murray's way, she sensed that Grandmother Cornelia, mother Agnes, Aunts Pauline and Sallie, Renee, and ER "were happy about all this." Murray imagined they were smiling the morning she donned her clerical collar, orange kente cloth stole, and Renee's crucifix. The night before Murray assisted with Communion for the first time, she dreamt she had given ER "some information she needed and she was very grateful for it." This dream had come on July 8, close to the fourteenth anniversary of Murray's July 14 visit with ER at Val-Kill, she noted in her journal.

Murray graduated from GTS with honors in 1976. Her master's thesis, "Black Theology and Feminist Theology: A Comparative Study," was a critical examination of two emerging theologies. Because black theologians ignored or dismissed women's contributions and concerns, while feminist theologians overlooked or brushed aside issues of race and class, Murray challenged both viewpoints. As one who had endured multiple oppressions, she argued that a theology of universal liberation and reconciliation was the only acceptable alternative.

. . .

ON SEPTEMBER 16, 1976, the 65th General Convention of the Episcopal Church officially approved the ordination of women. On January 8, 1977, Murray, dressed in a white robe that covered all but a few inches of her pants and thick-soled lace-ups, walked into Washington National Cathedral with fellow ordinands Carole Anne Crumley, Elizabeth Phenix Wiesner, Rayford W. Ellis, Joel A. Gibson, and John Leslie Rabb. Reverends Eleanor Lee McGee and Elizabeth Powell, who had been ordained before the change in church policy, were present and would be affirmed as well. This ceremony, witnessed by approximately two thousand congregants, marked "the end of a long series of firsts" for Murray, who was a seventh-generation Episcopalian.

Neither the snow nor the fifteen protesters outside the cathedral distributing circulars and holding placards condemning the "priestesses" deterred the jubilation inside. Murray was the last candidate to be consecrated. When Bishop William Creighton laid his hands on her forehead, "the sun broke through the clouds outside and sent shafts of rainbow-colored light down through the stained-glass windows." In that moment, she had become the first African American woman priest in the history of the Episcopal Church.

The warm ceremony and favorable press did not silence the opposition. The Coalition for the Apostolic Ministry, which insisted that Christian texts and traditions called exclusively for male priests and bishops, filed a complaint with Murray's local diocese. She also learned that John Thomas Walker, designated to succeed Creighton as the first African American bishop of the Diocese of Washington, was making insidious remarks about her sexuality behind her back. He was ready to accept women into the priesthood, but homosexuals were another matter. It mattered not that homosexuality had been removed from the *Diagnostic and Statistical Manual of Mental Disorders.* As far as the church was concerned, it was sin.

Although Walker's behavior upset Murray, it is not known if she ever confronted him directly. In an unsent letter dated March 14, 1977, she took him to task for his bias and the insinuation that there was a link between her sexuality and her mental health. "What do you really know about sexuality—heterosexuality, bi-sexuality, homosexuality, transexuality, unisexuality?" she asked. "What do you know about metabolic imbalance? Endocrine imbalance? The varieties of approach to mental health?"

After years of discrimination because of her race, gender, and sexuality, and after living through the nightmare of the McCarthy hearings, Murray leaned toward public embrace of who she was. She increasingly mentioned homosexual rights in her sermons, speeches, and other writings. To church friends, Murray said, "We bring our total selves to God, our sexuality, our joyousness, our foolishness, etc. etc."

Armed with a progressive perspective on gender and sexuality, she made inclusiveness the hallmark of her ministry. She also reached out to a new generation of scholars and activists. After the Feminist Press published the textbook *All the Women Are White, All the Blacks Are Men, But Some of Us Are Brave: Black Women's Studies,* in which the editors—Gloria T. [Akasha] Hull, Barbara Smith, and this author—called for the eradication of racism, anti-feminism, and homophobia in the academy and the larger society, Murray wrote to us on November 25, 1983. "Dear Sisters," she said, "if *Newsweek* [which had run a feature on women's studies ignoring the contributions of black women] doesn't see the value of your work, here's an 'Old Timer' who does. So be encouraged, *it can be done.*"

Notwithstanding the difficulties, Murray knew that her struggle paled in comparison to what others before her had faced. "My ordination as a Negro woman priest comes some 172 years after the first Afro-American male priest was ordained in 1804 at the age of 58," she wrote to friends. "I am only eight years older than he was at the time, and thankfully, my approval for admission to the priesthood has come one month after the absolute minimum of service required in the Diaconate. Absalom Jones, our first Black priest, had to wait ten years. The Holy Spirit in our Church moves slowly at times, but it *does* move."

The resistance to Murray was an omen for those who would follow her. Both Barbara Harris, an African American who became the first woman consecrated as a bishop, in 1989, and Gene Robinson, the first openly gay bishop approved by the General Convention, in 2003, would face hate mail and death threats during their tenure. The consecration of Mary Glasspool as the first openly lesbian bishop, in 2010, would be condemned by Archbishop of Canterbury Rowan Williams. Just as Murray paved the way for Harris, Robinson, Glasspool, and others, progressives would lay the ground for her elevation by the Episcopal Church to sainthood in July 2012, twenty-seven years after her death. By naming Murray to *Holy Women, Holy Men,* the General Convention of the Episcopal Church deemed that her life and contributions would be honored and celebrated on the anniversary of her death.

64

"God's Presence Is as Close as the Touch of a Loved One's Hand"

On February 13, a month after her ordination, Pauli Murray celebrated her first Holy Eucharist at the Chapel of the Cross in Chapel Hill, North Carolina. She was the first woman to perform the Eucharist at the old church and in the state of North Carolina. In the racially mixed congregation of six hundred sat journalist and UNC alumnus Charles Kuralt, who filmed the service and interviewed Murray for his popular CBS television series *On the Road.*

The elaborate lectern behind which Murray stood bore the name of her slaveholding great-aunt, Mary Ruffin Smith, who had bequeathed a portion of her inheritance to the Episcopal Diocese of North Carolina. The fragile Bible Murray held was a treasured gift from Smith to her niece, Murray's grandmother Cornelia, whose baptism as one of Smith's "five servant children" was recorded on December 20, 1858, in the church registry. The purple ribbon and dried flowers Murray used as a Bible bookmark had come with the bouquet Eleanor Roosevelt had sent thirty-three years ago when Murray graduated from Howard University School of Law.

"That the first woman priest to preside at the altar of the church to which Mary Ruffin Smith had given her deepest devotion should be the granddaughter of the little girl she had sent to the balcony reserved for slaves" was a remarkable irony that Murray felt deeply. It was indeed a "historic moment," she told Kuralt, in that she symbolized those who had suffered in the past because of "race, color, religion, sex (gender), age, sex preference, political and theological differences, economic and

The Reverend Dr. Pauli Murray (front) and unidentified speakers (seated at rear) at the Salute to Black Women program, Metropolitan Baptist Church, Washington, D.C., February 5, 1977. Murray carried her ministry into churches and nursing homes in Maryland, Massachusetts, New York, North Carolina, Pennsylvania, Virginia, and the nation's capital. *(Courtesy of Milton Williams)*

Murray with her dog Roy (left) and playing her organ (right), Alexandria, Virginia, 1976. She slept very little and considered television a waste of time. *(Courtesy of Milton Williams)*

social status, and other man-made barriers." These souls, she insisted, were "reaching out" through her in love and reconciliation.

Murray was the oldest practicing female Episcopal priest and still a maverick. She wore pants and ski caps for comfort. She carried her writing tools in a backpack wherever she went. After forced retirement at age seventy-two, she would continue to serve the aged, the sick, the shut-in, and those grieving the loss of loved ones. She was among the clergy who participated in the funeral services for Alice Paul, founder of the National Woman's Party and author of the original version of the Equal Rights Amendment, and for Dorothy Kenyon, who had been a role model and colleague.

Murray's sermons were an inspiring blend of Holy Scripture, poetry, philosophy, and personal narrative. Her favorite material came from Bible stories of women, like Mary Magdalene; Kahlil Gibran's *The Prophet;* the writings of Paul Tillich; and her experiences with Grandmother Cornelia, Aunts Pauline and Sallie, Renee, and ER. The spirit of "God's presence," Murray often said, "is as close as the touch of a loved one's hand."

Murray may have thought that becoming a priest would quiet her restless spirit and assuage her grief. This was not to be. Life was as intense as ever. Her longing for "a friend of the heart" remained unabated, as did her addiction to unfiltered cigarettes and strong coffee. Her small apartment, she quipped, was "a library with a few chairs."

Murray's loving embrace always included dogs. Six weeks after Doc died, she met Roy, a two-year-old black Labrador retriever, in a veterinarian's office, waiting to be put down after a hit-and-run driver had crushed his left hind leg. Murray could not bear the thought of Roy dying alone, so she took him home and nursed him. He rallied, and Murray had his leg surgically repaired. Roy would run, swim, and happily fetch sticks until his death, a decade later.

Murray at her home office in Alexandria, Virginia, 1976. Writing was Murray's salvation, and her tools were rarely more than an arm's length away. *(Courtesy of Milton Williams)*

65

"Hopefully, We Have Picked Up the Candle"

Doing "a creditable piece of writing" had always given Murray "a sense of self-worth," and she felt an urgent need to write a sequel to *Proud Shoes*. As she worked on what would become her autobiography, she sought to examine her life in historical perspective. Of the books Murray consulted on the twentieth century and the lives of Franklin and Eleanor Roosevelt, those by Stella K. Hershan and Joseph P. Lash touched her in a unique way.

Hershan's *A Woman of Quality,* published in 1970, was a collection of interviews with people who believed ER had changed the course of their lives. Hershan profiled people ER met by chance, such as cab drivers; those in whom she took a special interest, such as children, American and Israeli Jews, labor organizers, minorities, refugees, the disabled, and wounded soldiers; and those with whom she had worked, such as the staff and alumni of the Wiltwyck School, former members of her household staff, and her colleagues at the United Nations.

Hershan interviewed Murray for the chapter titled "The Negroes." Among the stories Murray recounted was the case of the black seamen accused of mutiny after the explosion at Port Chicago and ER's gallant, albeit unsuccessful, effort to convince the navy to grant them clemency. Murray "choked up" during the interview, and Hershan, an Austrian-born Jew who'd fled her homeland to escape the Nazis, became emotional, too. Both knew the heartache of injustice and the healing power of ER's accepting presence.

Murray knew Joseph Lash through ER and the network of progressives close to her. Born in New York City to Russian Jewish immigrant parents, Lash, like Murray, was a former student activist whom ER befriended in the late 1930s. A journalist with a keen sense of history, Lash had helped ER organize her papers before she donated them to the Franklin D. Roosevelt Presidential Library. Two years after ER's death, Lash published *Eleanor Roosevelt: A Friend's Memoir.* In 1971, he published *Eleanor and Franklin: The Study of Their Relationship Based on Eleanor Roosevelt's Private Papers,* for which he earned the Pulitzer Prize in biography. He followed with *Eleanor: The Years Alone* in 1972.

In *Eleanor and Franklin,* Lash excerpted the letter Murray wrote to FDR after his University of North Carolina address along with her poem "Mr. Roosevelt Regrets." Impressed with his work, Murray responded with an effusive letter. "Joe," she began, "it is magnificently beautiful! . . . I have to read slowly savoring each line and some of the sharply insightful passages. . . . You are an artist, writing lovingly, tenderly and gracefully. . . . This book will LIVE and do pride to Mrs. R's memory." Reading Lash's footnotes made Murray feel like "a miser," she confessed, for she had a large file of correspondence he had not seen. She had planned to give the documents to the FDR Library, but she "cherished Mrs. Roosevelt's letters so" that she had "been unable to part with them."

Lash was curious about Murray's file, and he asked if she would permit him to examine the correspondence, especially those with ER's handwritten postscripts and margin notes. "On the other hand," he wrote, "you are probably planning to write something yourself and if you want to save those letters for your own autobiography, I will understand fully a decision to keep your correspondence with Mrs. R. to yourself."

"Joe," Murray replied, "the great lesson Mrs. R. taught all of us by example was largesse, generosity—her heart seemed to me as big as all the world. . . . She belongs to history, and the impact of her spirit is sorely needed now in our sorrowful society which seems to have fallen on bad days in many respects. If there is anything in her correspondence with me or mine with her which will sharpen the impact of her great spirit of compassion, of caring for people, of keeping track of people no matter how busy she was—then use it now," Murray insisted. "I do not believe your use of such material will detract from anything I should write in the future—because our experiences are different and by the time I get around to full-time writing, history will have moved on. New insights will arise which will make my approach using the same material different from yours." On the chance that her literary agent "might not agree," Murray decided not to "consult her on this one."

When Murray began to write in earnest, Lash was at work on two collections of letters. *Love, Eleanor: Eleanor Roosevelt and Her Friends* was released in 1982, and *A World of Love: Eleanor Roosevelt and Her Friends, 1943–1962* appeared two years later. While he mentioned Murray in *A World of Love,* not one of the letters she and ER wrote to each other in their decades-long friendship appeared in full or excerpt in either collection. Considering the access Murray gave Lash, she must have been disappointed.

. . .

IN JULY 1982, Murray had emergency surgery at Johns Hopkins Hospital for a life-threatening intestinal blockage. Maida Springer-Kemp, who now lived in Pittsburgh, came to nurse Murray back to health. This crisis and the demands of her ministry thwarted Murray's writing. When the Eleanor Roosevelt Centennial Committee invited her to contribute to a book of essays, she was unable to participate. Even so, the outline of the project prompted Murray to write to the editors.

The first concern was "the absence of an author (so far as the names suggest)," Murray observed, "who is obviously a Negro/Black/Person of color/Afro-American—I prefer Negro. Given Mrs. Roosevelt's deep involvement in civil rights issues, it would be a grave oversight not to have a Negro author represented." (Murray recommended Pauline Redmond Coggs.) Another issue was the project's primary focus on ER's political life. "Mrs. Roosevelt was much more than a political animal," she maintained, and "the book would have more intrinsic value if the personal and the political are brought together in these essays as they were indeed reflected in her life."

. . .

ON DECEMBER 4, 1982, Murray, Lash, and Franklin D. Roosevelt Jr. joined a gathering of scholars, journalists, and former Roosevelt administration staffers at Hunter College for a conference on the role of the first lady. It was the first major conference on the subject. More than seven hundred people attended. Lash spoke from a biographer's perspective; Franklin Roosevelt, as a son.

Murray, introducing herself as a former "youthful challenger and critic" of ER's, recalled the early days of their relationship.

> For me, becoming friends with Mrs. Roosevelt was a slow, painful process, marked by sharp exchanges of correspondence, often anger on my side and exasperation on her side, and a gradual development of mutual admiration and respect. On the one hand, Mrs. Roosevelt was a mother figure to me; she and FDR were of the same generation as my own parents; they were also Episcopalians; they had six children as did my own parents, born roughly in the same period as the six Murray children. . . . I felt that Mrs. Roosevelt was a woman of deep religious commitment. And all these qualities made me feel very close to her in spite of myself.
>
> The result of my rebellion was that Mrs. Roosevelt thought of me as "a firebrand" who had done some "foolish things" and who should not "push too fast," while I took it upon myself to challenge her behavior in the area of race relations as an important figure and a part of an Administration which was moving too slow.

Previously, Murray had been reluctant to talk publicly about her friendship with ER. Here, Murray hit her stride. Of ER's impact on her life, she said,

> I learned by watching her in action over a period of three decades that each of us is culture-bound by the era in which we live, and that the greatest challenge to the individual is to try to move to the very boundaries of our historical limitations and to project ourselves toward future centuries. Mrs. Roosevelt, a product of late nineteenth century Victorianism, did just that, and she moved far beyond many of her contemporaries. I like to think that I am one of the young women of her time, touched by her spirit of commitment to the universal dignity of the human being created in the image of God (which we theologians call *imago dei*). Hopefully, we have picked up the candle that she lighted in the darkness and we are trying to carry it forward to the close of our own lives.

66

"Eleanor Roosevelt Was the Most Visible Symbol of Autonomy"

In 1984, Pauli Murray and Maida Springer-Kemp, both retired septuagenarians, embarked on "a joint venture in cooperative yet autonomous living." They moved into an old house with "twin apartments" in the North Point Breeze section of Pittsburgh. Maida lived on the first level, and Pauli occupied the upstairs unit. North Point Breeze was a friendly, racially integrated neighborhood, rich in architectural history, less than thirty minutes from downtown Pittsburgh. It was an ideal location for Murray, who loved to walk in Westinghouse Park with Christy, an elderly Doberman she adopted after Roy died, to the Homewood Branch of the Carnegie Library, and on the University of Pittsburgh campus.

Life in North Point Breeze nurtured Murray's writing. By the year's end, she had completed a draft of her autobiography and finished half the revisions her editor had recommended. Murray's social life was enriched by her relationships with Maida's son Eric Springer, who had become a distinguished attorney; his wife, Cecile, a highly regarded regional planner; and the congregation at the Church of the Holy Cross.

After years without sufficient funds or time for leisure travel, Pauli took an Amtrak train tour to Seattle with Maida. They stopped at the Wingspread Center in Racine, Wisconsin, for a black women's conference and a "joyful reunion" with Aileen Clarke Hernandez, who, like Patricia Roberts Harris, had participated in the Howard University student restaurant boycott. In Seattle, Pauli spoke at the Urban League's annual dinner, and the Coalition of Labor Union Women honored Maida at a luncheon.

When they were not being feted by their hosts—Mona H. Bailey, a former national president of Delta Sigma Theta sorority (Murray had become an honorary member), and the sorority's ninety-five-year-old cofounder Bertha Pitts Campbell—Pauli and Maida "gorged" themselves in first-class restaurants. On the way home, they visited Pauli's former editor, Elizabeth Kalashnikoff.

The "high point" of 1984 was Murray's participation in "The Vision of Eleanor Roosevelt: Past, Present, Future," a conference commemorating the centennial of ER's birth. This event was held at Vassar College on October 13–16 and was cohosted by the Eleanor Roosevelt Institute. Each session addressed one of ER's concerns: human rights, civil rights, women's rights, peace, or economic justice.

Among the presenters were Roosevelt family members; Joseph Lash and his wife, Trudy; Edna P. Gurewitsch, the wife of ER's personal physician David Gurewitsch; Henry Morgenthau III, the executive producer of *Prospects of Mankind,* which ER had hosted for public television; and Murray's friend Caroline Ware. Reverend Gordon Kidd, who had presided at the funerals of Franklin and Eleanor Roosevelt, led the Sunday convocation, at which Dorothy Height spoke and the West Point Gospel Choir sang. In addition to Murray and Height, the African American speakers included historian and U.S. civil rights commissioner Mary F. Berry, political scientist Charles Hamilton, and Bayard Rustin, director of the A. Philip Randolph Institute.

Murray joined ER's grandson John R. Boettiger, Edna Gurewitsch, Henry Morgenthau, former assistant secretary of labor Esther Peterson, and U.N. Association of the U.S.A. staffer Estelle Linzer on a plenary panel entitled "A Remembrance of Eleanor Roosevelt." Murray regaled the audience with memories of her first face-to-face conversation with ER the afternoon she hosted the National Sharecroppers Week delegation in her New York City apartment, ER's campaign inside the White House to save the life of Odell Waller, and the weekend ER braved Hurricane Hazel to keep a speaking engagement at Bard College.

ER's contribution to the modern women's movement was the subject of considerable debate. Some conferees claimed she was not a feminist by virtue of her opposition to the National Woman's Party and the Equal Rights Amendment. *Ms.* magazine cofounder Gloria Steinem disagreed. Because ER had used her power and position to fight injustice, Steinem argued, the former first lady was "definitely a feminist."

Murray had strong opinions about this issue, too, and she weighed in on the debate:

While Mrs. Roosevelt's brand of feminism did not lead her to give active support to the Equal Rights Amendment which she and many women reformers had earlier opposed for fear the adoption of ERA would undermine state protective labor laws for women, by the 1950's she had dropped her strong objections to a constitutional guarantee of equality. Also, while the [President's] Commission [on the Status of Women] itself did not recommend ERA, several of the women who worked with the Commission under her leadership, including myself, were the founders of the NOW which became the foremost advocate of ERA. . . .

Perhaps Mrs. Roosevelt's greatest contribution to feminism during the forty years, which spanned the period from securing the vote for women in 1920 to the resurgence of the women's movement in the 1960's, was the example she set. . . . Eleanor Roosevelt was the most visible symbol of autonomy and therefore the role model of women of my generation. Although she did not live to see many of the spectacular gains—both substantive and symbolic—women have made in the past two decades, her own life and work pointed the way and helped to set in motion forces which made these gains possible. Just as she became the First Lady of the World, in a very real sense she was also the Mother of the Women's Revolution.

Pauli Murray at the home of her Hunter College classmate Louise E. Jefferson, in Litchfield, Connecticut, circa May 1985. They had stayed in touch through the years and this is one of the last photographs taken before Murray's death. *(Photo by Louise E. Jefferson, Patricia Bell-Scott Collection)*

67

"All the Strands of My Life Had Come Together"

Pauli Murray's appearance at the Eleanor Roosevelt centennial conference proved to be her swan song. In December 1984, doctors discovered an obstruction in the bile duct leading into her pancreas. Preliminary tests indicated pancreatic cancer. Shortly after her admission to Pittsburgh's Presbyterian University Hospital on January 28, 1985, she lost consciousness. She was comatose for eight days and not expected to live. Her lung power was so diminished she had to use a breathing machine to keep pneumonia at bay. It took her a month before she could walk without assistance again. By the time she regained full awareness, she was only eighty-five pounds, twenty pounds below her ideal weight. "That I am among the living at all is a miracle of God's loving providence," she wrote in the spring to friends and family.

During Murray's extended hospitalization, her dog, Christy, died of old age. The loss of her pet, her failing health, and her fierce smoking addiction sent Murray into a tailspin. Determined to be seen as more than a cancer victim, she had a sign posted over her hospital bed that read, "Please refer to this patient as the Reverend Dr. Pauli Murray."

She came home on March 8 "to a shining place, flowers, and a 'fatted calf.'" This homecoming, the daily calls, the heartwarming prayers, the avalanche of telegrams and get-well cards, and the friends and family who came "in shifts" to help brought her to tears. "From here on out," she vowed, "it's a day at a time."

Having nearly succumbed on the operating table, Murray began to prepare for the inevitable. She sent the crucifix she wore at her ordination to Dovey Johnson Roundtree, a friend, fellow activist, and Howard University School of Law alumna who was assistant pastor at Allen Chapel African Methodist Episcopal Church, in Washington, D.C. Murray gave Maida an original painting by Louise Jefferson. And when Ruth Powell, co-leader of the 1943–44 Howard University student boycott campaign, flew to Pittsburgh to see Murray, she insisted that Powell take her wheeled luggage cart since she "wouldn't be needing it." Murray was correct. She would be too weak to attend the upcoming Hunter College graduation ceremony, where she, former Democratic vice presidential candidate Geraldine Ferraro, and artist Robert Motherwell would receive honorary doctorates.

Pauli had often prayed all night at the bedside of congregants and loved ones, as was the case when Maida's mother, Adina Stewart Carrington, passed. When Pauli drew her last breath, Maida was at her side. Pauli departed peacefully at home in Pittsburgh on July 1, 1985. She was seventy-four.

· · ·

PAULI MURRAY HAD BEEN a lifelong student of history, and she had often thought about how her life intersected with other agents of social change. She considered it no accident that the NAACP published the inaugural issue of *The Crisis,* under the editorship of "the great protagonist of civil rights" W. E. B. Du Bois, in the same month and year of her birth. It pleased her to discover "that the great Russian novelist and advocate of nonviolence, Leo Tolstoy . . . died within twenty-four hours" of her birth. That Murray's memorial service took place on the forty-third anniversary of the funeral of Odell Waller, the black sharecropper whose execution marked a defining moment in her relationship with Eleanor

Roosevelt, was another historical coincidence she would have surely noted.

On July 5, at eleven o'clock in the morning, 141 people attended a Mass of the Resurrection held, as Murray had requested, at the Washington National Cathedral. Murray's minister, Canon Junius F. Carter, officiated. Reverends Phoebe Coe, Becky Dinan, Doris Mote, Diane Shepard, Beverly Moore-Tasy, and Barbara Harris were cocelebrants. Canon Carter said of Murray, "The power she had and the effect her life had on all of us was a glorious experience." Murray's nephew Michael, who delivered a stirring tribute from the family, said, "It was Aunt Pauli's habit to speak the truth, no matter what the consequences." After the Mass, members of the Delta Sigma Theta sorority conducted their traditional Omega Omega farewell ritual in the courtyard.

Murray had asked that she be cremated and interred at the cathedral, but her ashes were buried in Brooklyn's Cypress Hills Cemetery, in a family plot with Aunts Pauline and Sallie, Renee Barlow, and Renee's mother, Mary Jane. This burial ground placed Murray in good company, for it was the site George Washington chose for a military fortification during the Revolutionary War. This cemetery was also the final resting place for Murray's hero, the baseball Hall of Famer and civil rights activist Jackie Robinson.

In the closing lines of her posthumously published autobiography, *Song in a Weary Throat: An American Pilgrimage,* Murray wrote,

> All the strands of my life had come together. Descendant of slave and of slave owner, I had already been called poet, lawyer, teacher, and friend. Now I was empowered to minister the sacrament of One in whom there is no north or south, no black or white, no male or female—only the spirit of love and reconciliation drawing us all toward the goal of human wholeness.

The quest for wholeness and the struggle for social justice brought the firebrand Pauli Murray and First Lady Eleanor Roosevelt together in friendship. The struggle continues to be nourished by the writings and records they left, the people they mentored, the organizations they cofounded, and the projects inspired by their examples.

ACKNOWLEDGMENTS

The nurturance and generosity of many people made it possible for me to write *The Firebrand and the First Lady.* I am grateful first to my parents, Dorothy and Louis Wilbanks Jr., my maternal grandparents, Roy and Marie Jewsome, and my paternal grandfather, Ollie Patton. They could not have known where my dreams or ambition would lead, yet they encouraged and supported me anyway.

I am grateful to Pauli Murray for affirming my early work as a feminist scholar and nudging me toward this project before I knew where I was going.

I am grateful to Charlotte Sheedy and Victoria Wilson, who believed in this project from day one. I offer heartfelt thanks for their patience and reassurance through all the years.

I thank Audrey Silverman, editorial assistant to Vicky Wilson. I thank Kathleen Fridella for her superb work as production editor.

Several people granted me interviews and access to private materials that enriched my understanding of Pauli Murray, Eleanor Roosevelt, and their friendship. I am indebted to:

Maida Springer-Kemp, for starting me out with a day-long interview and a home-cooked meal of stir-fried shrimp, garlic, onions, snow peas, and brown rice reminiscent of the savory dishes she and her mother, Adina Stewart Carrington, fed Pauli.

Pauline Redmond Coggs, for keen and psychologically rich observations of Murray and ER, both of whom she counted as close friends.

Grace Milgram, for recollections of the friendship between her former husband, Morris Milgram, and Murray, his friendship with ER, and the perils liberal activists faced during the Cold War.

Ruth Powell, for recollections of her days with Murray at Howard University and for treating me to a spontaneous rendition of the protest song she and her fellow female students composed and sang when they were jailed for sitting in the white section of a city bus. Powell, who was in her seventies when I met her, still moved "with the lilt of ballet dancer," as in the poem "Ruth," which Murray penned when they were in school.

Dovey Johnson Roundtree, for blessing this book project and urging me to write the truth.

Aileen Clarke Hernandez, for recollections of Howard University, Murray, ER, the early days of the EEOC and NOW, and for taking me under her wing.

Jean E. Friedman, for encouragement and recollections of her days with Murray at Benedict College.

Louise E. Jefferson, for invaluable photographs and correspondence.

Peggy McIntosh, for sharing her interview of her aunt Caroline F. Ware and her recollections of Ware and Murray.

Eric Springer, for recollections of his mother, Maida Springer-Kemp, and Murray, who was his mentor.

I also thank John Alan Creedy for recollections of the UNC campus response to Murray's application; Carole A. Crumley for recollections of the day she and Murray were ordained and Murray's subsequent work as a priest; Richard Sherman for recollections of his conversations with Morris Milgram; and Augusta Thomas for recollections of Murray in later life.

I am indebted to Pat McKenry, Mick Coleman, Lucie Fultz, Miriam DeCosta-Willis, and Charlotte Sheedy for encouraging critiques of the proposal out of which this book grew.

I benefited from a mountain of work by Eleanor Roosevelt scholars and owe special thanks to Allida M. Black, Maurine Beasley, Robert Cohen, and Blanche Wiesen Cook for heartening dialogue, letters, e-mails, and suggestions about possible sources.

My early vision of this project was nourished by discussions at the Women Writing Women's Lives Biography Seminar at the Graduate Center of the City University of New York. I thank Gail Hornstein for inviting me, Dorothy O. Helly for a warm welcome, Louise DeSalvo for her inspiring work, and Nell Irwin Painter—a historian turned visual artist—for her example of an art-centered later life.

I thank Sapphire for unwavering support, art sketchbooks, charcoal pencils, straight talk, and cheering me on as I learned to walk the writer's path.

I thank Janet Sims-Wood, who shared her encyclopedic knowledge of African Americans during World War II, as well as her home during my research trips to the Moorland-Spingarn Research Center; Miriam DeCosta-Willis, who sent a steady stream of helpful clippings and treated me to a tour of the Franklin Delano Roosevelt Memorial shortly after it opened in Washington, D.C.; and Lucie Fultz, who told me "not to sweat the deadline—focus on getting it right."

I thank Brenda Mitchell-Powell for her support, her belief in my work, and her uncanny intuition.

I thank Anna J. Williams for listening to passages of this work, illuminating discussion of women's developmental and health issues, and for helping to make my writing process and this book richer. I thank Margaret Cramer for sources on the treatment of thyroid disease and mood disorders in women.

I am grateful to Susan Ware for inviting me to write essays on Pauli Murray for *Notable American Women: A Biographical Dictionary—Completing the Twentieth Century* and the summer 2002 issue of the *Journal of Women's History;* Maurine Beasley for inviting me to write essays on Murray and the Odell Waller case for *The Eleanor Roosevelt Encyclopedia;* and Deb Chasman for inviting me to write the foreword to the Beacon Press edition of *Proud Shoes.* Each essay gave me a chance to consolidate my thinking.

I am grateful to the editorial collective of *SAGE: A Scholarly Journal on Black Women*—Beverly Guy-Sheftall, Jacqueline Jones Royster, Janet Sims-Wood, Miriam DeCosta-Willis, and Lucille P. Fultz—for the decade-long experience of coediting the journal and related publications. I am also grateful to Akasha Hull and Barbara Smith for the experience of coediting the first anthology in black women's studies. Both projects caught Pauli Murray's attention and hopefully made her proud.

I thank Bettye Collier-Thomas, Ralph Carlson, Adelaide Hill Cromwell, John D'Emilio, John Hope Franklin, John Inscoe, Werner M. Loval, Katy McCabe, Elizabeth Pleck, George Stoney, Patricia Sullivan, Dorothy Wick, and Milton Williams for feedback and encouragement.

For access to and assistance in locating primary materials, I thank the literary estates of Pauli Murray, Eleanor Roosevelt, and Lillian E. Smith, as well as the departments and people at the following institutions:

The Schlesinger Library, Radcliffe Institute, Harvard University, Reference Services, Ally Boland, Diana Carey, Anne Englehart, Sarah Hutcheon, Lynda Leahy, Ellen M. Shea, Amanda E. Strauss, and Susan Van Salis; Office of the Director and Sylvia McDowell.

Widener Library, Harvard University, Imaging Services, Evelyn Santana-Nola and Yuhua Li.

The Cumberland County Public Library, Fayetteville, North Carolina, and Wanda Hunter.

The Library of Congress, Veterans History Project, Megan Harris; Manuscripts Division, Bruce Kirby, Barbara Natanson, and Robin Rausch; Duplication Services, Rachel Mears and Tomeka Myers.

The Franklin D. Roosevelt Presidential Library and Museum, Archives Department, Robert Clark, Matthew Hanson, Virginia H. Lewick, Robert Park, Mark Renovitch, and Jay Teichmann.

New York Law School Mendik Library and William R. Mills.

New York Public Library, Reference Services.

New York State Library, Reference Services.

Princeton University, Seeley G. Mudd Manuscript Library, and Tom Rosko.

George Washington University, Eleanor Roosevelt Papers Project, Allida M. Black, and Christopher Brick; the Estelle and Melvin Gelman Library, Manuscripts Division, and Cheryl A. Chouiniere.

Wayne State University, Walter P. Reuther Library, Archives of Labor and Urban Affairs, William LeFevre, and Mary Joann Wallace.

Howard University, Moorland-Spingarn Research Center, University Archives, and Clifford L. Muse; Manuscripts Department and Joellen El-Bashir; References Services, Janet-Sims Wood; Office of Development and Alumni Affairs and Nesta H. Bernard.

The Library of Virginia, Archives.

The University of North Carolina at Chapel Hill, Louis Round Wilson Library, Special Collections, Southern Historical Collection, Keith Longiotti, David Moltke-Hansen, Matthew Turi, Tim West, and John White; Carolina Digital Library and Archives, Mike Millner, and Gary N. Pattillo; Alumni Records Office.

The University of North Carolina at Greensboro, Jackson Library, Reference Services, and Mark Schumacher.

The University of Georgia Library Interlibrary Loan Department, Hargrett Special Collections, Alexander Campbell King Law Library, Reference, and Thomas J. Striepe.

The Vassar College Library and Dean M. Rogers.

The Washington National Cathedral, Archives.

I also thank the New York State Parks staffer (unfortunately, I did not get his name) who responded to my telephone query by sending me copies of the *Tera Topics* newsletters.

For assistance with images, I thank: the Amistad Research Center, Tulane University, and Christopher Harter; the Associated Press and Matthew Lutts; Corbis; Cornell University, Industrial and Labor Relations School, Martin P. Catherwood Library, Kheel Center for Labor-Management Documentation and Archives, International Ladies' Garment Workers' Union Project, Katie Dowgiewicz and Melissa Holland; Durham County Library, North Carolina Collection, and Lynn Richardson; Getty Images; Harvard Law School Library, Historical and Special Collections, Public Service and Visual Collections, and Lesley Schoenfeld; Hunter College Libraries, Archives and Special Collections, and Julio Luis Hernandez-Delgado; Werner Loval; Milford Historical Society of Connecticut and Janice Broderick; the National Archives and Records Administration; National Archives for Black Women's History, Kenneth Chandler, Tazwell Franklin, and Kenvi Phillips; the National Park Service; the Naval Historical Foundation; *New Pittsburgh Courier* Archives and Eric Gaines; the Smithsonian Institution, National Museum of American History, Kenneth E. Behring Center, Archives Center, Mary Markey, and Kay Peterson; the University of Chicago Library, Julia Gardner, and Daniel Meyer; the University of Massachusetts, W. E. B. Du Bois Library, Special Collections and University

Archives, and Jeremy Smith; the Virginia Department of Corrections and Larry Taylor; and Milton Williams.

I thank Donna Alvermann, who went with me to an exhibition of hobo art at the Loudermilk Boarding House Museum in Cornelia, Georgia, behind which we found a spot where people still jump the rails; Juanita Johnson-Bailey, who joined me on a search for the old Camp Tera site and tours of Val-Kill and Springwood; and park ranger Geraldine C. Johnson, who made our tour of Val-Kill special.

I am indebted to several former students and research assistants, all of whom have become outstanding professionals in their own right. I am especially grateful to Carla Rae Abshire, research assistant extraordinaire. Her passionate interest in this story and her relentless pursuit of unanswered questions continued from start to finish. I am grateful to April L. Few-Demos, whose organizational skills and close reading of primary documents lit the path in the early years; Nina Lyon Jenkins, whose transcriptions made all the layers of an interview visible; Youn Mi Lee, whose meticulous handling of the documents eased my load; Kimberly Harper, for assistance with research on the Port Chicago case; Jessica Anderson, for assistance with research on "My Day"; and Kirk Philpot, who helped wherever he could until his death.

For basic research assistance, including travel, and support of my efforts to share my work in progress with other scholars and writers, I thank the Schlesinger Library for a summer honorary visiting fellowship in 1997 and the University of Georgia Willson Center for the Humanities and the Arts and Bettye Jean Craige for a fellowship in the spring of 1996 and a faculty seminar grant in the fall of 2007. I also thank the University of Georgia President's Venture Fund for a grant in 2000–2002.

It is my good fortune to belong to a supportive network of fellow writers. The White Car Gang of Athens, Georgia, affirmed my work as it evolved from rough to final draft. Genie Smith Bernstein walked me through doubt and never stopped reminding me "to let the reader be with Pauli and ER." Jim Murdoch shared his personal experience of Eleanor Roosevelt's magnetism and the impact of New Deal projects, such as the Tennessee Valley Authority. Dac Crossley gave me two "Adlai Stevenson for President" buttons, which are still tacked to the wall in my writing room. Harriette Austin helped me see the dramatic moments in the narrative.

I thank Carla Abshire, Elizabeth Bernstein, Genie Smith Bernstein, Jean E. Friedman, Jane Penland Hoover, Wayne Langston Perry, and Charles V. Underwood Jr. for reading multiple versions of my manuscript.

I am grateful to Pete Daniel, whose graduate course on African American history at the University of Tennessee changed the direction of my disciplinary orientation. I am grateful to Martin Lammon, who directed the 2001 and 2003 Arts and Letters workshops at Georgia College & State University, where I found inspiring teachers, receptive readers, and constructive critique. I thank

Al Perry, who directed the Winston-Salem Writers Conference in 2008, where I wrote with a circle of courageous writers.

I thank Harriette Austin, Annie Fahey, Philip Garrard, Jane Penland Hoover, Dinty Moore, Pat Schneider, and Carolyn Walker for writing workshops that challenged me to dig for narrative truth. I thank Frances Fifer, Christine Simmons Hicks, Fred A. Jones, Leroy Keith Jr., and Fred H. Singleton Jr. for encouraging my scholarly pursuits and love of language.

For support at important moments during the years it took to write this book, I thank Kizmet S. Adams, Joanne Allen, JoBeth Allen, Donna and Jack Alvermann, Maya Angelou, Patricia Arnold, Harriette Austin, Christina Baldwin, Deborah Bell, Lewis C. Bell Jr., Brenda Faye Bell-McAdams, Dawn Bennett-Alexander, Genie Smith Bernstein and Irwin Bernstein, Leanore and Randall Bramblett, Gene Brody, Gregory and Doretta Broughton, the Chattanooga, Tennessee, Howard High School Class of 1968, Pearl Cleage, Bronte Colbert, Evelyn Coleman, Bettye Collier-Thomas, Bettye Jean Craige, Margaret Cramer, Joyce Crawford, Dan Crawford and Van Shephard, Dac Crossley, Miriam DeCosta-Willis, Gina Dress, Terri Earl-Kulkovsky, Freddie Lee Fallins, Lucie Fultz, Marcia Ann Gillespie, Carl and Sara Glickman, Theodore Goetz, Doug Graf, Karen Hankins, Mike Healy, Wyler Hecht, Aileen Clarke Hernandez, Melody Higginbotham and her staff, bell hooks, Jane Penland Hoover, Pat King Hoveland, Sylvia Hutchinson, John Inscoe, David Earl Jackson, William Jackson, Patricia Kay Janes, Valerie Jean, Joel C. Jenkins, Juanita Johnson-Bailey and Marvin Bailey, Patricia Kalivoda, Monica Kucher and the staff at Good Hands Veterinary Hospital, Cheryl Legette, Patricia Lester, William Long Sr. and William Long Jr., Jacqueline Looney, Audre Lorde, Carol Jean Carter Lowery and Charles Lowery, Benjamin McAdams Sr., Sylvia McDowell, Donna McGinty, Pat McKenry, Angela Meltzer, Jessica Garris Miller, Brenda Mitchell-Powell, Diane Batts Morrow and John Morrow, Melissa A. Morse, Jim and Andrea Murdoch, Goldie Newsom, Ligaya and Onofre Paguio, Nell Irwin Painter, Margaret Ralston Payne, Robert W. Penland, Wayne Langston Perry, Kirk Philpot and Bernard Ferraro, Joseph and Elizabeth Pleck, Mary Lou Ponsell, Gleam Powell, Sharon J. Price, Paul B. Pruett, Kimberly Purnell, Regina M. Quick, John Shane Rayburn, Susan Reverby, Annice Ritter, Kate Rushin, Sapphire, Pat Schneider, Franklin Gregory Scott, Kirt Scott, Peter Shedd, Ann R. Silverman, Ronald Simpson, Janet Sims-Wood, Shelly Smith, Vivian Smith, Ana Maria Spagna, Maida Springer-Kemp, Robert E. Staples, Fred and Sharon Stephenson, Michelle Swagler, Mary Tatum, Crista Tinsley, Unity Athens Center for Spiritual Growth, Elvena Walker, Marian Walker, Charlotte Wallinga, Margaret Webber, Karen Weddle-West, Mark and Jan Wheeler, Dorothy Wilbanks, Anna J. Williams, and Patricia Underwood Williams.

This list of supporters would be incomplete without mention of my girls. Scarlett, the sweetest cocker spaniel in the world, died before I finished the book, and Pearl, my cunning rat terrier, joins me every morning in my writing chair. They listened to me read aloud, heard my complaints, accompanied me on daily walks, and kept vigil when I worked through the night.

This book is dedicated to four people, three of whom have passed away. Louis Wilbanks Jr., my father and a World War II navy veteran, always believed that our country would eventually get it right. Patrick McKenry, my beloved friend and colleague of three decades, comforted me when I faltered and pushed me when I needed to move forward. Hilda A. Davis, one of the first black college deans of women and Pauli Murray's contemporary, never stopped teaching me what it meant to be a friend.

Charles Vernon Underwood Jr., my husband, deserves a gold medal. Always at the ready, he untangled computer snafus, helped me locate and prepare images, checked every page multiple times, made sure I never wanted for a nutritious, home-cooked meal, and danced me across the finish line. He has made all the difference in my life. My love and deepest appreciation go to Charles.

NOTES

ABBREVIATIONS USED IN THE NOTES

AA	*Afro-American*
AAUN	American Association for the United Nations
ADW	*Atlanta Daily World*
CSM	*Christian Science Monitor*
CCC	Civilian Conservation Corps
CT	*Carolina Times*
DMH	*Durham Morning Herald*
DTH	*Daily Tar Heel*
ER	Eleanor Roosevelt
ERP	Eleanor Roosevelt Papers, Franklin D. Roosevelt Presidential Library and Museum
FDRL	Franklin D. Roosevelt Presidential Library and Museum
FDRP	Franklin Delano Roosevelt Papers, Franklin D. Roosevelt Presidential Library and Museum
HHFA	Housing and Home Finance Agency
JG	*Journal and Guide*
NAACP	National Association for the Advancement of Colored People
NYA	*New York Age*
NYAN	*New York Amsterdam News*
NYHT	*New York Herald Tribune*
NYP	*New York Post*
NYT	*New York Times*
PC	*Pittsburgh Courier*
PCSW	President's Commission on the Status of Women
PM	Pauli Murray
PMP	Pauli Murray Papers, Schlesinger Library, Radcliffe Institute for Advanced Study, Harvard University
RTD	*Richmond Times Dispatch*
SCHW	Southern Conference for Human Welfare
SNCC	Student Non-Violent Coordinating Committee
TT	*Tera Topics*
UC	University of California

UNC	The University of North Carolina
WDL	Workers Defense League
WDLC	Workers Defense League Collection
WP	*Washington Post*

INTRODUCTION

xiii "You need to know": PM to Pat[ricia Bell-Scott], December 12, 1983, in author's possession.

xiii "dratted autobiography": Ibid. Murray completed the manuscript, and Casey Miller and Kate Swift finished the remaining revisions. On their contributions, see Elizabeth Isele, "Casey Miller and Kate Swift: Women Who Dared to Disturb the Lexicon," *WILLA* 3 (1994): 8–10, accessed August 8, 2012, http://scholar.lib.vt.edu/ejournals/old-WILLA/fall94/h2-isele.html.

xiv "until late in 1984": PM to Pat[ricia Bell-Scott], December 12, 1983.

xiv "veterans who knew": Joseph P. Lash, *Eleanor and Franklin: The Story of Their Relationship Based on Eleanor Roosevelt's Private Papers* (New York: Norton, 1971), 523.

xiv "How come you give": PM, *Song in a Weary Throat: An American Pilgrimage* (New York: Harper & Row, 1987), 23.

xiv And I believe: The number of doctoral dissertations, master's theses, books and book chapters, journal articles, and essays devoted to some aspect of Pauli Murray's life and work has mushroomed since the 1990s. The Pauli Murray Project of the Duke Human Rights Center at the Franklin Humanities Center maintains a representative list of published works and related projects at http://paulimurrayproject.org.

xv "friendship with Mrs. R.": PM to Skipper [Caroline Ware], August 19, 1971, PMP.

xvi "fan": PM, interview by Thomas F. Soapes, February 3, 1978, FDRL.

xviii "a credit to Mrs. Roosevelt's": Maida Springer-Kemp, interview by author, Pittsburgh, Pennsylvania, July 15, 1995.

xviii "The Quarrel": PM, "The Quarrel," in *Dark Testament and Other Poems* (Norwalk, CT: Silvermine, 1970), 57.

xviii "further along the road": Blanche Wiesen Cook, *Eleanor Roosevelt*, vol. 1, *1884–1933* (New York: Viking, 1992), 7.

xix "women's caucus": PM to Dave and Mrs. ——, July 5, 1970, in author's possession.

xix "Eleanor Roosevelt lighted": PM to Dave and Mrs. ——, July 5, 1970.

xix "is a handshake across time": Richard Holmes, "Reflections on Biography" (Leon Levy Biography Lecture, Graduate Center, City University of New York, September 23, 2014).

PRELUDE: CAMP TERA, 1933–35

2 "I like this place": "Camp Red Tape Irks President's Wife: Disappointed on First Visit to Find Only 30 Jobless Women Living There," *NYT,* June 19, 1933.

3 "I sing of Youth": PM, "Youth, 1933," in *Dark Testament,* 51.

3 "We can not pass": ER, "Facing the Problems of Youth," *National Parent-Teacher Magazine* 29 (February 1935): 30.

3 Pauli Murray was sitting: For Murray's account of the Camp Tera experience, the events that led to her residency, and the first time she saw ER, see PM, *Song,* 94–97. This was not ER's first visit to the camp, as Murray thought. On the camp's opening, ER's first visit, and residents' reaction to her subsequent visits,

see "17 Jobless Women Enter New Camp: Rest Is the Only Thing on the Schedule, Now as Centre on Lake Tiorati Opens," *NYT,* June 11, 1933; "Mrs. Roosevelt Disappointed in Women's Camp: Finds Only 30 Jobless at Bear Mountain Haven for 200, Looks for Remedy," *NYHT,* June 19, 1933; "Camp Red Tape Irks President's Wife, *NYT*; Thomas W. Patton, "'What of Her?': Eleanor Roosevelt and Camp Tera," *New York History* 87, no. 2 (Spring 2006): 228–47; and *TT,* August 11, 1933; January 21, 1934; March 2, 1934; June 15, 1934; and July 15, 1934, in author's possession.

4 "slight figure": PM, *Song,* 79.

4 When Camp Tera opened: William E. Leuchtenburg, *Franklin D. Roosevelt and the New Deal, 1932–1940* (New York: Harper Torchbooks, 1963), 19; Robert S. McElvaine, *The Great Depression: America, 1929–1941* (New York: Times Books, 1993), 75, 187–88.

4 "to put people to work": "Text of New President's Address at Inauguration," *WP,* March 5, 1933.

4 One of the earliest: The Emergency Conservation Work Act, signed into law on March 31, 1933, gave birth to the CCC twenty-seven days after FDR took office. For a history of the CCC, see John A. Salmond, *The Civilian Conservation Corps, 1933–1942: A New Deal Case Study* (Durham, NC: Duke University Press, 1967).

4 It was the first time: Robert Stone, *American Experience,* "Civilian Conservation Corps," December 8, 2009 (Arlington, VA: Public Broadcasting Service Video, 2009), DVD.

4 By August 1935: Louis Easterling, "More Social Value in CCC Than Any Other U.S. Department," *Philadelphia AA,* September 19, 1936.

4 The majority lived: On the experience of black CCC enrollees, see Charles Johnson, "The Army, the Negro and the Civilian Conservation Corps: 1933–42," *Military Affairs* 36, no. 3 (October 1972): 82–88; and John A. Salmond, "The Civilian Conservation Corps and the Negro," *Journal of American History* 52, no. 1 (June 1965): 75–88.

4 "They never believed": Stone, "Civilian Conservation Corps."

4 The segregated and militaristic: On ER's opinions of the CCC and her advocacy for a women's counterpart, see Allida M. Black, *Casting Her Own Shadow: Eleanor Roosevelt and the Shaping of a Postwar Liberalism* (New York: Columbia University Press, 1996), 31; Blanche Wiesen Cook, *Eleanor Roosevelt,* vol. 2, *1933–1938* (New York: Viking, 1999), 88–91; and Martha H. Swain, *Ellen S. Woodward: New Deal Advocate for Women* (Jackson: University Press of Mississippi, 1992), 42–45.

4 The idea of women: See Swain, *Ellen S. Woodward,* 42–45; Susan Waldver-Morgan, "Young Women and the New Deal Camps and Resident Centers, 1933–1943," (PhD thesis, University of Indiana, 1982); Susan Ware, *Beyond Suffrage: Women in the New Deal* (Cambridge, MA: Harvard University Press, 1981), 112. On the concern of Camp Tera administrators about women's morality, see Harry Gersh, "She-She-She Camps: An Episode in New Deal History" (unpublished term paper, Harvard University, Cambridge, MA, spring 1979), Schlesinger Library, 17–18. Of the cultural concerns about women's camps, see Michele Mitchell, "A 'Corrupting Influence': Idleness and Sexuality During the Great Depression," in *Interconnections: Gender and Race in American History,* ed. Carol Faulkner and Alison M. Parker (Rochester: University of Rochester Press, 2012), 205–6.

5 Fueling her determination: ER, *On My Own* (New York: Harper & Brothers, 1937), 107–9; Blanche Wiesen Cook, *Eleanor Roosevelt,* 1:135–36; and Swain, *Ellen S. Woodward,* 42–45.

5   "women had been neglected": "Civil Works Help Pledged to Women: Mrs. Roosevelt at Parley Says," *NYT,* January 5, 1933.

5   Skeptics sarcastically dubbed: Gersh, "She-She-She Camps," 12–13, 20; and Waldver-Morgan, "Young Women and the New Deal Camps," 56.

5   She was disappointed: "Mrs. Roosevelt Disappointed in Women's Camp," *NYHT,* and "17 Jobless Women Enter New Camp," *NYT.*

5   To be eligible: Memorandum, "There Are Six Requirements for Women Going to Camp," June 19, 1933, ERP; "Mrs. Roosevelt Disappointed in Women's Camp," *NYHT*; and "Recruiting Speeded for Women's Camp: 65 to Be Enrolled by End of Week to Raise Total," *NYT,* June 20, 1933.

6   Stirred by estimates: "Civil Works Help Pledged to Women," *NYT,* and "First Lady Calls on Leaders to Help Unemployed Women," *WP,* November 21, 1933. For stories told by writer-activist Meridel Le Sueur and Hilda W. Smith, see Jane Kahramnidis, "The She-She-She Camps of the Great Depression," *History Magazine,* February-March 2008, 13. See Mark Barron, "A New Yorker at Large," *WP,* June 27, 1933, for a feature story on the hardships of Camp Tera residents. For accounts of unemployed homeless women, see Emily Hahn, "Women Without Work," *New Republic* 72, no. 981 (May 31, 1933): 63–65, and Thomas Minehan, "Girls on the Road," *Independent Woman* 13 (October 1934): 316–17, 335.

6   "There must be": "Mrs. Roosevelt Disappointed in Women's Camp," *NYHT.*

6   Within a month: "Recruiting Speeded for Women's Camp," *NYT*; "30 More Jobless Women Off for Camp Today: 'Mistaken Ideas' About Project Cleared," *NYT,* June 21, 1933; "Woman Camp Age Limit Is Raised from 35 to 40," *NYT,* June 22, 1933; and "129 More Women in Camp: 89 Now Getting Aid at Centre Fostered by Mrs. Roosevelt," *NYT,* June 24, 1933.

6   Native and immigrant: The background of residents was often described in *TT* and news stories, such as "Government Camp a Lure to Women," classified ad, *NYT,* July 30, 1933.

6   Camp Tera had twenty-six: *The Palisades Interstate Park, 1929–1947* (Harriman, NY: Commissioners of the Palisade Interstate Park, 1947), 7, and ER, "The Camp for Unemployed Women: A Novel American Experiment Under the Relief Administration," *World Today, Encyclopedia Britannica* 1 (October 1933): 1.

6   Whatever residents and staff: On ER's financial and material support, see "Women to Get Aid All Winter at Camp Tera," *NYHT,* October 19, 1933; "Turkey for Camp Tera Girls," *NYT,* December 1, 1933; "Mrs. Roosevelt Aids Camp," *NYT,* December 18, 1933; "Mrs. Roosevelt's 'Girls' in Camp to Get Presents," *NYT,* December 24, 1934; "First Lady Sends Check for Radio at Camp TERA," *NYT,* December 26, 1934; "Mrs. Roosevelt's Camp Goes in for Ice Sports," *NYT,* January 28, 1935; "$3,300 Gift by Mrs. Roosevelt to TERA Is Revealed in Final Audit of the Books," *NYT,* July 14, 1937; and Jessie I. Mills to ER, 11 July 1935, ERP. Appreciative mention of ER's support regularly appeared in *TT.*

6   Kate Smith: A photograph of Kate Smith and the radio she donated on June 21, 1933, can be found in the Bettmann/CORBIS archival collection as number BE083996.

6   This sensitivity: Lash, *Eleanor and Franklin,* 522. ER discussed her friendships with Mary McLeod Bethune, Walter White, Pauli Murray, and others in "Some of My Best Friends Are Negro," *Ebony,* February 1953, 16–20, 22, 24–26. ER's friendship with Murray is also mentioned in Black, *Casting Her Own Shadow,* 94–96, 110–11, 116; Cook, *ER,* 1:7; Cook, *ER,* 2:90, 565; Doris Kearns Goodwin, *No Ordinary Time: Franklin and Eleanor Roosevelt: The Home Front in World*

War II (New York: Simon & Schuster, 1994), 441, 443; and Lash, *Eleanor and Franklin,* 523–24, 675.

7   Charismatic and very dark-skinned: On Bethune's background and political career, see Joyce Ann Hanson, *Mary McLeod Bethune and Black Women's Political Activism* (Columbia: University of Missouri Press, 2003); Ida E. Jones, *Mary McLeod Bethune in Washington, D.C.: Activism and Education in Logan Circle* (Mount Pleasant, SC: History Press, 2013).

7   "always went running down": J. B. West with Mary Lynn Kotz, *Upstairs at the White House: My Life with the First Ladies* (New York: Coward, McCann & Geoghegan, 1973), 31–32. See also Lillian Rogers Parks with Frances Spatz Leighton, *The Roosevelts: A Family in Turmoil* (Englewood Cliffs, NJ: Prentice-Hall, 1981), 71, and ER, "Some of My Best Friends Are Negro," *Ebony,* on ER's affection for Bethune.

7   "Few heads of State": West with Kotz, *Upstairs at the White House,* 31–32.

7   White found an ally: Walter Francis White, *A Man Called White: The Autobiography of Walter White* (New York: Viking, 1948), 169–70.

7   Their efforts: Ibid., 179–80; Nancy J. Weiss, *Farewell to the Party of Lincoln: Black Politics in the Age of FDR* (Princeton: Princeton University Press, 1983), 104–19; and ER to Walter White, May 8, 1935, ERP.

7   What ER learned: ER, who had heard relatives refer to blacks as "pickaninnies" and "darkies" and had used these terms herself with affection, was stunned by the criticism of her language. See "Mrs. Roosevelt Refers to Triplets as Pickaninnies: First Lady Writes Letter to Virginian Who Named Boys for President," *Philadelphia AA,* January 19, 1935, and "Mrs. Roosevelt's Pickaninnies," *Philadelphia AA,* January 26, 1935. She apologized and pledged to change her behavior; see Lash, *Eleanor and Franklin,* 522.

8   "One of the colored girls": ER to William H. Matthews, August 18, 1933, ERP.

8   the situation had "changed": Matthews to ER, n.d., ERP.

8   Two tragedies marked: PM, *Song,* 11–13.

8   The second tragedy: Ibid., 9–10, 42–45.

9   "unpredictable attacks": Ibid., 10.

9   "dapper gentleman": Ibid., 45.

9   Unfortunately, a burly white: "Killing Insane Principal, Most Brutal in State's History," *Baltimore AA,* June 22, 1923.

9   "It was a common": "Slayer of Mad Teacher Gets Ten Years: Polish Guard Who Slew William Murray Is Tried at Ellicott City," *Baltimore AA,* September 28, 1923.

9   "an irrational fear": PM, *Song,* 58.

9   "she might go berserk": Ibid.

9   "The best I can do": *The Eagle* (Hillside High School yearbook, 1926), 17.

10   Rather than ride: PM, *Song,* 32.

10   "peanut gallery": Ibid.

10   Murray fell in love: Ibid., 65.

10   Murray's first choice: Ibid., 65–70.

10   "yellow-brown skin": Ibid., 69.

11   She entered Hunter College: PM, "A Working Student," *Hunter College Echo* (Christmas issue 1932): 42–44; PM, *Song,* 71–76, 87.

11   "the delicate balance": PM, *Song,* 69.

11   She lived for a while: Ibid., 74–77; PM, "A Working Student," *Hunter College Echo,* 42–44.

11   "nervous breakdown": PM, "A Working Student," *Hunter College Echo,* 43.

11   "It was a dreadful": PM, *Song,* 77.
11   "mutual loneliness": Ibid.
11   "Sexually inexperienced": Ibid.
11   Desperate for a change: Ibid., 77–81.
12   "I am the Highway": PM, "Song of the Highway," in *Negro: An Anthology,* ed. Nancy Cunard (London: Wishart, 1934), 93. This poem would be reprinted in PM, *Dark Testament,* 62–63.
12   "wanderlust": PM, *Song,* 82.
12   Murray's exuberance was: Ibid., 78–79.
12   Hundreds of thousands: Ibid., 79–81; Errol Lincoln Uys, *Riding the Rails: Teenagers on the Move During the Great Depression* (New York: Routledge, 2003); *Relief for Unemployed Transients: Hearings on S. 5121 Before a Subcommittee of the Committee on Manufacture, January 13 to 25, 1933* (Washington, DC: Government Printing Office); Thomas Minehan, "Girls of the Road," *Independent Woman* 13 (October 1934): 316–35; and Thomas Minehan, *Boy and Girl Tramps of America* (New York: Farrar and Rinehart, 1934).
12   "scout pants": PM, *Song,* 79.
12   Murray's adolescent build: In *Song,* 79, Murray suggests that she presented a male persona primarily for safety while riding the rails, but her private writings and photographs suggest that her clothing was an expression of identity. For further discussion, see Doreen Marie Drury, " 'Experimentation on the Male Side': Race, Class, Gender, and Sexuality in Pauli Murray's Quest for Love and Identity, 1910–1960" (PhD diss., Boston College, 2000); Doreen M. Drury, "Love, Ambition, and 'Invisible Footnotes' in the Life and Writing of Pauli Murray," *Souls: A Critical Journal of Black Politics, Culture & Society* 11, no. 3 (2009): 295–309. On Murray's childhood delight in wearing men's caps, see PM, interview by Genna Rae McNeil, February 13, 1976, interview G-0044, transcript, Southern Oral History Program Collection, #4007, University of North Carolina. For photographs and stories of black and white homeless women who dressed in men's clothing, see Minehan, "Girls of the Road," *Independent Woman;* Minehan, *Boy and Girl Tramps of America;* and "Young Girls 'Hobo' Way from Alabama to Chicago," *Chicago Defender,* September 21, 1929.
12   "so cinder-blackened": PM, *Song,* 81.
12   "jail-birds, veteran hoboes": PM, "Three Thousand Miles on a Dime in Ten Days," in *Negro: An Anthology,* ed. Nancy Cunard (London: Wishart, 1934), 90.
12   "the only one": Nancy Cunard to PM, January 15, n.d., PMP.
13   "boy-self": Nancy Cunard to PM, May 31, n.d., PMP.
13   Jefferson's self-discipline: PM, *Song,* 84.
13   Unemployment, which was: New York Temporary Commission on the Condition of the Colored Urban Population, *Second Report of the New York State Temporary Commission on the Condition of the Colored Urban Population to the Legislature of the State of New York, February 1939* (Albany, NY: J. B. Lyon, 1939), 233–36.
13   Margaret "Pee Wee" Inniss: PM, *Song,* 95–96. Pee Wee is mentioned as one of Camp Tera's earliest residents in "Government Camp a Lure to Women," *NYT.*
13   Murray was impressed: After Inniss wrote to ER of her desire to enroll in a course, ER sent a check for one hundred dollars. ER to Margaret A. Inniss, January 12, 1938, ERP.
14   "confrontation by typewriter": PM, *Song,* 96.
14   "narrow cubicle": Ibid., 95.

14 Surrounded by: For a description of the Bear Mountain area at the time Camp Tera was established and Murray was a resident, see Leon A. Dickinson, "Into Nearby Park Lands: Bear Mountain Territory Has Scenic Variety for Motorists," *NYT,* September 4, 1932. The activities and wildlife at the camp are chronicled in *TT.* See also "Camp for Needy Women Will Be Enlarged to Give Summer Vacations to 200 at Once," *NYT,* April 15, 1934; and "Mrs. Roosevelt's Camp Goes in for Ice Sports," *NYT,* January 28, 1935.

14 Life at Camp Tera: Throughout her life, ER took delight in being physically active. She loved to walk, swim, go horseback riding, and dance, all of which were options at the camp. Cook, *ER,* 1:94, and West with Kotz, *Upstairs at the White House,* 30.

14 Murray's favorite pastimes: On Murray's childhood delight in the outdoors, see PM, *Proud Shoes: The Story of An American Family* (New York: Harper & Brothers), 256.

14 "with a pen": PM, *Song,* 22.

14 The food at Camp Tera: "Government Camp a Lure to Women," *NYT.* Meals were often described in *TT.*

14 Thanks to the first lady: "Turkey Dinner Planned for Women at Camp Tera," *NYT,* November 25, 1934, and "Mrs. Roosevelt's 'Girls' in Camp to Get Presents," *NYT.*

14 Her sense of well-being: On Murray's relationship with Peg Holmes, see Drury, "'Experimentation on the Male Side,'" 81–100.

14 Peg was a round-faced: PM, *Song,* 96, 98–99.

14 "the second Babe Ruth": *TT,* May 5, 1934.

15 Her poem: PM, *"Poet's Memo," TT,* Christmas 1934, PMP.

15 "the tremor": PM, *Song,* 97.

15 "pretended to read": Ibid.

16 "never wanted to be": Lorena Hickok, "Just Plain 'Mrs. Roosevelt': Doesn't Want to Be Called 'First Lady,' " *WP,* November 10, 1932.

16 The prospect of what: Cook, *ER,* 2:445–47.

16 She tied her: Photographs and accounts of ER at Camp Tera indicate that she dressed smartly yet comfortably. See the photo at the beginning of the "Prelude" chapter of this book, the photo printed alongside the column "Mrs. Roosevelt Disappointed in Women's Camp," *NYHT,* and descriptions of ER's attire in *TT.*

16 "plain, ordinary Mrs. Roosevelt": Hickok, "Just Plain 'Mrs. Roosevelt,' " *WP,* November 10, 1932.

16 She had raised eyebrows: Lillian Rogers Parks and Frances S. Leighton, *It Was Fun Working at the White House* (New York: Fleet, 1969), 105; Catherine McKenzie, "Simple Fare for the White House: The Formal Dinner of Older Days Has Been Superseded by a Meal of Six Courses," *NYT,* December 9, 1934.

16 "dark": Ruby Black, *Eleanor Roosevelt: A Biography* (New York: Duell, Sloan and Pearce, 1940), 299.

16 "It may be bad politics": Ibid., 300.

17 Six years before: "Notables in Strike March: Mrs. F. D. Roosevelt Among Them—Eight Women Pickets Arrested," *NYT,* December 9, 1926.

17 Now that she was: Brigid O'Farrell, "A Stitch in Time: The New Deal, the International Ladies' Garment Workers' Union and Mrs. Roosevelt," *Transatlantic* 1 (2006), accessed August 3, 2013, http://transatlantica.revues.org/190, and Brigid O'Farrell, *She Was One of Us: Eleanor Roosevelt and the American Worker* (Ithaca, NY: Cornell University Press, 2010).

17   ER changed the complexion: "No Color Line at White House," *PC,* August 11, 1934; Parks with Leighton, *The Roosevelts,* 32–33, 92, 117; and West with Kotz, *Upstairs at the White House,* 19.

17   "destitute": Parks and Leighton, *It Was Fun Working at the White House,* 115.

17   "people who do things": "Mrs. Roosevelt a Driving Force in New Deal: First Lady's Life Crowded with Action," *WP,* March 4, 1934.

17   Had her husband: Lash, *Eleanor and Franklin,* 348.

17   At the suggestion of Hickok: Lorena Hickok influenced ER's thinking about her role as first lady, as well as issues of race, class, and gender. On the political impact of their early friendship, see Michael Golay, *American 1933: The Great Depression, Lorena Hickok, Eleanor Roosevelt, and the Shaping of the New Deal* (New York: Free Press, 2013).

17   She invited the public: ER, "I Want You to Write Me," *Woman's Home Companion,* August 1933, 4; Frances M. Seeber, "'I Want You to Write to Me': The Letters of Anna Eleanor Roosevelt," *Prologue* 19 (Summer 1987): 95; ER, "Mail of a President's Wife" (unpublished manuscript, 1939), ERP; and ER, "How I Handle My Mail," (unpublished manuscript, n.d.), ERP.

17   She braved the squalor: See Cook, *ER,* 2:129–52.

17   Mud coated: "Bonus Camp Viewed by Mrs. Roosevelt: Veterans Cheer First Lady as She Tells of Her War Service and Leads in Song," *NYT,* May 17, 1933.

17   "An able-bodied man": "Mrs. Roosevelt a Driving Force in New Deal," *WP.*

18   "standing at attention": PM, *Song,* 97.

18   Mills, who'd been an ambulance driver: This characterization of Mills's personality and regimentation at the camp are drawn from PM, *Song,* 96–97, and *TT.* The description of Mills's attire is based on news photographs, such as the one that appears in the "Prelude" chapter of this book.

18   "obsequious behavior": PM, *Song,* 97.

18   This time, Mills: Ibid.

18   Murray's friend Pee Wee: Inniss is mentioned in "Government Camp a Lure to Women," *NYT,* and *TT,* August 11, 1933.

18   But Mills expelled: PM, *Song,* 97. For accusations against the camp and ER's defense of it, see "Jane Addams Camp Is Assailed as 'Red': Legion Charges Federal Funds Are Used to Promote Communism at Center for Girls," *NYT,* July 3, 1936; "Communism Has Grip on Camps for Girls, Legion Post Reveals," *CSM,* July 3, 1936; "Communism Charged," *WP,* July 3, 1936; and "NYA Camp Not Red, First Lady Finds: After 3-Hour Visit with Girls at Suffern, She Holds Charge of Communism Unfounded," *NYT,* July 9, 1936.

18   It is also possible: On Mills's efforts to control the social life of campers and her eventual termination, see Michele Mitchell, "A 'Corrupting Influence,'" 205–6, and Patton, "'What of Her?': Eleanor Roosevelt and Camp Tera," 242–43.

18   After a five-week: PM, *Song,* 98.

1. "IT IS THE PROBLEM OF MY PEOPLE"

21   The clatter: This description of Pauli Murray's writing routine is drawn from Ruth Powell, interview by author, Mount Vernon, NY, February 5, 1996; Springer-Kemp, interview; and PM, *Song,* 108.

21   She had been forced: PM, *Song,* 108.

21   It was his first: William E. Leuchtenberg, "The Presidents Come to Chapel Hill," *Carolina Comments* 42, no. 2 (March 1994): 59–61.

22   The reports: Felix Belair Jr., "Roosevelt to Talk on Foreign Affairs: Aides Expect Declaration in President's Speech Tomorrow at Chapel Forum," *NYT,* December 4, 1938; and Felix Belair Jr., "World Will Hear Roosevelt Speak Today: Europe and South America on Radio Nets," *NYT,* December 5, 1938.

22   Thousands lined: "Thousands in Piedmont to See President Today When He Talks at U.N.C.: Roosevelt Party Will Entrain Here Following Speech," *DMH,* December 5, 1938; Robert H. Mason, "Steady Rain Falls on Crowd Outside Filled Gymnasium: Event Was to Have Been Held in Kenan Stadium," *DMH,* December 6, 1938; and "Overflow Throng Hears Roosevelt," *DMH,* December 6, 1938.

22   "liberal teaching": "Roosevelt's Address at Chapel Hill, N.C.: Recalls Theodore Roosevelt's Stand," *NYT,* December 6, 1938.

22   The "contradiction": PM, *Song,* 111.

22   "relieve": Ibid., 109.

22   "liberal institution": "Roosevelt Urges Nation to Continue Liberalism; Says World Looks to US No Turning Back: Discounting Election Reverses, He Holds New Deal Must Go On," *NYT,* December 6, 1938.

22   "proud and happy": Ibid.

23   "a vile form": "Roosevelt Address to Church Group," *NYT,* December 7, 1933, and "Filibuster Ended as Senate Shelves Anti-Lynch Bill: Vote of 58 to 22 to Lay Measure Aside for Relief Bill Taken on Motion by Barkley," *NYT,* February 22, 1938.

23   "lynchings and incidents": "President Wants Lynching Inquiries: Will Not Insist on Passage of Wagner Bill but Seeks Some Remedial Action," *NYT,* March 23, 1938.

23   "his tongue": Editorial, "A Christian Act," *NYAN,* April 2, 1938.

23   "an artful dodger": Editorial, "An Artful Dodger," *Chicago Defender,* April 2, 1938.

23   "You're too late": Editorial, "We Think It's Too Late," *Louisiana Weekly,* April 2, 1938.

23   Her introduction: PM, *Proud Shoes,* 1–2.

23   Since 1863: Robert L. Zangrando, *The NAACP Crusade Against Lynching, 1909–1950* (Philadelphia: Temple University Press, 1980), 6–7.

23   Murray's indignation: PM, *Proud Shoes,* 9–10, 218–23.

23   "his musket loaded": Ibid., 10.

23   "his feet first": Ibid., 262.

24   "buzzard circled": Ibid.

24   Six years later: "Killing Insane Principal, Most Brutal in State's History," *Baltimore AA.*

24   "purple": PM, *Song,* 56.

24   "split open like": Ibid.

24   The fight over: Harvard Sitkoff, "A Rift in the Coalition," in *A New Deal for Blacks: The Emergence of Civil Rights as a National Issue: The Depression Decade* (New York: Oxford University Press, 1978), 102–38.

24   After one day-long: ER, "My Day," September 11, 1936.

24   Southern segregation made: Parks with Leighton, *The Roosevelts,* 179. On FDR's and ER's feelings about Warm Springs, see William B. Rhoads, "Franklin D. Roosevelt and the Architecture of Warm Springs," *Georgia Historical Quarterly* 67, no. 1 (Spring 1983): 70–87.

25   She did not accompany: "First Lady Spikes Report She Plans Chapel Hill Trip," *DMH,* November 30, 1938.

25 SCHW was an interracial: Thomas A. Krueger, *And Promises to Keep: The Southern Conference for Human Welfare, 1938–1948* (Nashville: Vanderbilt University Press, 1967), 20–39, and Linda Reed, *Simple Decency and Common Sense: The Southern Conference Movement, 1938–1963* (Bloomington: Indiana University Press, 1991), 15–19.

25 "Mrs. Roosevelt arrived": Winifred Mallon, "Sweeping Moves Urged to Aid South: Direct Action, Largely by Federal Funds, Is Sought at Welfare Conference," *NYT,* November 23, 1938.

25 "universal education": ER, speech, SCHW, Birmingham, Alabama, November 23, 1938, excerpted in *Courage in a Dangerous World: The Political Writings of Eleanor Roosevelt,* ed. Allida M. Black (New York: Columbia University, 1999), 41.

25 Having walked into: ER to Lorena Hickok, November 23, 1938, ERP; Black, *Casting Her Own Shadow,* 40–41; and Lash, *Eleanor and Franklin,* 525–56.

25 The first lady's deft: Sitkoff, *A New Deal for Blacks,* 132.

25 "Sometimes actions": "Mrs. Roosevelt's Answer," *Philadelphia AA,* December 17, 1938.

25 After Camp Tera: PM, *Song,* 102–13.

26 "coziness with white": Ibid., 111.

26 "Dear President Roosevelt": PM to FDR, December 6, 1938, FDRP.

29 "Dear Mrs. Roosevelt": PM to ER, December 6, 1938, PMP.

29 The president's staff: J. W. Studebaker to PM, December 22, 1938, PMP, and Hilda W. Smith to PM, January 23, 1939, PMP.

30 "My dear Miss Murray": ER to PM, December 18, 1938, ERP.

30 "answered under": PM, *Song,* 112.

30 "I could not help": ER, "My Day," December 8, 1938.

30 "Are you free": Ibid.

2. "MEMBERS OF YOUR RACE ARE NOT ADMITTED"

31 On December 12, 1938: *State of Missouri ex rel. Gaines v. Canada,* 305 U.S. 337 (1938). For background on Lloyd L. Gaines and his case, see Richard Kluger, *Simple Justice: The History of* Brown v. Board of Education *and Black America's Struggle for Equality* (New York: Knopf, 2004), 202–13; Genna Rae McNeil, *Groundwork: Charles Hamilton Houston and the Struggle for Civil Rights* (Philadelphia: University of Pennsylvania Press, 1983), 143–51; Rawn James Jr., *Root and Branch: Charles Hamilton Houston, Thurgood Marshall, and the Struggle to End Segregation* (New York: Bloomsbury, 2010), 103–22; and Lloyd L. Gaines Collection, University of Missouri Law Library.

32 "substantially equal": *Missouri ex rel. Gaines v. Canada.*

32 Thrilled by the court's: PM to Lloyd Gaines, December 18, 1938, PMP.

32 By the time: Hilda W. Smith to PM, January 23, 1939, PMP.

32 "I am not authorized": William W. Pierson to PM, quoted in PM, *Song,* 115.

32 Unlike Thomas R. Hocutt: According to Richard Kluger, *Simple Justice,* 157–58, Hocutt's manner and less than stellar academic record further complicated his case.

33 Convinced that the scales: PM to Frank Porter Graham, December 17, 1938, PMP.

33 "How much longer": Ibid.

33 "It would be": Ibid.

33 Frank Graham, a native: Roland Giduz, "The 'Great Event' Is Revealed by 'Dr. Frank,'" *Alumni Review* 65 (September 1966): 8–11, and Leonard Schlup, "Frank

Porter Graham," in *The Eleanor Roosevelt Encyclopedia,* ed. Maurine H. Beasley, Holly C. Shulman, and Henry R. Beasley (Westport, CT: Greenwood, 2001), 210.

33 Eleanor Roosevelt's friendship: Leonard Schlup, "Frank Porter Graham," and "First Lady Speaks at Chapel Hill Rites: Mrs. Roosevelt Exhorts North Carolina Graduates to Work for the Underprivileged," *NYT,* June 12, 1935.

33 He had permitted: "University Is Made Subject of Attack in Petition to Governor Gardner," *Alumni Review* 21 (October 1932): 14, and Arnold Rampersad, *The Life of Langston Hughes,* vol. 1, *1902–1941: I, Too, Sing America* (New York: Oxford University Press, 1986), 224–25.

34 On learning: Warren Ashby, *Frank Porter Graham: A Southern Liberal* (Winston-Salem, NC: John F. Blair, 1980), 128–29.

34 His leadership of the SCHW: Ibid., 244–45.

34 "The black man is": Frank Porter Graham, SCHW speech manuscript, 1938, Frank Porter Graham Papers, Southern Historical Collection, UNC.

34 "It seems to me": Quoted in PM, *Song,* 107–8.

34 "aware of the inequities": Frank Porter Graham to PM, February 3, 1939, PMP.

34 "very fine letter": PM to Frank Porter Graham, February 6, 1939, PMP.

3. "WE HAVE TO BE VERY CAREFUL ABOUT THE PEOPLE WE SELECT"

35 When Murray saw: "Negress Applies to Enter Carolina: President Graham Out of Town, and Governor Refuses to Comment on Case," *DMH,* January 6, 1939.

35 "Rational members": Ibid.

35 "North Carolina does not": "Graham, Hoey Give Statements Concerning Negro Application: University Head Says Governor's Group Considering the Matter," *DTH,* January 7, 1939. See also Glenn Hutchinson, "Jim Crow Challenged in Southern Universities," *Crisis* 46, no. 4 (April 1939): 103.

35 "equality of opportunity": "Graham, Hoey Give Statements Concerning Negro Application," *DTH.*

35 Eager to share: PM to Governor Clyde R. Hoey, January 14, 1939, PMP.

35 The *Carolina Times:* "Woman Applicant to University of N.C. Tells Her Side of Story: Pauline Murray Releases to *Times* Letter Written President Frank Graham," *CT,* January 21, 1939.

36 "North Carolina will do": Editorial, "Graduate Courses for Negroes," *CT,* January 14, 1939.

36 The *Afro-American*: PM, "Did F.D.R. Mean It?," *Philadelphia AA,* January 14, 1939.

36 According to the *Daily Tar Heel*: Howard K. Beale, letter to the editor, *DTH,* January 11, 1939. Paul Green's comments at an interracial student forum are reported in "Lethargy Is Relative," *DTH,* February 19, 1939. For Murray's account of campus reaction, see PM, *Song,* 116–21, 123–24.

36 "asking too much": Howard W. Odum, "What Is the Answer? A Leading Sociologist Has a Plan," *Carolina Magazine* 6 (February 1939): 5–8.

36 Campus polls and debate: "Carolina Students Favor Admission," *JG* [January 2, 1939?], clipping, PMP; "Negro Applicant Seeks Student Opinion," *DTH,* February 5, 1939; "Graham, Hoey Give Statements Concerning Negro Application," *DTH;* "Leaders Favor Separate Negro Education: Graham Insists Assembly Must Solve Problem," *DTH,* January 8, 1939; "Graduate Voters Approve Admission of Negroes: Graham States One Is Pressing Entrance Claims," *DTH,* January 11, 1939; "U.N.C. Law Students Against Admitting Negroes to School," *DTH,* Janu-

ary 12, 1939; "Phi Against Negro Admission," *DTH,* January 18, 1939; "Odum Discusses Equal Education for All Races: Sociologist Says Two Viewpoints Must be Considered," *DTH,* February 8, 1939; and "Inter-racial Discussion Group Adopts Resolution to Admit Negro Graduates Immediately," *DTH,* February 15, 1939.

36   "tar and feather": "Negro Applicant Seeks Student Opinion," *DTH,* February 5, 1939.

36   "We are a conservative": John Alan Creedy, "We, the Hypocrites . . . ," *Carolina Magazine* 68, no. 4 (January 1939): 2.

36   "what sort of student": John Alan Creedy to PM, March 2, 1939, PMP.

36   Fifty-seven years later: John Alan Creedy to author, February 2, 1996.

36   "Please be careful": Mother [Pauline Fitzgerald Dame] to Lenie [PM], January 6, 1939, PMP.

36   Still teaching: PM, interview by McNeil.

36   "You can make it": Ibid.

37   "deeply respected friend": PM, *Song,* 119.

37   "Negroes could do": "Students Favor Negroes at U. of N.C.," *CT,* January 21, 1939. For a similar remark made by President James Shepard, see "Graduate School for Negroes Urged: North Carolina College for Race Stresses Need for Professional Training," *NYT,* January 8, 1939.

37   "deep-seated injustice": PM, *Song,* 120.

37   When Murray met: Ibid., 125–26.

37   "airtight": Ibid., 126.

37   "We have to be very careful": PM, interview by McNeil.

37   Radicalized by: For a discussion of Murray's experiences at Brookwood Labor College, her early labor activism, and the character of the school, see PM, *Song,* 105–7; 99–100, and Charles F. Howlett, *Brookwood Labor College and the Struggle for Peace and Social Justice in America* (Lewiston, NY: Edwin Mellen, 1993).

37   "to educate": PM, *Song,* 97.

37   "intellectual radicals": Ibid., 103. For a study of Jay Lovestone, see Ted Morgan, *A Covert Life: Jay Lovestone; Communist, Anti-Communist, and Spymaster* (New York: Random House, 1999).

38   "critique": PM, *Song,* 103.

38   "another form of segregation": Ibid.

38   A self-described individualist: Murray's belief in the sacredness of the individual and human diversity was rooted in her Christian faith and is articulated in her sermons. See Anthony Pinn, ed., *Pauli Murray: Selected Sermons and Writings* (Maryknoll, NY: Orbis Books, 2006).

38   Her assertive letters: Roy Wilkins to Walter White, January 21, 1939, NAACP Papers, Manuscript Division, Library of Congress.

38   "literary brilliance": See recommendations for Murray's admission to Brookwood Labor College, Ted Poston to Tucker P. Smith, August 4, 1936, and Lester B. Granger to Tucker P. Smith, August 12, 1936, WDLC.

38   They had been classmates: PM to Margaret "Peg" Holmes, February 21, 1977, PMP. William Murray was a student at Howard University School of Law between 1934 and 1935.

38   Because the association: Murray's case was not the only one NAACP leaders would sidestep. They did not back appeals for Claudette Colvin and Mary Louise Smith. Young, single, and poor, Colvin and Smith were arrested for defying Alabama's bus segregation law before Rosa Parks, whom NAACP officials saw as more acceptable. Colvin was pregnant at the time of her arrest, and Smith's father

was falsely rumored to be an alcoholic. Taylor Branch, *Parting the Waters: America in the King Years* (New York: Simon & Schuster, 1988), 123, 127.

39 "inner conflict": For Murray's characterization of her identity, see Pauli (Lenie) to Mother [Pauline Fitzgerald Dame], June 2, 1943, PMP. Despite Murray's rejection of the medical diagnosis of homosexuality as a mental disorder, she did refer to herself as homosexual or lesbian in conversations with Pauline Coggs, Ruth Powell, and Grace Milgram.

39 Murray's notes: PM, "Interview with Dr. —— [notes]," December 16, 1937, PMP; PM, "Questions prepared for Dr. Titley, Long Island 'Rest' Home—Amityville, New York," December 17, 1937, PMP.

39 "Simon-pure": PM, interview by McNeil.

39 As desperately as Murray: PM, *Song,* 126.

39 "personal defeat": Ibid., 128.

40 "precious creative energies": PM, "In Defense of Lloyd Gaines," *CT,* January 27, 1940, and PM, "Who Is to Blame for Disappearance of Gaines?," *Black Dispatch,* February 3, 1940.

40 "We Negroes can throng": Ibid.

40 "find Lloyd Gaines": Ibid.

40 Some blacks believed: See Lucile H. Bluford, "The Lloyd Gaines Story," *Journal of Educational Sociology* 32, no. 6 (February 1959): 242–46, and Chad Garrison, "The Mystery of Lloyd Gaines," *Riverfront Times,* April 4, 2007.

4. "I AM RESIGNING"

41 "The DAR may not think": Parks with Leighton, *The Roosevelts,* 103.

42 "On the clear understanding": "Lynch Bill Urged by Mrs. Roosevelt: Federal Measure Would Help, She Tells Negro Conference," *NYT,* January 13, 1939.

42 "moving": ER, "My Day," February 21, 1936.

42 "I am in complete": ER to Mrs. Henry M. Robert Jr., February 26, 1939, ERP.

42 "I have been debating": ER, "My Day," February 27, 1939.

43 After a group: "First Lady Also Sponsors Miss Anderson: Will 'Make Every Effort' to Attend Easter Recital," *WP,* April 6, 1939.

43 Over a hundred: "Justice Hughes Heads Sponsors of Marian Anderson Recital: Black, Swanson and Stokowski Also Among Notables on Honorary List," *WP,* April 4, 1939, and "Miss Hepburn Sponsors Anderson Fete: LaGuardia, McNary Are Added to List," *WP,* April 5, 1939.

43 The Easter Sunday concert: Edward T. Folliard, "Ickes Introduces Contralto at Lincoln Memorial; Many Officials Attend Concert," *WP,* April 10, 1939, and Ernest K. Lindley, "Voice from the Temple: Anderson Footnotes," *WP,* April 12, 1939.

43 Within weeks: Respondents who identified as Democrats and Republicans and who came from all regions of the United States except the South approved of ER's resignation, American Institute of Public Opinion, *The Gallop Poll: Public Opinion, 1935–1948,* vol. 1 (New York: Random House, 1972), 142.

43 "I have by now": ER, "Conquer Fear and You Will Enjoy Living," *Look* 3 (May 23, 1939): 7.

43 ER's personal standards: Parks with Leighton, *The Roosevelts,* 223, and ER, "My Day," May 26, 1939.

44 "great fun": Harold Faber, "Roosevelt Home Marks Royal Hot-Dog History," *NYT,* June 12, 1981. See also "Felix Belair Jr., "King Tries Hot Dog and Asks for More: And He Drinks Beer with Them—Uses Own Camera to Snap Guests

Photographing Him," *NYT,* June 12, 1939, and chapter 4 in Will Swift, *The Roosevelts and the Royals: Franklin and Eleanor, the King and Queen of England, and the Friendship That Changed History* (Hoboken, NJ: John Wiley, 2004), 128–51.

5. "WE . . . ARE THE DISINHERITED"

45 Compounding this challenge: On Murray's difficulties with the committee, see PM to Thyra Edwards, November 8, 1939, PMP, and "Communist Squabble Splits Harlem Group," *NYAN,* November 18, 1939.

45 Photographs of grief-stricken: See clipping of refugee children assisted by the Negro People's Committee enclosed with PM to ER, October 26, 1939, ERP.

46 The first lady had: "First Lady to Be Foster Mother of Boy, 12, Who Was Orphaned in the Spanish Conflict," *NYT,* April 16, 1939.

46 "propaganda of fear": "Mrs. Roosevelt Charges Intolerance Drive Against Refugees and Seeks Fund Sources," *NYT,* November 29, 1939.

46 "his sculptured figures": ER, "My Day," July 28, 1939.

46 "mention": PM to ER, October 26, 1939.

46 "Ethiopian question": Ibid.

46 She did call: ER, "My Day," November 8, 1939.

46 Her first communiqué: PM to FDR, December 2, 1939, FDRP.

46 White House press secretary: Stephen Early to PM, December 5, 1939, FDRP.

47 Murray's second letter: PM to ER, December 6, 1939, ERP.

47 Murray had left: PM, *Song,* 133–34; PM to Lester B. Granger, November 15, 1939, PMP; PM to Thyra Edwards, November 8, 1939; and "Communist Squabble Splits Harlem Group," *NYAN.*

47 "disapprove of": PM to Thrya Edwards, September 28, 1939, PMP.

47 The stress: On the strain of family responsibility, see memo, PM to Dr. Helen Rogers and Mrs. Blount (Southern Nurse) March 8, 1940, PMP.

47 "with the hope that": PM to ER, December 6, 1939, ERP.

47 "To the Editor": PM, letter to the editor, December 6, 1939, attached to PM to ER, December 6, 1939, ERP; quoted in PM, *Song,* 134.

48 "The other day": ER, "My Day," December 14, 1939.

49 "Will you kindly extend": PM to Malvina Thompson, December 21, 1939, PMP.

6. "IT WAS THE HIGHEST HONOR . . . TO MEET AND TALK WITH YOU"

51 In January, thousands: "Army of Sharecroppers Trek from Homes: Protest Missouri Landlords' Wage Plans," *NYT,* January 11, 1939, and "Sharecroppers Flee Shacks 2d Time in 2 Years: Mass Demonstration Against Conditions in Missouri," *WP,* January 11, 1939. For a detailed treatment of this demonstration, see Louis Cantor, *A Prologue to the Protest Movement: The Missouri Sharecropper Roadside Demonstration of 1939* (Durham, NC: Duke University Press, 1969).

51 The sight of displaced: "Rain, Snow Defied by Sharecroppers: Ragged 1,000 on Trek Seek Protection in Improvised Shelters and Tents," *NYT,* January 12, 1939; "Homeless Sharecroppers Face Disease in Roadside Camps," *WP,* January 12, 1939; and "Snow Discomforts Sharecroppers," *WP,* January 13, 1939.

51 Ironically, the Agricultural Adjustment Administration: Reports by the black press indicated that black sharecroppers were hardest hit by the Agricultural Adjustment Administration program. See, for example, "Negro Sharecroppers of South Suffer Under New Deal: Thousands Are Evicted From Cabins Formerly Occupied as Tenants," *Baltimore AA,* September 26, 1936.

51 "objectives": PM to ER, December 29, 1939, ERP.

51 "a chance for education": ER, "My Day," January 19, 1940.

51 She and the president: ER, "My Day," January 19, 1940, and Erik S. Gellman and Jarod H. Roll, "Owen Whitfield and the Gospel of the Working Class in New Deal America, 1936–1946," *Journal of Southern History* 72, no. 2 (May 2006): 303–48.

51 "broke off one": ER, "My Day," November 1, 1939.

52 "dread": ER, "My Day," June 28, 1939.

52 "lay the book": Ibid.

52 After she finished: "Mrs. Roosevelt Tours Mecca of Migrants: Inspects California Camps and Says Steinbeck Told Truth," *NYT*, April 3, 1940.

52 "to any of the government": ER to PM, January 5, 1940, PMP.

52 "flustered": PM, *Song*, 135.

52 "Oh, dear": PM, interview by Soapes.

52 "had prepared tea": PM, *Song*, 135.

52 "stammered like schoolgirls": Ibid.

52 "got up and bowed": Ibid.

52 "talking with an affectionate": Ibid.

52 "radiated an inner beauty": Ibid.

52 The first lady agreed: PM to ER, January 15, 1940, ERP; ER to PM, March 9, 1940, PMP; "First Lady to Give Prizes: Will Award Them to Students for Share-cropper Studies," *NYT*, February 4, 1940; and "Sharecroppers Week to Open," *NYT*, March 3, 1940.

52 "the conditions": Flyer, "National Sharecroppers Week: Contests for High School Students," 1940, WDLC.

52 "giddy with success": PM, *Song*, 135.

52 "It was the highest honor": PM to ER, January 15, 1940, ERP.

53 "We should surely": ER, "My Day," January 17, 1940.

53 ER loved the film: ER, "My Day," April, 13, 1940; and ER, "My Day," October 10, 1938.

53 "beliefs would be accepted": ER, "My Day," January 23, 1940.

53 "I reached the theater": ER, "My Day," January 24, 1940.

53 "tall, lanky": Ralph Matthews, "Abe's 'Double' Is Snubbed at Premier: Faces of Judges Red When Contest Winner Is Colored," *Philadelphia AA*, January 27, 1940.

53 "stewed over it": PM, *Song*, 137.

54 "I was disappointed": PM to ER, January 30, 1940, ERP.

7. "WHEN PEOPLE OVERWORK THEMSELVES, . . .
THEY MUST PAY FOR IT"

55 In Washington, D.C.: "Capital News in Brief: Benefit for Sharecroppers," *WP*, February 5, 1940, and "Sharecroppers to Meet Tonight," *WP*, March 8, 1940.

55 In New York City: "Sharecroppers Seek Aid: Campaign for $15,000 to Start Here Tomorrow Night," *NYT*, March 4, 1940; "Topics of Sermons That Will Be Heard in the Churches of the City Tomorrow," *NYT*, March 2, 1940.

55 More than 550: "First Lady Urges Sharecropper Aid: Calls for National Effort to Solve Problem as Campaign Gets Under Way," *NYT*, March 6, 1940.

55 The week before: Murray's medical records indicate that she was a patient at Bellevue Hospital on March 2, 1940. She was released in the custody of Adelene McBean. See "Notice to Adelene McBean," Department of Hospitals, Division of Psychiatry, Bellevue Hospital, March 2, 1940, PMP.

55 "migrant Okies": "First Lady Urges Sharecropper Aid," *NYT*.

55　"had talked at first hand": Ibid.

55　"problem": Ibid.

56　"quiet joy": PM to ER, March 7, 1940, ERP.

56　Unable to sleep: This characterization of Murray's hospitalization is drawn from her contemporaneous notes. See PM, "Summary of Symptoms of Upset—Pauli Murray," March 8, 1940, PMP, and memo, PM to Dr. Helen Rogers and Mrs. Blount.

56　"family matters": Memo, PM to Dr. Helen Rogers and Mrs. Blount.

56　As an unmarried daughter: Ibid.

56　"experimental theatre": Memo, PM to Dr. Helen Rogers, March 11, 1940, PMP.

56　"either falling in love": PM, "Summary of Symptoms of Upset."

56　"disappearance": Memo, PM to Dr. Helen Rogers and Mrs. Blount.

56　"was dressed in men's clothing": Report from Boston Office, Field Office File #140–3891, January 3, 1967, 2–3, U.S. Department of Justice, FBI, Subject: Anna Pauline Murray (140–33958); and Memorandum, Clyde Tolson to Cartha DeLoach, April 4, 1967, U.S. Department of Justice, FBI File, Subject: Anna Pauline Murray (140–33958).

57　"answer to true homosexuality": PM, "Questions Prepared for Dr. Titley, Long Island 'Rest' Home—Amityville, New York," December 17, 1937, PMP.

57　"a mother fixation": PM, "Interview with Dr. —— [notes]," December 16, 1937, PMP.

57　She convinced herself: Drury, " 'Experimentation on the Male Side.' " On the findings of a hysterosalpingogram, see John Randolph to Dr. W. Winters, July 31, 1942, PMP.

57　Now the suspicion: PM, interview by McNeil. For a discussion of Murray's frustration with her love life around the time of her hospitalization, see Drury, " 'Experimentation on the Male Side,' " 205–26.

57　"When people overwork": PM to ER, March 7, 1940, ERP.

57　"accepts people": ER, "My Day," February 26, 1940.

58　"helped people along": PM to ER, March 7, 1940.

58　omitted the most important: Ibid.

58　"There are basic rights": ER, "My Day," January 24, 1940.

58　"sitting in row 5": Ralph Matthews, "Abe's 'Double' Is Snubbed at Premier," *Philadelphia AA.*

58　"had slipped": Ibid.

58　"excellent": ER to PM, March 9, 1940, PMP.

58　"tentative invitation": PM to ER, March 15, 1940, ERP.

58　"swimming technique": memo, PM to Dr. Helen Rogers, March 11, 1940.

58　"Your lovely letter": PM to ER, March 15, 1940.

8. "MISS MURRAY WAS UNWISE NOT TO COMPLY WITH THE LAW"

61　"southern justice": PM, *Song,* 149.

61　"peppery, self-assertive": Ibid., 138.

62　"trouble": Ibid.; for Murray's account of the Petersburg bus incident and appeal, see ibid., 137–49. For the account of a white male passenger, see Herbert Garfinkel, "Color Trouble," *Opportunity,* May 18, 1940, 144–52. For a discussion of Murray's and Garfinkel's accounts, see Glenda Elizabeth Gilmore, *Defying Dixie: The Radical Roots of Civil Rights, 1919–1950* (New York: Norton, 2008), 322–25, and Rosalind Rosenberg, " 'Rights Talk' Revisited: Incidents in the Life of Pauli Murray," paper presented at Rice University Values in History Conference, Houston, TX, March 9, 2013.

62   "protruded into the floor": PM, *Song,* 138.

62   "a stabbing pain": Ibid.

62   "get out of his face": Ibid., 139.

62   "still behind": Ibid.

62   "You can't scare us": Garfinkel, "Color Trouble," 146.

63   "I'm a free American": Ibid., 147.

63   "good money": Ibid., 145.

63   "Why he did not hand": PM, *Song,* 141.

63   "half-carried": Ibid., 142.

63   That she was apparently dressed: Garfinkel, "Color Trouble," 144.

63   "under his breath": PM, *Song,* 142.

64   "treated for hysteria": Ibid.

64   "open toilet": Ibid., 143.

64   "sex and sexual gratification": Ibid., 145.

64   "stressing the injustice": Ibid.

64   "detailed Statement of Facts": Ibid., 146. For the original notes and diagrams, see "Petersburg Bus Incident—March 1940–May 16, 1940," PMP.

64   Their outlook: PM, *Song,* 146, and PM, interview by McNeil.

65   "devil's advocate": PM, *Song,* 148.

65   "the core of an issue": Ibid.

65   She suspected: PM and Adelene McBean to Robert Colley, n.d., PMP.

65   "slight," light-skinned "young man": Garfinkel, "Color Trouble," 144, 149.

65   Garfinkel's story was well: Gilmore, *Defying Dixie,* 325.

65   Murray dismissed: PM and Adelene McBean to Robert Colley; and Gilmore, *Defying Dixie,* 325.

65   Murray's "Color Trouble": PM, "Color Trouble," in *Dark Testament,* 30.

66   "Pauli Murray and traveling companion": ER to Governor James H. Price, March 17, 1940, ERP.

66   "Mrs. Roosevelt asks me": Malvina Thompson to Mrs. [Mildred] Fearing, April 10, 1940, PMP.

66   "what it meant": PM, *Song,* 147.

9. "WHERE WERE WE TO TURN FOR HELP?"

67   "They are very dear": PM to Odell Waller, January 23, 1941, WDLC.

67   One of the cases: For Murray's account of the Odell Waller case, see PM, *Song,* 150–76; PM and Murray Kempton, *"All for Mr. Davis": The Story of Sharecropper Odell Waller,* pamphlet reprinted in *The Rights of Man Are Worth Defending* (New York: Workers Defense League, 1942), 23–40; and PM, interview by McNeil. For a historical examination of the Odell Waller case, see Richard B. Sherman, *The Case of Odell Waller and Virginia Justice, 1940–1942* (Knoxville: University of Tennessee Press, 1992).

69   "ramshackle 1931 convertible": PM, *Song,* 152.

69   "Odell shot me": Quoted in Sherman, *The Case of Odell Waller,* 28; see also *Odell Waller v. Commonwealth of Virginia,* Record No. 2442, 178 Va. 294, 306; 16 S.E.2d 808 (Va., Oct. 13, 1941).

70   The sixty-six-year-old: On the background of Judge James Turner Clement and his role in the Waller case, see Sherman, *The Case of Odell Waller,* 20–32.

70 "a man charged": Quoted in Sherman, *The Case of Odell Waller*, 21; see also *Waller v. Commonwealth*, Record No. 2442, 178, 303.

70 His counsel's background: Sherman, *The Case of Odell Waller*, 19–20, and PM, *Song*, 157–58, 163.

71 "had to fight": PM, *Song*, 160.

71 "hear what she has to say": Ibid., 161.

71 "Gentlemen, I haven't": Ibid., 160.

71 "If men of God": Ibid., 162.

71 "fine young feller": Ibid.

71 "prayers and blessings": Ibid.

10. "WILL YOU DO WHAT YOU CAN TO HELP US?"

72 She had raised: PM, memorandum, "Funds Raised—Waller Defense Fund," November 12, 1940, WDLC.

73 "We want you": PM to Odell Waller, November 15, 1940, WDLC.

73 "I know I have": Odell Waller to PM, November 20, 1940, WDLC.

73 "Will you bring": PM to Malvina Thompson, November 20, 1940, ERP.

73 "Dear Mrs. Roosevelt": PM to ER, November 20, 1940, ERP.

74 "We have raised": PM to Odell Waller, November 28, 1940, WDLC.

75 "a great sense": ER, "My Day," January 10, 1939.

75 She was working: Hollinger F. Barnard, ed., *Outside the Magic Circle: The Autobiography of Virginia Foster Durr* (Tuscaloosa: University of Alabama Press, 1985), 156–58.

75 For ER to publicly: On the tension ER's advocacy for Waller created in the White House, see excerpt from Harry Hopkins's diary quoted in John Gunther, *Roosevelt in Retrospect* (New York: Harper & Brothers, 1950), 19. Another account from a black servant in the White House appears in Parks with Speighton, *The Roosevelts*, 174–75. On FDR's objection to ER's work against the poll tax, which was a central issue in the Waller case, see Barnard, ed., *Outside the Magic Circle*, 158.

75 "My dear Governor Price": ER to Governor [James H.] Price, November 30, 1940, ERP.

75 "wraithlike": PM, *Song*, 165.

75 "hands were scarred": Ibid.

75 "there was no one": Ibid.

75 "quavering voice": Ibid.

75 "worked like a slave": Ibid.

75 "When it was cold": Ibid., 155.

76 "I worked and I worked": Ibid., 165.

76 "Mrs. Waller is 65": PM to ER, November 25, 1940, ERP.

76 She had already broken: "First Lady Sets Precedent at House Inquiry: Criticizes Welfare Agencies of Washington," *NYT*, February 10, 1940. ER had previously testified before a House committee about the poor condition of welfare institutions in the District of Columbia.

76 She dazzled: James D. Secrest, "Mrs. Roosevelt Wins Inquiry into Migrant's Union Trouble," *WP*, December 11, 1940; "First Lady Favors Planning for Peace: She Tells Inquiry on Migrants It Will Bring Problems Best Brains Should Tackle Now," *NYT*, December 11, 1940; and PM to ER, December 4, 1940, WDLC. Despite the WDL's efforts and ER's advocacy for migrant workers, the Chirillos were evicted from the state of New York; see "3 'Relief Floaters' Are Ousted from State: Mamaroneck Cobbler and Sons Hail Trip," *NYT*, May 20, 1941.

76   "Mrs. Roosevelt asks me": Malvina Thompson to PM, December 9, 1940, ERP.

76   "Regret cannot give": Malvina Thompson to PM, December 11, 1940, WDLC.

77   "the oppressiveness": PM, *Song,* 167.

77   Murray yearned: PM to Odell Waller, January 3, 1941, WDLC.

77   "short, stocky": PM, *Song,* 166.

77   "I am as sorry": Ibid., 167.

77   "straightforwardness": Ibid., 166.

77   "There is a greater": PM to Odell Waller, January 23, 1941, WDLC.

11. "MIGHT AS WELL BECOME A LAWYER"

78   "resistance against": PM to Morris Milgram and David L. Clendenin, January 9, 1940, WDLC.

79   They spoke to: This description of the tour is drawn from Murray's account in PM, *Song,* 168, and from the correspondence, flyers, financial reports, itineraries, newsletters, photographs, press releases, and program handouts in the Odell Waller files, WDLC.

79   But she spoke: Springer-Kemp, interview by author.

79   She repeatedly urged: PM to Odell Waller, December 7 and 21, 1940, WDLC.

79   An irrepressible desire: Murray told an audience during the Waller tour that she yearned "to write like never before" when she returned home. PM, Vi Lewis, and Mother [Annie] Waller, audio recording, 1941, PMP.

80   "These boys": ER, "My Day," April 1, 1941.

80   In March, ER went: Todd Moye, *Freedom Flyers: The Tuskegee Airmen of World War II* (New York: Oxford University Press, 2010), 30–52.

80   "flagrant discrimination": Mary McLeod Bethune to FDR, October 17, 1939, Mary McLeod Bethune Papers; quoted in Audrey Thomas McCluskey and Elaine M. Smith, *Mary McLeod Bethune: Building a Better World; Essays and Selected Documents* (Bloomington: Indiana University Press, 1999), 240. On Bethune's role in the integration of women's military units, see Janet Sims-Wood, "'We Served America Too!': Personal Recollections of African American Women in the Women's Army Corps During World War II" (PhD diss., Union Institute, 1994).

80   "the Secret Service men": Quentin Smith, interview by Timothy J. Saunders, n.d., Quentin Smith Collection (AFC/2001/001/3001), Veterans History Project, American Folklife Center, Library of Congress.

81   ER had always loved: ER, "Flying Is Fun," *Collier's,* April 22, 1939, 15; and ER, "My Day," April 1, 1941.

81   "It was like being": "First Lady Flies with Miss Earhart: Aviatrix Pilots Mrs. Roosevelt, Who Feels 'On Top of World' on Night Hop to Baltimore," *NYT,* April 21, 1933.

81   ER encouraged: Minutes of the meeting of the Julius Rosenwald Fund, March 28, 1941, and "Notes on [Rosenwald] Fund Interests," June 23, 1941, ERP; and Frederick D. Patterson to ER, August 6, 1943, ERP.

81   "bless . . . the name": Carlton E. Spitzer, "Eleanor Roosevelt Saved Tuskegee Airmen," *Star Democrat,* February 6, 2011. See also J. Todd Moye, *Freedom Flyers,* 52.

81   In this tranquil: PM, *Song,* 177–80.

81   "avoided causes and politics": PM, journal, July 31, 1941, Mount Airy, PMP.

81   Murray had written: PM to Stephen Vincent Benét, October 1, 1939, PMP.

82   He responded: Benét to PM, [October 1939?], PMP.

82   "might as well become": PM, *Song,* 162.

82   "had what it takes": Ibid.

82 "I'm really a submerged writer": PM to Lillian Smith and Paula Snelling, September 1, 1942, PMP. Whether to be a lawyer or a writer was a question that plagued Murray for much of her life. Chapter 15 of PM, *Song,* 177–88, entitled "Writing or Law School?," explores this conflict. See also Patricia Bell-Scott, " 'To Write Like Never Before': Pauli Murray's Enduring Yearning," *Journal of Women's History* 14, no. 2 (Summer 2002): 58–61.

82 "Conflict": PM, "Conflict," in *Dark Testament,* 70.

82 "Without a trade": PM, *Song,* 166.

82 "didn't have the courage": PM to Lillian Smith, September 14, 1942, PMP.

12. "I HAVE DONE EVERYTHING I CAN POSSIBLY DO"

84 The delegation that went: Leon A. Ransom and Ted Poston, who were also members of the delegation, are not in the photograph.

84 When Murray organized: "Urge Roosevelt Fix Waller's Fate: 600 Signers Are on Petition Taken to White House for Intervention for Negro," *NYT,* July 2, 1942, and "Waller to Walk 'Last Mile,' " *Northern Virginia Daily,* July 2, 1942, clipping, WDLC.

85 A religious pacifist: On Murray's FOR affiliation and residency at the Harlem Ashram, see PM, *Song,* 201, and PM, diary, January 4, 5, and 6, 1941. See Nico Slate, *Colored Cosmopolitanism: The Shared Struggle for Freedom in the United States and India* (Cambridge, MA: Harvard University Press, 2012) on the relationship of black religious pacifists, including Murray, to the Indian freedom movement.

85 Between March 1941: See "Chronology of Events: Odell Waller," [1942?], WDLC; Sherman, *The Case of Odell Waller,* 74–179, provides a detailed summary of the appeal.

85 As the case made: "Harlem Will Pray to Save a Slayer: Churches Join Movement for New Trial for Odell Waller," *NYT,* May 26, 1942.

85 "to do whatever you can": PM to ER, May 18, 1942, ERP.

85 "I have heard lots": Odell Waller to ER, June 8, 1942, ERP.

86 In his piece: John Dewey, "The Case of Odell Waller: Supreme Court to Be Asked Again to Hear Negro's Petition," *NYT,* May 19, 1942.

86 "My dear Governor Darden": ER to Governor Colgate W. Darden Jr., June 2, 1942, ERP.

86 "bitterness": "Mrs. Roosevelt Intervenes," *Zanesville Times Recorder,* June 27, 1942, clipping, WDLC.

86 He was grieving: Parks with Leighton, *The Roosevelts,* 240–41.

86 "notes and messages": Ibid., 169.

86 "small basket": Kathleen McLaughlin, "She Who Has Made a Mute 'Office' Articulate Is Aide and Counselor to the President and a Definite Factor in the Political Campaign," *NYT,* July 5, 1936.

87 "personal and unofficial note: FDR to Governor Colgate W. Darden Jr., June 15, 1942, FDRP.

87 Among the expanding network: "Mrs. Coolidge Now Pleads for Waller," [Danville] *Bee,* June 26, 1942, clipping, WDLC.

87 The *New York Times* published: Pearl S. Buck, "Odell Waller's a Test Case: Prejudice, Politics, Poverty and Poll Tax Involved in Negro's Cause," *NYT,* May 30, 1942.

87 On June 16, Harlem residents: "Negroes to Fight Employment Bias: National Campaign to Start Tuesday to Press Demand for Equality in Jobs," *NYT,* June 13, 1942.

87 "beginning of a nationwide": "25,000 Storm Jim Crow Protest Confab," *ADW,* June 21, 1942.

87 "vast crowd": Ibid.

87 Twenty-four hours: "Waller Gets a Stay from Death Penalty: Darden Gives Negro 13 Days, Sets Commutation Hearing," *NYT,* June 19, 1942.

88 She learned that the governor: Colgate W. Darden Jr. was married to Constance Du Pont, daughter of the chemical company magnate Irénée Du Pont.

88 "a national figure": PM to Jessie Overholt, June 19, 1942, WDLC.

88 "political repercussions": Ibid.

88 "a convenient way": Ibid.

88 On June 28: Petition for a Presidential Commission of Inquiry in the Case of Odell Waller, June 15, 1942, WDLC.

88 To the veterans: "First Lady Says Allies Must Protect World," *RTD,* June 29, 1942.

88 "a number of questions": ER, "My Day," June 30, 1942.

88 "preaching racial unrest": W. Carl Spencer, letter to the editor, *Virginian-Pilot,* August 1942, clipping, WDLC.

88 Tens of thousands: "Waller Gets a Stay from Death Penalty," *NYT,* and "Appeals of 17,000 Fail as Waller Dies," June 12, 1942, clipping, WDLC. Forty-five years after Waller's execution, archivists at the Virginia State Library found fifteen boxes of correspondence that had not been processed, according to Sherman, *The Case of Odell Waller,* 241.

88 The pressure came closer: "Refuse Death Stay for Share Cropper: Four Supreme Court Justices Reject Plea for Odell Waller, Virginia Negro," *NYT,* June 28, 1942.

88 "pussyfooting": Editorial, "Justice Prevails," *Danville Register,* July 1, 1942.

88 "pertinent facts": Virginius Dabney, "The Waller Hearing Today," *RTD,* June 29, 1942.

88 The hearing began: "Odell Waller May Know Fate Today: Race Called Main Issue," *RTD,* June 30, 1942; "Governor Darden May Decide Fate of Odell Waller Today: Race Question Seen as the 'Main Issue' of Murder Case," *RTD,* June 30, 1942; J. A. Bowler, "Conflicts Found in Testimony: Persons from All Walks of Life Enter Pleas," *JG,* July 4, 1942, national edition; "Waller Hearing Lasts Eleven Hours," *JG,* July 4, 1942, home edition; and "Waller Hearing Lasts 11 Hours: Conflicts Found in Testimony," *Journal Guide and Newport News Star,* July 4, 1942. On the strategy of Waller's counsel, see Sherman, *The Case of Odell Waller,* 142–54.

89 Late the next day: Associated Press, "Darden Rules Waller Must Die: Holds Virginia Slayer's Trial Fair," *NYT,* July 1, 1942, and "Plea Rejected, Waller Faces Death: Two-Year-Old Case Brought to Close," *RTD,* July 1, 1942.

89 "a fair and impartial": "Odell Waller Received 'Fair and Impartial Trial,' Governor Declares in Statement Refusing Convicted Man's Appeal," *RTD,* July 1, 1942.

89 Murray would always believe: PM, *Song,* 171, and PM to J. Overholt, June 19, 1942.

90 Unable to see the president: "Urge Roosevelt Fix Waller's Fate," *NYT;* and "Waller to Walk 'Last Mile,'" *Northern Virginia Daily.*

90 "displayed contempt": PM, *Song,* 172.

90 Once the rumor spread: Ibid.

90 She, too, had been trying: For the tension between FDR and ER over the Waller case, see Parks with Leighton, *The Roosevelts,* 174–75, and Harry Hopkins's diary quoted in John Gunther, *Roosevelt in Retrospect* (New York: Harper & Brothers, 1950), 19.

90   "interfere again": Harry Hopkins's diary quoted in John Gunther, *Roosevelt in Retrospect,* 19.
90   "thought the Governor": Ibid.
90   "the five telephone": PM, *Song,* 173.
90   "Mr. Randolph, I have done": Ibid.
91   "went to the washroom": Ibid.

13. "THE PRESIDENT HAS LET THE NEGRO DOWN"

92   "alternating between periods": "Waller Breaks on Eve of Execution: Supreme Court Justices Refuse to Act as Fatal Day Nears," *Chicago Defender,* July 4, 1942, national edition.
92   "screen wire": "Odell Waller Goes Berserk as Death Date Nears," *JG,* July 4, 1942.
92   By the time: J. Andrew Bowler, "Long Stay on Death Row Ends: Condemns System Which Made His Crime Possible," *JG,* July 4, 1942, home edition.
92   "he didn't mind going": "Odell Waller Electrocuted: Body Sent to Pittsylvania," *RTD,* July 3, 1942.
92   "Mama, don't cry": Ibid.
92   "said goodbye": Ibid.
93   "This is Odell Waller speaking": For the original text with transcription, see "Appendix: Odell Waller's Dying Statement," in Sherman, *The Case of Odell Waller,* 191–94. Waller's dying statement was excerpted in several black newspapers, such as the *Philadelphia AA,* July 11, 1942.
93   At 8:35 a.m.: "Odell Waller Electrocuted," *RTD.*
93   He was the 156th: "Execution of Waller Set at 8 A.M.: Stay Is Asked of President," *RTD,* July 2, 1942, and J. Andrew Bowler, "Long Stay on Death Row Ends," *JG.*
93   Murray was haunted: PM, *Song,* 174.
93   "He Has Not Died": Murray's essay appeared in two installments: PM, "He Shall Not Have Died in Vain," *Call,* July 7, 1942, and PM, "Danger Signal," *Call,* July 31, 1942.
93   "Put it all down": This stanza appeared in an early version of the poem published as PM, "Dark Testament," *South Today* 8, no. 2 (Winter 1945): 28–36.
93   "With all the heartache": PM to ER, [July 4, 1942?], ERP.
94   "by foot, car, mule": Morris Milgram, "The Last Mile," *Workers Defense Bulletin* 2, no. 4 (Summer 1942): 2.
94   "Simple flowers": Layle Lane, "Land of the Noble Free," *NYA,* July 18, 1942.
94   "Thank God": Milgram, "The Last Mile," *Workers Defense Bulletin.*
94   "we're all in the death row": Ibid.
94   The only white person: Sherman, *The Case of Odell Waller,* 167; Morris Milgram, *"When It Was My Turn to Speak": A Journal to Mark the 35th Anniversary* (New York: Workers Defense League, 1971), 5.
94   He wept silently: Ibid.
94   "stressed the importance": Lane, "Land of the Noble Free," *NYA.*
94   "red earth": Ibid.
94   Overwhelmed with grief: PM, *Song,* 174.
94   "You take big people": "Appendix: Odell Waller's Dying Statement," in Sherman, *The Case of Odell Waller,* 194.
95   Two weeks after Waller's execution: PM, *Song,* 174, and "The Texas Lynching," *ADW,* July 19, 1942.
95   In Rome, Georgia: Cliff Mackay, "Rome Police Beat Roland Hayes," *ADW,* July 15, 1942.

95 "Waller's death": A. Philip Randolph, Channing H. Tobias, Layle Lane, Anna Arnold Hedgeman, Reverend William Lloyd Imes, Frank R. Crosswaith, Pauli Murray, Albert Hamilton, Leon A. Ransom, "open letter to President Franklin D. Roosevelt," July 16, 1942, PMP.

95 "You know as well": Ibid.

96 "throb of muffled drums": "Denouncing Poll Tax, Lynching, Jimcro, Hundreds Join Protest March, *People's Voice,* August 1, 1942, clipping, ERP, quoted in PM, *Song,* 175. For other descriptions of the Waller Protest Parade, see "Silent Parade Protests Wave of Killings," *Evansville Argus,* August 1, 1942, clipping, WDLC; this account was also informed by Springer-Kemp, interview by author.

96 "banner that went": Springer-Kemp, interview by author.

96 "We solemnly pledge": "Denouncing Poll Tax, Lynching, Jimcro," *People's Voice.*

96 "The significance of this": PM to ER, [August 1942?], note attached to "Denouncing Poll Tax, Lynching, Jimcro," *People's Voice.*

96 "There should be no such thing": "President's Wife Sounds Sympathy for Odell Waller," *Virginian-Pilot,* August 5, 1942, clipping, WDLC.

96 "Times without number": ER to A. M. Kroger, August 20, 1942, ERP.

96 Behind closed doors: Parks with Leighton, *The Roosevelts,* 175.

96 "If this were a white man": Ibid.

96 The WDL had raised: "Workers Defense League Schedule of Income and Expenditures Odell Waller Case, November 1, 1940–July 28, 1942," *Workers Defense Bulletin* 2, no. 4 (Summer 1942): 2.

14. "THE RACE PROBLEM IS A WAR ISSUE"

99 "rationalization": PM, *Song,* 189.

99 "As President of a nation": PM to FDR, July 23, 1942, ERP.

100 "race prejudice to imperialism": "Willkie Likens Race Prejudice to Imperialism," *WP,* July 20, 1942.

100 "You are very much": PM to FDR, July 23, 1942.

100 "Will you read this letter": PM to ER, July 23, 1942, ERP.

100 The first lady's indignation: For a discussion of ER's opposition to internment, see Allida M. Black, *Casting Her Own Shadow: Eleanor Roosevelt and the Shaping of a Postwar Liberalism* (New York: Columbia University Press, 1996), 142–47.

100 "If we can not meet": ER, "My Day," December 16, 1941.

100 "These people are good Americans": Quoted in Black, *Casting Her Own Shadow,* 143.

100 "children behind barbed wire": ER, "My Day," May 13, 1942.

100 She worked diligently: Black, *Casting Her Own Shadow,* 142–47.

100 "outburst": PM, *Song,* 193.

100 "Dear Miss Murray": ER to PM, August 3, 1942, PMP.

102 "Dear Mrs. Roosevelt": PM to ER, August 9, 1942, ERP.

104 "easier to talk": PM, *Song,* 193.

104 "for fear": Ibid.

104 "an affectionate hug": Ibid.

104 "wounds of interracial conflict": PM to ER, May 4, 1943, ERP.

104 "militant": PM, *Song,* 193.

104 "Mrs. R.": On ER asking young friends to address her as Mrs. R., see ER, "Some of My Best Friends Are Negro," *Ebony,* February 1953, 16–20, 22, 24–26.

104 "I cannot tell you": PM to ER, August 28, 1942, ERP.

105 Soviet delegate Lieutenant Lyudmila Pavlichenko: "Guerrilla Heroes Arrive for

Rally," *WP,* August 28, 1942, and Scott Hart, no title [profile of Pavlichenko], WP, August 29, 1942.

105   In a speech: "President's Call to Youth to Meet Problems of the War and the Future," *NYT,* September 4, 1942.

105   She showered the delegates: ER, "My Day," September 2 and 5, 1942, ERP.

105   "a ringleader": PM, *Song,* 194.

105   These resolutions: Ibid. See PM, "An American Negro Views the Indian Question," *Call,* September 4, 1942, for her discussion of the parallels between the fight for independence in India and the struggle for black civil rights in the United States.

105   "Pauli, I want to talk": PM, *Song,* 194.

105   "searching blue eyes": Ibid.

106   "The declaration": ER, "My Day," September 7, 1942.

15. "HE REALLY DIDN'T KNOW WHY WOMEN CAME TO LAW SCHOOL"

107   "the comparative freedom": PM, *Song,* 182.

107   The College of Liberal Arts: On the background of HU faculty during Murray's tenure, see Walter Dyson, *Howard University: The Capstone of Negro Education, a History: 1867–1940* (Washington, DC: Howard University Graduate School), 156–77, 219–38; Rayford W. Logan, *Howard University: The First Hundred Years, 1867–1967* (New York: New York University Press, 1967), 323–405; and PM, *Song,* 182, 200.

107   Ware, a New Englander: For Ware's background and her contributions as a historian, see Ellen Fitzpatrick, "Caroline F. Ware and the Cultural Approach to History," *American Quarterly* 43, no. 2 (June 1991): 173–98.

107   "whizzed around blind corners": PM, *Song,* 233.

107   "sanctuary for city-weary students": Ibid., 198.

107   "segregation laws": Ibid., 199.

107   "parallels between racism": Ibid.

107   They would examine: On the lifelong friendship and collaboration between Ware and Murray, see Anne Firor Scott, ed., *Pauli Murray and Caroline Ware: Forty Years of Letters in Black and White* (Chapel Hill: University of North Carolina Press, 2006).

109   Murray would seek his counsel: PM, *Song,* 228.

109   "unmercifully": Ibid., 182.

109   "cool and detached": Ibid., 148.

109   University policy constrained: Aileen Hernandez, interview by author, San Francisco, April 16, 1997.

109   "This is Political Science 183": Ibid.

109   It was the first step: Marva Rudolph, "Aileen Hernandez," in *Notable Black American Women,* ed. Jessie Carney Smith (Detroit: Gale Research, 1992), 491–94.

110   There were currently no women: PM, *Song,* 183, and J. Clay Smith Jr., "Appendix B: Pioneering Facts About Black Women Lawyers and Law Teachers," in *Rebels in Law: Voices in History of Black Women Lawyers* (Ann Arbor: University of Michigan Press, 2000), 277–78.

110   "trudging alone by herself": Ruth Powell, interview by author, Mount Vernon, NY, February 5, 1996.

110   "nice" young women: Aileen Hernandez, interview by author.

110   Murray, who had been: PM, interview by McNeil.

110 "he really didn't know why": PM, *Song,* 183; Murray identified Professor Ming in PM, interview by McNeil.

110 "to recite": Ibid.

110 "smoker": PM, *Song,* 182.

110 Murray could not fathom: Ibid., 184.

110 "I have no right": PM to Attorney Dobbins, November 7, 1941, PMP.

110 "the same policies of exclusion": Ibid.

110 "entered law school preoccupied": PM, *Song,* 238. On Murray's development as a legal activist and theorist, see Rosalind Rosenberg, "The Conjunction of Race and Gender," *Journal of Women's History* 14, no. 2 (Summer 2002): 68–73; Serena Mayeri, *Reasoning from Race: Race, Feminism, Law, and the Civil Rights Revolution* (Cambridge, MA: Harvard University Press, 2011); and Kenneth W. Mack, "The Trials of Pauli Murray," in *Representing the Race: The Creation of the Civil Rights Lawyer* (Cambridge, MA: Harvard University Press, 2012), 207–33.

111 In addition to Ware: PM, *Song,* 202–6, 185–88.

111 Murray also reconnected: On Morrow's background and her friendship with Murray, see PM to ER, June 30, 1954, PMP.

112 "It is difficult": PM [and Pauline Redmond], "Negro Youth's Dilemma," *Threshold* 2, no. 1 (1942): 8–11.

112 To protect Redmond: PM, *Song,* 185; Pauline Redmond Coggs, interview by author, Milwaukee, WI, February 28, 1996.

16. "MANY GOOD THINGS HAVE HAPPENED"

113 This campaign was set off: This description of the campaign and Murray's role as co-leader is drawn from PM, *Song,* 202–9; Powell, interview by author; and PM, comp., "Record of Howard University Student Civil Rights Campaign and Sit-ins, Washington, D.C., NAACP Civil Rights Committee 1943 and 1944, B. Ruth Powell, Chairman, Direct Action Committee" (unpublished scrapbook of clippings, planning documents, handwritten notes, and circulars assembled for Ruth Powell, n.d.), in Ruth Powell's possession. For press accounts, see Harry McAlpin, "Howard Students Picket Jim Crow Restaurant," *Chicago Defender,* April 24, 1943, and "Howard University Students Picket Force Restaurant to Drop Color Bar," *Baltimore AA,* April 23, 1943. See also PM, "A Blueprint for First Class Citizenship," *Crisis* 51, no. 11 (November 1944): 358–59, and Flora Bryant Brown, "NAACP Sponsored Sit-ins by Howard University Students in Washington, D.C., 1943–1944," *Journal of Negro History* 85, no. 4 (Fall 2000): 274–85.

114 "a torrent of resentment": PM, *Song,* 203.

114 "established": Ibid.

114 "nothing superficial": Powell, interview by author.

114 "the powder room": PM, *Song,* 202.

114 "sitting at her typewriter": Powell, interview by author.

114 "made more trips": Ibid.

114 "the heart of a poet": Ibid.

114 Yet Mr. Chaconas: Murray spelled the proprietor's name as "Chaconas," whereas April 1943 editions of the *Afro-American* newspaper use "Choconas."

114 "unsuspecting": PM, *Song,* 206.

114 On Saturday, April 17, 1943: PM, *Song,* 207–8.

115 While the mainstream press: On ER's friendship with Mordecai Johnson and Howard Thurman, see ER, "My Day," September 8, 1939; April 2, 1937; and Janu-

ary 23, 1941; Logan, *Howard University,* 395; and Howard Thurman, *With Head and Heart: The Autobiography of Howard Thurman* (New York: Harcourt Brace Jovanovich, 1979), 141, 146.

115 "Many good things": PM to ER, May 4, 1943, PMP.

115 Their placards: PM, *Song,* 207.

115 "induced": PM to ER, May 4, 1943.

115 "to help him": Ibid.

115 "discussion on Inter- and Intra-racial": Ibid.

115 "It was wonderful": Ibid.

115 "to discuss techniques": Ibid.

116 "full and equal opportunity": PM and Henry Babcock, "An Alternative Weapon," *South Today* 7 (Autumn-Winter 1942–43): 53–57.

116 Murray also enclosed: PM, "I Just Want to Eat, Mister," *Forty-Six: Freshman Assembly Bulletin* 2, no. 25 (May 1943): 1, 5–6.

117 For Eleanor Roosevelt: Cook, *ER,* 2:117.

117 "is well done": ER to PM, May 11, 1943, PMP.

117 At Murray's request: PM to ER, [May 13, 1943?], ERP, and Malvina Thompson to PM, May 17, 1943, PMP.

117 They called for: March on Washington Movement, *Proceedings of Conference Held in Detroit, September 26–27,* 1942.

117 MOWM's bold agenda: John D'Emilio, *Lost Prophet: The Life and Times of Bayard Rustin* (New York: Free Press, 2003), 57–58, and Albert W. Hamilton to A. Philip Randolph, July 16, 1942, PMP.

117 "sensation-mongering": Warren H. Brown's "A Negro Warns the Negro Press" appeared first in the *Saturday Review of Literature,* December 19, 1942, 5–6. It gained wider circulation and attention when it was reprinted in *Reader's Digest,* January 1943. PM may have included a clipping of the advertisement "*The Afro-American Newspapers Answer Reader's Digest* 'A Negro Warns the Negro Press,'" *WP,* January 17, 1943, a point-by-point response to Brown's attack, with the materials she sent to ER.

117 "temperate": ER to Walter White, January 4, 1943, ERP. This controversy is also discussed in Lash, *Eleanor and Franklin,* 673–74.

117 "that there are times": ER, "What Is Morale?," *Saturday Review of Literature* 25 (July 4, 1942): 12.

117 "Some of us thought": PM to ER, May 13, 1943, ERP.

118 "UNDERSTAND COMPLETION": PM to ER, telegram, May 29, 1943, PMP.

118 ER's long-standing affiliation: Brigid O'Farrell, "A Stitch in Time: The New Deal, the International Ladies' Garment Workers' Union and Mrs. Roosevelt," *Transatlantica* 1 (2006), accessed August 3, 2013, http://transatlantica.revues.org/190; see also Brigid O'Farrell, *She Was One of Us: Eleanor Roosevelt and the American Worker* (Ithaca, NY: Cornell University Press, 2010).

118 When Franklin Roosevelt reconstituted: "Fair Employment Body Named," *WP,* July 2, 1943. The other appointees were the Right Reverend Monsignor Francis J. Haas, chairman; John Brophy, Congress of Industrial Organizations; Milton P. Webster, Brotherhood of Sleeping Car Porters; Boris Shishkin, American Federation of Labor Economics; P. B. Young Sr., *Norfolk Journal and Guide;* and Samuel Zemurray, United Fruit Co.

118 Memorial Day: Coggs, interview by author; PM, *Song,* 195–97.

119 She called the White House: PM, *Song,* 196.

119   "wrinkled": Ibid.
119   "big magnolia tree": ER, "My Day," June 2, 1943.
119   "mini-reception": PM, *Song,* 197.
119   "spontaneous laughter": Ibid.
119   "tea for a few guests": ER, "My Day," June 2, 1943.
119   "She asked me": PM to Mother [Pauline Fitzgerald Dame], June 4, 1943.

17. "FORGIVE MY BRUTAL FRANKNESS"

120   "morally responsible": "Blood on Your Hands," *Jackson Daily News,* June 22, 1943.
120   Murray's unrelenting schedule: PM to Mother [Pauline Fitzgerald Dame], June 2, 1943, PMP.
120   "periods of crying": Dr. Brown, University Infirmary, Howard University, bedside notes, May 13, 1943, PMP.
120   "mental observation": PM to Mother [Pauline Fitzgerald Dame], June 2, 1943.
121   "emotional attachments": Ibid.
121   "terrific breakdowns": PM, "Questions prepared for Dr. Titley, Long Island 'Rest' Home—Amityville, New York," December 17, 1937, PMP.
121   "mad Murrays": PM to Mother [Pauline Fitzgerald Dame], June 2, 1943.
121   "pattern of life": Ibid.
121   "This little 'boy-girl' ": Ibid.
121   "done nothing": Ibid.
121   "legal genius": Ibid.
121   One topic was: "Shot While Playing with Roosevelt Lad: Chum of President's Grandson Is Victim of Rifle Bullet," *NYT,* June 7, 1943.
121   "wearing a rose": PM to ER, July 11, 1944, ERP.
121   "We cannot expect": PM to ER, June 7, 1943, ERP.
122   "four sons in the Army": Ibid.
122   Eleanor Roosevelt shared: Julieanne Phillips, "Carrie Chapman Catt," in *The Eleanor Roosevelt Encyclopedia,* ed. Maurine H. Beasley, Holly C. Shuman, and Henry R. Beasley (Westport, CT: Greenwood), 79–80, and Jason Berger, "Jane Addams," in *The Eleanor Roosevelt Encyclopedia,* ed. Beasley, Shuman, and Beasley, 1–3.
122   But the first lady did not share: John M. Craig, "Peace Movement," in *The Eleanor Roosevelt Encyclopedia,* ed. Beasley, Shuman, and Beasley, 396–98.
122   "It was very sad": ER to PM, June 12, 1943, ERP.
122   She had thirteen: PM to Mr. [Marvin H.] McIntyre, June 18, 1943, FDRP.
122   Some of her female friends: Powell, interview by author; Katie McCabe and Dovey Johnson Roundtree, *Justice Older Than the Law: The Life of Dovey Johnson Roundtree* (Jackson: University of Mississippi Press, 2009), 55–72.
123   In Mobile, Alabama: "Mobile Race Riot Laid to Company: OWI Taxes Alabama Shipbuilding Officers with Suppressing FEPC Ruling on Workers," *NYT,* June 13, 1943.
123   Clashes between: "Troops Curb Detroit Riots: 23 Are Dead; Governor Calls on Army for Help as Civil Authority Fails," *WP,* June 22, 1943.
123   In Los Angeles: "Los Angeles' Zoot War Called 'Near Anarchy': 'Black Widow' Girls Beat, Slash Woman," *WP,* June 11, 1943.
123   "the ugliest brand": "California: Zoot-Suit War," *Time,* June 21, 1943.
123   "question": International News Service, "Zoot Suit Riots Concern Mexico," *El Paso Herald-Post,* June 17, 1943.

123 Tempers also flared: PM to Mr. [Marvin H.] McIntyre, June 18, 1943.

123 Authorities in Beaumont: "Rape Sparks Race Rioting in Beaumont," *WP,* June 17, 1943.

123 Few public officials: Louis Martin, "Prelude to Disaster: Detroit," *Common Ground* 4 (Autumn 1943): 21–26; "Makes Race Riot Charges: Group to Aid Colored People Puts Onus on Detroit Officials," *NYT,* July 29, 1943; and "Los Angeles' Zoot War Called 'Near Anarchy,'" *WP.*

123 "personally proclaiming": "Blood on Your Hands," *Jackson Daily News.*

123 "white cabinet": PM to Mr. [Marvin H.] McIntyre, June 18, 1943.

124 "a determination": Ibid.

124 These alleged clubs: Caryn Neumann, "Eleanor Clubs," in *The Eleanor Roosevelt Encyclopedia,* ed. Beasley, Shuman, and Beasley, 157–58.

124 "a white woman": Howard W. Odum, *Race and Rumors of Race: Challenge to American Crisis* (Chapel Hill: University of North Carolina, 1943), 86.

124 The FBI found: "First Lady Says FBI Search for 'Eleanor Clubs' Futile," *WP,* September 23, 1942.

124 On August 2, 1943: "Harlem's Tragedy," *NYT,* August 3, 1943; William Pickens, "Harlem Riot: A Communication," *WP,* August 8, 1943; and "1943 Harlem Riot Killed 5, Hurt 500: It Began When a Policeman Shot a Negro Soldier," *NYT,* July 19, 1964. For in-depth discussion of the 1943 Harlem riot, see Harold Orlansky, *The Harlem Riot: A Study in Mass Frustration* (New York: Social Analysis, 1943); Dominic J. Capeci Jr., *The Harlem Riot of 1943* (Philadelphia: Temple University Press, 1977); and Nat Brandt, *Harlem at War: The Black Experience in WWII* (Syracuse, NY: Syracuse University Press, 1996), 183–215.

125 "tramped": PM, "And the Riots Came . . . ," *Call,* August 13, 1942.

125 "ostensibly for": Ibid.

125 "a woman carry": Ibid.

125 Her frustration: PM, "Harlem Riot," in PM, *Dark Testament,* 35, and PM, "And the Riots Came . . . ," *Call.*

125 "mealy-mouthed": PM, *Song,* 212.

125 "Mr. Roosevelt Regrets": PM, "Mr. Roosevelt Regrets," in *Dark Testament,* 34.

126 "heart sank": ER, "My Day," August 4, 1943, PMP.

126 "be stampeded": Ibid.

126 "unwelcome change": Quoted in Black, *Casting Her Own Shadow,* 92.

126 "I have your poem": ER to PM, July 26, 1943, PMP.

18. "I COUNT YOU A REAL FRIEND"

127 "What Can the Negro": "Freshmen Hear First Lady," *Hilltop,* January 29, 1944.

127 By the midsummer of 1943: Black, *Casting Her Own Shadow,* 92.

128 ER's days started: ER, *This I Remember* (New York: Harpers & Brothers, 1949), 295–310.

128 "mouth hanging open": Stella K. Hershan, *A Woman of Quality* (New York: Crown, 1970), 163.

128 "Mrs. Roosevelt made me": Ibid.

128 On January 14, 1944: "Freshmen Hear First Lady," *Hilltop.*

128 "I know that this will": Ibid.

128 "Don't get mad": This motto appears as the title of chapter 20 in PM, *Song,* 232.

128 Her answer: Ibid., 217–19.

129 Even as Murray: PM, "A Blueprint for First Class Citizenship," *Crisis,* and Brown, "NAACP Sponsored Sit-ins."

129   "moderately priced": PM, *Song,* 222.

129   "rigorous": Ibid.

129   "to indulge": PM and Ruth Powell, "Pledge," May 1, 1944, in PM, "Record of Howard University Student Civil Rights Campaign."

129   "such as making signs": PM, *Song,* 223.

129   "twos and threes": Ibid.

129   The demonstration produced: Ibid., 224.

129   "smartly dressed": Ibid.

130   "as a personal favor": Ibid.

130   "If the Army was afraid": Ibid.

130   "victory": Ibid.

130   They also saw her propensity: Powell, interview by author, and Dovey Johnson Roundtree, interview by author, Washington, DC, August 23, 1995.

130   Matters reached: See Logan, *Howard University,* 375–76, 379, on President Mordecai Johnson's treatment of William Hastie and Howard Thurman, who would eventually leave the university because of difficulties with the president. On Johnson's attitude toward women and his treatment of Lucy Diggs Slowe, the dean of women, who was the highest-ranking female administrator on campus, see Patricia Bell-Scott, " 'To Keep My Self-Respect': Dean Lucy Diggs Slowe's 1927 Memorandum on the Sexual Harassment of Black Women," *NWSA Journal* 9, no. 2 (Summer 1997): 70–76, and Patricia Bell-Scott, "The Business of Being Dean of Women: A Letter from Lucy Diggs Slowe to the Howard University Board of Trustees," *Initiatives* 54, no. 2 (1992): 35–41. For an extended discussion of Slowe's career and her struggle with Johnson and other male administrators over the treatment of women, see Lisa R. Rasheed, "Lucy Diggs Slowe, Howard University Dean of Women, 1922–1937: Educator, Administrator, Activist" (PhD diss., Georgia State University, 2010), and Carroll L. L. Miller and Anne S. Pruitt-Logan, *Faithful to the Task at Hand: The Life of Lucy Diggs Slowe* (Albany: State University of New York Press, 2012).

130   "suspend all activities": PM to ER, May 4, 1944, ERP.

130   At the reins: For Bilbo's position on race, see Theodore G. Bilbo, *Take Your Choice: Separation or Mongrelization* (Poplarville, MS: Dream House, 1946).

131   "Since I count you": PM to ER, May 4, 1944.

131   "second-hand": Ibid.

131   "Freedom of action": Ibid.

131   Murray asked permission: PM to Malvina Thompson, May 11, 1944, ERP.

131   "a slave in a small": "Open Letter to the Graduating Class of 1944," May 29, 1944, ERP.

19. "THE FLOWERS BROUGHT YOUR SPIRIT TO THE GRADUATION"

132   "tradition": PM, *Song,* 239.

132   "Your picture": quoted in PM, *Song,* 239.

133   "stinging gibes": PM, *Song,* 239.

133   "a source of": Ibid., 240.

133   "There's a limit": PM to Malvina Thompson, May 20, 1944, ERP.

133   "Seems to me": PM to ER, [May 20, 1944?], ERP.

133   "Dear Jim": FDR to Jim [James B. Conant], May 31, 1944, PMP.

134   FDR frequently employed: There are numerous accounts of FDR's efforts to avoid difficult conversations with gibes or storytelling. See, for example, Walter Francis White, *A Man Called White: The Autobiography of Walter White* (New

York: Viking, 1948), 168–69, and Jervis Anderson, *A. Philip Randolph: A Biographical Portrait* (New York: Harcourt Brace Jovanovich, 1973), 256–57.

134   The black servant: Powell, interview by author.
134   "in position": PM, "Notes on the Tea," written on *The Seventy-Sixth Annual Commencement Program,* Howard University, June 2, 1944, ERP.
134   "gawked": Ibid.
134   "tried to re-copy": Ibid.
134   "got caught": Ibid.
134   "posted around the room": Ibid.
134   "Ruth came out": Ibid.
134   "a bronze-colored [paper] clip": PM, *Song,* 197.
135   She inscribed: PM to ER, note on name card, June 1944, ERP.
135   On another card: PM to ER, note on name card, June 1944, ERP.
135   "With the wish": PM, "Notes on the Tea."
135   "The flowers brought": Ibid.
135   "reaction of one": "Open Letter to the Graduating Class of 1944," May 29, 1944.
135   "prepared to be": Ibid.
135   "put his finger": Ibid.
135   "the air is freest": Ibid.
135   "necessity for the North": Ibid.
136   "pet thesis": Ibid.
136   "his face grew": Ibid.
136   "Shall we move": Ibid.
136   "dank and suffocating": Ibid.
137   "A live lawyer": PM, interview by McNeil.
137   "shouted 'Oh My God!' ": PM to ER, June 4, 1941, ERP.
137   "with all the graduates": Ibid.
137   "removed the identification": Ibid.
137   In truth: For a press story about the bouquet, see Harry McAlpin, "Mrs. F.D.R. Sends Posies to Pauli for Commencement," *Philadelphia AA,* June 10, 1944.
137   "the honorary dinner": PM to ER, June 4, 1941.
137   "hot-footed it back": Ibid.
137   "I was much amused": ER to PM, June 8, 1944, PMP.
137   "more powerful": PM to ER, July 11, 1944, ERP.

20. "SO AT LAST WE HAVE COME TO D-DAY"

138   "the weariness that assails": ER, "My Day," April 7, 1944.
138   "to vote the Democratic": PM to President and Mrs. Roosevelt, June 4, 1944, ERP.
139   "I believe your great": Ibid.
139   "the unofficial Vice-President": Parks with Leighton, *The Roosevelts,* 221.
140   "Hope is a crushed stalk": PM, "Dark Testament," *South Today* 8, no. 2 (Winter 1945): 32.
140   "When you read it": PM to ER, June 7, 1944, ERP.
140   "Thank you for letting me": ER to PM, June 13, 1944, PMP.
140   This was reassuring: PM, interview by Blanche Wiesen Cook, October 19, 1983, PMP.
140   "This will introduce": ER to Flora Rose, June 5, 1944, PMP.
141   "recite the words": Lawrence Resner, "Country in Prayer: President on Radio Leads in Petition He Framed for Allied Cause," *NYT,* June 7, 1944.

141 "Almighty God": FDR, "D-Day Prayer," June 6, 1944, FDRP.

141 "So at last": ER, "My Day," June 7, 1944.

141 "eloquent": PM to ER, June 7, 1944, ERP.

21. "THIS HARVARD BUSINESS MAKES ME BRISTLE"

142 "The problem is": George H. Chase to FDR, June 5, 1944, FDRP.

142 "Dear Mr. Roosevelt": PM to FDR, June 17, 1944, FDRP.

143 "ruling that women": PM to Thomas Reed Powell and the Harvard Law School Committee on Graduate Studies, June 19, 1944, PMP.

143 "request": Ibid.

143 "personal factors": PM to A. Calvert Smith, June 24, 1944, PMP.

143 "'male slant'": Ibid.

143 "social factors": Ibid.

143 "liberal": Ibid.

144 "I'm sorry, Mrs. Roosevelt": PM to ER, July 22, 1944, ERP.

144 "Dear Pauli": ER to PM, July 3, 1944, PMP.

22. "YOU WOULDN'T WANT TO PUT FALA IN HERE"

148 "a black dog": ER, "My Day," October 18, 1944.

148 "see them off": ER, "My Day," August 12, 1944.

148 "with enthusiasm": PM to ER, July 11, 1944, ERP.

148 Mildred had taken: PM to ER, August 7, 1944, ERP.

148 "a full-sized trailer": PM, *Song*, 248.

148 "just finished": PM to ER, July 11, 1944.

149 Nonetheless, he: On Robert Fitzgerald as PM's first teacher, see PM, *Proud Shoes*, 1–3; on ER's admiration for her aunt Bye, see ER, *This Is My Story* (New York: Harper & Brothers, 1937), 50–51.

149 "fired at the First Lady": PM to ER, July 11, 1944.

149 "Los Angeles is a": ER to PM, July 23, 1944, PMP.

149 "You resisted this idea": PM to ER, July 11, 1944.

149 "Mrs R., the Negro soldiers": Ibid.

149 "opposed": ER to PM, July 23, 1944.

150 Hoarseness, sinusitis: Marquis Childs, "Washington Calling: Our Commander in Chief," *WP*, April 15, 1944; John H. Crider, "President's Health 'Satisfactory': Unique Report Made by McIntire; Roosevelt Health Is 'Satisfactory,'" *NYT*, April 5, 1944; "President Is Better but Remains Quiet: At Physician's Insistence, He Cancels Two Appointments," *NYT*, March 31, 1944; and "President Is Recovering: But Spends Some Time Abed, Still Weak from Influenza," *NYT*, January 4, 1944.

150 "the size of a hen's egg": Steven Lomazow and Eric Fettmann, *FDR's Deadly Secret* (New York: Public Affairs, 2009), 94. For a news story, see "Went Under Surgery, Roosevelt Discloses: But It Was Only for an Old Wen on His Head, He Says," *NYT*, February 5, 1944.

150 "unsteadiness of his hand": Harry McAlpin, "FDR as a White House Correspondent Saw Him," *Philadelphia AA*, April 21, 1945.

150 Rumors that FDR: John H. Crider, "Roosevelt Was Ill of Bronchitis, but Says That He Is Feeling Fine: Roosevelt Whips Bronchitis Attack," *NYT*, March 29, 1944, and Gladstone Williams, "Roosevelt Hurt by Treatment of Press," *Atlanta Constitution*, November 29, 1944.

150 Pronouncements about: Charles Hurd, "President's Health 'Excellent,' Admiral

McIntire Reports: Condition at 62 Is Above Average for His Age," *NYT,* June 9, 1944.

150   "if . . . so ordered": FDR to Robert E. Hannegan, July 11, 1944, FDRP.

150   "home on the Hudson": Ibid.

150   "run in the usual": Ibid.

150   "You are to be": PM to FDR, July 14, 1944, FDRP.

150   "There is no one": Ibid.

150   Committed to presenting: On PM as an early practitioner of literary journalism and literary nonfiction, see Patricia Bell-Scott, "Calling Out the Truth: Pauli Murray, Black Feminist Literary Journalist," paper presented at the Annual Meeting of American Journalism Historians Association Conference, Richmond, VA, October 2007), and Patricia Bell-Scott, foreword to *Proud Shoes,* by PM (Boston: Beacon, 1999), vi–x.

151   "I am glad to know": ER to PM, August 18, 1944, PMP.

151   The other item: South Crocker Street Property Owners to Mrs. Mildred M. Fearing and Pauli Murray, August 20, 1944, PMP.

151   "hot beds": See "Housing Shortage, Bronzeville–Little Tokyo," Los Angeles Online History, accessed May 24, 2012, http://www.bronzeville-la.com/index .php?option=com_content&task=view&id=31&Itemid=2; and Los Angeles Urban League Records, 1939–1945, Charles E. Young Research Library, University of California, Los Angeles.

151   The font: PM, note on South Crocker Street Property Owners to Fearing and PM, August 20, 1944, ERP.

151   "I wish you could see": PM to ER, August 23, 1944, ERP.

152   With police protection: PM, *Song,* 254.

152   "That rent notice": ER to PM, August 30, 1944, PMP.

152   "returned to normal conditions": PM, *Song,* 243–44.

152   "indefinable male egoism": Quoted in PM, *Song,* 243.

152   "Definitely plan": PM to ER, August 22, 1944, ERP.

23. "THIS LETTER IS CONFIDENTIAL"

153   As the 1944 presidential: On criticism of ER, see Pamela Tyler, " 'Blood on Your Hands': White Southerners' Criticism of Eleanor Roosevelt During World War II," in *Before* Brown: *Civil Rights and White Backlash in the Modern South,* ed. Glenn Feldman (Tuscaloosa: University of Alabama, 2004), 96–115.

153   "to associate with workers": ER, "My Day," September 26, 1944.

153   "The story does me": Ibid.

153   Such a program: ER, "My Day," August 22, 1944, and ER, "My Day," August 23, 1944.

153   "wilder in her attempts": ER, "My Day," August 23, 1944.

153   "No one is more conscious": Ibid.

153   "the essential thing": Ibid.

154   "the idea of a year's": PM to ER, August 25, 1944, ERP.

154   "You know, we could": Ibid.

154   "complete knowledge": Catherine Stallworth to ER, August 18, 1944, ERP.

154   "Much that is said": ER to Catherine Stallworth, August 26, 1944, ERP.

154   "The Negro is not": PM, "Social Equality Needs Definition," *Los Angeles Sentinel,* September 14, 1944.

154   "Dear Pauli": ER to PM, October 3, 1944, PMP.

156 "Your young friend": Rose quoted in ER to PM, August 30, 1944, PMP.

156 "It does worry me": PM to ER, September 9, 1944, ERP.

156 "You are right we should": ER to PM, September 21, 1944, PMP.

24. "THE WHOLE THING HAS LEFT ME VERY DISTURBED"

157 "policy of discrimination": PM to ER, October 27, 1944, ERP.

157 The Port Chicago Fifty: For an in-depth treatment, see Robert L. Allen, *The Port Chicago Mutiny: The Story of the Largest Mass Mutiny Trial in U.S. Naval History* (New York: Amistad, 1989).

158 "mass trial": NAACP, *Mutiny? The Real Story of How the Navy Branded 60 Fear-Shocked Sailors as Mutineers* (New York: NAACP Legal Defense and Educational Fund, 1945), 2.

158 "for general service": "Navy Combat Units Opened to Negroes: Knox Says They Will Be Put in 'Reserve Components' with Promotion Rights," *NYT,* April 8, 1942. On the problems black seamen faced during FDR's presidency and the war, see Richard E. Miller, *Messman Chronicles: African Americans in the U.S., 1932–1943* (Annapolis, MD: Naval Institute Press, 2003), and Doris Kearns Goodwin, *No Ordinary Time: Franklin and Eleanor Roosevelt: The Home Front in World War II* (New York: Simon & Schuster, 1994), 166–67, 169, 328–30.

158 Even after Doris "Dorie" Miller: See Miller, *Messman Chronicles,* 285–318.

158 Of the fourteen hundred: PM, *Song,* 257; PM to ER, October 27, 1944; and NAACP, *Mutiny?,* 5.

158 The year before: Allen, *The Port Chicago Mutiny,* 44.

158 Shortly after ten o'clock: Ibid., 56–66. For photographs and documents related to the Port Chicago case, see "Frequently Asked Questions: Port Chicago Naval Magazine Explosion, 1944," U.S. Department of Navy, Navy Historical Center, accessed August 30 2012, http://www.history.navy.mil/photos/pl-usa/pl-ca/pt-hgo.htm; http://www.history.navy.mil/faqs/faq80–1.htm.

159 The cleanup: Allen, *The Port Chicago Mutiny,* 66–68, and NAACP, *Mutiny?,* 8.

159 The survivors: Allen, *The Port Chicago Mutiny,* 72–74.

159 "I am willing": William Glaberson, "WWII Mutineer Pardoned," *Houston Chronicle,* December 24, 1999.

159 "When men are shocked": NAACP, *Mutiny?,* 8.

160 "a neurotic": Ibid.

160 "This is not fifty": Allen, *The Port Chicago Mutiny,* 119.

160 "her silent presence": PM, *Song,* 257.

160 Ten received: NAACP, foreword to *Mutiny?,* i.

160 "The whole thing": PM to ER, October 27, 1944, ERP.

160 "terrible disaster": Edna Seixas to James K. Forrestal, October 25, 1944, PMP.

160 "with extreme interest": ER to PM, November 4, 1944, PMP.

160 "Please read because": Memorandum, ER to FDR, November 4, 1944, attached to ER to PM, November 4, 1944.

160 "how, in following the letter": ER to PM, November 4, 1944.

161 "the verdict": Ibid.

161 "special care": Allen, *The Port Chicago Mutiny,* 132.

161 On November 15, 1944: Ibid., 127.

161 On December 23, 1999: William Glaberson, "Sailor from Mutiny in '44 Wins a Presidential Pardon: End to Case That Became a Race Benchmark," *NYT,* December 24, 1999.

25. "I SHALL SHOUT FOR THE RIGHTS OF ALL MANKIND"

162   "had suffered from exclusion": PM, *Song,* 259.

162   In October 1944: Ibid., 258–61.

163   "coffee and cigarettes": Ibid., 259.

163   "heart-to-heart": PM to ER, March 30, 1945, ERP.

163   "friendship and peace": Ibid.

163   "The real crux": Ibid.

163   "persuasion" and "spiritual resistance": PM, "An American Credo," *Common Ground* 5, no. 2 (1945): 24.

163   "When my brothers": Ibid.

163   "somewhere in Marianas Islands": PM, *Song,* 255.

163   "liked it very much": ER to PM, March 23, 1945, PMP.

163   "released from the 'racial struggle' ": PM to ER, March 30, 1945.

163   In addition to: Ibid.

164   "place where anything": ER, "My Day," March 28, 1945.

26 "I PRAY FOR YOUR STRENGTH AND FORTITUDE"

165   "mind's eye": PM to ER, April 16, 1945, ERP.

165   "I will be": ER to PM, April 5, 1945, PMP.

165   "I hope that you will": "Report of President Roosevelt in Person to the Congress on the Crimea Conference: The Scene in Congress as the President Made His Address Yesterday," *NYT,* March 2, 1945.

166   "the entire time": Ibid.

166   "The Roosevelts are not": Ibid.

166   "It is not fitting": Winston Churchill, "Death of President Roosevelt," Hansard, House of Commons Debate, April 13, 1945.

166   "Every American": "Tributes to President Roosevelt by Leaders: The Final Resting Place of Franklin D. Roosevelt," *NYT,* April 13, 1945.

166   "Men will thank God": Editorial, "Franklin D. Roosevelt," *NYT,* April 13, 1945.

166   "Negroes cried publicly": "Mr. Roosevelt Is Dead," *PC,* April 21, 1945.

166   "Since Abraham Lincoln": "Roosevelt Mourned as Best Friend of Race Since Lincoln and Willkie, " *PC,* April, 21, 1945.

166   "Little people": "D.C. Citizens Recall How FDR Broke Precedents," *Baltimore AA,* April 21, 1945.

166   "the removal of Mrs. Roosevelt": "Mr. Roosevelt Is Dead," *PC.*

166   "necessarily restrained": Ibid.

167   "noted champion": Maethelda Morris, "Era Ends for Mrs. Roosevelt," *Washington AA,* April 21, 1945.

167   The Philadelphia *Afro-American*: "Human Interest Stories in Mrs. Roosevelt's Life," *Philadelphia AA,* April 14, 1945.

167   "entire adult life": PM to ER, April 20, 1945, ERP.

167   "tough western idealism": PM to ER, July 30, 1944, ERP.

167   "Dear Mrs. Roosevelt": PM to ER, April 12, 1945, ERP.

168   Her grief: Lash, *Eleanor and Franklin,* 722.

168   With tears streaming: Photographer Ed Clark captured this image of Graham Jackson, which was published in *Life,* April 17, 1945.

168   Rowan County Pleasant Grove Baptist: Louis Lomax, "Return Trip of President Described by AFRO Writer," *Washington AA,* April 21, 1945, and Harry McAlpin, "Tan Yanks Walk Before Caisson," *Philadelphia AA,* April 21, 1945.

169   "We wish the great": PM to ER, April 16, 1945, ERP.

169   "President Roosevelt": PM, "The Passing of F.D.R.," in *Dark Testament,* 36–37.

27. "THE PROBLEM NOW IS HOW TO CARRY ON"

171   When the weather permitted: ER, "My Day," September 18, 1939.

171   "little red light": ER, "My Day," April 21, 1945.

171   The next morning: "Roosevelt Family Leaves the White House; 20 Army Trucks Carry Belongings Away," *NYT,* April 21, 1945.

171   "Perhaps, in His wisdom": ER, "My Day," April 17, 1945.

172   "on its own merits": ER, "My Day," April 19, 1945.

172   "he refused to complete": "D.C. Citizens Recall How FDR Broke Precedents," *Baltimore AA.*

172   "the delicate balance": Ibid.

172   The *Courier:* Editorial, "The Price We Pay," *PC,* October 28, 1944, national edition.

172   In contrast to Eleanor Roosevelt: "First Lady Silent on Press Parleys: President Says Conferences Will Be Decided on Later," *NYT,* April 18, 1945, and Charles Nutter, "Her Quiet Stay in Missouri Sets Pattern for Mrs. Truman," *WP,* August 12, 1945.

172   "Negroes, as with Labor": PM to ER, April 20, 1945, ERP.

173   "small group": Ibid.

173   "This bill would give": ER, "My Day," April 30, 1945.

173   "Discrimination in": "Truman Backs Bill for Fair Job Policy: He Urges Rules Committee to Let House Vote on Making Hiring Practice Permanent," *NYT,* June 6, 1945.

173   "I feel you are": PM to ER, June 6, 1945, ERP.

173   She rebuffed: ER, "My Day," April 19, 1945.

174   "Have you ever considered": PM to ER, June 6, 1945, ERP.

174   "I have never considered": ER to PM, June 18, 1945, PMP.

174   "You are sweet": Ibid.

28. "JUST KNOW HOW CHERISHED YOU ARE TO SO MANY"

177   "the field of public service": "Awards to Twelve Outstanding Women of 1946," *Aframerican Woman's Journal* (March 1946): 17. Also honored were Lieutenant Colonel Charity Edna Adams, Women's Army Corps; Justice Jane Matilda Bolin, New York City Court of Domestic Relations; Helen Gahagan Douglas, U.S. representative from California; Virginia Foster Durr, civil rights activist; Florence Jaffray Harriman, diplomat; Lois Mailou Jones, artist; Catherine D. Lealtad, director of the United Nations Relief and Rehabilitation Administration; Arenia Cornelia Mallory, educator; Agnes Ernst Meyer, writer; and Eslanda Goode Robeson, activist and writer.

177   "the first American Negro woman": "Women Labor Leaders Are Going to England to Good-Will Exchange with 4 from There: Guest at Luncheon Here," *NYT,* January 10, 1945.

177   The publication of her thesis: PM, "The Right to Equal Opportunity in Employment," *California Law Review* 33 (1945): 388–433.

178   "created an untenable situation": PM, *Song,* 268.

178   After discussing her situation: PM to Frank Murphy, June 5, 1946, PMP.

178   But there were: Frank Murphy to PM, June 10, 1946, PMP.

178   Having just read: PM, *Song,* 264.

179   "felt a great responsibility": ER, "My Day," December 22, 1945.

179   "that he was writing": James B. Reston, "UNO Delegates Confirmed but Policy Is Challenged: Fulbright Attacks 'Political Awards,' Asks Experts to Give Continuity to Foreign Plans—Bilbo Criticizes Mrs. Roosevelt," *NYT,* December 21, 1945.

179   Notwithstanding the Senate's: Ibid.; and ER, *On My Own* (New York: Harper & Brothers, 1937), 39.

179   She worried: ER, *On My Own,* 39–41.

179   "a sincere desire": ER, "My Day," December 22, 1945.

179   ER spent most: ER, *On My Own,* 40–42.

179   Reporters clamored: "U.S. Division Denied by Mrs. Roosevelt: In Her First Press Conference in London She Doubts That Churchill Wants UNO Post," *NYT,* January 14, 1946.

179   A crowd lined: "Six Women Lead in UNO Assembly: Mrs. Roosevelt as Delegate Is One of Most Popular at London Sessions," *NYT,* January 14, 1946.

180   "with other nations'": ER, *On My Own,* 47.

180   "a common problem": Ibid.

180   She presented: Mary Hornaday, "Delegates to UNO Urge Women to Seek Roles in World Affairs: Role for Women Train Children," *CSM,* February 9, 1946.

180   "The whole of Europe": ER, "Address at the Opening Campaign Rally Women's Division of the United Jewish Appeal of Greater New York" (New York, February 20, 1946), ERP.

180   "I had a most interesting": ER to PM, February 28, 1946, PMP.

180   "perpetual motion": PM to ER, April 9, 1946, ERP.

181   She pitched the idea: PM to ER, April 21, 1946, ERP.

181   "straight in the eye": PM to ER, April 9, 1946, and Caroline F. Ware, interview by Peggy McIntosh, n.d., in Peggy McIntosh's possession.

181   "Dear Mrs. Roosevelt": PM to ER, April 9, 1946.

29. "GLAD TO HEAR THE OPERATION WAS SUCCESSFUL"

183   Pauli Murray returned: PM, *Song,* 270.

184   "an enlarged and enflamed": PM to ER, April 19, 1947, ERP.

184   "glad to hear": ER to PM, April 23, 1947, PMP.

184   She found herself: PM, *Song,* 270–73.

185   "Being a woman": PM to Mother [Pauline Fitzgerald Dame], June 18, 1946, PMP.

185   "errand girl": PM, *Song,* 273.

185   One particularly demeaning: Ibid., 274.

185   The goal of the: See John D'Emilio, *Lost Prophet: The Life and Times of Bayard Rustin* (New York: Free Press, 2003), 131–32, for a discussion of the planning team and campaign; and *Morgan v. Virginia,* 328 U.S. 373 (1946).

186   "veterans": PM to ER, May 5, 1947, ERP.

186   Rustin and Murray had first: PM, interview by Robert E. Martin, August 17 and 19, 1968, transcript, RJB 290, Ralph J. Bunche Oral History Collection, Moorland-Spingarn Research Center, Howard University, Washington, DC, and PM, *Song,* 201.

186   "thinking through each possibility": PM to ER, May 5, 1947.

186   "insane": Bayard Rustin, interview by unknown interviewer, February 13, 1970, audiocassette, RJB 534, Ralph J. Bunche Oral History Collection, Moorland-Spingarn Research Center, Howard University, Washington, DC.

186   "You will recognize": PM to ER, May 5, 1947.

186   "flower gardens": PM, *Song,* 277.

187   Sleep-deprived: "Mrs. Roosevelt Hits Car as She Dozes at Wheel," *WP,* August 15, 1946, and "Mrs. Roosevelt 'Dozes Off,' Is Hurt in Triple Car Crash: Mrs. Roosevelt's Car and One of Machines It Hit," *NYT,* August 15, 1946.

187   "about halfway up": "Mrs. Roosevelt Badly Bruised, She Reveals," *WP,* August 17, 1946.

187   "I am a little sad": ER, "My Day," January 16, 1947.

187   "protruding": "Mrs. Roosevelt Badly Bruised, She Reveals," *WP.*

30. "I HOPE TO FOLLOW THE ROOSEVELT TRADITION"

188   "Good Government": PM, *Song,* 281.

188   "It would be an unspeakable": "Text of President's Message: Text," *WP,* March 13, 1947.

188   "My superficial understanding": PM to ER, March 14, 1947, ERP.

189   "for relief and rehabilitation": ER, "My Day," March 15, 1947.

189   "repressive": ER, "My Day," March 27, 1947.

189   "They need a mind": PM to ER, June 19, 1948, ERP.

189   "the birth of a new democracy": PM to Mother [Pauline Fitzgerald Dame], [1948?], PMP.

189   "Mrs. R. sat": Ibid.

189   "It was different": Ibid.

189   "history in the making": Ibid.

189   In the summer of 1948: ER to PM, August 16, 1948, PMP.

190   "in mind": Ibid.

190   Franklin offered: Franklin D. Roosevelt Jr. to ER, n.d., ERP.

190   The Liberal Party was: For a study that examines black women's participation, including Murray's, in New York City politics, see Julie A. Gallagher, "African American Women and Power Politics in New York City, 1944–1972," *Journal of Women, Politics & Policy* (Fall 2007), 101–30. For a study of the Liberal Party during the period when Murray ran for office, see Gerald David Weintraub, "The Liberal Party of New York State, 1944–1956" (master's thesis, Brown University, 1957).

190   In 1949, Murray agreed: For Murray's account of her campaign, see PM, *Song,* 279–82. See also Yevette Richards, *Maida Springer: Pan-Africanist and International Labor Leader* (Pittsburgh: University of Pittsburgh Press, 2000), 90–91.

190   Operating on a budget: PM, *Song,* 281.

190   "little blue-and-white fliers": Ibid.

190   "called for more traffic lights": Ibid.

190   "I think it is more": Ted Poston, "Miss Murray Delays Study at Harvard," *NYP,* October 26, 1949.

191   "I have drawn so much": PM to ER, November 17, 1949, ERP. Maida Springer underscored ER's influence on Murray in a note acknowledging the donation, Maida Springer to ER, October 21, 1949, ERP.

191   "If successful": PM to ER, November 17, 1949.

191   "Please use your nicest": PM to ER, October 21, 1949, ERP.

191   During the campaign: PM to Dean Erwin H. Griswold, October 10, 1949, PMP.

191   "crowds at her nightly": Poston, "Miss Murray Delays Study at Harvard," *NYP.*

191   "a prestigious nonpartisan body": PM, *Song,* 281.

191   "I've waited years": Poston, "Miss Murray Delays Study at Harvard," *NYP.*

31. "I COULDN'T WAIT TO GIVE YOU ONE OF THE FIRST COPIES"

192   On March 26, 1949: "Murray-Wynn Marital Affair—Annulment Proceedings,"
      1943–49, PMP.
192   The impetus for the project: PM, *Song*, 283–93; Thelma Stevens had been work-
      ing for civil rights years before she hired Murray for the *States' Laws* project. See
      Thelma Stevens, interview by Bob Hall and Jacquelyn Hall, February 13, 1972,
      Interview G-0058, Southern Oral History Program, University of North Caro-
      lina, Chapel Hill.
192   "carry an intrinsic argument": PM, *Song*, 286.
192   "developed a ritual": Ibid.
192   She found solace: PM to ER, June 29, 1950, ERP.
193   "the best of Christian-Judaeo-Democratic": Ibid.
193   "beyond all doubt": Associated Press, "Statement on Korea," *NYT*, June 28, 1950.
193   "I think of you": PM to ER, June 29, 1950.
193   "influence over the Northern Koreans": ER, "My Day," July 1, 1950.
193   "the first effort": PM, comp. and ed., *States' Laws on Race and Color and Appen-
      dices: Containing International Documents, Federal Laws and Regulations, Local
      Ordinances and Charts* (Cincinnati: Women's Division of Christian Service,
      Board of Missions and Church Extension, Methodist Church, 1951), 6.
194   "to publish or distribute": Ibid., 18.
194   "I couldn't wait": PM to ER, March 8, 1951, ERP.
194   "the bible": PM, *Song*, 289.
194   "a primary source": Ibid., 288.
195   "Dear 'Mrs. Rovel'": PM to ER, March 26, 1951, ERP.
195   "nasty": Ibid.
195   "to take care": PM to ER, March 26, 1951, ERP.
195   "a sprig of lilacs": ER to PM, May 15, 1951, PMP.
195   "own health situation": PM to ER, March 26, 1951, ERP.
195   "I have known Miss Murray": ER to David Morse, June 14, 1951, PMP.
195   "I guess this just isn't": PM to ER, June 23, 1951, ER.
195   "that she had to quickly": Springer-Kemp, interview by author.

32. "I HAVE TO STAND OR FALL WITH THE PEOPLE WHO KNOW ME"

196   In March 1952: PM, *Song*, 294–98.
197   "had a penchant": Ibid., 271.
197   "affiliated with twenty-eight": William S. White, "McCarthy Says Miss Kenyon
      Helped 28 Red Front Groups: Tells Names," *NYT*, March 9, 1950.
197   "little people": Ibid.
197   "knowingly identified": Ibid.
197   "an unmitigated liar": Doris Greenberg, "Miss Kenyon Calls McCarthy a 'Liar':
      Denies Ties to Red Fronts and Terms Him Coward for Use of Congressional
      Immunity," *NYT*, March 9, 1950.
198   "to stick it out": PM, *Song*, 271.
198   In the state of Washington: Jane Sanders, *Cold War on the Campus: Academic Free-
      dom at the University of Washington, 1949–1964* (Seattle: University of Washington
      Press, 1979).
198   These attacks: See Ronald E. Magden, "The Schuddakopf Case, 1954–1958:
      Tacoma Public Schools and Anticommunism," *Pacific Northwest Quarterly* 89,
      no. 1 (Winter 1997–98): 4–11.

198 "if there was anything": PM to Messrs. Lloyd K. Garrison, Lester B. Granger, William H. Hastie, Elmer A. Carter, A. Phillip Randolph, Morris Milgram, Thurgood Marshall, Will Maslow, Miss Maslow, Miss Thelma Stevens, Dr. Caroline F. Ware and Mrs. Franklin D. Roosevelt, May 6, 1952, PMP.

198 "an outspoken critic": Ibid.

198 "knowingly joined": Ibid.

198 "infiltrated or were": Ibid.

198 "for the record": Ibid.

198 "a recommendation from someone": PM, *Song,* 296.

198 "that as a person": PM to Messrs. Lloyd K. Garrison et al., May 6, 1952.

199 "produce a casual reference": Ibid.

199 The May 14, 1951: U.S. House Committee on Un-American Activities, *Guide to Subversive Organizations and Publications* (Washington, DC: U.S. Government Printing Office, 1951).

199 "several years": ER to Milton R. Konvitz, [May?] 1952, ERP.

199 "qualifications": PM to Messrs. Lloyd K. Garrison et al., May 6, 1952.

199 "they felt they ought": Ibid.

199 "I share with you": Milton R. Konvitz to ER, May 7, 1952, ERP.

199 "the unhappy go-between": PM, *Song,* 297.

200 "think and to differ": ER, "Address to the Americans for Democratic Action Convention" (Washington, DC, April 2, 1950), ERP.

200 "The day I'm afraid": Ibid.

200 "If all of": ER, "My Day," March 11, 1950.

200 "absolutely furious": PM to Skipper [Caroline Ware], May 10, 1952, PMP.

200 "One has to go on": Ibid.

200 "exaggerated stories": William Worthy, "In Cloud-Cuckoo Land," *Crisis* 59 (April 1952): 226–30.

200 "race riots": Ibid.

200 "dishonest": Ibid.

201 "It was wonderful": PM to ER, May 9, 1952, ERP.

33. "I COULD WRITE IN PRIVACY WITHOUT INTERRUPTION"

205 "shadowy inference": PM, *Song,* 297.

205 "earliest and most enduring": Ibid., 298.

205 "the germ": Stephen Vincent Benét to PM, [October 1939?], PMP.

206 "do some more": Stephen Vincent Benét to PM, [1944?], PMP

206 "rolled a sheet": PM, *Song,* 298.

206 "I could write": Ibid., 299.

206 "dedicated to becoming": PM, journal, [1954?], PMP.

206 Together, they would occasionally: PM to Skipper [Caroline Ware], August 1, 1954, PMP.

206 The reputations: On the prejudice and discrimination Bayard Rustin suffered at the hands of white conservatives, as well as black civil rights leaders, because of his sexuality, see D'Emilio, *Lost Prophet,* 338–39.

207 She had been studying: For a discussion of Murray's review of the scientific literature, her correspondence with doctors, her personal notes, and her identity development vis-à-vis the social context of her life, see Drury, "'Experimentation on the Male Side.'"

207 Murray's family background: Ibid.

207 "the long way": ER, *On My Own,* 96.

207   "going through this pass": ER, "My Day," February 28, 1952.
207   "hated to leave": ER, "My Day," March 22, 1952.

34. "we consider you a member of the family"

208   "happy to have the picture": ER to PM, January 26, 1953, PMP.
208   "beautiful blue pool": Pauline F. Dame [and PM?] to Dear ———, August 19, 1952, PMP. Although Murray's copy of this document is marked as "letter from Pauline F. Dame," the format, font, and style strongly suggest that it was typed, cowritten, and edited by Murray.
209   "raising and training": Ibid.
209   "talked politics": Ibid.
209   "liberal civil rights record": PM, *Song,* 306.
209   "white plain marble": Pauline F. Dame [and PM?] to Dear ——— August 19, 1952.
209   "flat marker level": Ibid.
209   "little kiltie": Ibid.
210   "My Sallie gave birth": Ibid.
210   "It's not the best": PM to ER, June 6, 1954, ERP.

35. "i was deeply moved that you counted me among your close friends"

211   Although he pledged: "Text of Eisenhower Inaugural Address Pledging Search for Peace," *NYT,* January 21, 1953.
211   He had carried: PM, *Song,* 306.
211   That the new president: On Eisenhower's reluctance to criticize Joseph McCarthy or defend General George C. Marshall, whom McCarthy had attacked, see W. H. Lawrence, "Eisenhower Scores President on Reds: Supports McCarthy; In Tour of Wisconsin, General Asserts He Backs Senator's Aims Not His Methods," *NYT,* October 4, 1952.
211   Inside, Murray was mentioned: ER, "Some of My Best Friends Are Negro," *Ebony,* February 1953, 16–20, 22, 24–26.
211   "social equals": Ibid., 16.
211   "One of my finest": Ibid.
212   "I think there were times": Ibid.
212   "really close friends": Ibid.
212   "I howled": PM to ER, January 21, 1953, ERP.
212   "I had always thought": Ibid.
212   "I am glad": ER to PM, January 26, 1953, PMP.
212   "ran, gathered momentum": Eleanor Roosevelt II, *With Love, Aunt Eleanor: Stories from My Life with the First Lady of the World* (Petaluma, CA: Scrapbook Press), 78.
212   Malvina Thompson died: "Malvina Thompson Dies in Hospital, 61: Confidential Secretary to Mrs. Roosevelt 25 Years Served—in Albany and Washington," *NYT,* April 13, 1953.
213   "Her standards were high": ER, "My Day," April 14, 1953.
213   "I will miss her terribly": ER to PM, [April 1953?], ERP.

36. "i know how much this decision means to you"

214   "For those of us": PM to ER, June 1, 1954, ERP.
215   "I think I can": PM, letter to the editor, *NYT,* May 21, 1954.
215   "I could not let": PM to ER, June 1, 1954.

215   "I know how much": Ibid.
215   She was astonished: PM, *Song,* 255.
215   "in an inferior social: Quoted in PM, *Song,* 254. For the complete essay, see PM, "Should the Civil Rights Cases and *Plessy v. Ferguson* Be Overruled?," 1944, PMP.
215   "no legal precedents": PM, *Song,* 254.
215   "violence to the personality": Ibid.
215   Their experiments: On the Clarks, their research, and the *Brown* case, see Richard Kluger, "The Doll Man and Other Experts," in *Simple Justice* (New York: Knopf, 1976), 315–45, and Mamie K. Phipps Clark, "The Development of Consciousness of Self in Negro Pre-School Children" (master's thesis, Howard University, 1939).
216   "To separate them": *Brown v. Board of Education of Topeka et. al.,* 347 U.S. 483 (1954).
216   "rubbish": PM to ER, June 1, 1954, ERP.
216   "If legalities must be observed": Ibid.
216   "delighted": ER, "My Day," May 20, 1954.
216   "one of the arguments": Ibid.
216   "One can no longer": Ibid.
216   "I have been thinking": ER, "My Day," June 5, 1954.

37. "I CANNOT LIVE WITH FEAR"

218   Eventually, 214 witnesses: *Executive Sessions of the Senate Permanent Subcommittee on Investigations of the Committee on Government Operations,* 83rd Cong. 972 (1953) (introduction by Donald A. Ritchie, Senate Historical Office), Volume 1. Made public in 2003.
218   Hughes, who testified: *Executive Sessions of the Senate Permanent Subcommittee on Investigations of the Committee on Government Operations,* 83rd Cong. 972 (1953) (statement of Langston Hughes, American writer), vol. 2. Made public in 2003.
219   "undeviating follower": Ibid., 983.
219   "Goodbye Christ": After his Senate appearance, Hughes would avoid mention of "Goodbye Christ," which was published in the November-December 1932 issue of the *Negro Worker,* and "Put Another 'S' in the USA" (sometimes titled as "One More 'S' in the U.S.A."), which appeared in the *Daily Worker,* April 2, 1934. Both the *Negro Worker* and the *Daily Worker* were Communist-sponsored publications.
219   "older": *Executive Sessions of the Senate Permanent Subcommittee,* 83rd Cong. 991 (statement of Hughes).
219   "A portion of a poem": Ibid., 989.
219   "not very representative": Ibid., 992.
219   Cohn, a homosexual: For an example of Cohn's treatment of a gay male witness who was one of the most influential accounting professionals in the country, see *Executive Sessions of the Senate Permanent Subcommittee,* 83rd Cong. 411 (1953), (statement of Eric L. Kohler, consulting accountant), vol. 1. Made public in 2003.
220   The Harlem Suitcase: PM to ER, October 26, 1939, ERP.
220   "protest poetry": PM to Walter Lowenfels, September 14, 1967, PMP.
220   She had even considered: PM, *Song,* 88–89.
220   The New Jersey Anti-Communist League: "Jersey School Bars Dr. Bethune: Charge Links Her to Subversives; Meeting of Englewood Legion's Auxiliary Off to Let Negro Leader Clear Herself," *NYT,* April 25, 1952.
220   Dorothy Boulding Ferebee: See *Executive Sessions of the Senate Permanent Subcommittee on Investigations of the Committee on Government Operations,* 83rd Cong.

1298 (1953) (statement of Dorothy Boulding Ferebee, medical director, Howard University, and president, National Council of Negro Women), vol. 2. Made public in 2003.

220   That Caroline Ware: Anne Firor Scott, ed., *Pauli Murray and Caroline Ware: Forty Years of Letters in Black and White* (Chapel Hill: University of North Carolina Press, 2006), 75.

220   "Most of these investigations": ER, "My Day," June 12, 1954.

220   "If we continue": ER, "My Day," June 4, 1954.

220   "Mary McLeod Bethune": ER, "My Day," May 3, 1952.

220   "no question": ER, "My Day," May 28, 1954.

221   The fear fostered by: ER, "My Day," August 9, 1952.

221   "I have always thought": ER, "My Day," October 29, 1947.

221   "like garbage": PM to Pauline Redmond Coggs, June 5, 1954, ERP.

221   "derogatory material": Ibid.

221   "As a serum": PM to Ralph Bunche, June 10, 1954, PMP.

221   One of her first: Ibid.

221   "operatives": PM to Pauline Redmond Coggs, June 5, 1954.

221   "behind one's back": Ibid.

221   "personal history": Ibid.

221   "an experimental lobotomy": Ibid.

221   "I cannot live": Ibid.

221   Murray and Coggs had made: Pauline Redmond Coggs, interview by author, Milwaukee, WI, February 28, 1996.

221   "I call it a frightened": PM to Pauline Redmond Coggs, June 5, 1954.

222   "Since the Supreme Court": PM to ER, June 6, 1954, ERP.

38. "SOME FEAR-MONGERS MAY FEEL THAT EVEN PRESIDENT EISENHOWER MIGHT BE A SECURITY RISK"

223   "There appears to be": PM to ER, June 30, 1954, ERP.

223   "flesh was literally shaking": PM to Lillian Smith, June 11, 1954, PMP.

223   "an over-active thyroid": PM to Thelma Stevens, June 12, 1954, PMP.

224   "'a panty-waist'": PM to ER, June 13, 1954, PMP.

224   "a blessing": PM to Thelma Stevens, June 12, 1945.

224   "But how hard it is": Lillian Eugenia Smith, *The Journey* (Cleveland: World, 1954), 85; quoted in PM to Pauline Redmond Coggs, June 5, 1954, PMP.

224   "well and strong": ER to PM, June 15, 1954, PMP.

224   "lost a great deal": PM to ER, June 17, 1954, PMP.

224   "drop in": ER to PM, June 19, 1954, PMP.

224   Like Murray, ER: ER to Lillian Smith, July 24, 1954, Lillian Smith Papers, Hargrett Rare Books and Manuscript Library, University of Georgia.

224   "such a request": Helen Gandy to PM, June 10, 1954, U.S. Department of Justice, FBI, Subject File: Anna Pauline Murray (140-0-3505).

225   According to an internal office: Memorandum, L. N. Conroy to Mr. A. Rosen, June 10, 1954, U.S. Department of Justice, FBI, Subject File: Anna Pauline Murray (140-0-3505).

225   "front men": PM to ER, June 30, 1954, ERP.

225   "received less housing": Ibid.

226   "ridiculous": Ibid.

226   Murray believed: Coggs, interview by author.

226 "behavior, activities": Dwight D. Eisenhower, "Executive Order 10450—Security Requirements for Government Employment," Exec. Order No. 10450, 18 Federal Register, 2489 (April 27, 1953).

226 "Sexual perversion": Ibid.

226 Thus, homosexuals: For an in-depth discussion, see David K. Johnson, *The Lavender Scare: The Cold War Persecution of Gays and Lesbians in the Federal Government* (Chicago: University of Chicago Press, 2004), and Lillian Faderman, *Odd Girls and Twilight Lovers: A History of Lesbian Life in Twentieth-Century America* (New York: Penguin, 1992), 139–58.

226 "illness, including any mental condition": Dwight D. Eisenhower, "Executive Order 10450—Security Requirements for Government Employment."

227 "women's achievements": ER, "My Day," June 19, 1954.

227 "wished so much": Ibid.

39. "what i have to say now is *entirely personal*"

228 Word of ER's presence: PM to ER, July 4, 1954, ERP.

228 "like a little happy elf": Ibid.

228 "PERSONAL AND CONFIDENTIAL": Ibid.

229 Halfway through: Powell, interview by author.

229 "What I have to say": PM to ER, July 4, 1954.

230 What is known: ER, *This Is My Story,* 256–59.

230 "Griselda moods": Ibid., 149. For the perspectives of ER's biographers on her experience of depression, see Cook, *ER,* 1:235; Cook, *ER,* 2:269; Goodwin, *No Ordinary Time,* 89–95; Joseph P. Lash, *A World of Love: Eleanor Roosevelt and Her Friends, 1943–1962* (New York: Doubleday, 1984), 55–56; and Lash, *Eleanor and Franklin,* 237–38.

230 "prayerfully": PM to ER, July 4, 1954.

230 "You have one idea": ER to PM, July 7, 1954, PMP.

231 "can now well afford": PM to Channing Tobias, July 28, 1954, PMP.

40. "what a wonderful weekend it was"

232 "indomitable courage": PM, *Song,* 293.

232 "example": Ibid.

232 "laugh-and-cry": PM to Skipper [Caroline Ware], July 21, 1954, PMP.

233 "If it would not": PM to ER, July 10, 1954, ERP.

233 ER welcomed: ER to PM, July 13, 1954, PMP.

233 On Friday, October 15, 1954: PM, *Song,* 291–93.

233 The first reports: This description of Hurricane Hazel is drawn from the Associated Press, "Hurricane Smashes Haiti Cities: Toll Is Heavy; Storm Moves North," *NYT,* October 14, 1954; "Carolina Beaches Ravaged by Hazel: 6 Dead, Houses Washed Away," *NYT,* October 16, 1954; "Virginia Hard Hit," *NYT,* October 16, 1954; "Old Mount Vernon Tree Is Added to Hazel's Toll," *NYT,* October 21, 1954; Wayne Phillips, "100-Mile Wind Here Leaves Three Dead: Cottages and Church Steeple Are Victims of Hurricane's Battering Winds," *NYT,* October 16, 1954; Russell Porter, "Death Toll Is 39: Scores Hurt, Thousands Homeless," *NYT,* October 16, 1954; and William R. Conklin, "Hurricane's Toll Increases to 118," *NYT,* October 17, 1954.

233 "stepped on a live wire": Porter, "Death Toll Is 39," *NYT.*

233 "swept over its": Phillips, "100-Mile Wind Here Leaves Three Dead," *NYT.*

233   "sped along the parkways": PM, *Song,* 291.

233   "Hurry up, girls": Ibid.

234   She read excerpts: Ibid., 292.

234   "apparition": Ibid.

234   "towel-turbaned": Ibid.

234   "There's a swimming pool": Ibid., 293.

234   "came out and stared": Ibid.

234   Later, over lunch: Ibid.

234   "what a wonderful weekend": PM to ER, October 25, 1954, ERP.

41. "YOU MIGHT . . . COMMENT FROM THE SPECIAL WOMAN'S ANGLE"

235   "was very disturbed": PM to Skipper [Caroline Ware], October 29, 1954, PMP.

235   "something was wrong: Ibid.

235   "budgetary considerations": National Committee Against Discrimination in Housing, "Fact Sheet on Case of Dr. Frank S. Horne," [August 1955?], ERP. In addition to the fact sheet, Murray's packet to ER included clippings of Charles Abrams, "Segregation, Housing, and the Horne Case," *Reporter* 13, no. 5 (October 6, 1955), 30–33; Ted Poston, "CSC Ignored Horne's Backers on Firing," *NYP,* November 22, 1955; and "'Freeze' On in Racial Housing Posts—11 Jobs Vacant," *NYP,* November 25, 1955.

235   Morrow and Horne were replaced: Poston, "CSC Ignored Horne's Backers on Firing," *NYP.*

235   "you might": PM to ER, September 5, 1955, ERP. To this letter, Murray attached "Memorandum on Corienne R. Morrow," August 25, 1955, which described Morrow's background and career, in addition to a press release about the Horne-Morrow case issued by the National Urban League, August 25, 1955, ERP.

236   "one of the top-level": PM to ER, September 5, 1955.

236   "the outlook": Ibid.

236   Joining a chorus: See Abrams, "Segregation, Housing, and the Horne Case," *Reporter;* Barrow Lyons, "Patronage Hangover," *Washington Post and Times Herald,* August 14, 1955; Charles Abrams, "Discrimination in Housing: Reinstatement of Racial Relations Service Officials Is Asked," *NYT,* August 23, 1955; and "Reinstate Horne, Urban League Asks," *Washington Post and Times Herald,* August 26, 1955.

236   "There are very few": ER, "My Day," August 17, 1955.

236   "budgetary reasons": Ibid.

236   "to go slow": Ibid.

236   "Dr. Horne's case": ER, "My Day," September 30, 1955.

236   Encouraged by ER's advocacy: PM to ER, October 23, 1955, ERP.

236   The pressure forced: "HHFA Aide Wins Fight on Firing," *Washington Post and Times Herald,* November 3, 1955.

237   "You're a real darling": PM to ER, October 3, 1955, ERP.

42. "I CANNOT AFFORD TO BE A PIKER"

238   "To Mrs. Roosevelt": PM, inscription on the back of photograph, December 3, 1955, ERP.

239   "last ceremonial": PM, *Song,* 303.

239   "I don't think": Ibid.

239   "the psalms": Ibid., 304.

239   "defend her": Ibid. Only masculine pronouns appear in the original text.
239   "burial undergarments": Ibid.
239   "slipped away peacefully": Ibid.
239   "fortitude": PM to ER, November 6, 1955, ERP.
240   After the burial: Ibid.
240   "even more precious": Ibid.
240   "an Alice-blue": Ibid.
240   "chased": Ibid.
240   "If Mrs. R. has": Ibid.
240   "You are very brave": ER to PM, December 10, 1955, PMP.
240   As she walked: PM to Marian MacDowell, November 10, 1955, MacDowell Colony Papers, Manuscript Division, Library of Congress.
240   "marvelous tradition": PM to ER, November 6, 1955.
240   "little snapshot": PM to ER, December 5, 1955, ERP.
241   "It's my most": PM to ER, December 16, 1955, ERP.
241   "delightful": ER to PM, December 12, 1955, PMP.
241   After the Civil Service: "HHFA Aide Restored to Duty, Fired," *Washington Post and Times Herald,* November 16, 1955.
241   "heart": PM to ER, December 3, 1955, ERP.
241   "blond, blue-eyed": PM, *Song,* 14.
241   "This is an inside story": PM to ER, December 16, 1955.
241   "If the rest": ER to PM, December 27, 1955, PMP.
241   "Did I ever tell you": PM to ER, December 16, 1955.

43. "THERE APPEARS TO BE A CLEAVAGE"

245   "Civil rights": PM, *Song,* 308.
246   The general assembly: John D. Morris, "Virginia Passes Integration Curb: Senate Approves Bill, 38 to 1," *NYT,* December 4, 1955.
246   Louisiana legislators: "Ban on Mixed Athletic Events Finally Passed," *Baton Rouge Morning Advocate,* July 6, 1956.
246   Mississippi governor: "Segregation Pressed: Governor of Mississippi Says Schools Will Not Integrate," *NYT,* September 13, 1956, and "Coleman School View: Mississippi's Governor Says Closings Are Possible," *NYT,* October 6, 1958.
246   On March 12: *Southern Manifesto on Integration,* 102 Cong. Rec. 4459-4460 (1956) (statement of Sen. Walter F. George).
246   "a clear abuse": Ibid.
246   "parallels": PM to Bobby [Corienne R. Morrow], January 24, 1956, PMP.
246   "*Proud Shoes* is": Ibid.
246   "sad but true": ER to PM, January 26, 1956, PMP.
246   "to proceed gradually": "Favors Integration," *Charleston (SC) News and Courier,* February 8, 1956.
247   The governor's relations: Averill Harriman and Adlai Stevenson, "Comments by Harriman and Stevenson on Integration: 'Ultimate' Test Seen," *NYT,* February 13, 1956, and Lawrence E. Davies, "Stevenson Urges Candidates Ban Integration Issue: Sees No Greater Disservice Than Exploiting Tension," *NYT,* February 13, 1956.
247   Incensed by Stevenson's: "Wilkins Scores Stevenson," *NYT,* February 13, 1956.
247   "To Negro Americans": Roy Wilkins, *Standing Fast: The Autobiography of Roy Wilkins* (New York: Viking, 1982), 231.

247 "running away": A. H. Raskin, "Meany Chides Candidate for 'Running Away' on Segregation: Meany Censures Stevenson Stand Also," *NYT,* February 15, 1956.

247 Eager to de-escalate: "Mrs. FDR Explains Adlai's 'Moderation,'" *Philadelphia AA,* August 18, 1956.

247 "The record": ER, "My Day," February 17, 1956.

247 "mores faster than people": PM, *Song,* 310.

247 "secondary to winning": Ibid., 309.

247 "Dear Mrs. Roosevelt": PM to ER, February 16, 1956, ERP.

248 "close association": Ibid.

248 "My dear Pauli": PM to ER, February 22, 1956, PMP.

249 "Much as I love": PM to Bobby [Corienne R. Morrow], January 24, 1956. The title of ER's article was actually "Some of My Best Friends Are Negro," and not "Negroes" as Murray wrote to Corienne Morrow.

249 "She is a regular": Ibid.

250 "encouragement and understanding": PM to ER, July 13, 1956, ERP.

250 "troubles": PM to ER, April 12, 1956, ERP.

250 "providential": PM to ER, May 21, 1956, ERP.

250 "I am so sorry": ER to PM, May 22, 156, PMP.

250 "clung to life": PM, *Song,* 305.

250 "to the typewriter": Ibid.

250 "Cut adrift": Ibid.

44. "YOU'RE A BIT OF A FIREBRAND YOURSELF"

251 "not one student": ER, "My Day," March 12, 1956.

251 In Montgomery: "Buses Boycotted over Race Issue: Montgomery, Ala., Negroes Protest Woman's Arrest for Defying Segregation," *NYT,* December 6, 1955.

251 In Tuscaloosa: "Negro Student Admitted," *NYT,* February 1, 1956.

251 Lucy's first day: "Miss Lucy Goes to College," *NYT,* February 6, 1956, and E. Culpepper Clark, *The Schoolhouse Door: Segregation's Last Stand at the University of Alabama* (New York: Oxford University Press, 1993).

252 "Keep 'Bama White": Clark, *The Schoolhouse Door,* 62–68.

252 "Hey, hey": Wayne Phillips, "Miss Lucy's Education: Segregation Test Case," *NYT,* February 12, 1956.

252 On Monday: Phillips, "Miss Lucy's Education," *NYT.*

252 "Let's kill her!": Tiya Miles, "Autherine Lucy Foster," in *Black Women in America: An Historical Encyclopedia,* ed. Darlene Clark Hine (New York: Carlson, 1993), 448.

252 When university officials: Peter Kihss, "Negro Co-ed Is Suspended to Curb Alabama Clashes," *NYT,* Feburary 7, 1956.

252 She invited Rosa Parks: ER, "My Day," May 14, 1956.

252 "They must have known": "Students Praised for Lucy Support: Mrs. Roosevelt Cites 500 Who 'Dared' to Sign Petition at University of Alabama," *NYT,* March 25, 1956.

252 "the Negroes' right": "Civil Rights Lag Scored at Rally: Speakers in Garden Assail Congress and Political Leaders on Progress," *NYT,* May 25, 1956.

252 Notwithstanding the turmoil: Virginia Foster Durr, *Outside the Magic Circle: The Autobiography of Virginia Foster Durr,* ed., Hollinger F. Barnard (Tuscaloosa: University of Alabama Press, 1985), 279–80, 291.

252 "courage": PM to Dr. [Omer] Carmichael, September 11, 1956, PMP.

253 "outstandingly good job": ER, "My Day," September 15, 1956.
253 Murray handed: PM to ER, September 18, 1956, ERP.
253 "I am very happy": ER to PM, September 24, 1956, PMP.
253 ER promised: ER to PM, October 8, 1956, and ER to PM, September 24, 1956, PMP.
253 Black voters: Leo Egan, "Negro Shift Aids Maryland G.O.P.: Trend in Baltimore Is More Definite Than Elsewhere," *NYT,* October 12, 1956, and Layhmond Robinson Jr., "Democrats Face Negro Vote Loss: A Sizable Switch to G.O.P. Could Hurt," *NYT,* November 2, 1956.
253 "We're for Eisenhower": *PC,* November 3, 1956.
253 "We like both Ike": *Philadelphia AA,* October 27, 1956.
253 ER campaigned: Allida M. Black, *Casting Her Own Shadow: Eleanor Roosevelt and the Shaping of a Postwar Liberalism* (New York: Columbia University Press, 1996), 109–15, presents an analysis of ER's strategy along with a discussion of the views of earlier historians and biographers.
253 "What moderation": "Mrs. FDR Explains Adlai's Moderation," *Philadelphia AA.*
253 In an effort to keep: Black, *Casting Her Own Shadow,* 113–14.
253 "I do not think": "Mrs. FDR Explains Adlai's Moderation," *Philadelphia AA.*
254 Only after a soul-searching: PM, *Song,* 310.
254 When Powell announced: Russell Baker, "Powell, Switching, Backs Eisenhower," *NYT,* October 12, 1956.
254 "the moral leadership": PM to Adlai Stevenson, October 17, 1956, ERP.
254 "egghead": ER, "My Day," December 12, 1953.
254 "One of the reasons": PM to ER, November 1, 1956, ERP.

45. "YOU CAUGHT THE FEELING I HAD IN MIND"

255 "the courage": ER, "My Day," October 23, 1956.
255 "a gallant book": Henrietta Buckmaster, "Indomitable Family," a review of *Proud Shoes* by PM, *NYT,* October 21, 1956.
255 "loved": Langston Hughes to PM, October 20, 1956, PMP.
255 "I have finished": ER to PM, October 8, 1956, ERP.
256 For its title: PM, introduction to new edition of *Proud Shoes* (New York: Harper & Row, 1978), viii.
256 "blue-eyed": PM, *Proud Shoes* (New York: Harper & Row, 1956), 65.
256 Having grown up: PM, introduction to *Proud Shoes* (1978), vii.
256 "past associations": PM, *Song,* 294.
257 Murray's personal identification: PM, introduction to *Proud Shoes* (1978), xiv. For an extended discussion of identity as a theme in *Proud Shoes,* see Darlene O'Dell, "Face of the Tombstones," in *Sites of Memory: The Autobiographies of Katharine Du Pre Lumpkin, Lillian Smith, and Pauli Murray* (Charlottesville: University Press of Virginia, 2001), 104–43. See also Jean M. Humez, "Pauli Murray's Histories of Loyalty and Revolt," *Black American Literature Forum* 24, no. 2 (1990): 315–55.
257 "What a story!": J. Saunders Redding's blurb appeared on the jacket of the 1956 edition. An expanded version appears on the jacket of the 1978 edition.
257 "You have done": Quoted in PM to ER, July 13, 1956, ERP. An excerpt of Lillian Smith's telegram appeared as a blurb on the book jacket of the 1956 edition.
257 "effective use": Byron R. Bryant, "The New Books," a review of *Proud Shoes* by PM, *San Francisco Chronicle,* December 9, 1956.

257 "told with an uncanny": Margot Jackson, "A Negro Writes of Civil War, Slavery," a review of *Proud Shoes* by PM, *Akron Beacon Journal,* October 12, 1956.

257 "a Civil War story": Ted Poston, "A Truly American Family," a review of *Proud Shoes* by PM, *NYP,* October 21, 1956.

257 "Outstanding Books of 1956": *New York Herald Tribune,* December 2, 1956.

257 "100 copies per week": PM to Skipper [Caroline Ware], December 2, 1956, PMP.

257 "anyone interested": ER, "My Day," October 23, 1956.

257 "intangibles": PM, *Proud Shoes,* (1956), 246.

258 "They had little": Ibid., 246–47.

258 "Your review": PM to ER, [October 1956?], ERP.

258 "The cause for": Jane Speights, "Only Half Picture Painted: Serves No Useful Purpose," a review of *Proud Shoes* by PM, *Clarion-Ledger and Jackson Daily News,* October 14, 1956.

258 "objectivity": Frank Hains to Ramona Herdman, October 15, 1956, ERP.

258 "It's amazing": PM to ER, [October 1956?].

46. "I NEVER CEASE TO MARVEL AT THE GREATNESS OF YOUR HUMANITY"

259 "professional opportunity": PM, *Song,* 311.

260 "It's too bad": PM to Skipper [Caroline Ware], December 2, 1956, PMP.

260 "Aunt Pauli": Ibid.

260 Seated around: Ibid.

260 "emptying the ashtrays": PM to ER, December 5, 1956, ERP.

260 "bits of cookies": PM to Skipper [Caroline Ware], December 2, 1956.

260 "eyes popped": Ibid.

260 "calmly munching": Ibid.

261 "I never cease": PM to ER, December 5, 1956.

261 "I shall never forget": Ibid.

261 "One for my billfold": Ibid.

261 "By contact": Ibid.

47. "OUR FRIENDSHIP PRODUCED SPARKS OF SHEER JOY"

262 "sandlot player": PM, *Song,* 311.

262 "triple minority": Ibid., 312.

262 "corporate mergers": Ibid.

262 "earned the right": PM to Skipper [Caroline Ware], December 2, 1956.

263 "the totem pole": Ibid.

263 "I've been so busy": PM to ER, January 20, 1957, ERP.

263 "was rumored": PM, *Song,* 313.

263 "awkwardness": Ibid.

263 "essence of courtesy": Ibid.

263 "staring foolishly": Ibid., 314.

263 "grindstone": Ibid., 312.

263 Murray found an ally: For Murray's characterization of this relationship, see PM, "To Those Who Loved Irene Barlow," March 7, 1973–March 13, 1973, PMP, and PM, "What I Learned from Irene Barlow," March 12, 1973, PMP.

263 "the managing partner": Ibid., 314.

263 "pronounced to rhyme": PM, *Song,* 314.

263 "threadbare hand-me-down": Ibid., 315.

264   Consequently, the clerical staff: PM, interview by Blanche Wiesen Cook, October 19, 1983.
264   "job kept her": PM, *Song,* 314–15.
264   "spasms of laughter": Ibid., 316.
264   "Now don't get up": Ibid.
264   "Oh, blast": Ibid.
264   "shot out of a cannon": PM, "What I Learned from Irene Barlow."
264   "firm confidences": Ibid.
264   "less the rough diamond": Ibid.
264   "our friendship produced": PM, *Song,* 316.
264   "relationship a special quality": Ibid.
264   She likened their bond: PM, "What I Learned from Irene Barlow."
264   "strong-willed": Ibid.
264   "I think she loved": Ibid.
265   This relationship proved: PM, journal, June 24, 1973, PMP.
265   "neglected clothing": PM, "What I Learned from Irene Barlow."
265   "gift of this friendship": PM, journal, September 3, 1973, PMP.

48. "YOU CAN SAY WE HAD A FRIENDLY CONVERSATION, BUT WE DIFFER"

266   ER arrived: ER, "My Day," March 26, 1957.
266   From Casablanca: ER, "My Day," March 27–30, 1957; April 1–6, 8–11, 1957.
267   "a beautiful orange": ER, "My Day," April 9, 1957.
267   The longing of Moroccan: ER, "My Day," April 6, 1957.
267   This interest: PM, *Song,* 318, and Yevette Richards, *Maida Springer: Pan-Africanist and International Labor Leader* (Pittsburgh: University of Pittsburgh Press, 2000), 106, 206.
267   She took Maureen Corr: ER, "My Day," September 10, 1957.
267   "wanted to get as far": ER, *On My Own* (New York: Harper & Brothers, 1958), 198.
267   "under local anesthesia": A. David Gurewitsch, *Eleanor Roosevelt: Her Day; A Personal Album* (New York: Quadrangle/New York Times Book Co., 1974), 139.
268   "flared up": ER, "My Day," October 8, 1957.
268   "had a friendly conversation": ER, "My Day," October 5, 1957.
268   "street-cleaning": ER, *On My Own,* 199.
268   "I think I should die": Ibid., 193.

49. "THE CHIPS ARE REALLY DOWN IN LITTLE ROCK"

269   White supremacists: Daisy Bates, *The Long Shadow of Little Rock: A Memoir* (New York: David McKay, 1962), 61.
270   "blood will run": Ibid.
270   "It will be easier": Ibid., 63.
270   Fearing the worst: Ibid., 64–65.
270   The following morning: Ibid., 73.
270   A woman spat: Ibid., 75.
270   The guardsmen: Ibid., 71, 74.
270   "out of place": PM, *Song,* 39.
270   "too frightened to scream": Ibid., 38.
270   On September 24: Anthony Lewis, "President Sends Troops to Little Rock, Federalizes Arkansas National Guard," *NYT,* September 25, 1957, and W. H. Lawrence,

"Eisenhower 'Disappointed' by Impasse at Little Rock," *NYT,* September 20, 1957.

271 "patience and forbearance": John Jasper, "Ike's 'Be Patient' Speech 'Shocking': Was He so Poorly Informed?," *Philadelphia AA,* May 24, 1958, and "No Time for Patience," *AA,* June 21, 1958, national edition.

271 "mob rule": Anthony Lewis, "President Sends Troops to Little Rock," *NYT.*

271 "How can they draw": Louis S. Lomax, "Pupils Want Mrs. Bates Included," *Philadelphia AA,* June 7, 1958.

271 "Mrs. Bates and the nine": Ibid.

271 "Mrs. Bates is": Ibid.

272 "Just as a baseball": PM to Spingarn Award Committee, NAACP, May 30, 1958, PMP.

272 The stories about: See Louis S. Lomax, "Pupils Want Mrs. Bates Included"; "9 Spurn Spingarn: Pupils Want Mrs. Bates Included," *AA,* June 7, 1958, national edition; "Little Rock Students Reject NAACP Award Because Mrs. Bates Was Ignored," *PC,* June 7, 1968; and "Ten Spingarn Medals," June 28, 1958, *AA* National Edition.

272 In June 1958: Milton Bracker, "Little Rock Nine Get Racial Honor: Eight from School Join Girl Here as Harriman Hails Them at Union's Fete," *NYT,* June 13, 1958; Milton Bracker, "Official Here Hails Little Rock 9 as Crusaders for Equal Rights," *NYT,* June 15, 1958; "Busy Schedule for Little Rock Nine in New York City," *Baltimore AA,* June 14, 1958; and "Little Rock 9 see 'Jamaica,' Meet Stars," *Philadelphia AA,* June 21, 1958.

272 "see every movement": PM to ER, June 16, 1958, ERP.

273 Fourteen-year-old: This description of the Little Rock Nine and Daisy Bates is drawn from Ted Poston's series "Nine Kids Who Dared," *NYP,* October 20–November 1, 1957, and "A Woman Who Dared: Mrs. Daisy Bates," *NYP,* November 3, 1957, which Murray read and shared with ER. Murray and Poston had been friends since the 1930s, and she put great stock in his perspective. On Poston's contributions as a journalist, see Kathleen A. Hauke, *Ted Poston: Pioneer American Journalist* (Athens: University of Georgia Press, 2000).

273 The audience responded: PM to Dr. [Channing] Tobias, July 4, 1958, PMP.

273 Murray managed: PM to ER, June 16, 1958.

273 "a perfectly mad": Ibid.

273 "a catchy pseudonym": Ibid.

273 Murray sent a ten-dollar: PM to Mr. [L. C.] Bates, *PC,* June 28, 1958, and PM to Mr. [Robert M.] Ratcliffe, *PC,* June 28, 1958.

273 "The chips are": PM to ER, June 16, 1958.

273 "for an advertising space": ER to Gentlemen [*Arkansas State Press*], June 21, 1958, ERP.

274 "This group has made": ER, "My Day," June 24, 1958.

274 ER condemned: ER, "My Day," August 23, 1958.

274 "I think instead": Ibid.

274 "the world has changed": ER, "My Day," August 4, 1958.

274 "The old doctrine": Ibid.

274 On June 21, 1958: Clifton Wells, "School Board Granted Delay of 2½ Years: Little Rock Gets Stay on Schools," *Washington Post and Times Herald,* June 22, 1958.

274 "a clear national policy": Joseph A. Loftus, "Negro Leaders Confer with President

and Rogers at White House: 4 Negro Leaders See Eisenhower" *NYT,* June 24, 1958, and "That White House Conference," *PC,* July 5, 1958.

274   "economic resources": PM to Dr. [Channing] Tobias, July 4, 1958.

50. "DISCRIMINATION DOES SOMETHING INTANGIBLE AND HARMFUL"

276   His recent projects: Murray enclosed the following articles about Concord Park and Greenbelt Knoll with PM to ER, January 20, 1957, ERP: "Democracy Comes to the Suburbs," *Ebony,* February 1957, 17; "Study Shows Both Races Happy in Mixed Community," *Ebony,* February 1957, 18–19, and "Quakers, Negroes, Jews Cooperated in Raising Capital," *Ebony,* February 1957, 20–22.

276   In fact, Milgram: Morris Milgram, introduction to *Dark Testament and Other Poems,* by PM (Norwalk, CT: Silvermine, 1970), 4–5. See also the dedication and introduction to *Good Neighborhood: The Challenge of Open Housing* by Morris Milgram (New York: Norton, 1977), 5, 11–15.

277   "sometime soon": ER to PM, January 28, 1957.

277   MCD was a for-profit: On Milgram, MCD, and related projects, see Morris Milgram, "Pioneer in Integrated Housing," interview by Mary Jo Deering, July 21, 1976, Oral History Program, George Washington University Library, Washington, DC, and Milgram, *Good Neighborhood.*

277   "I am sure that": ER, "My Day," October 20, 1958.

277   ER had seen him: ER, "My Day," September 12, 1958.

277   "I can think of nothing": ER, "My Day," October 20, 1958.

278   Although he would: Harry Belafonte, *My Song* (New York: Knopf, 2011), 191–93.

278   "thanked her profusely": Ibid., 192.

278   "walking away from a battle": Ibid.

278   "Now I am waiting": ER, "My Day," July 15, 1958.

278   "This play has been": ER, "My Day," May 2, 1959.

51. "THERE ARE TIMES WHEN A LEGAL BRIEF IS INADEQUATE"

279   The first, which was detailed: Ted Poston, "A Story of Two Little Boys in Carolina," *NYP,* November 10, 1958. For James Thompson's account, see " 'The Kissing Case' and the Lives It Shattered," *StoryCorps,* National Public Radio, April 29, 2011; see also Conrad Lynn, "The Kissing Case," in *There Is a Fountain* (Westport, CT: Lawrence Hill, 1979), 141–57.

279   "put a stop": Lynn, *There Is a Fountain,* 156.

279   The second incident: Howard Smead, *Blood Justice: The Lynching of Mack Charles Parker* (New York: Oxford University Press, 1988).

280   "What made the recent": ER, "My Day," June 17, 1959.

280   The chance of a fair: Smead, *Blood Justice,* 19–21.

280   "The cornered and trapped": See PM, "For Mack C. Parker," in *Dark Testament,* 39.

280   "that most difficult": See PM, "Collect for Poplarville," in *Dark Testament,* 38.

280   "Dark Testament": PM, "Dark Testament," in *Dark Testament,* 12–27, and PM, "Psalm of Deliverance," in *Dark Testament,* 41–47.

280   "strong and stirring": ER to PM, June 2, 1959, ERP.

280   "There are times": PM to ER, May 6, 1959, PMP.

281   "the 'shape of things' ": PM, "Benét and Cullen—Poets Who Died Young," February 2, 1946, PMP.

281   She reviewed: Martin Luther King Jr. to Marie Rodell, November 17, 1957, MLK

Papers. The contract was probably for King's first book, *Stride Toward Freedom: The Montgomery Story* (New York: Harper & Row, 1958).

281   Murray favored: The summary attached to PM to ER, February 23, 1959, was a typewritten copy of Anthony Lewis, "Integration Plan Offered in South," *NYT,* February 16, 1959, ERP.

281   "If you would use": PM to Senator [Lyndon Baines] Johnson, February 23, 1959, PMP.

52. "THAT GRANDDAUGHTER MUST BE A CHIP OFF THE VENERABLE BLOCK"

282   It amused ER: ER, "My Day," May 4, 1959.

282   An avid reader: ER, "My Day," March 23, 1959.

283   ER's reading material: Ibid.

283   "sapphire blue": ER, "My Day," April 6, 1959.

283   "special brilliance": ER, "My Day," April 15, 1959.

283   "fountains and the benches": ER, "My Day," April 16, 1959.

283   "close watch": Hal Cooper, "But Even She Gets Tired," *Washington Post and Times Herald,* April 8, 1959.

283   "People forget": Ibid.

283   On more than one: Ibid.

283   "awkward": Ibid.

283   Murray giggled: PM to ER, April 21, 1959, ERP.

284   "It is not yet clear": Ibid.

284   "a former YWCA gal": PM to ER, February 23, 1959, ERP.

284   Third, ER had close: Roger Streitmatter, *Empty Without You: The Intimate Letters of Eleanor Roosevelt and Lorena Hickok* (New York: Free Press, 1998); Kristie Miller, "Esther Everett Lape," in *The Eleanor Roosevelt Encyclopedia,* ed. Beasley, Shuman, and Beasley, 301–4; and Roger Streitmatter, "Elizabeth Fisher Read," in ibid., 429–31.

284   A week earlier: Homer Bigart, "Employees Strike at Six Hospitals: Service Goes On," *NYT,* May 9, 1959.

285   "all economic issues": PM to ER, June 3, 1959.

285   "It seems to me": ER, "My Day," May 13, 1959.

53. "NOTHING I HAD READ OR HEARD PREPARED ME"

289   Late in the fall: PM, *Song,* 318.

289   Even Howard University: J. Clay Smith Jr., "Appendix B: Pioneering Facts About Black Women Lawyers and Law Teachers," in *Rebels in Law: Voices in History of Black Women Lawyers* (Ann Arbor: University of Michigan Press, 2000), 278.

290   "a desk lawyer": PM, *Song,* 318.

290   Springer's work: Ibid., and Yevette Richards, *Maida Springer: Pan-Africanist and International Labor Leader* (Pittsburgh: University of Pittsburgh Press, 2000), 106, 206–7.

290   In addition to her: PM, *Song,* 318.

290   "Nothing I had read": Ibid., 321.

290   While the countryside: Ibid., 323.

291   Murray suffered: Ibid., 324.

291   "three times a day": Ibid., 323.

291   "cut his hair short": PM, travelogue and progress report to family and friends, July 10, 1962, PMP.

291 "entrenched custom": PM, *Song,* 324.

291 "an angry-looking gash": Ibid., 325.

291 "dignity and lack of obsequiousness": Ibid., 324.

291 "politically controversial": Ibid., 334.

292 "with bright-blue covers": Ibid., 335.

292 She adopted an American-style: Ibid., 335–37.

292 "switched from English": Ibid., 336.

292 "We used to accept": Ibid., 338.

54. "IT IS A BIT OF A PEST TO HAVE TO KEEP STILL"

294 Murray saw these sit-ins: PM, *Song,* 200.

294 "Heed Their Rising Voices": "Heed Their Rising Voices," advertisement, *NYT,* March 29, 1960.

294 She criticized: ER, "My Day," October 28, 1960.

294 She applauded: ER, "My Day," February 19, 1960.

294 Two years earlier: Black, *Casting Her Own Shadow,* 117–19.

294 "If I blew up": "Mrs. Roosevelt Addresses Mixed Group Despite Telephone Bomb Threat," *Ocala Star-Banner,* March 15, 1960.

294 She had always loved: Cook, *ER,* 1:399, 473.

294 Not surprisingly: "Professor Roosevelt," *NYT,* October 5, 1959.

295 "I managed to get": ER to PM, April 11, 1960, PMP.

295 The governor: "Stevenson Avers He'd Still Accept: Telegram to Mrs. Roosevelt Expresses Willingness to Run If He Is Drafted," *NYT,* June 12, 1960, and "Stevenson Seen Ready to Approve Draft Move: Stevenson Seen Accepting Draft," *Washington Post, Times Herald,* June 12, 1960.

295 Yet she did not believe: Black, *Casting Her Own Shadow,* 191.

295 She finally agreed: Douglas Cornell, "Kennedy, Mrs. FDR Make Peace: Nominee Scores Senate Version of Aged-Care Plan," *Washington Post, Times Herald,* August 15, 1960.

295 Sally, Nina's younger sister: "John Roosevelt's Daughter, 13, Dies After a Fall: President's Grandchild Faints on Adirondack Hike," *NYT,* August 13, 1960.

295 "was a great blow": ER to PM, October 3, 1960, PMP.

296 utilize Stevenson: ER, "My Day," August 17, 1960, and Black, *Casting Her Own Shadow,* 190–91.

296 "a quick mind": ER, "My Day," August 17, 1960.

296 He would have: ER to Mary Lasker, August 15, 1960, ERP.

296 "I thought of you": PM to ER, September 5, 1960, ERP.

296 "I see you've finally": Ibid.

55. "I HOPE YOU WERE NOT IN DANGER"

297 In Ghana: For Murray's account, see PM, "A Question of Identity," in PM, *Song,* 318–32, and PM, "Teaching in Ghana," in PM, *Song,* 333–43. For a scholarly assessment of Murray's experience and political developments in Africa during her residency, see Kevin K. Gaines, "Pauli Murray in Ghana: The Congo Crisis and an African American Woman's Dilemma," in *African Americans in Ghana: Black Expatriates and the Civil Rights Era* (Chapel Hill: University of North Carolina Press, 2006), 110–35.

297 "the Africans, too": PM, letter to the editor, *Washington Post, Times Herald* [draft], August 20, 1960, attached to PM to ER, September 5, 1960, ERP.

297 "Africa is certainly": ER to PM, October 3, 1960, PMP.

298   Not even the distinguished: Brian Urquhart, *Ralph Bunche: An American Life* (New York: Norton, 1993), 308.

298   "a sense of history": Maida Springer to President Kwame Nkrumah, February 25, 1959 (quoted in Richards, *Maida Springer,* 207).

298   Her suspicion: PM, *Song,* 339.

298   He was awed: Ibid., 337.

299   A Jew who had: PM, interview by McNeil, February 13, 1976, Interview G-0044, transcript, Southern Oral History Program Collection, #4007, UNC.

299   The text he and Murray: Leslie Rubin and PM, *The Constitution and Government of Ghana,* no. 1 of Law in Africa (London: Sweet & Maxwell, 1961).

299   "I am beginning": PM, *Song,* 332.

299   "Africans are no longer": Ibid.

56. "READ THAT YOU HAD A BAD CASE OF FLU"

300   ER hoped: ER, "My Day," May 24, 1961.

300   Eleanor Roosevelt had brought: Black, *Casting Her Own Shadow,* 192.

300   "If I am right": ER, "My Day," November 2, 1960.

300   ER arrived early: Joseph P. Lash, *Eleanor: The Years Alone* (New York: Norton, 1972), 300–301, and Black, *Casting Her Own Shadow,* 192.

301   It must have pleased: W. H. Lawrence, "Nation Exhorted: Inaugural Says U.S. Will 'Pay Any Price' to Keep Freedom," *NYT,* January 21, 1961.

301   "We observe today": "Text of President Kennedy's Inaugural Address," *Washington Post, Times Herald,* January 21, 1961.

301   "our last best hope": Ibid.

301   "My fellow Americans": Ibid.

301   "glad" that ER: PM to ER, June 1, 1961, ERP.

301   Murray took comfort: Ibid.

301   "This is still": Marie Smith, "Mrs. FDR Pushes Women Toward New Frontier," *Washington Post, Times Herald,* March 14, 1961.

301   When the president's: Lash, *Eleanor: The Years Alone,* 318–19, and ER, "My Day," October 18, 1961.

302   "Guns never really change": ER, "My Day," May 1, 1961.

302   "the present drift": ER, "My Day," November 3, 1961.

302   "He seems a little slow": PM to ER, June 1, 1961.

302   "You'll be pleased": Ibid.

302   ER had aplastic anemia: Questions about the cause and nature of ER's illness, as well as the quality of care she received, would linger for years after her death. For an assessment of her medical records, see Barron H. Lerner, "Revisiting the Death of Eleanor Roosevelt: Was the Diagnosis of Tuberculosis Missed?," *International Journal of Tuberculosis and Lung Disease* 5 (2001): 1080–85.

302   "As one gets older": David E. Lilienthal, *Journals of David Lilienthal,* vol. 4: *The Road to Change, 1955–59* (New York: Harper & Row, 1969), 298.

303   Kennedy named her: "Mrs. Roosevelt Nominated for U.N.," *NYT,* March 1, 1961, and Lash, *Eleanor: The Years Alone,* 316.

303   "two old legs": ER to Adlai Stevenson, April 19, 1961 (quoted in Lash, *Eleanor: The Years Alone,* 316).

303   "didn't want to talk": Ibid.

303   "I am delighted": ER to PM, June 6, 1961, PMP.

303   Their homecoming: PM, *Song,* 344–45.

303   "space capsule": PM, travelogue, July 10, 1962.

303　"private office": Ibid.

303　"three times": PM, *Song,* 345.

304　The law school student body: Ibid.

304　"almost single-handedly": Eleanor Holmes Norton, introduction to PM, *Song in a Weary Throat: An American Pilgrimage* (New York: Harper & Row, 1987).

304　"I was delighted": ER to PM, September 11, 1961, PMP.

57. "I AM AS WELL AS ANYONE CAN BE AT MY AGE"

305　"is to find how": ER, "My Day," February 16, 1962.

305　"I have no idea": ER, "My Day," November 20, 1961.

306　"with the responsibility": Exec. Order No. 10980, 26 Federal Register 12059 (December 16, 1961).

306　"self-protection": William McPherson, "JFK Backs Equal Job Status at Commission's First Meeting," *Washington Post, Times Herald,* February 14, 1962.

306　"The other and more": Ibid.

306　The PCSW went to work: ER, "My Day," February 16, 1962.

306　The group's plans: For a detailed summary of the PCSW, its subcommittees, and a listing of members, see Margaret Mead and Frances Balgley Kaplan, *American Women: The Report of the President's Commission on the Status of Women* (New York: Charles Scribner's Sons, 1965).

307　Because Murray had: PM, *Song,* 349–52.

307　"puppy with two tails": PM, travelogue, July 10, 1962.

307　The steroid prednisone: Lash, *Eleanor: The Years Alone,* 321–22, and Lerner, "Revisiting the Death of Eleanor Roosevelt," *International Journal of Tuberculosis and Lung Disease.*

307　One especially meaningful: Clarence Hunter, "Panel Hears How South Harassed Rights Groups," *Washington Evening Star,* May 26, 1962.

58. "WOULD YOU PLEASE BRING ME A GLASS OF LEMONADE?"

308　Pauli Murray was: PM to ER, June 26, 1962, ERP, and PM, *Song,* 350.

308　A few days before: Lash, *A World of Love,* 549–50.

309　Most of the youths: See Floyd Patterson with Milton Gross, *Victory over Myself* (New York: Bernard Geis, 1962), 24, and Claude Brown, *Manchild in the Promised Land* (New York: Macmillan, 1965), ii, vi, 79–80, for their remembrances of Wiltwyck and Eleanor Roosevelt.

309　ER's friend Harry Belafonte: Belafonte, *My Song,* 194.

309　Like all the boys: For photographs of the Val-Kill picnics ER hosted for the Wiltwyck boys, as well as accounts of these events, see Lash, *Eleanor: The Years Alone,* 307; A. David Gurewitsch, *Eleanor Roosevelt: Her Day,* 74–79; and Eleanor Roosevelt II, *With Love, Aunt Eleanor,* 128–29.

309　She loved these: Lash, *A World of Love,* 549–50.

309　The magician John Mulholland: ER, "My Day," July 13, 1962.

309　"in her car": PM to Maureen [Corr], September 9, 1968, ERP.

310　Joining Murray: PM, *Song,* 350.

310　"a swarm of children": PM to Maureen [Corr], September 9, 1968.

310　"Pauli, if you are going": PM, *Song,* 350.

310　"personal favor": Ibid.

310　"overjoyed": PM to Maureen [Corr], September 9, 1968.

310　"felt close enough": PM, *Song,* 350.

310　Unaware that ER: Lash, *Eleanor: The Years Alone,* 324.

310   "had the privilege": PM to Maureen [Corr], September 9, 1968.
310   "to touch her": Ibid.
310   "felt like the fat lady": Ibid.
310   "slightly stooped": Ibid.

59. "WE SHALL BE WORKING DOUBLY HARD TO CARRY ON"

311   "a great light": PM, *Song,* 351.
311   On August 3, 1962: Lerner, "Revisiting the Death of Eleanor Roosevelt," *International Journal of Tuberculosis and Lung Disease,* 1081. For ER's account of her hospitalization, see ER, "My Day," August 13, 1962.
311   "all the new friends": Memorandum, PM to All the New Friends of Kwaku Baah, August 8, 1962, ERP.
312   "Did anybody ever": PM to ER, August 7, 1962, ERP.
312   "My uncle": ER to PM, August 29, 1962, PMP.
312   "had a miserable": Ibid.
312   She continued: See ER, "My Day," August 6, 1962; September 12, 1962; September 26, 1962; September 3, 1962; September 14, 1962; and September 7, 1962.
312   "Staying aloof": ER, *Tomorrow Is Now* (New York: Harper & Row, 1963), 19.
312   "clouds the judgment": Ibid., 25.
312   Nonetheless, she stayed: Lash, *Eleanor: The Years Alone,* 325–26, and ER, "My Day," August 15, 20, and 22, 1962.
313   ER was hospitalized again: Lerner, "Revisiting the Death of Eleanor Roosevelt," *International Journal of Tuberculosis and Lung Disease,* 1081–82.
313   "A Proposal to Reexamine": PM, "A Proposal to Reexamine the Applicability of the Fourteenth Amendment to State Laws and Practices Which Discriminate on the Basis of Sex Per Se," December 1962, PMP.
313   ER had once opposed: ER, "My Day," August 12, 1937; June 1, 1946; November 18, 1946; February 2, 1950; and June 7, 1951.
313   "The important thing": PM to ER, October 2, 1962, ERP.
313   "Mrs. Roosevelt is still": Maureen Corr to PM, October 10, 1962, FDRL.
313   Murray, introduced: "Life of Wife of Astronaut Is Recounted," *NYT,* October 12, 1962.
313   "Grace Under Pressure": PM, "Grace Under Pressure" (address, All-Women Conference, National Council of Women of the United States, October 11, 1962), attached to PM to ER, October 12, 1962, ERP.
314   "Dear Mrs. Roosevelt": PM to ER, October 12, 1962, ERP.
315   "stretcher-borne": Lash, *Eleanor: The Years Alone,* 330.
315   The autopsy and later reevaluation: Lerner, "Revisiting the Death of Eleanor Roosevelt," *International Journal of Tuberculosis and Lung Disease,* 1082–83.
316   "It is just so difficult": PM to Maureen Corr, November 4, 1962, FDRL.
316   "kept a private vigil": PM, *Song,* 351.
316   "example of doing": Ibid.
316   On November 7, 1962: For the statement ER's physicians issued after her death, see Henry Grossman, "Mrs. Roosevelt Dies at 78 After Illness of Six Weeks," *NYT,* November 8, 1962.
316   "One of the great ladies": Ibid.
316   "Her life was one": Martin Luther King Jr. to Roosevelt Family, November 8, 1962, ERP.
316   "We Have Lost": "We Have Lost a Great Friend," *Baltimore AA,* November 10, 1962.

316 "A hushed silence fell": Ernestine Cofield, "Mrs. Roosevelt Loved by All," *Chicago Defender,* November 10, 1962.

316 "low-hanging dark clouds": PM, *Song,* 351.

317 "In the death": Milton Bracker, "Burial in Hyde Park Garden Next to Grave of Husband: 3 Presidents at Mrs. Roosevelt's Rites," *NYT,* November 11, 1962.

60. "MRS. ROOSEVELT'S SPIRIT MARCHES ON"

321 Pauli Murray was among: PM, *Song,* 353–54; Dorothy I. Height, " 'We Wanted the Voice of a Woman to Be Heard': Black Women and the 1963 March on Washington," in *Sisters in the Struggle: African American Women in the Civil Rights–Black Power Movement,* ed. Bettye Collier-Thomas and V. P. Franklin (New York: New York University Press, 2001), 83–91; and Lynne Olson, *Freedom's Daughters: The Unsung Heroines of the Civil Rights Movement from 1830 to 1970* (New York: Scribner, 2001), 283–90.

321 "fell in line": PM, *Song,* 354.

322 A week before: Anna Arnold Hedgeman, *The Trumpet Sounds: A Memoir of Negro Leadership* (New York: Holt, Rinehart & Winston, 1964), 178–80.

322 "The men seemed": Height, " 'We Wanted the Voice of a Woman to Be Heard,' " in *Sisters in the Struggle,* 86.

322 "She's not speaking": Ibid., 87.

322 Women reporters, barred: "Newswomen Hit Press Club 'Bias,' " *Washington Post, Times Herald,* August, 22, 1963.

322 "As one who": PM, "Letters to the Editor: Discrimination," *Washington Post, Times Herald,* August 24, 1963.

323 "It seems appropriate": Ibid.

323 "the utilization": "March Chief Answers Press Club," *Washington Post, Times Herald,* August 26, 1963.

323 "the fact that": Ibid.

323 They added: PM, *Song,* 353; Rosa Parks with Jim Haskins, *Rosa Parks: My Story* (New York: Dial, 1992), 165–66; and Hedgeman, *The Trumpet Sounds,* 178–80.

323 Randolph honored: "Six to Be Honored," *Washington Post, Times Herald,* August 28, 1963. Those mentioned were Rosa Parks; Daisy Bates; Diane Nash Bevels, field secretary, Student Non-Violent Coordinating Committee; Myrlie Evers, widow of slain civil rights leader Medgar Evers; Gloria Richardson, chair, Cambridge, Maryland, Non-Violent Action Committee; and the widow of Herbert Lee, a Mississippi farmer and father of nine who was shot and killed in retaliation for his voter registration work with SNCC.

323 Some of the women: See Hedgeman, *The Trumpet Sounds,* 180; Dorothy Height, *Open Wide the Freedom Gates: A Memoir* (New York: Random House, 2003), 145–46, and Parks, *My Story,* 165–66, on their feelings about the treatment of women.

323 "What you may not know": PM to Mary Ransom Hunter, September 25, 1963, PMP.

324 "It was bitterly": Sue Cronk, "Women Given a Backseat," *Washington Post, Times Herald,* November 16, 1963.

324 "secondary, ornamental roles": Ibid.

324 The assertion: Ibid.

324 "All Negroes": Ibid.

324 "no sign of remorse": Height, " 'We Wanted the Voice of a Woman to Be Heard,' " in *Sisters in the Struggle,* 88.

324 "take a hard look": Ibid.

324   "that women's rights were": PM to Bayard Rustin, September 9, 1970, PMP.
324   Her indignation: Bayard Rustin to PM, September 17, 1971, and PM to Bayard Rustin, September 19, 1971.
324   "never in this life": Springer-Kemp, interview by author.
325   This disagreement resulted: Richards, *Maida Springer,* 263–64, and Springer-Kemp, interview by author.
325   "that human rights are": PM to Mary Ransom Hunter, September 25, 1963.
325   House conservatives: For a discussion of the debate and political maneuvers related to the inclusion of Title VII in the 1964 Civil Rights Act, see Jo Freeman, "How 'Sex' Got into Title VII: Persistent Opportunism as a Maker of Public Policy," in *We Will Be Heard: Women's Struggles for Political Power in the United States* (Lanham, MD: Rowman & Littlefield, 2008), 171–90.
325   In any case, Murray: PM, *Song,* 355–58.
326   "there were few": PM, "Memorandum in Support of Retaining the Amendment to H.R. 7152. Title VII (Equal Employment Opportunity) to Prohibit Discrimination in Employment Because of Sex," 1964, PMP.
326   "Title VII without": Ibid.
326   "If it is true": Carolyn Lewis, "Dream Haunts Practical Poet," *Washington Post, Time Herald,"* December 11, 1966.
326   "to discuss the matter": PM, *Song,* 357.
326   "checked this matter out": Quoted in PM, *Song,* 358.
326   "To you comes": Quoted in PM, *Song,* 357.
326   "You'll be amused": PM to Lloyd K. Garrison, September 17, 1964, PMP.
327   "registered but independent": PM, letter to the editor, *NYT,* October 21, 1971.

61. "I HAVE BEEN A PERSON WITH AN INDEPENDENT INQUIRING MIND"

328   Twenty-one years: PM, "Roots of the Racial Crisis: Prologue to Policy" (PhD diss., Yale Law School, 1965).
328   Now in possession: On the paucity of African American women law professors, see J. Clay Smith Jr., "Appendix B: Pioneering Facts About Black Women Lawyers and Law Teachers," in *Rebels in Law: Voices in History of Black Women Lawyers* (Ann Arbor: University of Michigan Press, 2000), 277–83.
329   "with a clumsy gait": PM, *Song,* 363.
329   She signed: PM, *Human Rights U.S.A.: 1948–1966* (Cincinnati: Service Center, Board of Missions, Methodist Church, 1967).
329   She worked: U.S. Department of Justice, FBI File, Subject: Anna Pauline Murray, (140-33958).
329   In 1966, Kenyon and Murray: PM, *Song,* 363–65; *White v. Crook,* 251 F. Supp. 401 (DCMD Ala.1966).
329   Ginsburg would pay: Ruth Bader Ginsburg, interview by William Treanor, C-SPAN, February 4, 2015, http://www.c-span.org/video/?324177-1/discussion-supreme-court-justice-ruth-bader-ginsburg. When historian Anne Firor Scott asked Ginsburg to share her thoughts about Murray and Kenyon, she wrote, "When I authored the brief for appellant Sally Reed in the turning point gender discrimination case, *Reed v. Reed,* 404 U.S. 71 (1971) I placed Pauli's name on the cover together with Dorothy Kenyon's. Both women had urged, a decade and more earlier, arguments that courts were not prepared to hear until the 1970s." Quoted in Anne Firor Scott, *Pauli Murray and Caroline Ware: Forty Years of Letters in Black and White* (Chapel Hill: University of North Carolina Press, 2006),

138–39. For editorial comment on Ginsburg's tribute to Kenyon and Murray, see Linda K. Kerber, "Judge Ginsburg's Gift," *WP,* August 1, 1993.

329   "to assure equal job": Edith Evans Asbury, "Protest Proposed on Women's Jobs: Yale Professor Says It May Be Needed to Obtain Rights," *NYT,* October 13, 1965.

329   Friedan, who was: PM, *Song,* 365–68.

330   Disagreement over the process: PM to Kathryn Clarenbach, November 21, 1967, PMP; PM to Al [Reitman], November 24, 1969, PMP; and PM, journal, November 21, 1967, PMP. For historical comment, see Susan M. Hartmann, "Pauli Murray and the 'Juncture of Women's Liberation and Black Liberation,'" *Journal of Women's History* 14, no. 2 (Summer 2002): 74–77.

330   She would publicly: PM to Aileen Clarke Hernandez, August 7, 1971, PMP.

330   At the same time: PM, *Song,* 361–62, 367–68.

331   During her tenure: Aileen Hernandez, interview by author, San Francisco, April 16, 1997

331   "number one objective": Luther Holcomb, interview by Dana Whitaker, April 28, 2000, http://www.eeoc.gov/eeoc/history/35th/voices/oral_history-luther_holcomb -dana_whitaker.wpd.html.

331   "second place": Ibid.

331   Frustration with the: Ashbury, "Protest Proposed on Women's Jobs," *NYT.*

332   When it became: PM, interview by McNeil.

332   "Jane Crow and the Law": PM and Mary O. Eastwood, "Jane Crow and the Law: Sex Discrimination and Title VII," *George Washington Law Review* 34, no. 2 (December 1965): 232–56.

332   "organizational affiliations": PM to Stephen N. Shulman, April 18, 1967, PMP.

332   "factors": Ibid.

332   "That I have been": Ibid.

333   Murray was described: U.S. Department of Justice, FBI File, Subject: Anna Pauline Murray (140-33958).

333   "she was a homosexual": Memorandum, Clyde Tolson to Cartha DeLoach, April 4, 1967, U.S. Department of Justice, FBI File, Subject: Anna Pauline Murray (140-33958).

333   "was to determine": Ibid.

333   "challenge . . . her affiliation": Ibid.

333   "This has been": PM, journal, May 11, 1967, PMP.

333   "no longer young": PM, journal, April 26, 1967, PMP.

333   "a has-been": PM, journal, May 11, 1967.

333   "not part of anyone's": PM, journal April 19, 1967, PMP.

333   "as a Commissioner": PM, journal, April 22, 1967, PMP.

333   "try to be": Ibid.

333   "personality and talents": PM, journal, June 17, 1968.

334   "civil rights, women, politics": PM, journal, April 24, 1967, PMP.

62. "MRS. R. SEEMED TO HAVE BEEN FORGOTTEN"

335   In the wake: Jack Bass and Jack Nelson, *The Orangeburg Massacre* (New York: World, 1970).

336   Jean E. Friedman: Jean E. Friedman, discussion with author, Athens, Georgia, October 16, 2006; Jean E. Friedman, telephone interview with author, August 17, 2010; and Jean E. Friedman, "Personal Reflections on Community and the Writing of American Religious History," in *Autobiographical Reflections on Southern*

Religious History, ed. John B. Boles (Athens: University of Georgia Press, 2001), 177–92.

336　"in the open air": PM, *Song,* 393.

336　Seeking the solace: Ibid., 388.

336　"holding her glasses": PM to Maureen Corr, September 9, 1968, FDRL.

336　"the baskets of canes": Ibid.

336　"wood fire burning": Ibid.

336　"writing table": Ibid.

336　"Dear Maureen": Ibid.

337　"a kind of rebirth": Ibid.

337　"psychically close": Ibid.

337　"would frown upon": Ibid.

337　"who loved her": Ibid.

337　Convinced that her: PM, *Song,* 378–79.

337　"exciting, tormenting": Ibid., 389.

338　She also challenged: On Murray's role in the development of a women's studies program, the appointment of a committee on the status of women, and the filing of an EEOC complaint that charged the university with discriminating against women in its retirement rate schedule, thereby violating Title VII, see Joyce Antler, "Pauli Murray: The Brandeis Years," *Journal of Women's History* 14, no. 2 (Summer 2002): 78–82.

338　"impatient young Black Militants": PM, *Song,* 389.

338　"separate dormitories": Ibid., 396.

338　"white liberal colleagues": PM to Dave and Mrs. ———, July 5, 1970, in author's possession.

338　"to the memory": PM, *Dark Testament,* 1.

338　"brilliance and conceptual power": PM to Marie Rodell, June 29, 1970, PMP.

338　She was disappointed: PM, journal, July 2, 1970, PMP.

338　This time, readers: For a discussion of the reception to *Proud Shoes* in 1956 and 1978, see Patricia Bell-Scott, foreword to *Proud Shoes: The Story of An American Family,* by PM (Boston: Beacon, 1999), vii–x.

339　*Roots* "dwells": Jack Hicks, "A State of Uneasy Peace," review of *Proud Shoes,* by PM, *Nation,* December 16, 1978, 680.

339　"not a spinoff": Larry Swindell, "Not a Spinoff on 'Roots' but a Splendid Forerunner," review of *Proud Shoes,* by PM, *Philadelphia Inquirer,* September 14, 1978.

339　Murray was happy: PM to Naomi Burns, September 5, 1978, PMP.

339　With adequate marketing: PM to Marie Rodell, August 5, 1970, PMP.

339　On June 19, 1970: *Discrimination Against Women: House Committee on Education and Labor, Discrimination Against Women: Hearings Before the Special Subcommittee on Education of the Committee on Education and Labor,* 91st Cong. 328 (June 19, 1970) (statement of Dr. Pauli Murray, Professor of American Studies, Brandeis University).

339　"If anyone should ask": Ibid., 335.

339　Three months later: Barbara Campbell, "Girl Denied Spot on Boys' Team Takes Complaint to Rights Unit," *NYT,* September 26, 1970.

339　For years, Marshall: Dovey Johnson Roundtree, interview by author, Washington, DC, August 23, 1995.

339　"I know what": Ibid.

339　"work on the Bench": Thurgood Marshall to PM, October 11, 1961, PMP.

339　Now an old hand: "Available for Court," *NYT,* September 28, 1971.

340 She believed that her: Eleanor Blau, "63 and an Activist, She Hopes to Become an Episcopal Priest," *NYT,* February 11, 1974.

63. "THE MISSING ELEMENT . . . IS THEOLOGICAL"

341 "self-destructive": Grace Milgram, interview by author, Washington, DC, November 8, 1997.

342 "authentic selfhood": See PM, "Synthesis: Theology, Feminism, and the Law: The Impact upon a Creative Writer," in Pinn, ed., *Pauli Murray: Selected Sermons and Writings,* 207.

342 Murray's religious education: See Anthony B. Pinn, *Becoming "America's Problem Child": An Outline of Pauli Murray's Religious Life and Theology* (Eugene, OR: Pickwick, 2008). For a biography that focuses on Murray's religious development, see Sarah Azaransky, *The Dream Is Freedom: Pauli Murray and American Democratic Faith* (New York: Oxford University Press, 2011).

342 "prime movers": PM, *Song,* 48.

342 "a child of destiny": Ibid., 70.

342 "prophetic": Ibid.

342 "The missing element": PM to Family and Friends, [20 December 1973?], PMP.

342 Murray was fully aware: PM, *Song,* 369–73, 417–19.

342 On January 10: Ibid., 373–75, 419–25.

343 "uncontrollable sobs": Ibid., 423.

343 "talking to Renee": PM, "To Those Who Loved Irene Barlow," March 7, 1973–March 13, 1973, PMP.

343 "kissed her goodbye": Ibid.

343 "flanked on each end": Ibid.

343 The public memorial: Ibid.

343 "the closest person": Ibid.

343 Pauli's efforts: PM, *Song,* 425, and PM, journal, August 8, 1973, and June 9, 1974, PMP.

343 "together to comfort": PM, journal, July 8, 1973, PMP.

343 However, the call: PM, *Song,* 426.

343 Renee had designated Pauli: PM, journal, August 9, 1973, PMP.

343 Murray was the oldest: PM, *Song,* 427–32.

344 "in limbo": Ibid., 427.

344 "With the prayer": PM to Bishop Paul Moore, inscription in PM, *Dark Testament,* Christmas 1973, Keller Library Archives, General Theological Seminary.

344 "abrasive": PM, *Song,* 428.

344 However, Murray's calls: Ibid., 430, and Earnest E. Pollock to PM, March 19, 1974, PMP.

344 "If you have to": PM to Ernie [Earnest E. Pollock], March 21, 1974, PMP.

344 "If I can't take": Ibid.

344 "Church politics": PM to Pat[ricia Roberts Harris] and Bill [William Beasley Harris], December 25, 1976, Patricia Roberts Harris Papers, Manuscript Division, Library of Congress.

345 "the most rigorous": PM, *Song,* 427.

345 "were happy about": PM, journal, July 8, 1973, PMP.

345 "some information": Ibid.

345 Her master's thesis: For a published version, see PM, "Black Theology and Feminist Theology: A Comparative View," *Anglican Theological Review* 60 (1978): 3–23.

345   On January 8, 1977: Marjorie Hyer, "Episcopal Priests Ordained," *WP,* January 9, 1977, and PM, *Song,* 434–35.

345   "the end of a long": Betty Anne Williams, Associated Press, January 8, 1977, a.m. cycle.

345   "priestesses": Hyer, "Episcopal Priests Ordained," *WP.*

346   "the sun broke through": PM, *Song,* 435.

346   The Coalition: James C. Wattley to Mr. Secretary, January 13, 1977, PMP.

346   "What do you really": PM to Johnny Walker, March 14, 1977, PMP.

346   She increasingly mentioned: See Pinn, ed., *Pauli Murray: Selected Sermons and Writings,* 33, 82, 158, 191.

346   "We bring our total": PM to Jim and Mary, February 4, 1971, PMP.

346   "Dear Sisters": PM to Dear Sisters [Gloria T. Hull, Patricia Bell-Scott, and Barbara Smith], November 25, 1983, in author's possession. For the reflections of two scholars who interviewed Murray in 1983, see Leila J. Rupp and Verta Taylor, "Pauli Murray: The Unasked Question," *Journal of Women's History* 14, no. 2 (Summer 2002): 83–87.

347   "My ordination": PM to Family and Friends, December 21, 1976, Special Collections, William R. Perkins Library, Duke University.

347   Barbara Harris: Michael Paulson, "Episcopal Pioneer Reflects on Debate," Boston .com, November 1, 2003, accessed August 3, 2013, http://www.boston.com/ news/local/massachusetts/articles/2003/11/01/episcopal_pioneer_reflects_on _debate, and Mark Memmott, "First Gay Episcopal Bishop Says Death Threats 'Strengthened My Faith,'" November 10, 2010, All Things Considered, National Public Radio, accessed August 3, 2013, http://www.wgbhnews.org/post/first-gay -episcopal-bishop-says-death-threats-strengthened-my-faith.

347   The consecration: CNN Wire Staff, "Archbishop of Canterbury Slaps Episcopal Church for Openly Gay Bishop," CNN World, May 28, 2010, accessed August 3, 2013, http://religion.blogs.cnn.com/2010/05/28/archbishop-of-canterbury -punishing-episcopal-church.

347   By naming Murray: Dawn Baumgartner Vaughn, "Episcopalians Celebrate Saint Pauli Murray: She Worked for Justice for All," *Herald-Sun,* July 3, 1913.

64. "GOD'S PRESENCE IS AS CLOSE AS THE TOUCH
OF A LOVED ONE'S HAND"

348   On February 13: PM, *Song,* 435; the sermon she gave appears as PM, "Healing and Reconciliation," in Pinn, ed., *Pauli Murray: Selected Sermons and Writing,* 81–87.

348   "five servant children": PM, *Song,* 435.

348   "That the first woman": Ibid.

348   "historic moment": Charles Kuralt, *On the Road with Charles Kuralt* (New York: Putnam, 1985), 30.

348   "race, color, religion": PM, "Healing and Reconciliation," in Pinn, ed., *Pauli Murray: Selected Sermons and Writing,* 82.

350   "reaching out": Kuralt, *On the Road with Charles Kuralt,* 30.

350   She wore pants: PM to Bill [William Beasley Harris] and Pat [Patricia Roberts Harris], October 20, 1982, Patricia Roberts Harris Papers, Manuscript Division, Library of Congress.

350   She was among: "Alice Paul, Advocate of Votes for Women, ERA, Eulogized," *WP,* July 21, 1977; and "Celebrating Women's History Month: Five Notable Women at the ACLU," American Civil Liberties Union, August 9, 2013, http://www.aclu .org/FilesPDFs/five%20notable%20women%20of%20the%20aclu.doc.

350　Murray's sermons: For a cross section of Murray's sermons, see Pinn, ed., *Pauli Murray: Selected Sermons and Writing,* and Bettye Collier-Thomas, ed., *Daughters of Thunder: Black Women Preachers and Their Sermons, 1850–1979* (San Francisco: Jossey-Bass, 1998), 221–76.

350　"God's presence": PM, "The Gift of the Holy Spirit," in Pinn, ed., *Pauli Murray: Selected Sermons and Writing,* 23.

350　"a friend of the heart": PM, journals, December 28, 1974; December 31, 1974; and April 2, 1976; and PM to Louise Jefferson, February 27, 1984, PMP.

350　"a library with a": Michele Burgen, "Rev. Dr. Pauli Murray: Scholar, Activist, First Black Female Episcopal Priest, She's Now Satisfied to Live Day to Day," *Ebony,* September 1979, 112.

350　Murray's loving embrace: On the dog Roy, see PM to Aileen Hernandez and Wilma Heide, July 20, 1970, PMP. Roy is also mentioned and appears in a full-page photo with Murray in Harriet Jackson Scarupa, "The Extraordinary Faith of Pauli Murray," *Essence* 91 (December 1977): 107–10.

65. "HOPEFULLY, WE HAVE PICKED UP THE CANDLE"

351　"a creditable piece": PM, journal, December 23, 1968, PMP.

352　Among the stories: Stella K. Hershan, *A Woman of Quality* (New York: Crown, 1970), 158–59.

352　"choked up": PM to Stella Hershan, October 25, 1968, PMP.

352　Both knew the heartache: Hershan to PM, October 20, 1968, PMP.

352　In *Eleanor and Franklin:* Joseph P. Lash, *Eleanor and Franklin: The Study of Their Relationship Based on Eleanor Roosevelt's Private Papers* (New York: Norton, 1971), 523–34; 675.

352　"Joe," she began: PM to Joseph P. Lash, October 5, 1971, PMP.

352　"a miser": Ibid.

352　"cherished Mrs. Roosevelt's": PM to FDR Library, November 5, 1971, PMP.

352　"On the other hand": Joseph P. Lash to PM, October 17, 1971, PMP.

352　"Joe," Murray replied: PM to Joseph P. Lash, October 21, 1971, PMP.

353　While he mentioned: Lash, *A World of Love,* 266, 493.

353　In July 1982: PM to Family and Friends, August 11, 1982, Patricia Roberts Harris Papers, Manuscript Division, Library of Congress.

353　This crisis: Caroline F. Ware, epilogue to PM, *Song.*

353　Even so, the outline: On the project in question, see Joan Hoff-Wilson and Marjorie Lightman, *Without Precedent: The Life and Career of Eleanor Roosevelt* (Bloomington: University of Indiana Press, 1984).

353　"the absence": PM to Majorie Lightman, December 15, 1983, PMP.

354　On December 4, 1982: Judy Klemesrud, "The 42 First Ladies: Their Place in History," *NYT,* December 6, 1982.

354　"youthful challenger": For a published version of the presentation Murray made at the Hunter College Conference on First Ladies, see PM, "Challenging Mrs. R.," *Hunter Magazine,* September 1983, 21–23.

354　"For me": Ibid., 22.

66. "ELEANOR ROOSEVELT WAS THE MOST VISIBLE SYMBOL OF AUTONOMY"

355　"a joint venture": PM, Greetings [to Family and Friends], December 1984, in author's possession. Maida Springer had married James Horace Kemp in 1965. He died in December 1983.

355   "twin apartments": Ibid.
355   By the year's end: Ibid.
355   "joyful reunion": Ibid.
356   "gorged": Ibid.
356   "high point": Ibid.
356   Among the presenters: For the program, see "The Vision of Eleanor Roosevelt: Past, Present, Future," October 12–16, 1984, Conference Program, Vassar College Archives, Poughkeepsie, NY.
356   Murray regaled: PM, "Remembrance of Eleanor Roosevelt" (unpublished manuscript, September 1984), PMP.
356   Some conferees claimed: Judy Klemesrud, "Mrs. Roosevelt Never Considered Herself a Feminist," *Anchorage Daily News,* November 8, 1984, 26.
356   "definitely a feminist": Ibid.
357   "While Mrs. Roosevelt's": PM, "Remembrance of Eleanor Roosevelt."

67. "ALL THE STRANDS OF MY LIFE HAD COME TOGETHER"

358   "That I am among": PM to Grace Milgram, April 2, 1985, in author's possession.
359   During Murray's extended: Springer-Kemp, interview by author.
359   "Please refer": Ibid.
359   "to a shining place": PM to Grace Milgram, April 2, 1985.
359   "in shifts": Ibid.
359   "From here on out": Ibid.
359   She sent the crucifix: Dovey Johnson Roundtree, interview by author. For Roundtree's career, see McCabe and Roundtree, *Justice Older Than the Law.* Roundtree is also profiled in chapter 3 of Sims-Wood, "'We Served America Too!'"
359   Murray gave Maida: Springer-Kemp, interview by author.
359   "wouldn't be needing it": Powell, interview by author.
359   She would be too weak: George W. Goodman, "Ferraro, at Hunter Graduation, Assails U.S. Cuts in Education," *NYT,* May 30, 1985.
359   Pauli had often prayed: PM, *Song,* 433–34.
359   When Pauli drew: Zachary Smith, "Memorial Services for Dr. Pauli Murray," *Washington AA,* July 9, 1985.
359   "that the great Russian: PM, *Song,* 2.
360   "The power she had": Smith, "Memorial Services for Dr. Pauli Murray," *Washington AA.*
360   "It was Aunt Pauli's habit": Ibid.
360   Murray had asked: Springer-Kemp, interview by author.
360   "All the strands": PM, *Song,* 435.

INDEX

Page numbers in *italics* refer to illustrations.

"Thorough and engaging. . . . Our lives are richer for the accounting of their friendship in this important book." —*The Washington Post*

In 1938, the twenty-eight-year-old Pauli Murray wrote a letter to the president and first lady, Franklin and Eleanor Roosevelt, protesting racial segregation in the South. Eleanor wrote back. So began a friendship that would last for a quarter-century, as Pauli became a lawyer, a principal strategist in the fight to protect Title VII of the 1964 Civil Rights Act, and a cofounder of the National Organization for Women, and Eleanor became a diplomat and first chair of the United Nations Commission on Human Rights.

Two decades in the making, and drawing on letters, journals, diaries, and interviews, this monumental work shows how the relationship between a writer-turned-activist and the first lady not only had a profound effect on each of their lives, but also impacted the struggle for social justice.

"Tremendous." —*The New York Times Book Review*

"[Written] with the grace, compassion and diligent attention to detail that characterized both of its principal subjects. . . . 'The Firebrand' is someone whose inspiration is sorely needed." —*USA Today*

"A definitive biography of Murray, a trailblazing legal scholar and a tremendous influence on Mrs. Roosevelt." —*Essence*

U.S. $17.00 Can. $23.00   Biography

Cover design by Janet Hansen

Cover images: (left) Anna Pauline (Pauli) Murray, 1933,
Courtesy Archives & Special Collections, Hunter College
Libraries, Hunter College; (right) Eleanor Roosevelt, Science
Source / Getty Images

ISBN 978-0-679-76729-9

www.vintagebooks.com